# Developmental Disabilities: Etiology, Assessment, Intervention, and Integration

## Dedication

This book is dedicated to the graduate students who have, over the years, provided assessment, teaching, direct care, observation, interventions, staff training, and emotional support for the consumers and staff of the Pre-vocational Assessment Training and Habilitation Program (P.A.T.H.) and its earlier sister program the Social Transition and Employment Program (S.T.E.P.) of the Behavior Analysis Program at the University of Nevada, Reno, as they provided service, managed, taught, researched, and learned about developmental disabilities. They are the future.

Mark Adams, Kate Benedict, Kimberly Berens, Nick Berens, Jeremy Biesbrouck, Michele Bishop, Kendra Brooks-Rickard, Cindy Blackledge, Lisa Britton, Alaina Bumstead, Eric Burkholder, Jackie Chotiner, Amy Christensen, Mike Clayton, Tina Clayton, Sean Coriaty, Diana Delgado, Mark Dixon, Janice Doney, Ed Dyer, Dixie Eastridge, Chris Empey, Deirdre Fitzgerald, Eric Fox, Deborah Fredericks, Julianne Gallinat, Stewart Goulder, Heather Grada, Brian Gaunt, Fernando Guerrero, Ramona Houmanfar, Cristin Harrison, Thomas Higbee, Neleatta Houchins, Ken Huntley, Kristin Maglieri, Marianne Jackson, Becky Johnson, Don Karr, Amy Kenzer, Cristine Kim, Jennifer King, Heidi Landaburu, Duane Lord, Ken Macaleese, Mary Maragakas, Travis McNeal, Charna Mintz, Adel Najdowski, Jill Pellicciarini-Hilton, Becky Penrod, James Porter, Curt Reed, Ruth Anne Rehfeldt, David Richards, N. Joe Rodrigues, Kim Romick, David Sayers, Jacob Singer, Maria Stevenson, Ruth Steinagle, Jay Summers, Mark Swain, Jonathan Tarbox, Rachel Tarbox, Yukiko Washio, Tim Weil, David Wilder, and Ginger Wilson.

# Developmental Disabilities: Etiology, Assessment, Intervention, and Integration

Edited by

**W. Larry Williams**
*University of Nevada, Reno*

CONTEXT PRESS

Reno, NV

Developmental Disabilites: Etiology, Assessment, Intervention, and Integration

Paperback   pp. 363

Distributed by New Harbinger Publications, Inc.

Library of Congress Cataloging-in-Publication Data

Developmental disabilities : etiology, assessment, intervention, and integration /
edited by W. Larry Williams.
    p. cm.
  ISBN-13: 978-1-878978-49-3 (pbk.)
  ISBN-10:  1-878978-49-7 (pbk.)
 1. Developmental disabilities. I. Williams, W. Larry.
  RC451.4.M47D48 2004
  618.92'8588–dc22

                                                    2004007738

                              © 2004 Context Press
                        933 Gear Street, Reno, NV  89503-2729

Printed in the United States of America

# Table of Contents

# Introduction

The field of Developmental Disabilities (DD) is ever changing. And the rate of change appears exponential if one looks back beyond the meteoric change rate during the past 50 years in the scientific and sociological milestones achieved in the western world, to both the advances and atrocities that defined the original field of Mental Retardation (MR) at the beginning of the 20th Century. It was at that time, of course, that the earliest modern understandings of what became known as "normal" human development and functioning were established following the medical and educational discoveries in France and later Europe during the 18th and 19th Centuries (Hickson, Blackman, & Ries, 1995; Pessotti, 1984; Williams, 1999). However, if one studies this past one soon discovers that whereas great change has occurred in the "technical" field, many of the "political" issues have survived and resurfaced again and again over the centuries. Indeed, perhaps the most significant changes in the field, those concerning the accessible treatment, education, social role and acceptance of persons with DD into the "mainstream" have only recently begun to be established, especially in North America via large scale social change and legislation. Ironically, it is also perhaps these more recent advances in the "people" aspects of the DD field that have often overshadowed and on occasion have seemed to represent opposition to the many scientific medical, psychological and educational advances that have been realized in recent years. In order for the field to advance, it is crucial that its overarching philosophical movement fully embrace and encourage scientific advances. Notwithstanding the crucial role of political and sociological positioning in the field, such positioning should not be confused with, nor substitute medical, psychological and educational treatments.

This book represents an attempt to describe developments in the DD field from a perspective that recognizes the importance of both the "people" issues and the "technical" advances that have, in many instances, made the former possible. Accordingly, it presents contributions from many of the best researchers, clinicians, educators and service administrators in the field concerning what we currently know regarding the causes of, assessment of, and interventions for persons with a wide variety of developmental disabilities and / or mental retardation. It is not by accident that much of this work is from a behavior analytic perspective. Appropriately, the book also provides descriptions of recent developments from some of the most recognized leaders on issues of integration and accessibility of psychological and educational services.

The first section (chapters 1, 2, & 3) describe current knowledge from basic research. There have been huge advances realized even in the past ten years in the area of genetics, in particular the completion of the mapping of the human genome. Chapter one provides us with the implications of recent genetic discovery for our understanding of the myriad causes of DD and the related condition of Mental Retardation. Chapter two expands on this by providing the implications of the genetics of DD and MR to behavioral phenotypes and the ever closing gap between genetic and biological knowledge and psychological functioning. Chapter three provides an example of the exciting advances being made in basic behavioral research into human learning processes. It is these discoveries that are now providing educational procedures that have represented a breakthrough in teaching technologies for persons with all levels of mental retardation and especially children diagnosed with autism.

The second and largest section of the book concentrates on a variety of assessment and treatment issues for a variety of populations with DD or related MR. Chapters 4, 5, 6, & 7 provide state-of-the-art summaries and analyses of research and clinical practice in the areas of Pharmacology, Behavioral Functional Analysis, , specific assessment and treatment strategies for tic and repetitive movement disorders, and the assessment of people's abilities to discriminate different types and complexities of auditory and visual stimuli.

Medications and their use for a variety of conditions with people with DD have long been central to the field and simultaneously surrounded by controversy, variations in treatment team's knowledge of their effects, and lacking in solid research specifically with the DD population. Chapter 4 provides a concise description of the history and recent advances in pharmacological research as it relates to DD and provide some "eye-opening" facts regarding the relative lack of scientific knowledge in this field that is at the heart of current clinical treatment for this population.

Chapter 5 updates the reader on perhaps the most significant assessment method in behavior analysis - Functional Analysis (FA). Based on the seminal original research of Brian Iwata and his colleagues (Iwata et al., 1982; 1994) this chapter provides crucial new information and procedures regarding the proper use of this technology that should assist the reader in understanding the purpose of functional analysis and the subtleties in conducting a proper assessment.

Chapter 6 describes the state-of-the-art assessment and treatment methods for Tic and repetitive movement disorders. The chapter represents a rare compilation of an extensive clinical research line, essentially pioneered by the authors on the assessment and treatment of these disorders.

Chapter 7 provides a much needed overview and summary into a now well demonstrated hierarchy of discrimination abilities in persons with DD. This still relatively unknown phenomenon has profound implications for teaching and clinical assessment and interventions as well as providing an area of cross research related to basic behavioral learning processes and recent discoveries of phenomena such as "Equivalence" (Sidman & Tailby, 1982; Sidman, 1994) and Relational Frame Theory (Hayes, Barnes-Holmes, & Roche, 2001).

Probably no other application in behavior analysis has been greater than the well documented effectiveness of behavioral assessment and teaching strategies to alleviate the conditions associated with Autism. Accordingly, chapters 8 and 9 address the behavior analytic approach to assessment and training for this population. Chapter 8 describes what is known from such a behavior analytic perspective and provides a description of a state-of-the-art educational and clinical service for children diagnosed with autism. Central to the recent behavioral advances in the treatment of autism is the teaching of language. Chapter 9 is an outstanding theoretical and clinical description of a language analysis and intervention method that is being shown to be extremely effective in establishing language in persons with DD and in particular in children with autism spectrum disorder.

Chapters 10, 11, & 12 are concerned with areas within the DD field that have not traditionally received a lot of attention, and yet are crucial to our eventual understanding of the functioning of the "whole" person. Emotion is central to the human condition and considerably at play in psychopathological disturbance. As Psychopathology co-occurring with Mental Retardation has only been clinically possible to diagnose since the early 1980s, there is much need for research into assessment and treatment for this population. In a similar way, surprisingly little has been discovered regarding emotional functioning for persons diagnosed with DD and yet most in the field recognize its crucial role in appropriate social interaction and in anger management.

Chapter 10 is one of two chapters concerning what is known regarding emotional states and DD. This chapter describes research on the abilities of persons with DD to recognize emotional states in others via facial expressions, a phenomenon known to be universal in humans. Chapter 11 describes a new approach to Dual Diagnosis (co-occurring mental illness and mental retardation). This chapter co-authored by one of the leading researchers in the field and his colleagues describes a new approach that is definitely founded in a "people first" approach. Chapter 12 addresses the phenomenon of depression for persons with DD. It provides a review of the area and the implications of new research in Relational Frame Theory for assessment and intervention in depression. Perhaps no other issue will change the field of DD more than the recognized fact that the population is aging and that soon there will be a significant increase in not only the number of older people in general but an increase in older persons who also have DD. Chapter 13 describes the issues and current and needed research in the area of gerontology and DD. The chapter provides an important overview from researchers well established in this new and developing area of DD.

Chapters 14, 15 & 16 provide updates and overviews of three large areas in DD- special education, person centered service development and technology transfer. Chapter 14 provides an overview of the recent advances and issues in special education and in particular the recent legislation now in place in this area.

A much welcomed analysis and description of the issues, necessities, and methods of expanding the person centered service delivery position are described in Chapter 15. This chapter is exemplary of the previously mentioned need for "people" and "technical" issues to be championed together, not against one another. Finally, chapter 16 provides an update on a long standing issue in service delivery - technology transfer. In particular it describes what we know concerning staff training and the literature of management intervention in the field.

In summary, the field of DD continues to evolve. Recent changes have been "ocean-voyages" compared to those observed over many centuries. Significant changes in societal education about and acceptance of persons with DD and advances in legislation represent the most drastic in all recorded history. It is suggested that these major advances in the "people" or political aspects of the field have perhaps overshadowed and in recent years on occasion even seemed to represent opposition to the technical side of the field. However, breakthroughs have been made in the medical, psychological and educational areas in DD. The future of persons with DD will be best enhanced by a field that does not choose "people" or "technical" positions but rather "people" AND "technical" positions. This book is an attempt at promoting such a field.

W. Larry Williams, Ph.D.
*University of Nevada, Reno*

## References

Hayes, S. C., Barnes-Holmes, D., & Roche, B. (Eds.). (2001). *Relational frame theory: A post Skinnerian account of language and cognition* (1st ed.). New York: Kluwer academic/Plenum Publishers.

Hickson, L. H., Blackman, L. S., & Reis, E. M. (1995). *Mental retardation: Foundations of educational programming.* Needham Heights, MA: Allyn & Bacon

Iwata, B. A., Dorsey, M. F., Slifer, K. J., Bauman, K. E., & Richman, G. S. (1994). Toward a functional analysis of self injury. *Journal of Applied Behavior Analysis, 27,* 197-209. *(Reprinted from Analysis and Intervention in Developmental Disabilities, 2, 3-20, 1982).*

Pessotti, I. (1984). *Deficiencia mental: da supersticão a ciência.* São Paulo: Editora da Universidade de Sao Paulo.

Sidman, M. (1994). *Equivalence relations and behavior: A research story.* Boston: Author's Cooperative.

Sidman, M., & Tailby, W. (1982). Conditional discrimination vs. matching-to-sample: An expansion of the testing paradigm. *Journal of the Experimental Analysis of Behavior, 37,* 5-22.

Williams, W. L. (1999). *An introduction to mental retardation and developmental disabilities.* Homewood, IL: High Tide Press.

# Chapter 1

# Advances in the Genetics of Developmental Disabilities

Albert E. Chudley

*Department of Pediatrics and Child Health, and Department of
Biochemistry and Medical Genetics, University of Manitoba, and Section
of Genetics and Metabolism, Children's Hospital,
Winnipeg, Manitoba, Canada*

Developmental disabilities (DD) represent a concern for affected individuals, their families, public health, and society. It is estimated that between 1% and 3% of North Americans meet the cognitive and functional criteria for a diagnosis of mental retardation (McLaren & Bryson, 1987; Massey & McDermott, 1995; Murphy et al., 1995; Stevenson, 1996). Mild degrees of intellectual disabilities account for the majority (20-30 per 1,000 compared to 3-4 per 1,000 for moderate to severe degrees of handicap) (Schaefer & Bodensteiner, 1992). Many more individuals, collectively as many as 15% of a school age population, exhibit other DD such as autism spectrum disorders (ASD) attention deficit hyperactivity disorder (ADHD), selective language disorders, dyslexia, and other specific learning disorders with or without behavioral difficulties. The reduced productivity and limitations on self-care and self-direction as well as the need for specialized care, support, supervision and education can be viewed as significant emotional and financial burdens.

The evaluation of a child with developmental disabilities is complex. Ideally it involves the collaborative efforts of a team of professionals that often includes physicians, pediatricians, child development specialists, psychologists, psychiatrists, clinical geneticists, speech and language pathologists, occupational therapists, educational specialists, therapists, and social workers, among others. Clinical geneticists have expertise in recognizing a variety of genetic and teratogenic disorders that contribute substantially to the etiology of DD. Recently the attention to behavioral phenotypes, identified through collaboration and forged alliances in clinical and research efforts amongst geneticists, psychologists, and psychiatrists, has improved the characterization of syndromes and led to the earlier recognition of many genetic disorders (Dykens, 1995; Finucane et al., 2003; Skuse, 2000; Donnai & Karlimoff-Smith, 2000; Flint, 1998; Swillen et al., 2000; Ozonoff et al., 2000). Syndrome identification and determination of etiology are important if prevention, intervention and management are to be optimized for affected children and their families.

Many individuals with DD have a multifactorial causation, involving interaction between the environment and genetic factors. Recent research initiatives in molecular biology and the discoveries arising from the Human Genome Project will soon identify the genetic basis of most human genetic diseases. Gene discovery will help psychologists and geneticists better understand normal neurobiology and phenotypes associated with DD. This will lead to strategies for more effective treatment, through gene manipulation or drug therapy developed from the study of protein genomics or "proteomics".

In this chapter, I review some recent advances in genetics that have enhanced our ability to understand, diagnose and manage individuals affected by DD, including a review of genetic factors in intellectual disabilities/mental retardation, ASD, ADHD and some specific learning disorders.

## The Human Genome Initiative and Beyond

Mendel is credited with being the father of genetics, based on his discovery of single gene inheritance and "laws of heredity" from his studies on plants (Chudley, 1998). These discoveries were reported in 1865, but received limited attention until their rediscovery in 1900. Over fifty years later, and fifty years ago, Crick and Watson reported on the structure of DNA in 1953. Their discovery was one of the most significant findings in biology over the past century. The correct human chromosome number of 46 was not confirmed until 1956. In 1966 the genetic code was determined. In 1990 the Human Genome Initiative was established to sequence the genome of *Homo sapiens*. Convergence of the two technological revolutions, in biology and in informatics, drove the project forward in a more rapid time frame than originally anticipated. A "working draft" of the 3 billion base pair sequence of the human genome and a physical map were completed in 2001 (McPherson et al., 2001; Lander et al., 2001). The publication was released on the 192nd anniversary of Charles Darwin's birth on February 12. This was a massive undertaking on a scale that has been unparalleled in science, and the published sequence has been given an almost mystical quality by being referred to by some as the Book of Life. Now that we have the sequence information on all the 30,000 or so genes in the human genome, molecular geneticists and biologists will determine their function and purpose over the next several decades (functional genomics). This is no small task as we now more fully realize that genes do not always work solo, but frequently they interact with other genes in concert. Furthermore there have been concerns about how the information is to be used on a population basis. Concerns regarding privacy, confidentiality, and discrimination against person, employment, medical, disability, or life insurance are beginning to be appreciated. Fears of reductionism or determinism beliefs, that we now fully understand humans because we know the genome make-up, or that "we are what our genes are" were also addressed. Research has shown that our phenotypes are not hard-wired, and that the genotype may predict a phenotype to a probability, not a certainty. As part of the initiative, the ethical, legal, and societal implications of genome discovery have been given an important priority for research funding (McKusick, 2002).

Results of the project showed a wide variation in sequence, with about 1% of the gene sequences showing differences between individuals. Most of these have little to no effect on the phenotype, as they involve a single base pair in a non-coding region of a gene, or single base pair changes that do not change the amino acid sequence of the protein. However genetic variations in coding regions of genes that are involved in protein products or gene regulation and result in an amino acid change may affect the phenotype, ranging from subtle changes in the phenotype to sometimes serious disease. Only about 2% of the genome is transcribed into RNA, which is modified, released into the cytoplasm, and translated into its corresponding protein. Some of the remaining 98% of the DNA is transcribed into RNA but no protein is produced. This so-called junk DNA may have important biological function. Introns of the RNA are spliced out and not released from the nucleus; exonic regions (coding region of a gene) are released from the cell nucleus into the cytoplasm for translation into amino acids and their proteins. Recent evidence revealed that some introns may regulate the expression of other genes (Eddy, 2001).

In the "old" medical genetics paradigm, we identified the phenotype and searched for the culpable gene. In the "new" post-genome paradigm we have the gene and we need to search for a phenotype and disease that results when the gene is altered in its sequence and/or function. This is referred to as reverse genetics. The switch from identifying genes to determining their function, (i.e., functional genomics) has begun (Phillips et al., 2002; Plomin & Crabbe, 2000). The major areas of research strategies are: gene manipulation (using gene knock out techniques in mice and lower animals to establish the phenotype after altering or eliminating expression of a particular gene); gene expression profiling (determining which genes are being expressed at different times in development in various organs and tissues through microarrays that monitor thousands of genes simultaneously as indexed by the presence mRNA); proteomics (the study of proteins resulting from translation of RNA). This is complex because some genes have several different protein products resulting from altered splicing, and after translation proteins can be modified with multiple functions. For each gene with a single intron, there could be at least 3 modified proteins produced each having a different function (Banks et al. 2000).

How this might apply to human DD and psychopathology is challenging as many studies of functional genomics use lower animals as subjects for research, and begin with genomics and work up to the phenotype. Attempting to study more subtle cognitive disorders in humans such as autism, communication and language problems is clearly problematic. Plomin and Crabbe (2000) have suggested a top-down level of analysis that considers the behavior of the whole organism. The term behavioral genomics has been coined to emphasize this top-down psychological level of analysis toward understanding gene function.

## Gene Localization and Discovery

Mendel predicted that 2 genes would segregate independently and be inherited independently, but he was unaware that genes are located on chromosomes. Although independent assortment is the usual rule, some genes are linked because of their close placement together on the same chromosome. Two genes located close to each other on the same chromosome are more likely to be passed down as a package during meiosis. Two genes located on the same chromosome but far apart are more likely to segregate independently because of crossing over at meiosis or 2 genes on different chromosomes will segregate independently. Another factor is that for any given gene there are DNA sequence variations. Each variation of the gene is called an allele. Some genes have multiple alleles, which usually have no impact on the phenotype and occur at specific frequencies in the population. They are referred to as polymorphisms. These DNA polymorphisms or "markers" are useful for linkage analysis i.e. attempting to link a particular gene to a particular DNA marker. Using this approach, geneticists have successfully studied families with single gene or monogenic disorders (dominant or recessive patterns of inheritance) and used DNA markers and statistical analyses to eventually locate the region on a particular chromosome where the gene in question is found. This is referred to as genetic linkage analysis. Further molecular analysis, including positional cloning and a search for mutations in candidate genes in that region are undertaken to eventually locate the gene. Candidate studies examine genes implicated in the disorder. Those candidate genes that have a relevant pathophysiological process are called functional candidates, whereas positional candidate genes are those genes that are close to or within cytogenetic rearrangements found in some patients with the disorder. This method is useful only for genetic disorders in which the gene is a major factor in the disease and the gene is highly penetrant (Nussbaum et al., 2001; Anderson, 2002). Most genetic diseases, including autism, ADD, and learning disabilities have a more complex pattern of inheritance and involve more than one gene that determines the expression of the disease, and may require the presence of certain environmental triggers (Plomin & McGuffin, 2003; Plomin et al., 1994). These more complex traits in which multiple genes are responsible requires a more sensitive quantitative approach to analysis such as quantitative trait locus (QTL) analysis (Bishop & Sham, 2000; Risch, 2000; Anderson & Dominiczak, 2002).

Sib-pair QTL linkage analysis allows one to determine whether sharing alleles for a particular DNA marker makes sibs more similar phenotypically. If sibs affected with a particular complex genetic disorder are more often found to share the same DNA markers than the unaffected sibs, this provides strong evidence for the location of a susceptibility gene in those families that are studied (Figure 1.1). Another method is called association or linkage disequilibrium. Association is the correlation between a particular allele and a trait in the population. Linkage disequilibrium can also be defined as the preferential association of a disease gene with particular alleles at closely linked markers, and may result from a founder effect (Nussbaum et al., 2001). This method allows the detection of QTLs that account for much smaller amounts of variance than linkage (Plomin & McGuffin, 2003). Association studies involve the fine mapping of areas of suggestive linkage. These studies identify alleles that occur at different frequencies in affected versus control samples. The frequency of parental alleles that are not transmitted to affected offspring are used as internal controls (Figure 1.2).

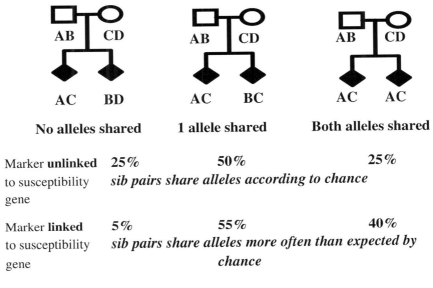

*Figure 1.1: Affected Sib-Pair Method of Linkage, that relies on the co-segregation of disease with marker alleles in families with multiple affected individuals. Black diamonds depict sibs affected by same genetic disorder. (Adapted from Maestrini et al., 2000).*

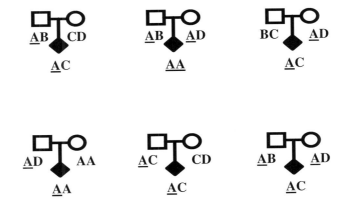

The "A" allele is transmitted from heterozygous parent to affected child 7/8ths of the time. 4/8ths would be expected by chance.

*Figure 1.2: Transmission Disequilibrium Test, a form of Association analysis. In a population the frequency of a particular allele is significantly higher in affected individuals (black diamonds) than in controls. (Adapted from Maestrini et al., 2000).*

Genome screens use between 300-400 highly polymorphic markers (often microsatellite markers—short repeats of certain bases found predictably throughout the genome) or single nucleotide polymorphisms (or SNPs, of which there are thousands, evenly spaced throughout the genome) typed in an affected relative pair sample. Allele sharing linkage analysis is used to identify markers at which affected relative pairs share alleles more often than expected by chance. A statistically significant increase in sharing implies that the marker may be linked to a nearby susceptibility locus.

## Inheritance Patterns—Old Concepts and New Discoveries

Traditional views of the segregation of genes are based on Mendel's concepts of patterns of inheritance [autosomal dominant (AD), autosomal recessive (AR) and X-linked recessive or dominant (XL)]. The concept of Mendelian inheritance remains valid for many single gene disorders, but new twists and exceptions to the rule have radically changed our understanding of gene expression, mutation and inheritance patterns (Austin & Hall, 1992; Zlotogora, 1998).

Mutations most often result in an inactive gene product. The resulting loss of 50% of gene product usually does not lead to disease. However, in some genes, mutations that lead to a reduction to 50% of the gene product will result in an abnormal phenotype or disease, which is termed *haploinsufficiency*. Some mutations lead to a gain-of–function and may even increase gene dosage: such mutations can alter the protein product leading to increased or different protein activity (and loss of regulatory properties of the protein) thereby resulting in disease. Dominant negative mutations involve mutant genes that interfere with the wild type allele. This often involves multimeric protein structures. Some mutations result in the production of toxic protein alterations that accumulate in the cell and result in cell death.

Autosomal dominant (AD) inheritance implies that an affected heterozygote parent passes on the gene to half of his or her offspring, and they in turn express the trait or disease. AD inheritance is notorious for a wide variation in expression for heterozygote carriers, with some being more severely affected than others, or some having different phenotypic effects or complications even within the same family. Many AD inherited disorders do not show complete penetrance i.e. only a proportion of those with the mutation will express the phenotype at all. Both these events occur frequently, implying that other factors, either in the environment or other modifying genes are influencing the phenotype and/or gene expression. Stable transmission of gene expression patterns to daughter cells, in the absence of any change in DNA content or sequence is one form of epigenetic regulation, whereby changes in phenotype are transmitted without a change in genotype. This is usually the result of chromatin structure or DNA modification (through the methylation of cytosine bases on the DNA). Other exceptions include normal parents having children with AD inherited disease. This is explained by the occurrence of a new AD mutation in a parental germ cell prior to conception, with a predicable low risk of recurrence to the parents for having other affected children. An exception is those couples who have *gonadal mosaicism* (in which there are two genetically different types of germ cells in an individual). These individuals are at risk for having other affected children, despite the fact that the parents do not carry the mutation in their somatic cells.

Some AD traits or disorders show a phenomenon referred to as *anticipation*, wherein the trait or disease is more severe and is expressed at an earlier age in subsequent generations. This phenomenon was first described for myotonic dystrophy, and was initially believed to represent a bias in ascertaining affected families. This AD myopathy is characterized by myotonia (reduced ability to relax a muscle contraction), progressive muscular dystrophy, cataracts, reduced fertility, male pattern baldness. This phenomenon is biologically based. The commonest form of myotonic dystrophy was determined to be a trinucleotide repeat disorder, whereby there is an expansion of CTG triplet repeats during meiosis in the 3' untranslated region of a protein kinase gene (*DMPK*) gene resulting in a more severe molecular effect on gene expression (Brooke et al., 1992). Normal alleles have 5 to 30 repeats; mildly affected individuals have 50 to 80 copies and severely affected children have over 2000 repeat copies. Either parent can transmit an amplified copy, but generally only females can have offspring with massive expansion that leads to the severe congenital form of myotonic dystrophy. Children with congenital myotonic dystrophy often are mentally retarded and display severe breathing and feeding problems in early life (Roig et al., 1994). Some die early because of complications of the disease. Several neurologically based genetic disorders have mutations characterized by expansion of repeats, including other AD disorders (Huntington disease, the group of Spinocerebellar ataxias), the AR neurodegenerative disorder Freidreich's ataxia, and at least 2 forms of X-linked mental retardation, Fragile X syndrome (FRAXA type) and Fragile XE (FRAXE type).

AR inheritance implies that both parents are heterozygous for the same disease causing allele, and are phenotypically normal (since the wild allele is dominant to the mutant allele), and 25% of their offspring will be homozygous affected. Many forms of mental retardation and inborn errors of metabolism are inherited in this way. Families at greater risk are those whose parents are consanguineous (related as cousins), or families where the parents are of the same ethnic background or come from an isolated community. The closer the relationship the higher the probability of a couple having a child with an AR inherited disorder. Exceptions exist to this rule. In rare cases only one parent is heterozygous for a recessive gene. The affected child is homozygous, and both mutant genes are from one parent. This is called of *uniparental disomy* (UPD). The most likely mechanism is due to a trisomic rescue. This begins with meiotic nondisjunction in one gamete that results in a embryo trisomic for that chromosome. Most often the trisomic embryo is not viable. However a second mutational event occurs with the loss of the chromosome from the parent who contributed only one homologue, leaving the embryo with two copies of the chromosomes from the parent in which the nondisjunction occurred. If both chromosomes from the parent who carries the mutation are identical (i.e. the non-disjunction occurred during meiosis II), the AR disorder will be fully expressed in the rescued embryo. There are several other explanations for this that are reviewed in detail elsewhere (Cook, Lam, & Mueller, 2002).

X-Linked recessive inheritance implies that males are almost exclusively affected, transmission occurs through unaffected or carrier females, male to male transmission is not observed, and affected males transmit the trait to their grandsons through their obligate carrier daughters. Sometimes carrier females partially manifest features of the trait. This is generally the result of *unfavorable Lyonization* and non-random or skewed X inactivation. Women have 2 X chromosomes; there usually is an equal proportion of either of the two X chromosomes active in any given cell – skewing from this results in expression of disease if a proportionately greater number of cells carrying the X-linked mutation are active. Since females with Turner syndrome (45, X) have only one X chromosome, they express an X-linked recessive trait fully and resemble hemizygous affected males.

X-linked dominant families are usually identified by an excess of affected females, together with the other features found for X-Linked recessive inheritance. It is often difficult to determine whether a disorder is dominant or recessive for X-linked traits since many females with X-Linked recessive conditions show mild expression. This is especially the case with the Fragile X (FMR1 or FRAXA) syndrome. The disorder was first described in a case report in 1969 (Lubs, 1969). He noted a marker X or fragile site on the X chromosome in a family with 3 affected males and their carrier mother. The boys had prominent ears. Subsequent reports emphasized other common clinical features, such as a connective tissue dysplasia with loose joints, autistic-like behavior and macro-orchidism in adult males (Fig. 1.3). The pattern of inheritance was an irregular X-linked pattern, as there was the frequent occurrence of variably affected females in families (30%, which is much more than expected for X-linked recessive inheritance, but also less than for an X-linked dominant disorder). In addition, phenotypically normal males can transmit the gene to their phenotypically normal daughters who are at risk for having affected sons. This puzzle was solved with the discovery that the Fragile X syndrome is due to an unstable *trinucleotide repeat* involving the expansion of a CGG trinucleotide repeat in the 5' untranslated region of the *FMR1* gene. The Fragile X syndrome is one of the most common inherited causes of moderate to severe mental retardation in males and affects about 1 in 4000 males. It is also a common cause of learning disability in females (Turner et al., 1996). Males have characteristic physical and behavioral features (Chudley & Hagerman, 1987; Sutherland, Geez, & Mulley, 2002). After the discovery of the gene it became evident that there were 3 states to the gene: normal with 6 to 50 CGG repeats; premutation with partial expansion of 55 to 200 CGG repeats; fully expanded mutations with over 200 CGG repeats (Rousseau et al., 1991; Verkerk et al., 1992; Yu et al., 1992). In the full mutation state the gene product, called FMR protein, is absent. This appears to be due to extensive methylation of the gene in the 5' expanded CGG region, and methylation of cytosine bases represses gene transcription. Expansion only occurs in oogenesis in premutation carrier females. Exceptions do exist. About 5% or fewer males with the Fragile X syndrome have normal CGG repeat size but no detectable levels of the

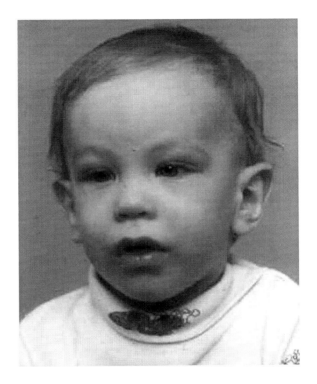

*Figure 1.3: Fragile X male at age 3 years. Note the large head, prominent forehead, wide ears, epicanthal folds (skin crease in corner of eye) and mild coarse facial features.*

FMR protein (FMRP). Small intragenic loss-of-function mutations (Lugenbeel et al., 1995), as well as larger deletions (Meijer et al., 1994) in the *FMR1* gene have been identified. FMRP is an RNA binding protein associated with translating polyribosomes, but the exact function is unknown (Bardoni et al., 2000). FMRP is expressed in many tissues, and is most abundant in neurons where it appears to play a role in the structural and functional maturation of synapses (Weiler & Greenough, 1999). Brains of patients with the Fragile X syndrome and from Frm1 knockout mice show abnormal dendritic spines illustrating the important role FMRP plays in synapse formation and function (O'Donnell & Warren, 2002). The expanded CGG repeat is contained in the regulatory region of the FMR1 gene and causes transcriptional inactivation. Since the mutation spares the coding region of the FMR1 gene, this potentially would allow synthesis of a normal protein if transcription could be restored. Pharmacological regimens using DNA demethylating and histone hyperacetylating drugs may be used as future treatments of the fragile X syndrome (Chiurazzi & Neri, 2001).

From our knowledge of inheritance it has been assumed that genes from both parents play an equal role in early development. Surprised again! Genes from paternal and maternal genomes are not necessarily functionally equal. Through a process of differential epigenetic modifications, there is silencing during development of a select few regions of the genome in one parent or the other. This process is known as *genomic imprinting* and leads to the functional hemizygosity of a small number of genes, as only the paternal or maternal allele is expressed. A maternally imprinted gene means that a maternal allele is inactivated, and a paternally imprinted gene means that a paternal allele is inactivated. The basis to imprinting is accomplished through DNA methylation and through different chromatin structure organization. In humans, we expect an unusual inheritance pattern to exist with a trait that is due to an imprinted gene. The pattern shows equal numbers of affected males and females through several generations, but the transmission is through only one sex, and the disorder appears to skip generations.

Two examples of human diseases that have been confirmed to be due to disruption of genomic imprinting in some cases, are the "sister" imprinted disorders of Prader-Willi syndrome (PWS) and Angelman syndrome (AS) (Cassidy et al., 2000). PWS is a disorder characterized by short stature, hypotonia, hyperphagia, hypogonadism, dysmorphic facial features, small hands and feet, mild mental impairment, and some behavioral difficulties (Fig. 1.4). AS is characterized by severe mental retardation, ataxia and spasticity, microcephaly, lack of speech development, and unusual behavior including inappropriate laughter. Because of the features of jerky movements of the limbs and the frequent laughter, the condition was given the unfortunate title of the Happy Puppet syndrome (Fig. 1.5). Deletions involving a small region of chromosome 15 between bands q11 and q13 are seen in about 70% individuals with PWS and the same deletion is found in about 60% of AS patients. Parental origin studies showed that in PWS the deletion always involves the paternal chromosome 15, whereas in AS the deletion is always the chromosome 15 of maternal origin. In about 30% of PWS and 3% of AS cases, in whom no deletion is detectable, the 15q11-13 region or the whole chromosome 15s originate from only one parent, i.e. uniparental disomy (UPD). In the PWS as the result of UPD, the parental 15 q11-13 contribution is always maternal, whereas it is always paternal in the AS individuals due to UPD. In 2-3% of PWS and 7-9% of AS, abnormalities in methylation patterns exist in the 15q11-13 region, and a mutation in the imprinting center has been identified.. The critical region for PWS involves certain genes believed to be responsible for the phenotype. The small ribonucleoprotein associated polypeptide N (*SNRPN*), needin (*NDN*), zinc finger protein 127 (*ZNF 127*), and imprinted in Prader-Willi (*IPW*) genes are all preferentially expressed on the paternal chromosome (Christian et al., 1998; Jiang et al., 1998). Mutations in the E6-AP ubiquitin protein ligase gene (*UBE3A*) are associated with some non-deletion cases of AS. UBE3A has a tissue specific pattern of imprinting and is preferentially expressed by the maternal allele in the brain (Vu & Hoffman, 1997).

*Digenic inheritance* is another recently identified but complex mechanism that has helped to elucidate genotype-phenotype correlations that have been elusive in

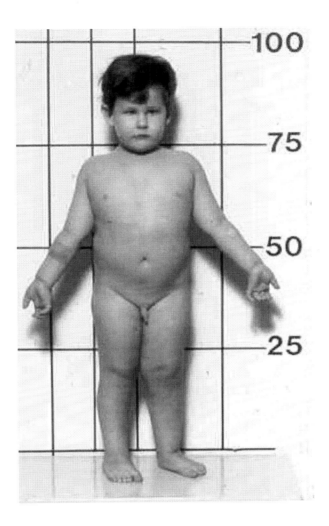

*Figure 1.4: Five year old male with Prader-Willi syndrome.*
*Note short stature, obesity, long narrow face with close set eyes.*

certain disorders (Scriver, 2002; Ming & Muenke, 2002). In this form of inheritance, two loci are involved; affected individuals usually carry mutations involving 2 different genes. Retinitis pigmentosa (RP) presents with progressive visual loss, night blindness, and pigmentary defects in the retina. RP is genetically heterogeneous with over 20 mutations having been identified. This mechanism was first identified when individuals affected by RP were noted to be heterozygous for two different recessive genes (Kajiwara et al., 1994). RP families were identified with apparent AD inherit-

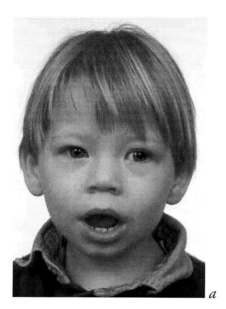
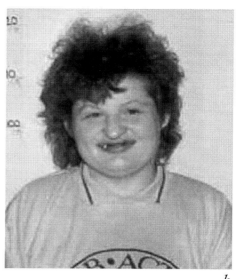

*a*                                                                    *b*

*Figure 1.5: (a) Young boy with Angelman syndrome who presented with ataxia, absent speech and motor delay, and a happy disposition, confirmed deletion involving chromosome 15q12. (b) Adult with severe MR, and facial features typical of Angelman syndrome.*

ance and reduced penetrance. However molecular testing identified both affected and unaffected members with mutations in the *peripherin/RDS* gene. Affected individuals were also heterozygous for a mutation in the *ROM1* gene. Both genes encode polypeptide subunits of an oligomeric transmembrane protein complex present at the photoreceptor outer segment disc rims. The mutant *peripherin/RDS* protein can assemble with the wild type *ROM1* to form structurally normal complexes, but cannot assemble with the mutant *ROM1* protein. The result is the loss of function and expression of RP when individuals are heterozygous at both genes.

Other disorders showing digenic inheritance include some forms of hereditary nonsyndromic deafness involving mutations in the *GJB2* gene encoding connexin 26 and the *GJB6* gene encoding connexin 30, as well as *DFNA12* and *DFNA2*. Bardet-Biedl syndrome (BBS) is an AR disorder characterized by mental retardation, retinal degeneration, polydactyly, and obesity. At least six different loci have been identified, with 4 genes identified *BBS1, BBS2, BBS4, BBS6* (Sheffield et al., 2001). Mutations in *BBS6* are found in the McKusick-Kaufman syndrome (an AR inherited disorder associated with polydactyly in both sexes affected and polydactyly and hydrometrocolpos in affected females). In four families with BBS, some affected family members were homozygous for mutations in one of the mutated *BBS2* genes and were heterozygous for *BBS6*. An unaffected individual in one of the families was homozygous for the *BBS2* and had two normal *BBS6 alleles,* whereas the affected individual had one mutated allele for *BBS6*, and two mutant alleles for *BBS2*, suggesting "triallelic inheritance" (Katsanis et al., 2000).

Holoprosencephaly (HPE) is a common developmental anomaly of the fore-brain that is etiologically heterogeneous, with both environmental and genetic causes. In familial forms of HPE, there can be a wide variation in expression with mild hypertelorism and normal intelligence in some, to severe brain anomalies and severe mental retardation and early lethality in others (Nanni et al., 2000). Mutations in the Sonic Hedgehog (*SHH*) gene were the first of several genes implicated in the cause of familial HPE. Based on animal studies and some preliminary human data, it appears digenic inheritance may explain the variability of expression in some familial cases of HPE (Ming & Muenke, 2002).

Transmission of DNA material does not only depend on chromosomal inheritance. Mitochondria have their own DNA (mDNA) that is processed and replicated autonomously from the chromosomal nuclear DNA. In addition to the tRNA and rRNA that are encoded within mDNA, there are genes for 12 other structural proteins. These genes code for mitochondrial enzyme subunits, and mutations in these genes can result in diseases that impair the function of many organ systems, and especially the central nervous system. This is based on the fact that mitochondria have a central role in a variety of cellular processes including generation of cellular energy by oxidative phosphorylation, production of toxic reactive oxygen species, and regulation of initiation of apoptosis (programmed cell death) through the activation of the mitochondrial permeability transition pore. Mitochondrial diseases present with a family tree that is typical of *maternal inheritance*, in which the disease is transmitted solely from mothers to most of their offspring. Affected males do not transmit to their children or grandchildren, since essentially all of our mDNA comes from the oocyte. Examples of mitochondrial DNA mutations leading to disease in humans include Kearns-Sayre syndrome, Leber hereditary optic neuropathy, several forms of encephalomyopathies, [e.g. myoclonic epilepsy and ragged-red-fiber disease (MERRF)], some forms of Leigh disease, mitochondrial myopathy, encephalopathy, lactic acidosis, and stroke-like episodes (MELAS). These disorders are usually multi-system, progressive and catastrophic in nature. The diagnosis involves a thorough metabolic work-up and confirmation by analysis of the disease-specific mutation in the mDNA. A more thorough review of mitochondrial diseases can be found elsewhere (Wallace & Lott, 2002).

## Genetic Causes of Intellectual Disabilities/Mental Retardation

Mental retardation (MR) is a lifelong disability characterized by impairment of cognitive and adaptive skills. Estimates of the prevalence of MR vary, but it affects approximately 1-3% of the population (Stevenson, 1996; McLaren & Bryson, 1987; Massey & McDermott, 1995). MR can be the outcome of brain malformations and brain malfunction and can result from genetic influences, environmental exposures, or a combination of the two. Determining the etiology of MR is important and beneficial for many reasons such as answering how to properly manage, prognosticate, and prevent disease complications. For the affected individual, a diagnosis allows appropriate medical and non-medical therapies; identifies appropriate referrals; provides anticipatory guidance for associated complications or functional disabilities; helps direct educational planning and eliminates unnecessary testing and evaluations. For the parents, a diagnosis aids in providing more targeted advocacy, support group contact and family networking, reproductive counseling, carrier testing, and prenatal diagnosis.

For the genetic assessment of individuals with MR it is estimated that about 40-50% will have an etiologic diagnosis (Chudley et al., 1990; Majnemer & Shevell, 1995; Anderson et al., 1996; Curry et al., 1997; Battaglia et al., 1999; Hunter, 2000) (Table 1.1). Through further advances in molecular diagnostics including molecular cytogenetics, subtelomeric *fluorescent in situ hybridization* (FISH) screening, comparative genomic hybridization, *spectral imaging or karyotyping* (SKY) to name a few, it is likely that the proportion of MR individuals identified with a genetic diagnosis will increase substantially over the next few decades (Battaglia & Carey, 2003).

When a clinical geneticist is asked to evaluate an individual with MR, the challenge is enormous. For example, the number of separate entries in the Online Mendelian Inheritance in Man (OMIM) for the key words "mental retardation" is 1027. Guidelines for an approach to the genetic evaluation of the individual with MR have been published (Curry et al., 1997), and recently updated (Battaglia & Carey, 2003). The clinician takes a thorough history, including details of the pregnancy, labor and delivery, medical history of the individual and immediate family members, and review of a three-generation family tree making note of ethnic and racial origins. The physical examination entails an assessment of major and

| ETIOLOGY | PERCENTAGE |
|---|---|
| Chromosomal abnormalities | 4-28 |
| Recognizable syndromes | 3-7 |
| Known single gene conditions | 3-9 |
| CNS malformations | 7-17 |
| Complications of prematurity | 2-10 |
| Teratogenic disorders | 5-13 |
| Cultural-familial MR | 3-12 |
| Metabolic | 1-5 |
| Provisionally unique single gene syndromes | 1-5 |
| Unknown | 30-50 |

\* Modified from Curry et al., 1997

*Table 1.1: Etiology of MR \**

minor anomalies, dysmorphic features, and a careful measurement of appropriate facial and body landmarks. This helps direct the laboratory (molecular, cytogenetic, metabolic) or neuroimaging [Computed Tomography (CT) scan, Magnetic Resonance Imaging (MRI) scan] assessments that may follow. An assessment of the parents is sometimes necessary, and a review of family photographs is frequently revealing of familial traits or the presence of a genetic syndrome in other family members. Reviewing videotapes of the child at different stages may confirm certain behavioral traits, abnormal movements or disturbed gait and evidence of progression/ regression of the disease. Clinicians cannot always rely on their experience in recognizing patterns of malformations and in identifying the hundreds of multiple congenital anomalies/ metal retardation (MCA/MR) syndromes. Fortunately there are up-to-date internet and standalone data base references on CD-ROM with illustrations of patients that help clinicians to identify a specific syndrome (Evans, 1995; van Steensel & Winter, 1998). These "smart" programs include the London Dysmorphology Database (Winter & Baraitser, 1998), and the POSSUM (Pictures of Standardized Syndromes and Unknown Malformations) database (Bankier & Keith, 1989). There are several excellent reference texts that aid in syndrome diagnosis. Examples include Smith's Recognizable Patterns of Human Malformations (Jones, 1996); Syndromes of the Head and Neck (Gorlin et al., 2001); Emery and Rimoin's Principles and Practice of Medical Genetics (Rimoin et al., 2002), and X-linked Mental Retardation (Stevenson et al., 2000).

## Mendelian Disorders and Intellectual Disability/Mental Retardation

Most conditions associated with severe degrees of MR that are inherited as Mendelian traits tend to be inherited in an autosomal recessive or X-linked recessive pattern. There are autosomal dominant inherited disorders that lead to MR, but they often represent a minority proportion and one end of the spectrum of variation in expression of those carrying the mutant gene. In general, autosomal dominantly inherited MR disorders have less severe degrees of handicap. The autosomal dominantly inherited disorders that lead to more severe intellectual handicap often arise as the result of new germ cell mutations in non-carrier parents, and the affected individuals tend not to have offspring, thus limiting the likelihood of transmitting the disorder to future generations. Many of the AR disorders with MR are caused by inborn errors of metabolism with specific biochemical enzyme deficiencies (Kahler & Fahey, 2003), or are the result of major CNS malformations. A few examples of autosomal dominantly and recessively inherited disorders associated with MR in which genes have recently been identified are listed in Table 1.2 (Fig. 1.6, 1.7).

Much progress has been made in identifying and localizing X-linked genes responsible for X-Linked forms of mental retardation (XLMR). This is based on the fact that there is a 30% excess of males with MR, epidemiological data, and the observation of XLMR entries in the OMIM database. Many question the apparent overrepresentation of X-linked genes involved in intelligence, arguing that this is a bias in ascertainment, in that identifying X-linked families with MR is more obvious

| DISORDER | INHERITANCE & PREVALENCE | MAJOR PHYSICAL FEATURES | BEHAVIORAL FREATURES & DEGREE OF MR | GENE(S) |
|---|---|---|---|---|
| Tuberous sclerosis | AD 1:6,000 children (50-80% are due to new mutations) | Seizures (half with infantile spasms), facial angiofibromas (adenoma sebacium), shagreen patches, hypomelanotic macules, gingival and nail fibroma, cortical tubers in brain, tumors in kidney, bone, heart | MR in 50%, usually mild but sometimes severe, Verbal disability, autistic traits, aggressive and hyperactive, sleep dosrders, ADHD, | *TSC1, TSC2* Proteins produced are hamartin and tuberin, both expressed in neurons |
| Neurofibromatosis Type 1 | AD 1 in 3000 children (50% are due to new mutations) | Café-au –lait spots, peripheral neurofibromas, axillary and inguinal freckling, Lisch nodules of iris, optic nerve gliomas and other tumors | Learning disability in 60%, mild MR in ~15%, poor attention and short term memory, poor coordination | *NF1* Protein is neurofibronin, involved in cell growth and differentiation |
| Noonan syndrome | AD ~1 in 2000 children (50% are due to new mutations | Short stature, congenital heart disease, bleeding disorder in half, wide spaced and down-slanted eyes, broad forehead, triangle face with coarse facial features, low set ears, broad short neck, sometimes confused for Turner syndrome | Mild MR in about 25%, many tend to be clumsy, stubborn, irritable, some have communication difficulties | *PTPN11* (found in half patients studied) gene encodes the non-receptor-type protein tyrosine phosphatase SHP-2 |
| Sotos syndrome | AD 90% are due to new germ cell mutations 1 in 10,000 children | An overgrowth syndrome characterized by a distinctive facial appearance with frontal bossing and | Mild and moderate learning disabilities and mild MR in some, social | *NSD1* mutations identified in a minority of cases and are more likely to |

*Table 1.2: Select genetic disorders with autosomal dominant and autosomal recessive inheritance.*

| DISORDER | INHERITANCE & PREVALENCE | MAJOR PHYSICAL FEATURES | BEHAVIORAL FREATURES & DEGREE OF MR | GENE(S) |
|---|---|---|---|---|
| Sotos syndrome | | balding, high arched palate, pointed chin, height and head circumference >97th percentile, long skull, advanced bone age | problems and anxious behaviour are most prominent characteristics. Some aggression, with usually poor coordination and hypotonia | be familial with a milder phenotype, many involve a microdeletion incorporating the *NSD1* at 5q35, tend to be more severe and are isolated cases in families |
| Rubinstein-Taybi syndrome | AD Great majority are new mutations. 1 in 50,000 children | Short stature, microcephaly, beaked nose, slightly malformed ears, a highly arched palate, anti-mongoloid slant of eyes, heavy or highly arched eyebrows, small head, broad thumbs and/or great toes | Modertae to severe MR, severe speech delay | *CBP* encodes the transcriptional coactivator CREB-binding protein, coactivator in cyclic AMP-regulated gene expression. Most are due to point mutations, some and 10% are due to microdeletions encompassing the gene. |
| Smith-Lemli-Opitz syndrome | AR 1 in 20,000 to 40,000 live births | Low birth weight, short stature, microcephaly, micrognathia, cleft palate, polydactyly, ambiguous male genitalia, congenital heart disease, brain | Severe mental retardation, although some milder cases have been identified suggesting a wide phenotypic variability, self-injurious and | *DHCR7* sterol delta-7-reductase gene |

*Table 1.2: Continued*

| DISORDER | INHERITANCE & PREVALENCE | MAJOR PHYSICAL FEATURES | BEHAVIORAL FREATURES & DEGREE OF MR | GENE(S) |
|---|---|---|---|---|
| Smith-Lemli-Opitz syndrome | | malformations, seizures, low cholesterol, elevated 7-dehydrocholesterol | aggressive behavior | |
| Non-specific AR MR (Molinari syndrome) | AR Rare, and likely genetically heterogeneous with multiple loci | Non-specific MR, spasticity, microcephaly, strabismus and nystagmus, consanguineous parents often a factor, one of several forms of nonspecific AR MR. | | *PRSS12* Neurotrypsin may be a regulatory protease, possibly serving as an element in an extracellular regulatory cascade |
| Nijmegen breakage syndrome | AR rare | Short stature, microcephaly, sloped forehead, prominent mid-face, upslanted eyes, long nose, high risk of infections and cancer, chromosome instability and excessive breakage on exposure to radiation and alkylating agents | MR is mild and progresses with age | *NBS1* Nibrin protein also called p95 protein. Involved in repair of double stranded breakage in DNA |
| Zellweger syndrome | AR 1 in 50,000 several variants | Failure to thrive, seizures, abnormal cortical development, hypotonia, face reminiscent od Down syndrome infants, intahepatic biliary dysgenesis, stippled epiphyses, | Severe MR, death usually in the first year or two of life | PEX1, PEX 3, PEX 6, PEX 12, PXR1, PXMP3. These genes identified are involved in coding for proteins for peroxisome |

*Table 1.2: Continued*

| DISORDER | INHERITANCE & PREVALENCE | MAJOR PHYSICAL FEATURES | BEHAVIORAL FREATURES & DEGREE OF MR | GENE(S) |
|---|---|---|---|---|
| Zellweger syndrome | | elevated very long chain fatty acids | | membrane and peroxisomal biogenesis |
| Marinesco-Sjogren syndrome (also called congenital cataracts facial dysmorphism neuropathy (CCFD) | AR Rare, 1 in 100,000 | Cerebellar ataxia, dysarthria, cataracts, microcephaly, short stature, myopathy, cerebellar atrophy | Mild MR | CCFDN |

*Table 1.2: Continued*

and easier than recognizing MR in individuals due to other autosomal modes of inheritance. Even after correction for ascertainment bias, it appears that MR is 3.1 times more frequently associated with X-Linked genes than autosomes (Zechner et al., 2001).

In addition to the Fragile X syndrome, there are over 200 XLMR disorders identified; they are categorized as being syndromic XLMR (MRXS) and non-syndromic/non-specific XLMR (MRX) (Stevenson et al., 2000; Stevenson, 2000; Chiurazzi et al., 2001; Meloni et al., 2002; Toniolo, 2000). Collectively, they represent approximately 5% of all MR (Toniolo, 2000). As of 2003, of the 66 MRX disorders, 57 have been mapped, and 9 have had a causative gene identified (Meloni et al., 2002), and in all forms of XLMR there are over 25 that have been cloned and a further 60 or so that have been regionally mapped (Stevenson, 2000; Chiurazzi et al., 2001). The web page http://xlmr.interfere.it/home.htm maintained by Pietro Chiurazzi will keep readers up to date with new information on XLMR genes. Table 1.3 lists some examples of some MRXS and MRX forms of XLMR.

Several MRX disorders have been caused by mutations in genes that produce proteins (oligophrenin 1, PAK3, alpha PIX) that interact directly with Rho GTPases (Toniolo 2000). Brains in MR individuals frequently show abnormalities in dendrites and dendritic spines. Rho GTPases are key signaling proteins that coordinate changes in the actin cytoskeleton that is essential for neurite outgrowth and migration and regulation of synaptic connectivity (Ramakers et al., 2002). Recent evidence has demonstrated that several MR syndromes such as Rubinstein-Taybi syndrome (Fig. 1.8), alpha-thalassemia/XLMR syndrome or XLMR-Hypotonic Face syndrome (Fig. 1.9), Rett syndrome (Fig. 1.10), and Coffin-Lowry syndrome have been associated with mutations in genes involved in chromatin remodeling. These mutations lead to deregulation of DNA transcription, resulting in chaotic and uncontrolled protein production causing dysfunction in macromolecular processes and profound changes in cognitive function (Johnson, 2001).

| XLMR DISORDER | CLINICAL FEATURES & BIRTH INCIDENCE | GENE EXPRESSION IN BRAIN | LOCUS LOCATION & GENE | FUNCTION |
|---|---|---|---|---|
| Fragile X mental retardation 1 (FRAXA) | Macrocephaly, prominent wide ears, large testes, connective tissue dysplasia, moderate MR, autistic features in ~10%. 1 in 4000 males. Variable expression in full mutation females. | Ubiquitous, but especially concentrated in neurons of the hippocampus and cerebellum | Xq27.3 *FMR1* | RNA binding protein associated with mRNA transport, and translating polyribosomes; Absence of FMR protein impairs synaptic maturation |
| Fragile X mental retardation 2 (FRAXE) | Non-specific, mild MR. 1 in 20,000 to 30,000 males | Neocortex, Purkinge cells, hippocampus | Xq27.3 *FMR2* | Nuclear protein, putative transcription activator |
| XLMR-Hypotonic Face (Also known as alpha thalassemia-MR syndrome [ATXR]; allelic syndromes include: Juberg-Marsidi, Sutherland-Haan, Smith-Fineman-Meyers and Chudley-Lowry syndromes.) | Severe to moderate MR, microcephaly, large mouth, hypotonic and coarse face, small nose, low-set ears, widely spaced teeth, genital anomalies, skeletal abnormalities, scoliosis, severe expressive language delays, some have HgBH inclusions on peripheral blood smear. 1 in 15,000 to 20,000 (estimated) | Pattern of expression of the gene in the newborn mouse (especially the expression in particular regions of the brain: optical lobe, frontal cortex, hippocampus and cerebellum), as well as the expression in human tissues. | Xq13.3 ATRX locus *XH2* | Might be involved in neuronal differentiation and testicular development. ATRX is part of a large multiprotein complex similar in size to the SWI/SNF complex, and is considered a chromatin remodeling protein |

*Table 1.3: Some examples of X-Linked Mental Retardation syndromes.*

| XLMR DISORDER | CLINICAL FEATURES & BIRTH INCIDENCE | GENE EXPRESSION IN BRAIN | LOCUS LOCATION & GENE | FUNCTION |
|---|---|---|---|---|
| X-Linked Hydrocephalus (allelic with MASA: Mental retardation, Aphasia, Shuffling gait, Adducted thumbs) | Hydrocephalus, aqueduct of Sylvius stenosis, agenesis of the corpus callosum, cortical spinal tract hypoplasia, mental retardation and spasticity, flexion deformities of the thumbs. 1 in 30,000 male livebirths. | L1CAM is found primarily in the nervous system of several species and may be more aptly called a neural recognition molecule. | Xq28 *L1CAM* | L1 cell adhesion molecule is one of a subgroup of structurally related integral membrane glycoproteins belonging to a large class of immunoglobulin superfamily cell adhesion molecules (CAMs) that mediate cell-to-cell adhesion at the cell surface. (Kenwrick et al., 2000) |
| Rett syndrome. | X-linked dominant; lethal and rare in males. Regression before 18 months, microcephaly, severe dementia, progressive encephalopathy, seizures, microcephaly, autistic features, characteristic mid-line hand wringing, short stature, gait ataxia and apraxia with dystonia. | MeCP2 appears to be expressed ubiquitously by neurons. | Xq 28 *MECP2* (The same gene has been associated with MRX 16 and MRX 79). | Truncated Mecp2 protein in mice localized normally to heterochromatic domains in vivo, histone H3 hyperacetylated. Mouse model of RTT, the chromatin architecture is abnormal and gene expression may be misregulated. MeCP2 binds primarily, but not exclusively, to methylated DNA, and it is thought to regulate gene expression, chromatin composition, and chromosomal architecture. |

*Table 1.3: Continued*

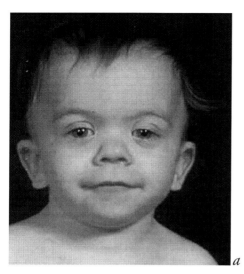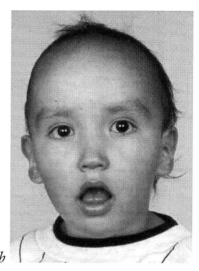

*a*    *b*

*Figure 1.6: Some autosomal dominant conditions associated with DD. (a) Child with Noonan syndrome. Note broad forehead and triangular face, down-slanted palpebral fissures, wide set eye, low set ears and short neck. (b) Sotos syndrome (cerebral gigantism). Child with a large head, receding hair line, prominent forehead, down slanted eyes, pointed chin.*

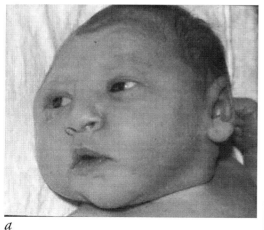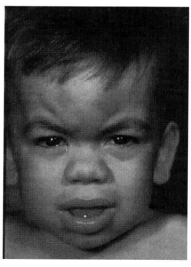

*a*

*b*

*Figure 1.7: Some autosomal recessively inherited conditions associated with DD. (a) Child with primary microcephaly. Note small cranium with sloped forehead and redundant scalp skin. (b) Child with severe delay, coarse facial features. Biochemical studies confirm evidence of one form of mucoploysaccharidosis (type 1—Hurler syndrome).*

Recent breakthroughs have shown that genes responsible for many MR syndromes encode for proteins involved in signaling pathways which regulate cytoskeleton organization, synaptic vesicle transport and, maybe, other cellular functions. MRX can be conceptualized as disorders resulting from perturbed genes required for processes such as the remodeling, establishment and stabilization of connections between neuronal cells. Such processes are crucial for the development of intellectual and cognitive functions. As these functions evolve mainly in postnatal stages through contact with diverse stimuli and environments, a potential therapeutic approach could be envisioned (Chelly, 1999). The real challenge over the next 50 years is to understand the neurobiology and to develop pharmacological agents that target cellular signaling pathways implicated in MRX or counteract or correct the effects of derangement in cellular metabolism of many other inherited disorders.

## Chromosomal Disorders Intellectual Disability/Mental Retardation

The presence of additional (duplication) or missing (deletion) of a whole chromosome or parts of a chromosome (aneuploidy) leads to an imbalance in genetic information within the cell, and this in turn results in either a deficiency or over-expression of gene product(s). This gene dosage imbalance leads to develop-

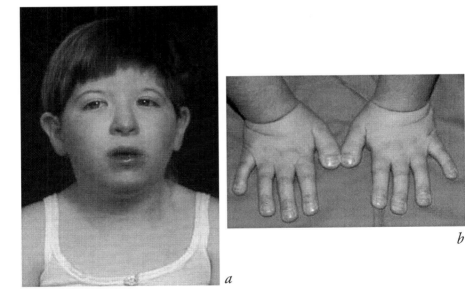

*Figure 1.8: (a) Child with typical features of Rubinstein-Taybi syndrome (RTS). Note epicanthal folds of eye, down-slanted eyes, a short beaked nose, small jaw. (b) Hands from patient with RTS. Note broad distal phalanges, especially involving the thumbs.*

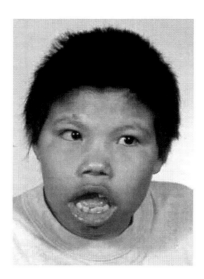

*Figure 1.9: Child with XLMR-hypotonic face. Note small nose, wide, open mouth, flat nasal bridge, and telecanthus (increased distance between inner canthi of the palpebral fissure).*

ment errors that manifest as congenital malformations, and almost invariability, in brain dysfunction and cognitive impairment. There are scores of aneuploid syndromes associated with variable degrees of cognitive impairment. The first and most common disorders recognized were the autosomal and sex chromosomal aneuploidies including for example Trisomy 21 (Down syndrome), Trisomy 18 (Edwards syndrome), 4p deletion (Wolf-Hirschorn syndrome), 5p deletion (Cri-du-Chat syndrome) and Klinefelter syndrome (47, XXY), Triple X syndrome (47, XXX) to name a few. These disorders were recognized using light microscopy and directly visualizing the chromosome structures by developing a karyotype to confirm either a numerical or structural abnormality. With improved techniques and high-resolution cytogenetic analysis, small, subtle deletions and duplications in almost every region of all the 23 pairs of chromosomes were soon discovered to be associated with abnormal phenotypic expression. The reader is referred to other sources for a clinical review of Down syndrome, other autosomal trisomies, structural abnormalities of the autosomes (Tomie, 2002; Spinner & Emanuel, 2002; Schinzel, 1994), and sex chromosome abnormalities (Allanson & Graham, 2002).

Through the Human Genome Initiative some advances have been made in correlating genotype with abnormal phenotypic expression, and determining genes responsible for the clinical abnormalities and developmental abnormalities in chromosome syndromes such as Down syndrome (DS). Essentially the whole of chromosome 21 with approximately 200 genes has been sequenced, and several candidate genes have emerged as possibly explaining the reasons for the Down

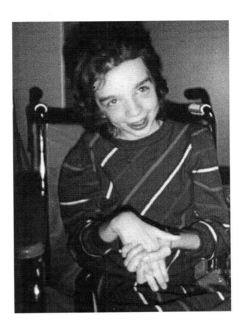

*Figure 1.10: Twelve year old girl with Rett syndrome. Note the normal appearing face and midline washing position of her hands. (Courtesy of Drs. Patrick MacLeod and Giovanna de Amorim).*

syndrome phenotype. Comparison of human chromosome 21 genes with mouse chromosome 21 homologues is one strategy in further understanding gene function and the pathogenetic mechanisms in DS, its evolution and cause of DS (Gardiner et al., 2002; Reymond et al., 2002). It is hoped that selectively altering gene expression may ameliorate some of the manifestations of cognitive impairment in DS. DS appears to involve numerous gene products and this interaction and interplay may well determine the outcome of the disease. Transcription factors, reactive oxygen species and apoptosis related proteins are potential candidates that play a significant role in DS. Therapeutic modalities that target these factors including antioxidants and caspase inhibitors might have some benefit in alleviating the symptoms of DS (Lubec & Engidawork, 2002). It remains unclear whether the DS phenotype is simply due to gene dosage effects and over expression of certain proteins. Recent data showing unaltered expression of six proteins on chromosome 21 in fetal DS brain suggest that the existence of the trisomic state is not involved in abnormal development of fetal DS brain and that the gene dosage effect hypothesis is not sufficient to fully explain the DS phenotype (Cheon et al., 2003). Currently the neurochemical and pathogenetic basis to DS is unknown.

Over the past decade there have been extraordinary rapid developments in molecular cytogenetics. These developments have helped identify several recogniz-able multiple congenital anomalies/mental retardation (MCA/MR) syndromes of previously unknown etiology. Many have been demonstrated to be due to submi-

*Figure 1.11: Child with Williams syndrome. Note up-slanted eyes, short midface, long philtrum, thick lips, long neck with sloped shoulders.*

croscopic deletions or duplications. Identification required specific DNA sequence probes directed to the region in question. Several of these so-called contiguous gene syndromes have a pattern of clinically distinctive features. The diagnosis can be confirmed by specific probes using fluorescent *in situ* hybridization (FISH). Some of these disorders and their chromosomal location are listed in Table 1.4.

Williams syndrome is an uncommon (1 in 20,000 births) MCA/MR syndrome that can be diagnosed by using commercially available FISH probes to confirm a deletion that involves the elastin gene. In this disorder, there is a distinct facial appearance. The face is characterized by a flat nasal bridge, epicanthic folds, anteverted nares, a wide mouth with thick lips, prominent cheeks, a long philtrum, curly hair, a raspy voice, short distal ends of the digits, reduced subcutaneous fat, a long neck and sloped shoulders (Fig. 1.11). Patients may have some neurological problems with poor gross and fine motor ability. They also have a high frequency of cardiac anomalies and often a narrowing of the aorta just distal to the aortic valve (supravalvular aortic stenosis) or peripheral pulmonic stenosis. Other vascular defects include stenoses of other vessels including renal, carotid, subclavian, and mesenteric arteries. There have been reports of early myocardial infarction and cerebral stenosis resulting in stroke. Infants may be irritable and have an elevated serum calcium. They tend to have growth problems, and variable degrees of MR. They have a specific cognitive profile characterized by over friendliness—the so-called cocktail personality, anxiety, attentional difficulties and poor social judgement skills. They have an uneven linguistic profile and near normal scores in face processing. Some have demonstrated exceptional musical talents. The vascular and cardiac anomalies may be explained by haploinsufficiency of the elastin gene.

| Syndrome | Chromosome segment deleted |
|---|---|
| Williams syndrome | 7q11.23 |
| Langer-Gideon Syndrome | 8q24.1 |
| WAGR (Wilms tumor, Aniridia, Genitourinary anomalies, mental Retardation) syndrome | 11p13 |
| Prader-Willi/Angelman syndromes | 15q12 |
| Rubinstein-Taybi syndrome | 16p13.3 |
| Smith-Magenis syndrome | 17p11.2 |
| Miller-Dieker syndrome | 17p13.3 |
| Alagille syndrome | 20p11.23 |
| Velocardiofacial syndrome/Di George syndrome | 22q11.2 |

*Table 1.4: Some chromosome deletion syndromes identifiable by FISH analysis.*

However, the critical region is complex, and encompasses at least 30 or more genes and pseudogenes that have yet to be thoroughly delineated in terms of their phenotypic expression. Some of the other genes included in the deletion region are: *LIMK1*- a protein tyrosine kinase that is expressed in the brain cortex and required for actin depolymerization. Haploinsufficiency of *LIMK1* may alter axonal guidance; Syntaxin1 A (*STX1A*) encodes a component of synaptic apparatus; *RFC2* encodes a sub-unit of replication factor C complex involved in DNA replication; *WBSCR9/WSTF* may be a transcriptional factor; *CPETR1* and *CPETR2* are believed to be involved in cell signaling; *GTF3* is a transcription factor that regulates skeletal gene expression (reviewed in Francke, 1999; Donnai & Karmiloff-Smith, 2000). Diagnosis can be confirmed in over 90% of the affected individuals using a FISH probe specific for the elastin gene (Fig. 1.12).

Chromosome 22q11 deletion is another contiguous gene disorder with a characteristic face and predicted multi-system involvement. Over 10 years ago it was recognized that some infants with DiGeorge syndrome (DGS) (severe conotruncal congenital heart defects, hypoparathyroidism and immune deficiency with facial anomalies) and the condition velocardiofacial syndrome (VCFS) were both associated with submicroscopic deletions of 22q11.2 (Driscoll et al., 1992). The estimated birth incidence of both disorders combined is about 1 in 5000. The features are variable and they overlap. VCFS can be characterized by a variety of heart defects (such as tetralogy of Fallot, or ventricular septal defects), velopharyngeal insufficiency (hypernasal speech, impaired palate movement and coordination), cleft palate, mild to moderate DD, and psychiatric disturbance in adolescence and adulthood. The face in VCFS usually shows hooded eyelids, malar recession, a long nose with a bulbous tip and a variety of other internal organ malformations (Fig. 1.13). The deletion spans between 1.5 and 3 megabases, and involves the loss of several structural genes, some important in cardiac development. Tbx1 is the main candidate gene for the cardiac defects involved in (DGS/VCFS). Jerome and Papaioannou (2001) found that mice heterozygous for the Tbx1, which encodes a

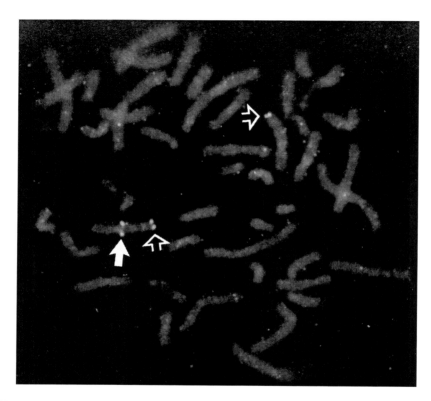

*Figure 1.12: Metaphase spread from a patient with Williams syndrome. FISH using an elastin (ELN) gene probe and another control probe specific for the tip of the short arm of chromosome 7. Note that the lower left chromosome 7 is positive for the control probe (open arrow top) and the ELN probe (large solid arrow), whereas the chromosome 7 at the top right has only the control probe (open arrow), and is missing the DNA region where the ELN probe normally binds. This is evidence for a submicroscopic deletion in that region of one chromosome 7 and confirms the clinical diagnosis of Williams syndrome.*

transcription factor of the T-box family had a high incidence of cardiac outflow tract anomalies. Tbx1-/- mice displayed a wide range of developmental anomalies encompassing almost all of the common DGS/VCFS features, including hypoplasia of the thymus and parathyroid glands, cardiac outflow tract abnormalities, abnormal facial structures, abnormal vertebrae and cleft palate. On the basis of this phenotype in mice, they proposed that *TBX1* in humans is a key gene in the etiology of DGS/VCFS.

Adults with 22q11 deletion have significant impairments in visuoperceptual ability (Visual Object and Space Perception Battery), problem solving and planning (Tower of London) and abstract and social thinking (Comprehension WAIS-R). It is likely that haploinsufficiency (reduced gene dosage) of a neurodevelopmental

*Figure 1.13: Child with velocardiofacial syndrome who is FISH positive for a deletion of a probe specific to the 22q11.2 region. Note the hooded eyes, small nose with a bulbous tip, dysplastic ears, and small mouth. His growth showed short stature and a small head circumference (microcephaly).*

gene or genes mapping to chromosome 22q11 underlies the cognitive deficits observed in individuals with VCFS (Henry et al., 2002). Patients with 22q11 deletion are at significant risk for psychiatric disorders as well, with one in four developing schizophrenia, and one in six developing major depressive disorders (Maynard et al., 2002). Using case control, simplex families (trios), and functional studies, De Luca et al. (2001) provided evidence for association between schizophrenia and a single nucleotide functional polymorphism, -277A/G, located within the non-coding region upstream the first exon of the *UFD1L* gene. The results of their study are supportive of *UFD1L* involvement in the neurodevelopmental origin of schizophrenia and contribute in delineating etiological and pathogenetic mechanism of the schizophrenia subtype related to 22q11.2 deletion syndrome. Lachman et al. (1996) suggested that catechol-O-methyltransferase (*COMT*), which is found in the critical region may be involved in the neurobehavioral phenotype of VCFS. They identified a polymorphism in the *COMT* gene that leads to a valine–>methionine substitution at amino acid 158 of the membrane-bound form of the enzyme. Homozygosity for COMT158met leads to a 3-4-fold reduction in enzymatic activity, compared with homozygotes for COMT158val. They suggested that in a population of patients with VCFS, there is an apparent association between the low-activity allele, COMT158met, and the development of the rapid-cycling form of bipolar spectrum disorder.

Subtelomeric regions are gene rich, and these regions are more prone to aberrations from illegitimate pairing and crossover. These regions tend to be lightly stained on chromosome analysis, and smaller deletions are easily missed on routine examination. Cryptic deletions have been found in subtelomeric regions of chromosomes. Deletions in these regions result in severe mental retardation. Over the past few years studies using *multiplex FISH* (M-FISH). M-FISH allows visualization of the 24 different human chromosomes in a unique color using a combination of probes. Many cases of previously unexplained, idiopathic MR have demonstrated deletions. In many studies, from 5% to 10% of idiopathic MR cases will demonstrate cryptic deletions or rearrangements (Dawson et al., 2002; Knight et al., 1999; Uhrig et al., 1999; Xu & Chen, 2003). Testing by M-FISH for subtelomeric deletion is quite laborious and costly. A high throughput screening technique, called muliplex amplifiable probe hybridization (MAPH), may offer a large scale screening of telomeric copy number as a means to select patients for FISH or M-FISH analysis (Hollox et al., 2002).

*Comparative genomic hybridization* (CGH) is a technique that provides genome-wide screening for chromosomal imbalance by direct DNA hybridization. CGH may prove useful in the delineation of smaller gene duplications or deletions, and will help define boundaries of know chromosome deletions (Kirchhoff et al., 2001). Spectral imaging or karyotyping (SKY) is a form of high resolution multi-color banding and chromosome painting. SKY can help refine and identify the origin of cytogenetic anomalies, and also can screen for cryptic rearrangements (Schrock et al., 1996; Ried et al., 1998; Chudoba et al., 1999; Riordan et al., 2002). Other advanced techniques that may play an important role in clinical genetics and the assessment of individuals with suspected cryptic chromosome deletions or duplications include microarrays (which is a genome-wide analysis of copy number changes of genomic DNA), microdissection (which allows removal of defined chromosome regions and is useful in the molecular identification of small ring chromosomes, rearrangements, deletions and complex rearrangements) and primed *in situ* labeling (PRINS) (can be used in place of FISH to diagnose microdeletions) (Xu & Chen, 2003).

## Developmental Disorders Associated with Complex Inheritance

## Autism Spectrum Disorders

Autism is a heterogeneous group disorders associated with severe, chronic impairments in social and language development, accompanied by rigid and repetitive behaviors, and restricted activities (Folstein & Rosen-Sheidley, 2001; Dawson et al., 2002). Autism Spectrum Disorders (ASD) includes autism, Pervasive Developmental Disorder-not otherwise specified (PDD-NOS), plus Asperger syndrome, Rett syndrome, and Childhood Disintegrative Disorder. The prevalence of autism has been estimated to be between 2-5 per 10,000, with a male to female sex ratio of 4:1. More recent prevalence studies suggest rates of at least 1 in 1000, to as high as 6 per 1000, which may in part be due to changing diagnostic criteria, and inclusion of the whole spectrum of disorders (Gillberg & Wing, 1999; MRC, 2001). Fombonne (1999) reviewed 23 epidemiological surveys of autism published in the English language between 1966 and 1998. The author noted that prevalence rates significantly increased with publication year, which he believed reflected changes in case definition and improved recognition; no evidence was found for a secular increase in the incidence of autism. In eight surveys, Fombonne noted rates for other forms of pervasive developmental disorders to be two to three times higher than the rate for autism, with a minimum estimate of 18.7 per 10,000 for all forms of pervasive developmental disorders (PDD). Chakrabarti and Fombonne (2001) surveyed an English district from 1998 to 1999 and determined prevalences were 16.8 per 10 000 for autistic disorder and 45.8 per 10 000 for other PDDs. The University of California's Medical Investigation of Neurodevelopmental Disorders Institute concluded that previous misclassification of some cases of autism as mental retardation or secular changes in the proportion of cases born in California were not likely to have contributed to the observed increase in the prevalence of autism in that state (http://news.ucdmc.ucdavis.edu/mindepi study.html). Croen et al. (2002), using statistics on Californian children born with autism in 1989-1994, noted increased risks for males, multiple births, and children born to black mothers, with an increased risk as maternal age and maternal education increased. Children born to immigrant mothers had similar or decreased risk compared with California-born mothers. They concluded that environmental factors associated with these demographic characteristics may interact with genetic vulnerability to increase the risk of autism.

Environmental factors that have been suggested to be related to autism include maternal hypothyroidism, prenatal exposure to thalidomide, valproic acid, alcohol, congenital CMV and rubella infections, and MMR vaccination (Folstein &.Rosen-Sheidley, 2001). The perception of a rising prevalence and "epidemic" created some degree of hysteria amongst the general public, and the call for further studies, leading to many searching for causes with limited plausibility. Many sound epidemiological studies in the past few years have addressed this possible link between MMR and autism and inflammatory bowel disease. Studies from the US, UK, Sweden, and Finland have all failed to demonstrate a link MMR vaccinations to autism (Madsen et al., 2002; Elliman & Bedford, 2002), although a link to bowel disorders remains uncertain (Horvath & Perman, 2002; Torrente et al., 2002).

ASD are recognized to have a genetic component from several lines of evidence. Twin studies show higher concordance rates for monozygotic (MZ) twins than for dizygotic (DZ) twins (Bailey et al., 1995). Approximately 80% of MZ twins are concordant compared to 10% of DZ twins, with a heritability of over 90% (Folstein & Rutter, 1977). In families, the recurrence in sibs with non-syndromic forms of ASD is about 5-10% (Ritvo et al., 1989; Chudley et al., 1998; Chudley et al., 1999). Recent studies have confirmed a significantly increased expression of the traits anxious, impulsive, aloof, shy, over-sensitive, irritable and eccentric among the autism relatives with evidence of different profiles for male and female relatives and for parents and adult children, and that particular personality traits may aggregate in the family members of autistic individuals and that some of these traits may be a manifestation of the liability to autism (Murphy et al., 2000). In addition, macrocephaly has been seen in a higher than expected proportion of autistic children and adults and their relatives (Lainhart et al., 1997; Bolton et al., 2001; Chudley et al., 1998). Other studies show both microcephaly and macrocephaly are over-represented in the autistic population (Fombonne et al., 1999). A variety of other neuroanatomical abnormalities have been described, including abnormalities of the cerebellum (Allen & Courchesne, 2003; Fatemi et al., 2002).There is also the association of autistic features in Mendelian disorders such as Fragile X syndrome, Tuberous Sclerosis, untreated pheylketonuria (PKU), Rett syndrome (Fombonne 1999; Chudley et al., 1998). Also, the occurrence of chromosome abnormalities have been identified in some ASD individuals (Gillberg, 1998; Prasad et al., 2000), or excess chromosome breakage and fragility (Arrieta et al., 2002; Jayakar et al., 1986). Finally and more recently, molecular genetic studies have identified regions within the genome that harbor susceptibility genes, or in which molecular rearrangements are present in certain regions of the genome, as well as specific candidate genes (Folstein & Rosen-Sheidley, 2001; Lauritsen & Ewald, 2001; Turner et al., 2000). And perhaps in relation to the above noted increased chromosome fragility, Yu et al., (2002) studied segregation patterns of short tandem repeat polymorphic markers from four chromosomes in 12 families and revealed null alleles at four marker sites that were the result of deletions ranging in size from 5 to >260 kb. Common deletions appeared to be specific to autism kindreds and may potentially be autism-susceptibility alleles. Alternatively, they hypothesized that autism-susceptibility alleles elsewhere cause the deletions detected here, possibly by inducing errors during meiosis.

Reports of autism induced by thalidomide and valproic acid exposures (Christianson et al., 1994; Stromland et al., 1994) provides evidence that the disease may result from an injury at the time of closure of the neural tube (Rodier et al., 1996). The human data suggest that the initiating lesion includes the motor cranial nerve nuclei. To test this hypothesis, Rodier et al. (1996) examined motor nuclei in the brainstem of a human autistic case postmortem, and the brain exhibited near-complete absence of the facial nucleus and superior olive along with shortening of the brainstem between the trapezoid body and the inferior olive. Hoxa-1 gene knockout mice, in which pattern formation of the hindbrain is disrupted during neurulation, shows similar abnormalities. Experimental data from rats exposed to valproic acid in utero confirm that CNS injuries occurring during or just after neural tube closure can lead to a selective loss of neurons derived from the basal plate of the rhombencephalon. The study added new lines of evidence that place the initiating injury for autism around the time of neural tube closure. A study by Ingram et al. (2000) suggested that a (His)73(Arg) polymorphism (A:G) in HOXA1 contributes substantially to a liability for autism. Devlin et al. (2002) studied 68 individuals diagnosed with Autism Spectrum Disorders and found a significant dearth of G homozygotes and biased transmission of G alleles from parents to affected offspring, especially from mothers. Because the connection between

HOXA1 and liability to autism was considered compelling, Devlin and his colleagues attempted to replicate this finding using a larger, independent sample from the Collaborative Programs of Excellence in Autism (CPEA) network. They found no obvious sex-biased allele transmission. Although they could not exclude the possibility that the samples in the two studies are intrinsically different, their data argued against a major role for HOXA1 (His)73(Arg) in liability to autism.

Genome wide screens have identified several locations on the human genome that suggest linkage signals to autism. Most of these studies involved different methodologies and identified different genome regions. These studies suggested several autosomal regions including chromosomes 1p, 2q, 4p, 7q, 13q, 15q, and 16p (reviewed in Folstein & Rosen-Sheidley, 2001; International Molecular Genetic Study of Autism Consortium, 2001). The excess of males in the affected population has led to suggestions that an X-linked locus could play a role in the causation of autism or a related pervasive developmental disorders (Hallmayer et al., 1995).

Despite the excess of males, no strong linkage to the X chromosome has been confirmed (Schutz et al., 2002). However, some reports suggest Xq may contain genes relevant to autism (Skuse et al., 1997). Skuse et al. (1997) studied 80 females with Turner syndrome and a single X chromosome, in 55 of which the X was maternally derived (45,X[m]) and in 25 it was of paternal origin (45,X[p]). Members of the 45,X[p] group were significantly better adjusted, with superior verbal and higher-order executive function skills, which mediate social interactions. Their observations suggest a genetic locus exists for social cognition, which is imprinted and is not expressed from the maternally derived X chromosome. Eight females with partial deletions of the short arm of the X chromosome were investigated and results indicate that the putative imprinted locus escapes X-inactivation, and probably lies on Xq or close to the centromere on Xp. If expressed exclusively from the paternal X chromosome, the existence of this locus could explain why 46,XY males (in whom the X chromosome is always maternal in origin) are more vulnerable to developmental disorders of language and social cognition, such as autism, than are 46,XX females. Donnelly et al. (2000) described autism in a girl with Turner syndrome in which the X chromosome was maternal in origin. This offers further support to the notion that the parent-of-origin of the X chromosome influences social cognition.

Recently, French geneticists identified a form of X-linked MR in which there were several affected males in a large kindred with MR with or without autism or pervasive development disorder (Laumonnier et al., 2004). A 2 base pair deletion was found in the *Neuroligin 4* gene (*NLGN4*). Neuroligins are required for proper cell-cell interactions through binding to beta-neurexins. As the neuroligins are enriched at excitatory synapses, the authors believe that a defect in synaptogenesis may lead to deficits in cognitive development and communication processes. Clearly some types of autism and mental retardation appear to have common genetic origins.

Several candidate regions and genes have been linked to ASD. Chromosome 15q11-q13 has been identified as a strong candidate region because of the frequent occurrence of chromosomal abnormalities in that region and numerous suggestive linkage and association findings (Folstein & Rosen-Sheidley, 2001). A novel statistical approach called ordered-subset analysis (OSA), can help identify a homoge-neous subset of families that contribute to overall linkage at a given chromosomal location to help in the fine mapping and localization of the susceptibility gene within a chromosomal area. Shao et al., (2003) showed increased linkage evidence for the 15q11-q13 region, at the GABRB3 locus, from a logarithm of the odds (LOD) score of 1.45 to a LOD score of 4.71 (usually anything over a LOD score of 3 in an autosomal region is highly suggestive of linkage). These results narrowed the region of interest on chromosome 15 to an area surrounding the gamma-aminobutyric acid-receptor subunit genes, a potential candidate gene for autism. Buxbaum et al. (2002) also confirmed a role for genetic variants within the GABA receptor gene complex in 15q11-13 in autistic disorders.

Other neurotransmitter pathways, involving the neurotransmitter genes them-selves or their receptors have also generated much interest as candidate genes causing autism. These include serotonin and the 5-hydroxytryotamine transporter gene The promoter polymorphism of the serotonin transporter gene (HTT) is of special interest in autism in light of the consistent finding of platelet hyperserotonemia of autism (Anderson et al., 2002), the treatment effects of serotonin reuptake inhibitors, and the role of serotonin in limbic functioning and neurodevelopment (Tordjman et al., 2001). Tordjman and colleagues believe that HTT promoter alleles by themselves do not convey risk for autism, but, rather, modify the severity of autistic behaviors in the social and communication domains.

Some families with autistic children have a low level of serum dopamine beta-hydroxylase (DbetaH), which catalyzes the conversion of dopamine to norepineph-rine, Robinson et al. (2001) examined the DBH gene as a candidate locus in families with two or more children with autism spectrum disorder using the affected sib-pair method. They suggest that lowered maternal serum DbetaH activity results in a suboptimal uterine environment (decreased norepinephrine relative to dopamine), which, in conjunction with genotypic susceptibility of the fetus, results in autism spectrum disorder in some families.

Zhang et al. (2002) examined a polymorphic trinucleotide repeat (CGG/GCC) within the human Reelin gene (RELN) as a candidate gene for ASD). This gene encodes a large extracellular matrix protein that orchestrates neuronal positioning during corticogenesis. Their case-control and affected sib-pair findings did not support a role for RELN in susceptibility to ASD, but the more powerful family-based association study demonstrated that RELN alleles with larger numbers of CGG repeats may play a role in the etiology of some cases of ASD, especially in children without delayed phrase speech.

Cohen et al., (2003) studied an upstream variable-number tandem repeat region polymorphism (uVNTR) in the monoamine oxidase A (MAOA) promoter region and the phenotypic expression of autism in children. They found that children with the low-activity MAOA allele had both lower intelligence quotients and they were more severely affected with autistic behavior than children with the high-activity allele. The authors speculate that functional MAOA-uVNTR alleles may be a genetic factor in the severity of expression in some autistic males.

Since between 15-30% of children with ASD will develop a seizure disorder, an attempt was made to look at molecular variants in the sodium channel genes, since a susceptibility locus for autism was mapped near a cluster of voltage-gated sodium channel genes on chromosome 2. Weiss et al. (2003) studied 117 multiplex autism families. Only six families carried variants with potential effects on sodium channel function. Five coding variants and one lariat branchpoint mutation were each observed in a single family, but were not present in controls. The variant R1902C in SCN2A is located in the calmodulin binding site and was found to reduce binding affinity for calcium-bound calmodulin. R542Q in SCN1A was observed in one autism family and had previously been identified in a patient with juvenile myoclonic epilepsy (Weiss et al., 2003).

Research efforts have intensified in the hunt to solve the mystery of autism. Results of research to date have confirmed the importance of both environmental and genetic factors, and that the answers to this complex group of disorders will also be complex. It appears that multiple genes, each one a risk factor for a component of these complex disorders, together with other genes and other risk factors account for the extent of the disease expression. These genes act as non-deterministic risk factors for autism expression, and with an increasing risk being conferred by a greater number of genes. Some genes may have an effect on a continually distributed phenotype. Developing quantitative measures of the various components of the syndrome may eventually lead to a better understanding and prediction of the disorder (Dawson et al., 2002).

## Attention Deficit Hyperactivity Disorder

Attention Deficit Hyperactivity Disorder (ADHD) is one of the most common childhood conditions with a significant impact on the affected child's ability to learn, and symptoms and signs persist into adulthood in many. It is associated with conduct problems, academic underachievement and substance abuse. It is estimated that between 2% and 10% of the population are affected (Bauermeister et al., 1994). The diagnosis involves the presence of inattentiveness and/or hyperactivity and impulsivity as a pervasive impairment, that is, impairment in more than 1 setting. (American Psychiatric Association, 1994). Like ASD, the cause is heterogeneous, males are more often affected than females, there is familial clustering, and inheritance is complex. Family, twin and adoption studies confirm a genetic susceptibility, although environmental factors are also important in causation (Faraone & Doyle, 2002).

Based on the premise of a dominant or co-dominant gene inheritance and results of segregation analysis in families, molecular genetic studies were undertaken to identify susceptibility genes or regions on the genome. Molecular genetic studies suggest that three genes may increase the susceptibility to ADHD: the D4 dopamine receptor gene, the dopamine transporter gene, and the D2 dopamine receptor gene (Faraone & Biederman, 1998; Kirley et al., 2002). One study used affected-sib-pair analysis in 203 families to localize the first major susceptibility locus for ADHD to a 12-cM region on chromosome 16p13 (LOD score 4.2) (Smalley et al., 2002). The region overlaps with one region showing linkage to autism, in which inattention and hyperactivity are common. The authors suggest that variations in a gene on 16p13 may contribute to common deficits found in both ADHD and autism.

Dopaminergic, serotonergic and nor-adrenergic pathways have been implicated to be associated with ADHD. Monoamine oxidase A (MAOA) which is involved in the degradation of all three of these neurotransmitters has been suggested as a strong candidate gene for ADHD, but evidence has been weak at best (Lawson et al., 2003). The pattern of neuropsychological deficits found in ADHD children implicate executive functions and working memory; this pattern is similar to what has been found among adults with frontal lobe damage, which suggests that the frontal cortex or regions projecting to the frontal cortex are dysfunctional in at least some ADHD children. Moreover, neuroimaging studies implicate frontosubcortical pathways in ADHD. Notably, these pathways are rich in catecholamines, which have been implicated in ADHD by the mechanism of action of stimulants–the class of drugs that effectively treats many ADHD children. To date, human studies of the catecholamine hypothesis of ADHD have been equivocal. Recent research has further supported the concept that serotonin pathways, in addition to dopamine, may be involved in the development of attention deficit hyperactivity disorder (ADHD) (Kent et al., 2002; Quist et al., 2003).

The role of environmental susceptibility factors should not be discounted. Approximately 80% of children with Fetal Alcohol Spectrum Disorder (FASD) exhibit features of ADHD. FASD individuals also have complex learning disabilities, especially a mixed receptive-expressive language disorder with deficits in social cognition and communication, working memory problems, and a mathematics disorder. ADHD in children with FASD often differs from that of children without FASD. For children with FASD, ADHD is more likely to be the earlier-onset, inattention subtype, with co-morbid developmental, psychiatric, and medical conditions (O'Malley & Nanson, 2002). Sustained attention processing defects in early childhood has been observed in children with prenatal cocaine exposure with a long-lasting disruption of the brain systems relevant to arousal and attention (Bandstra et al., 2001). Since these drugs are commonly abused in pregnancy, and in the case of FASD the prevalence in some American metropolitan areas is at least 9 per 1000 and higher in other at risk populations, the role of teratogens especially in children presenting with ADHD and other more complex learning and executive function deficits has to be considered (Sampson et al., 1996).

## Specific Reading Disability (Dyslexia) and Other Learning Disorders

Specific Reading Disability (SRD), also known as dyslexia, is common, and affects from 5-10% of school-aged children, with a male excess of 3 or 4 to 1. Affected children typically are normally intelligent and have a disproportionate difficulty with reading and spelling. The disability persists into adulthood. Family studies using powerful segregation analysis, and twin studies (MZ concordance 68% compared to DZ concordance of 38%) confirm an inherited predisposition, and it appears to be multifactorial and probably polygenic (DeFries & Alarcon, 1996; Smith et al., 2002).

Linkage analysis in families with SRD using lod score approach and sib pair analysis demonstrate several regions in the genome suggestive of culpable loci, including chromosome regions 1p36, 2p12-16, 6p21.3, 6q13-16, 15 cen, 15q21 (Smith et al., 2002). Several studies have consistently found evidence for a quantitative-trait locus (QTL) within the 17 Mb (14.9 cM) that span D6S109 and D6S291 on chromosome 6p21.3-22, and the region was further more narrowly defined to a 4Mb region (Kaplan et al., 2002). It is evident that, like autism and ADHD, SRD is a heterogeneous, complex disorder that is strongly influenced by genetic factors.

Specific language impairment (SLI) is similar to SRD in that it is a diagnosis of exclusion. SLI is not simple but may involve specific expressive or receptive deficits in one or several of the global language domains (phonology, morphology, syntax, semantics, and pragmatics). SLI is common, and affects between 6% and 8% of school age children (Tomblin et al., 1997). As in ASD, ADHD, and SRD, the greatest genetic liability is having a Y chromosome. Male to female ratios is 3 to 1. Familial clustering is present, heretability is high, and twin studies show higher concordance rates amongst MZ compared to DZ twins (MZ=0.96; DZ=0.69) (Tomblin & Buckwalter, 1998).

Lai et al. (2001) in the U.K. studied a unique three-generation family, in which a severe speech and language disorder is transmitted as an AD trait. Previous work suggested that the region 7q31 on chromosome 7 may harbor a gene specific to SLI. They identified a point mutation in affected members of the family that alters an invariant amino-acid residue in the forkhead domain of FOXP2, and suggest that this gene is involved in the developmental process that culminates in speech and language. Subsequently the same group studied several more FLI and ASD families searching for variants of this gene, and concluded that coding-region variants in FOXP2 do not play a role in autism or more common forms of language impairment (Newbury et al., 2002).

## Conclusions

The Human Genome Project and other clinical discoveries have accelerated our ability to identify genes responsible for many afflictions of humanity. Molecular technology has brought back into the limelight protein chemistry, and the new discipline of proteomics. Our ability to identify the genetic etiology of individuals with DD will be enhanced by the collaboration of molecular and medical geneticists, physicians, psychologists and psychiatrists. Earlier and more accurate clinical and laboratory diagnoses will provide families and individuals more options related to prevention, carrier testing, prenatal diagnosis, and treatment interventions. Breakthroughs in our understanding of the mechanisms by which genes interact with each other and with the environment will be realized. Within the next few decades, more targeted, cost-efficient diagnostic and treatment options will unfold for many of the disorders leading to DD. Ultimately, the goal to improve the quality and productivity of the lives of those individuals living with DD will be achieved.

## Acknowledgments

Thanks to my mentors in medicine and genetics who inspired me to choose the study of children with disabilities as a research focus. It has been a privilege to observe and participate in the remarkable advances in the field of clinical genetics over the past three decades and witness the benefits derived for families and the children living with intellectual disability. A special thanks is extended to Dr. Dickie Yu, who renewed my interests in children with autism, and to Drs. Jeannette Holden and Cheryl Rockman-Greenberg who critically reviewed the chapter. Thanks to the Children's Hospital Foundation, Inc., Winnipeg, and an Interdisciplinary Health Research Team (IHRT) grant #RT-43820 from the Canadian Institutes of Health Research (CIHR) (P.I. Dr. Jeanette Holden) and the Autism Spectrum Disorders Canadian-American Research Consortium who supported, in part, the development of this chapter.

## References

Allanson, J. E., & Graham, G. E. (2002). Sex chromosome abnormalities. In D. L. Rimoin, J. M. Connor, R. E. Pyeritz, & B. R. Korf (Eds.), *Emory and Rimoin's principles and practice of medical genetics 4th edition* (pp. 1184-1201). London: Churchill Livingstone.

Allen, G., & Courchesne, E. (2003). Differential effects of developmental cerebellar abnormality on cognitive and motor functions in the cerebellum: an fMRI study of autism. *American Journal of Psychiatry, 160,* 262-273.

American Psychiatric Association. (1994). *Diagnostic and statistical manual of diagnostic disorders (4th ed.).* Washington, D.C.: Author.

Anderson, G. M., Gutknecht, L., Cohen, D. J., Brailly-Tabard, S., Cohen, J. H., Ferrari, P., et al. (2002). Serotonin transporter promoter variants in autism: functional effects and relationship to platelet hyperserotonemia. *Molecular Psychiatry, 7,* 831-836.

Anderson, N. H. (2002). Analysis of genetic linkage. In D. L. Rimoin, J. M. Connor, R. E. Pyeritz, & B. R. Korf (Eds.), *Emory and Rimoin's principles and practice of medical genetics 4th edition* (pp. 133-148). London: Churchill Livingstone.

Anderson, N. H., & Dominiczak, A. F. (2002). Genetic analysis of complex traits. In D. L. Rimoin, J. M. Connor, R. E. Pyeritz, & B. R. Korf (Eds.), *Emory and Rimoin's principles and practice of medical genetics 4th edition* (pp. 410-424). London: Churchill Livingstone.

Anderson, G., Schroer, R. J., & Stevenson, R. E. (1996). Mental retardation in South Carolina II: Causation. *Proceedings of the Greenwood Genetics Center, 15,* 32-44.

Arrieta, I., Nunez, T., Martinez, B., Perez, A., Telez, M., Criado, B., et al. (2002). Chromosomal fragility in a behavioral disorder. *Behavioural Genetics, 32,* 397-412.

Austin, K. D., & Hall, J. G. (1992). Nontraditional inheritance. *Pediatric Clinics of North America, 39,* 335-348.

Bailey, A., Le Couteur, A., Gottesman, I., Bolton, P., Simonoff, E., Yuzda, E., & Rutter, M. (1995). Autism as a strongly genetic disorder: Evidence from a British twin study. *Psychological Medicine, 25,* 63-77.

Bandstra, E. S., Morrow, C. E., Anthony, J. C., Accornero, V. H., & Fried, P. A. (2001). Longitudinal investigation of task persistence and sustained attention in children with prenatal cocaine exposure. *Neurotoxicology and Teratology, 23,* 545-559.

Bankier, A., & Keith, C. G. (1989). POSSUM: the microcomputer laser-videodisk syndrome information system. *Ophthalmic Paediatric Genetics, 10,* 51-52.

Banks, R. E., Dunn, M. J., Hochstrasser, D. F., Sanchez, J. C., Blackstock, W., Pappin, D. J., & Selby, P. J. (2000). Proteomics: new perspectives, new biomedical opportunities. *The Lancet 2000, 356*(9243), 1749-1756.

Bardoni, B., Mandel, J. L., & Fisch, G. S. (2000). FMR1 gene and fragile X syndrome. *American Journal of Medical Genetics, 97,* 153-163.

Battaglia, A., Bianchini, E., & Carey, J. C. (1999). Diagnostic yield of the comprehensive assessment of developmental delay/mental retardation in an institute of child neuropsychiatry. *American Journal of Medical Genetics, 82,* 60-66.

Battaglia, A., & Carey, J. C. (2003). Diagnostic evaluation of developmental delay/mental retardation: An overview. *American Journal of Medical Genetics, 117C,* 3-14.

Bauermeister, J., Canino, G., & Bird, H. (1994). Epidemiology of disruptive behavior disorders. *Child and Adolescent Psychiatric Clinics of North America. 3,* 177-194.

Bishop, T., & Sham, P. C. (2000). *Analysis of multifactorial disease.* London: Bios.

Bolton, P. F, Roobol, M., Allsopp, L., & Pickles, A. (2001). Association between idiopathic infantile macrocephaly and autism spectrum disorders. *The Lancet, 358*(9283), 726-727.

Brook, J. D., McCurrach, M. E., Harley, H. G., Buckler, A. J., Church, D., Aburatani, H., et al. (1992). Molecular basis of myotonic dystrophy: expansion of a trinucleotide (CTG) repeat at the 3' end of a transcript encoding a protein kinase family member. *Cell 68,* 799-808.

Buxbaum, J. D., Silverman, J. M., Smith, C. J., Greenberg, D. A., Kilifarski, M., Reichert, J., et al. (2002). Association between a GABRB3 polymorphism and autism. *Molecular Psychiatry, 7,* 311-316.

Cassidy, S. B., Dykens, E., & Williams, C. A. (2000). Prader-Willi and Angelman syndromes: sister imprinted disorders. *American Journal of Medical Genetics, 97,* 136-146.

Chakrabarti, S., & Fombonne, E. (2001). Pervasive developmental disorders in preschool children. *Journal of the American Medical Association, 285,* 3093-3099.

Chelly, J. (2000). MRX review. *American Journal of Medical Genetics, 94,* 364-366.

Cheon, M. S., Kim, S. H., Yaspo, M. L., Blasi, F., Aoki, Y., Melen, K., & Lubec, G. (2003). Protein levels of genes encoded on chromosome 21 in fetal Down syndrome brain: Challenging the gene dosage effect hypothesis (Part I). *Amino Acids , 24,* 111-117.

Chiurazzi, P., & Neri, G. (2001). Pharmacological reactivation of inactive genes: the fragile X experience. *Brain Research Bulletin, 56*, 383-387.

Chiurazzi, P., Hamel, B. C., & Neri, G. (2001). XLMR genes: update 2000. *European Journal of Human Genetics, 9*, 71-81.

Christian, S. L., Bhatt, N. K., Martin, S. A., Sutcliffe, J. S., Kubota, T., Huang, B., et al. (1998). Integrated YAC contig map of the Prader-Willi/Angelman region on chromosome 15q11-q13 with average STS spacing of 35 kb. *Genome Research, 8*, 146-157.

Christianson, A. L., Chesler, N., & Kromberg, J. G. (1994). Fetal valproate syndrome: clinical and neuro-developmental features in two sibling pairs. *Developmental Medicine and Child Neurology, 36*, 361-369.

Chudley, A. E. (1998). Genetic landmarks through philately—Gregor Johann Mendel (1822-1884). *Clinical Genetics, 54*, 121-123.

Chudley, A. E., Gutierrez, E., Jocelyn, L. J., & Chodirker, B. N. (1998). Outcomes of genetic evaluation in children with pervasive developmental disorder. *Journal of Developmental and Behavioral Pediatrics, 19*, 321-325.

Chudley, A. E., Dawson, A. J., Chodirker, B. N., & Jocelyn, L. J. (1999). Children with PDD need to be evaluated by clinical geneticists. Pervasive developmental disorder. *Journal of Developmental and Behavioral Pediatrics, 20*, 72-73.

Chudley, A. E., & Hagerman, R. J. (1987). Fragile X syndrome. *Journal of Pediatrics, 110*, 821-831.

Chudley, A. E., Ray, M., Evans, J. A., & Cheang, M. (1990). Possible association of rare autosomal folate sensitive fragile sites and idiopathic mental retardation: a blind controlled population study. *Clinical Genetics, 38*, 241-256.

Chudoba, I., Plesch, A., Lorch, T., Lemke, J., Claussen, U., & Senger, G. (1999). High resolution multicolor-banding: a new technique for refined FISH analysis of human chromosomes. *Cytogenetics and Cell Genetics, 84*, 156-160.

Cohen, I. L., Liu, X., Schutz, C., White, B. N., Jenkins, E. C., Brown, W. T., & Holden, J. J. (2003). Association of autism severity with a monoamine oxidase A functional polymorphism. *Clinical Genetics, 64*, 190-197.

Cook, J., Lamb, W., & Mueller, R. F. (2002). Mendelian inheritance. In D. L. Rimoin, J. M. Connor, R. E. Pyeritz, & B. R. Korf (Eds.), *Emory and Rimoin's principles and practice of medical genetics 4th edition* (pp. 104-124). London: Churchill Livingstone.

Croen, L. A., Grether, J. K., & Selvin, S. (2002). Descriptive epidemiology of autism in a California population: who is at risk? *Journal of Autism and Developmental Disorders, 32*, 217-224.

Curry, C. J., Stevenson, R. E., Aughton, D., Byrne, J., Carey, J. C., Cassidy, S., et al. (1997). Evaluation of mental retardation: recommendations of a Consensus Conference: American College of Medical Genetics. *American Journal of Medical Genetics, 72*, 468-477.

Dawson, A. J., Putnam, S., Schultz, J., Riordan, D., Prasad, C., Greenberg, C. R., et al. (2002). Cryptic chromosome rearrangements detected by subtelomere assay in patients with mental retardation and dysmorphic features. *Clinical Genetics, 62,* 488-494.

Dawson, G., Webb, S., Schellenberg, G. D., Dager, S., Friedman, S., Aylward, E., & Richards, T. (2002). Defining the broader phenotype of autism: Genetic, brain, and behavioral perspectives. *Development and Psychopathology, 14,* 581-611.

De Luca, A., Pasini, A., Amati, F., Botta, A., Spalletta, G., Alimenti, S., et al. (2001). Association study of a promoter polymorphism of UFD1L gene with schizophrenia. *American Journal of Medical Genetics, 105,* 529-533.

DeFries, J. C., & Alarcon, M. (1996). Genetics of specific learning disability. *Mental Retardation and Developmental Disabilities Research Review, 2,* 39-47.

Devlin, B., Bennett, P., Cook, E. H., Jr., Dawson, G., Gonen, D., Grigorenko, E. L., et al. (2002). No evidence for linkage of liability to autism to HOXA1 in a sample from the CPEA network. *American Journal of Medical Genetics, 114,* 667-672.

Donnai, D., & Karmiloff-Smith, A. (2000). Williams syndrome: from genotype through to the cognitive phenotype. *American Journal of Medical Genetics, 97,* 164-171.

Donnelly, S. L., Wolpert, C. M., Menold, M. M., Bass, M. P., Gilbert, J. R., Cuccaro, M., et al. (2000). Female with autistic disorder and monosomy X (Turner syndrome): parent-of-origin effect of the X chromosome. American Journal of Medical Genetics (Neuropsychiatric Genetics) *96,* 312-316.

Driscoll, D. A., Spinner, N. B., Budarf, M. L., McDonald-McGinn, D. M., Zackai, E. H., Goldberg, R. B., et al. (1992). Deletions and microdeletions of 22q11.2 in velo-cardio-facial syndrome. *American Journal of Medical Genetics, 44,* 261-268.

Dykens, E. M. (1995). Measuring behavioral phenotypes: provocations from the "new genetics". *American Journal on Mental Retardation, 99,* 522-532.

Eddy, S. R. (2001). Non-coding RNA genes and the modern RNA world. *Nature Reviews Genetics, 2,* 919-929.

Elliman, D. A., & Bedford, H. E. (2002). Measles, mumps and rubella vaccine, autism and inflammatory bowel disease: advising concerned parents. *Paediatric Drugs 4,* 631-635.

Evans, C. D. (1995). Computer systems in dysmorphology. *Clinical Dysmorphology, 4,* 185-201.

Fatemi, S. H., Halt, A. R., Realmuto, G., Earle, J., Kist, D. A., Thuras, P., & Merz, A. (2002). Purkinje cell size is reduced in cerebellum of patients with autism. *Cellular and Molecular Neurobiology, 22,* 171-175.

Faraone, S. V., & Biederman, J. (1998). Neurobiology of attention-deficit hyperactivity disorder. *Biological Psychiatry, 44,* 951-958.

Faraone, S. V., & Doyle, A. E. (2002). Attention deficit hyperactivity disorder. In D. L. Rimoin, J. M. Connor, R. E. Pyeritz, & B. R. Korf (Eds.), *Emory and Rimoin's principles and practice of medical genetics 4th edition* (pp. 2866-2872). London: Churchill Livingstone.

Finucane, B., Haas-Givler, B., & Simon, E. W. (2003). Genetics, mental retardation, and the forging of new alliances. *American Journal of Medical Genetics, 117C,* 66-72.

Flint, J. (1998). Behavioral phenotypes: conceptual and methodological issues. *American Journal of Medical Genetics, 81,* 235-240.

Folstein, S. E., & Rosen-Sheidley, B. (2001). Genetics of autism: complex aetiology for a heterogeneous disorder. *Nature Reviews in Genetics, 2,* 943-955.

Folstein, S. E., & Rutter, M. (1977). Infantile autism: a genetic study of 21 twin pairs. *Journal of Child Psychology and Psychiatry, 18,* 297-321.

Fombonne, E. (1999). The epidemiology of autism: a review. *Psychological Medicine, 29,* 769-786.

Fombonne, E., Roge, B., Claverie, J., Courty, S., & Fremolle, J. (1999). Microcephaly and macrocephaly in autism. *Journal of Autism and Developmental Disorders, 29,* 113-119.

Francke, U. (1999). Williams-Beuren syndrome: genes and mechanisms. *Human Molecular Genetics, 8,* 1947-1954.

Gardiner, K., Slavov, D., Bechtel, L., & Davisson, M. (2002). Annotation of human chromosome 21 for relevance to Down syndrome: gene structure and expression analysis. *Genomics, 79,* 833-843.

Gillberg, C. (1998). Chromosomal disorders and autism. *Journal of Autism and Developmental Disorders, 28,* 415-425.

Gillberg, C., & Wing, L. (1999). Autism: not an extremely rare disorder. *Acta Psychiatrica Scandinavia, 99,* 399-406.

Gorlin, R. J., Cohen, M. M., Jr., & Hennekam, R. C. M. (2001). *Syndromes of the Head and Neck.* Oxford Monographs on Medical Genetics, No. 42. 4th ed. New York: Oxford University Press.

Hallmayer, J., Hebert, J. M., Spiker, D., Lotspeich, L., McMahon, W. M., Petersen, P. B., et al. (1996). Autism and the X chromosome. Multipoint sib-pair analysis. *Archives in General Psychiatry, 53,* 985-989.

Henry, J. C., van Amelsvoort, T., Morris, R. G., Owen, M. J., Murphy, D. G., & Murphy, K. C. (2002). An investigation of the neuropsychological profile in adults with velo-cardio-facial syndrome (VCFS). *Neuropsychologia, 40,* 471-478.

Hollox, E. J., Atia, T., Cross, G., Parkin, T., & Armour, J. A. (2002). High throughput screening of human subtelomeric DNA for copy number changes using multiplex amplifiable probe hybridisation (MAPH). *Journal of Medical Genetics, 39,* 790-795.

Horvath, K., & Perman, J. A. (2002). Autistic disorder and gastrointestinal disease. *Current Opinions in Pediatrics, 14,* 583-587.

Hunter, A. G. (2000). Outcome of the routine assessment of patients with mental retardation in a genetics clinic. *American Journal of Medical Genetics, 90,* 60-68.

Ingram, J. L., Stodgell, C. J., Hyman, S. L., Figlewicz, D. A., Weitkamp, L. R., & Rodier, P. M. (2000). Discovery of allelic variants of HOXA1 and HOXB1: genetic susceptibility to autism spectrum disorders. *Teratology, 62,* 393-405.

International Molecular Genetic Study of Autism Consortium (IMGSAC). (2001). A genomewide screen for autism: strong evidence for linkage to chromosome 2q, 7q, and 16p. *American Journal of Human Genetics, 69,* 570-581.

Jayakar, P., Chudley, A. E., Ray, M., Evans, J. A., Perlov, J., & Wand, R. (1986). Fra(2) (q13) and inv(9) (p11q12) in autism: causal relationship? *American Journal of Medical Genetics, 23*(1-2), 381-392.

Jerome, L. A., & Papaioannou, V. E. (2001). DiGeorge syndrome phenotype in mice mutant for the T-box gene, Tbx1. *Nature Genetics, 27,* 286-291.

Jiang, Y., Tsai, T. F., Bressler, J., & Beaudet, A. L. (1998). Imprinting in Angelman and Prader-Willi syndromes. *Current Opinion in Genetics and Development, 8,* 334-342.

Johnson, C. A. (2000). Chromatin modification and disease. *Journal of Medical Genetics, 37,* 905-915.

Jones, K. L. (Ed.). (1996). *Smith's recognizable patterns of human malformations* (5th ed.). Philadelphia: W. B. Saunders, Inc.

Kahler, S. H., & Fahey, M. C. (2003). Metabolic disorders and mental retardation. *American Journal of Medical Genetics, 117C,* 31-41.

Kajiwara, K., Berson, E. L., & Dryja, T. P. (1994). Digenic retinitis pigmentosa due to mutations at the unlinked peripherin/RDS and ROM1 loci. *Science 264(5165),* 1604-1608.

Kaplan, D. E., Gayan, J., Ahn, J., Won, T. W., Pauls, D., Olson, R. K., DeFries, J. C., et al. (2002). Evidence for linkage and association with reading disability on 6p21.3-22. *American Journal of Human Genetics, 70,* 1287-1298.

Katsanis, N., Beales, P. L., Woods, M. O., Lewis, R. A., Green, J. S., Parfrey, P. S., et al. (2000). Mutations in MKKS cause obesity, retinal dystrophy and renal malformations associated with Bardet-Biedl syndrome. *Nature Genetics, 26,* 67-70.

Kent, L., Doerry, U., Hardy, E., Parmar, R., Gingell, K., Hawi, Z., Kirley, A., et al. (2002). Evidence that variation at the serotonin transporter gene influences susceptibility to attention deficit hyperactivity disorder (ADHD): analysis and pooled analysis. *Molecular Psychiatry, 7,* 908-912.

Kirchhoff, M., Rose, H., & Lundsteen, C. (2001). High resolution comparative genomic hybridisation in clinical cytogenetics. *Journal of Medical Genetics, 38,* 740-744.

Kirley, A., Hawi, Z., Daly, G., McCarron, M., Mullins, C., Millar, N., et al. (2002). Dopaminergic system genes in ADHD: toward a biological hypothesis. *Neuropsychopharmacology, 27,* 607-619.

Knight, S. J., Regan, R., Nicod, A., Horsley, S. W., Kearney, L., Homfray, T., et al. (1999). Subtle chromosomal rearrangements in children with unexplained mental retardation. *The Lancet, 354*(9191), 1676-1681.

Lachman, H. M., Morrow, B., Shprintzen, R., Veit, S., Parsia, S. S., Faedda, G., et al. (1996). Association of codon 108/158 catechol-O-methyltransferase gene polymorphism with the psychiatric manifestations of velo-cardio-facial syndrome. *American Journal of Medical Genetics, 67,* 468-472.

Lai, C. S., Fisher, S. E., Hurst, J. A., Vargha-Khadem, F., & Monaco, A. P. (2001). A forkhead-domain gene is mutated in a severe speech and language disorder. *Nature, 413,* 519-523.

Lainhart, J. E., Piven, J., Wzorek, M., Landa, R., Santangelo, S. L., Coon, H., & Folstein, S. E. (1997). Macrocephaly in children and adults with autism. *Journal of the American Academy of Child and Adolescent Psychiatry, 36,* 282-290.

Lander, E. S., Linton, L. M., Birren, B., Nusbaum, C., Zody, M. C., Baldwin, J., et al. (2001). Initial sequencing and analysis of the human genome. *Nature, 409*(6822), 860-921.

Laumonnier, F., Bonnet-Brilhaut, F., Gomot, M., Blanc, R., David, A., Moizard, M-P., et al. (2004). X-linked mental retardation and autism are associated with a mutation in the *NLGN4* gene, a member of the Neuroligin Family. *American Journal of Human Genetics, 74,* 552-557.

Lauritsen, M., & Ewald, H. (2001). The genetics of autism. *Acta Psychiatrica Scandinavia, 103,* 411-427.

Lawson, D. C., Turic, D., Langley, K., Pay, H. M., Govan, C. F., Norton, N., et al. (2003). Association analysis of monoamine oxidase A and attention deficit hyperactivity disorder. *American Journal of Medical Genetics, 116*(1 Suppl), 84-89.

Lubec, G., & Engidawork, E. (2002) The brain in Down syndrome (TRISOMY 21). *Journal of Neurology, 249,* 1347-1356.

Lubs, H. A. (1969). A marker X chromosome. *American Journal of Human Genetics, 21,* 231-244.

Lugenbeel, K. A., Peier, A. M., Carson, N. L., Chudley, A. E., & Nelson, D. L. (1995). Intragenic loss of function mutations demonstrate the primary role of FMR1 in fragile X syndrome. *Nature Genetics, 10,* 483-485.

Madsen, K. M., Hviid, A., Vestergaard, M., Schendel, D., Wohlfahrt, J., Thorsen, P., et al. (2002). MMR vaccination and autism—a population-based follow-up study. [Danish]. *Ugeskrift for Læger, 164,* 5741-5744.

Maestrini, E., Paul, A., Monaco, A. P., & Bailey, A. (2000). Identifying autism susceptibility genes. *Neuron, 28,* 19-24.

Majnemer, A., & Shevell, M. I. (1995). Diagnostic yield of the neurologic assessment of the developmentally delayed child. *Journal of Pediatrics, 127,* 193-199.

Massey, P. S., & McDermott, S. (1995). State-specific rates of mental retardation: Prevalence, associated disorders, and etiology. *Morbidity and Mortality Weekly Report, 45,* 61-65.

Maynard, T. M., Haskell, G. T., Lieberman, J. A., & LaMantia, A. S. (2002). 22q11 DS: genomic mechanisms and gene function in DiGeorge/velocardiofacial syndrome. *International Journal of Developmental Neurosciences, 20*(3-5), 407-419.

McKusick V. A. (2002). History of medical genetics. In D. L. Rimoin, J. M. Connor, R. E. Pyeritz, & B. R. Korf (Eds.), *Emory and Rimoin's principles and practice of medical genetics 4th edition* (pp. 3-36). London: Churchill Livingstone.

McLaren, J., & Bryson, S. E. (1987). Review of recent epidemiological studies of mental retardation: prevalence, associated disorders, and etiology. *American Journal on Mental Retardation, 92,* 243-54.

McPherson, J. D., Marra, M., Hillier, L., Waterston, R. H., Chinwalla, A., Wallis, J., et al. (2001). A physical map of the human genome. *Nature, 409*(6822), 934-941.

Meijer, H., de Graaff, E., Merckx, D. M., Jongbloed, R. J., de Die-Smulders, C. E., Engelen, J. J., et al. (1994). A deletion of 1.6 kb proximal to the CGG repeat of the FMR1 gene causes the clinical phenotype of the fragile X syndrome. *Human Molecular Genetics, 3,* 615-620.

Meloni, I., Muscettola, M., Raynaud, M., Longo, I., Bruttini, M., Moizard, M. P., et al. (2002). FACL4, encoding fatty acid-CoA ligase 4, is mutated in nonspecific X-linked mental retardation. *Nature Genetics, 30,* 436-440.

Ming, J. E., & Muenke, M. (2002). Multiple Hits during Early Embryonic Development: Digenic Diseases and Holoprosencephaly. *American Journal of Human Genetics, 71,* 1017-1032.

*MRC: Review of Autism research. Epidemiology and Causes.* (2001). Medical Research Council report. United Kingdom. http://www.mrc.ac.uk/index/public_interest/ public-topical_issues/public-autism-main_section/public-autism_review.htm

Murphy, C. C., Yeargin-Allsopp, M., Decoufle, P., & Drews, C. D. (1995). The administrative prevalence of mental retardation in 10-year-old children in metropolitan Atlanta, 1985 through 1987. *American Journal of Public Health, 85,* 319-23.

Murphy, M., Bolton, P. F., Pickles, A., Fombonne, E., Piven, J., & Rutter, M. (2000). Personality traits of the relatives of autistic probands. *Psychological Medicine 30,* 1411-1424.

Nanni, L., Schelper, R. L., & Muenke, M. T. (2000). Molecular genetics of holoprosencephaly. *Frontiers in Biosciences, 1,* D334-342.

Newbury, D. F., et al. and the International Molecular Genetic Study of Autism Consortium. (2002). FOXP2 is not a major susceptibility gene for autism or specific language impairment. *American Journal of Human Genetics, 70,* 1318-1327.

Nussbaum, R. L., McInnes, R. R., & Willard, H. F. (Eds.). (2001). *Thompson & Thompson Genetics in Medicine.* Philadelphia: W. B. Saunders, Inc.

O'Donnell, W. T., & Warren, S. T. (2002). A decade of molecular studies of fragile X syndrome. *Annual Reviews in Neurosciences, 25,* 315-338.

O'Malley, K. D., & Nanson, J. (2002). Clinical implications of a link between fetal alcohol spectrum disorder and attention-deficit hyperactivity disorder. *Canadian Journal of Psychiatry; 47,* 349-354.

*Online Mendelian Inheritance in Man, OMIM* (TM). McKusick-Nathans Institute for Genetic Medicine, Johns Hopkins University (Baltimore, MD) and National Center for Biotechnology Information, National Library of Medicine (Bethesda, MD), 2000. World Wide Web URL: http://www.ncbi.nlm.nih.gov/omim/

Ozonoff, S., Williams, B. J., Rauch, A. M., & Opitz, J. O. (2000). Behavior phenotype of FG syndrome: cognition, personality, and behavior in eleven affected boys. *American Journal of Medical Genetics, 97,* 112-118.

Phillips, T. J., Belknap, J. K., Hitzemann, R. J., Buck, K., J., Cunningham, C., L., & Crabbe, J. C. (2002). Harnessing the mouse to unravel the genetics of human disease. *Genes Brain and Behaviour, 1,* 14-26.

Plomin, R., & Crabbe, J. (2000). DNA. *Psychology Bulletin, 126,* 806-828.

Plomin, R., & McGuffin, P. (2003). Psychopathology in the postgenomic era. *Annual Reviews in Psychology, 54,* 205-228.

Plomin, R., Owen, M. J., & McGuffin, P. (1994) The genetic basis of complex human behaviors. *Science, 264*(5166), 1733-1739.

Prasad, C., Prasad, A. N., Chodirker, B. N., Lee, C., Dawson, A. K., Jocelyn, L. J., & Chudley, A. E. (2000). Genetic evaluation of pervasive developmental disorders: the terminal 22q13 deletion syndrome may represent a recognizable phenotype. *Clinical Genetics, 57,* 103-109.

Quist, J. F., Barr, C. .L, Schachar, R., Roberts, W., Malone, M., Tannock, R., et al. (2003). The serotonin 5-HT1B receptor gene and attention deficit hyperactivity disorder. *Molecular Psychiatry, 8,* 98-102.

Ramakers, G. J. (2002). Rho proteins, mental retardation and the cellular basis of cognition. *Trends in Neurosciences 25,* 191-199.

Reymond, A., Marigo, V., Yaylaoglu, M. B., Leoni, A., Ucla, C., Scamuffa, N., et al. (2002). Human chromosome 21 gene expression atlas in the mouse. *Nature, 420*(6915), 582-586.

Ried, T., Schrock, E., Ning, Y., & Wienberg, J. (1998). Chromosome painting: a useful art. *Human Molecular Genetics, 7,* 1619-1626.

Riordan, D., Vust, A., Wickstrom, D. E., Brown, J., Chudley, A. E., Tomkins, D., et al. (2002). Identification of a dup(5)(p15.3) by multicolor banding. *Clinical Genetics, 61,* 277-282.

Roig, M., Balliu, P. R., Navarro, C., Brugera, R., & Losada, M. (1994). Presentation, clinical course, and outcome of the congenital form of myotonic dystrophy. Pediatric *Neurology 11,* 208-213.

Rousseau, F, Heitz, D., Biancalana, V., Blumenfeld, S., Kretz, C., Boue, J., et al. (1991). Direct diagnosis by DNA analysis of the fragile X syndrome of mental retardation. *New England Journal of Medicine, 325,* 1673-1681.

Risch, N. J. (2000). Searching for genetic determinants in the new millennium. *Nature, 405*(6788), 847-856.

Ritvo, E. R., Jorde, L. B., Mason-Brothers, A., Freeman, B. J., Pingree, C., Jones, M. B., et al. (1989). The UCLA-University of Utah epidemiologic survey of autism: recurrence risk estimates and genetic counseling. *American Journal of Psychiatry 146,* 1032-1036.

Robinson, P. D., Schutz, C. K., Macciardi, F., White, B. N., & Holden, J. J. (2001). Genetically determined low maternal serum dopamine beta-hydroxylase levels and the etiology of autism spectrum disorders. *American Journal of Medical Genetics, 100,* 30-36.

Rodier, P. M., Ingram, J. L., Tisdale, B., Nelson, S., & Romano, J. (1996). Embryological origin for autism: developmental anomalies of the cranial nerve motor nuclei. *Journal of Comprehensive Neurology, 370,* 247-261.

Sampson, P. D., Streissguth, A. P., Bookstein, F. L., Little, R. E., Clarren, S. K., Dehaene, P., et al. (1996). Incidence of fetal alcohol syndrome and prevalence of alcohol-related neurodevelopmental disorder. *Teratology, 56,* 317-326.

Schaefer, G. B., & Bodensteiner, J. B. (1992). Evaluation of the child with idiopathic mental retardation. *Pediatric Clinics of North America 39,* 929-943.

Schinzel, A. (1984). *Human Cytogenetics Database.* Oxford Medical Database Series. New York: Oxford University Press.

Schrock, E., du Manoir, S., Veldman, T., Schoell, B., Wienberg, J., Ferguson-Smith, M. A., et al. (1996). Multicolor spectral karyotyping of human chromosomes. *Science, 273*(5274), 494-497.

Schutz, C. K., Polley, D., Robinson, P. D., Chalifoux, M., Macciardi, F., White, B. N., & Holden, J. J. (2002). Autism and the X chromosome: no linkage to microsatellite loci detected using the affected sibling pair method. *American Journal of Medical Genetics, 109,* 36-41.

Scriver, C. R. (2002). Why mutation analysis does not always predict clinical consequences: explanations in the era of genomics. *Journal of Pediatrics, 140,* 502-506.

Sheffield, V. C., Nishimura, D., & Stone, E. M. (2001). The molecular genetics of Bardet-Biedl syndrome. *Current Opinion in Genetics and Development, 11,* 317-321.

Shao, Y., Cuccaro, M. L., Hauser, E. R., Raiford, K. L., Menold, M. M., Wolpert, C. M., et al. (2003). Fine Mapping of Autistic Disorder to Chromosome 15q11-q13 by Use of Phenotypic Subtypes. *American Journal of Human Genetics, 72,* 539-548.

Skuse, D. H. (2000). Behavioural phenotyoes: What do they teach us? *Archives of Diseases in Childhood, 82,* 222-225.

Skuse, D. H., James, R. S., Bishop, D. V., Coppin, B., Dalton, P., Aamodt-Leeper, G., et al. (1997). Evidence from Turner's syndrome of an imprinted X-linked locus affecting cognitive function. *Nature, 387,* 705-708.

Smalley, S. L., Kustanovich, V., Minassian, S. L., Stone, J. L., Ogdie, M. N., McGough, J. J., et al. (2002). Genetic linkage of attention-deficit/hyperactivity disorder on chromosome 16p13, in a region implicated in autism. *American Journal of Human Genetics, 71,* 959-963.

Smith, S. D., Gilger, J. W., & Pennington, B. F. (2002). Dyslexia and other specific learning disorders. In D. L. Rimoin, J. M. Connor, R. E. Pyeritz, & B. R. Korf (Eds.), *Emory and Rimoin's principles and practice of medical genetics 4th edition* (pp. 2827-2865). London: Churchill Livingstone.

Spinner, N. B., & Emanuel, B. S. (2002). Deletions and other structural abnormalities of the autosomes. In D. L. Rimoin, J. M. Connor, R. E. Pyeritz, & B. R. Korf (Eds.), *Emory and Rimoin's principles and practice of medical genetics 4th edition* (pp. 1202-1238). London: Churchill Livingstone.

Stevenson, R., E. (1996). Mental retardation: Overview and historical perspective. *Proceedings of the Greenwood Genetics Center, 15,* 19-25.

Stevenson, R. E. (2000). Splitting and lumping in the nosology of XLMR. *American Journal of Medical Genetics, 97,* 174-82

Stevenson, R. E., Schwartz, C. E., & Schroer, R. J. (2000). *X-linked mental retardation.* Oxford Monographs on Medical Genetics. New York: Oxford University Press.

Stromland, K., Nordin, V., Miller, M., Akerstrom, B., & Gillberg, C. (1994). Autism in thalidomide embryopathy: a population study. *Developmental Medicine and Child Neurology, 36,* 351-356.

Sutherland, G. R., Gecz, J., & Mulley, J. C. (2002). Fragile X syndrome and other causes of X-linked mental handicap. In D. L. Rimoin, J. M. Connor, R. E. Pyeritz, & B. R. Korf (Eds.), *Emory and Rimoin's principles and practice of medical genetics 4th edition* (pp. 2801-2826). London: Churchill Livingstone.

Swillen, A., Vogels, A., Devriendt, K., & Fryns, J. P. (2000). Chromosome 22q11 deletion syndrome: update and review of the clinical features, cognitive-behavioral spectrum, and psychiatric complications. *American Journal of Medical Genetics, 97,* 128-135.

Tomblin, J. B., & Buckwalter, P. R. (1998). Heritability of poor language achievement among twins. *Journal of Speech, Language and Hearing Research, 41,* 188-199.

Tomblin, J. B., Records, N. L., Buckwalter, P., Zhang, X., Smith, E., & O'Brien, M. (1997). Prevalence of specific language impairment in kindergarten children. *Journal of Speech, Language and Hearing Research, 40,* 1245-1260.

Tomie, J. L. (2002). Down syndrome and other autosomal trisomies. In D. L. Rimoin, J. M. Connor, R. E. Pyeritz, & B. R. Korf (Eds.), *Emory and Rimoin's principles and practice of medical genetics 4th edition* (pp. 1129-1183). London: Churchill Livingstone.

Toniolo, D. (2000). In search of the MRX genes. *American Journal of Medical Genetics, 97,* 221-227.

Tordjman, S., Gutknecht, L., Carlier, M., Spitz, E., Antoine, C., Slama, F., et al. (2001). Role of the serotonin transporter gene in the behavioral expression of autism. *Molecular Psychiatry, 6,* 434-439.

Torrente, F., Ashwood, P., Day, R., Machado, N., Furlano, R. I., Anthony, A., et al. (2002). Small intestinal enteropathy with epithelial IgG and complement deposition in children with regressive autism. *Molecular Psychiatry, 7,* 375-382.

Turner, G., Webb, T., Wake, S., & Robinson, H. (1996). Prevalence of Fragile X syndrome. *American Journal of Medical Genetics, 64,* 196-197.

Turner, M., Barnby, G., & Bailey, A. (2000). Genetic clues to the biological basis of autism. *Molecular Medicine Today, 6,* 238-244.

Uhrig, S., Schuffenhauer, S., Fauth, C., Wirtz, A., Daumer-Haas, C., Apacik, C., et al. (1999). Multiplex-FISH for pre- and postnatal diagnostic applications. *American Journal of Human Genetics, 65,* 448-462.

van Steensel, M. A., & Winter, R. M. (1998). Internet databases for clinical geneticists—an overview. *Clinical Genetics, 53,* 323-330.

Verkerk, A. J., deVries, B. B., Niermeijer, M. F., Fu, Y. H., Nelson, D. L., et al. (1992). Intragenic probe used for diagnostics in fragile X families. *American Journal of Medical Genetics, 43,* 192-196.

Vu, T. H., Hoffman, A. R. (1997). Imprinting of the Angelman syndrome gene, UBE3A, is restricted to brain. *Nature Genetics, 17,* 12-13.

Wallace, D. C., & Lott, M. T. (2002). Mitochondrial genes in degenerative diseases, cancer and aging. In D. L. Rimoin, J. M. Connor, R. E. Pyeritz, & B. R. Korf (Eds.), *Emory and Rimoin's principles and practice of medical genetics 4th edition* (pp. 299-409). London: Churchill Livingstone.

Weiler, I. J., & Greenough, W. T. (1999). Synaptic synthesis of the Fragile X protein: possible involvement in synapse maturation and elimination. *American Journal of Medical Genetics, 83,* 248-252.

Weiss, L. A., Escayg, A., Kearney, J. A., Trudeau, M., MacDonald, B. T., Mori, M., et al. (2003). Sodium channels SCN1A, SCN2A and SCN3A in familial autism. *Molecular Psychiatry, 8,* 186-194.

Xu, J., & Chen, Z. (2003). Advances in molecular cytogenetics for the evaluation of mental retardation. *American Journal of Medical Genetics, 117C,* 15-24.

Yu, S., Mulley, J., Loesch, D., Turner, G., Donnelly, A., Gedeon, A., et al. (1992). Fragile-X syndrome: unique genetics of the heritable unstable element. *American Journal of Human Genetics, 50,* 968-980.

Yu, C. E., Dawson, G., Munson, J., D'Souza, I., Osterling, J., Estes, A., et al. (2002). Presence of large deletions in kindreds with autism. *American Journal of Human Genetics, 71,* 100-115.

Zhang, H., Liu, X., Zhang, C., Mundo, E., Macciardi, F., Grayson, D. R., et al. (2002). Reelin gene alleles and susceptibility to autism spectrum disorders. *Molecular Psychiatry, 7,* 1012-1017.

Zechner, U., Wilda, M., Kehrer-Sawatzki, H., Vogel, W., Fundele, R., & Hameister, H. (2001). A high density of X-linked genes for general cognitive ability: a runaway process shaping human evolution? *Trends in Genetics, 17,* 697-701.

Zlotogora, J. (1998). Recessive or dominant? Reclassification in the molecular age. *Clinical Genetics, 53,* 423-425.

# Chapter 2

# Behavioral Phenotypes In Neurodevelopmental Disabilities: Implications for Research and Intervention

**W. J. McIlvane**
*University of Massachusetts Medical School*
**C. K. Deutsch**
*University of Massachusetts Medical School
& Harvard Medical School*

This chapter considers the concept of the behavioral phenotype in relationship to the scientific study of and clinical/educational support for persons with mental retardation and other developmental disabilities (MR/DD). It is worth noting that the word "phenotype" derives from the Greek for the display (*phainen*) of a type or character (*typus*), capturing the notion of an organism's distinctive characteristics. Both genes, the environment, and their interactions play a role in shaping the phenotype, including its behavioral dimensions. Thus, the phenotype may be differentiated from the genotype, the latter being the set of genetically coded, heritable instructions that guide cellular processes involved in an organism's development and functioning.

Within the MR/DD field, the role of genetic influences on behavior was not emphasized for much of the latter part of the 20th century. There was acknowledgment that certain intellectual disabilities had a genetic component, for example, Down syndrome is most often associated with a third copy of the 21st chromosome. However, there are many other circumstances that affect the phenotype, including impoverished environments that do not provide adequate stimulation, malnutrition, exposure to toxic environments that produce genetic and/or structural abnormalities, premature birth, and so on.

Perhaps for this reason (among others), scientists and clinicians have tended to conceptualize intellectual disabilities mainly in functional terms. For example, the American Association on Mental Retardation has endorsed the following definition: "Mental retardation is a disability characterized by significant limitations both in intellectual functioning and in adaptive behavior as expressed in conceptual, social, and practical adaptive skills. This disability originates before age 18" (AAMR,

2002). As the AAMR definition indicates, mental retardation is defined in terms of impaired functioning relative to an implied reference population. When a standardized evaluation of intellectual functioning is employed (e.g., a *Stanford-Binet*, Roid, 2003), the reference population is explicit – the population with which the evaluation instrument was normed. A given individual's intellectual functioning is evaluated as significantly limited when the intelligence quotient yielded by test performance is 70-75 or lower. Analogous procedures are used to evaluate adaptive behavior (e.g., *Vineland Adaptive Behavior Scales*, Sparrow, Balla, & Cicchetti, 2001).

To what extent is etiology relevant in classifying an individual as having an intellectual disability according to the AAMR definition? Perhaps surprisingly, the answer is "not at all." For example, although Down syndrome is frequently associated with intellectual disability, there are some persons with trisomy 21 who score higher than 75 on IQ tests and who function well in daily life despite their atypical genetic status. The situation is similar with autism, an apparently heritable disorder associated with atypical language, social behavior, and interests (see McIlvane, Bristol, & Alexander, 1998 for a comprehensive review of this disorder). Although the majority of persons with autism also have mental retardation (Bailey et al., 1996), there is a variant on the autism spectrum, termed Asperger's syndrome, in which intellectual functioning and most aspects of adaptive behavior are not globally impaired.

Given that the MR/DD field has tended to emphasize functional characteristics, it is not surprising that much psychological/behavioral research sought answers to functional questions such as "In what ways do persons with intellectual disabilities function differently from persons without disabilities?" A typical approach has been to compare the performance of large groups of etiologically heterogeneous individuals who do and do not have mental retardation on some task of interest. The resulting data are then used to make statements concerning such disabilities in general (see Ellis, 1979, for a compendium of research within this tradition). For example, it has been reported that persons with intellectual disabilities tend to be more perseverative and less behaviorally flexible than persons without disabilities (Ellis & Dulaney, 1991).

In parallel, special educators have sought to develop interventions that would help persons with intellectual disabilities function in a more typical fashion. The goal has been to remove or bypass barriers to adaptive functioning via skillful teaching. Texts on psychoeducational intervention for this population (e.g., Maurice, Green, & Luce, 1996) suggest broadly effective strategies based on findings from studies of diagnostically heterogeneous samples, typically large group studies or small-N single-case design studies of the type characteristic of applied behavior analysis (Barlow & Hersen, 1984).

Implicit in the practice of studying diagnostically heterogeneous samples is the assumption that behavioral variability due to diagnostic status is not a critical concern. On its face, researchers have adopted either or perhaps both of the following assumptions: (1) Diagnosis and any associated behavioral phenotypes do not strongly determine behavioral variability, and thus the effects can be safely discounted. (2) While diagnosis and associated behavioral phenotypes may be a significant source of behavioral variability, statistical treatment of data may be used to control/manage it; one can still obtain findings with broad generality to the statistically "average" person with an intellectual disability.

Although arguments based on these two assumptions may be reasonable, only the first seems to provide a rationale for extrapolating group research findings to the level of the individual. It was pointed out long ago (e.g., Sidman, 1960) that group analyses are informative at the individual level only to the extent that the individual is representative of the group. For example, the statement "Dunking a basketball is an extremely rare ability" is true when applied to the population of humans as a group. The fact that statistics for the population as a whole would show that the statistically average person cannot dunk tells us only that – it tells us nothing useful for predicting the average ability of players in the National Basketball Association or the likely ability of an individual player.

In the case where the focus is the individual, and the individual is or may not be representative of the general population, scientific methods and clinical/educational supports must be comparably individualized. In research, this requirement was part of the inspiration for developing the single-case experimental designs that were mentioned earlier. Generally speaking, behavioral variability at the individual level is managed by experimental procedures that control for or eliminate its primary sources. For example, because single-case designs involve only comparing a participant with him/herself, participant and associated state variables do not vary and thus are not a source of concern. Perhaps this is one reason why behavioral phenotypes are all but unmentioned in the literature of basic and applied behavior analysis, which features extensive use of single-case design strategies.

Although the single-case approach has been broadly useful and effective on a case-by-case basis, the approach has certain limitations. Just as it is difficult to extrapolate from the group to the individual, so too is it difficult to extrapolate from the individual to the group. For example, suppose one develops an intervention that has been routinely effective with several individual cases of self-injurious behavior. To what extent, will that intervention prove more generally effective? The answer to this particular question cannot be known unless one also knows the degree to which the individuals who were treated are truly representative of the larger group of persons who exhibit self-injurious behavior.

Notably, both the research and intervention literatures in the MR/DD field have demonstrated that intervention procedures may be quite variable in their effects across individuals. For example, it has been understood for some time that the motivations for self-injurious behavior may be different in different individuals (e.g., Symons et al., 1999). For this reason, a "general" approach to intervention has to conduct case-by-case analysis of environmental contingencies that maintain behavior (e.g., Iwata et al., 1994), so as to inform the applied behavior analyst about which of a number of intervention strategies are likely to be effective.

Within the functionalist perspective just described, to what extent must one consider behavioral phenotypes when designing research and/or intervention procedures? As noted earlier, if the effects of behavioral phenotype are negligible or small, perhaps such effects can be safely ignored. However, if behavioral phenotype could be an important determinant of performance, then one is obligated to consider it. The next section will selectively review the current literature on behavioral phenotypes to allow the reader to begin to evaluate whether or not his/her interest warrants such consideration. For readers interested in follow-up studies in the field of genetics, we will briefly introduce some of the relevant terminology that is used in the field of medical genetics.

## Behavioral Phenotypes: A Brief Introduction

### Terminology

Early on, John and Lewis (1966) used the term "endophenotype" to describe the *internal* rather the more easily observed outward appearance of an organism. Thus, the original sense of the word, which has been adopted in recent years by geneticists, was to indicate a phenotype not observable to the naked eye. Gottesman and Gould (2003) suggest that it should be applied only to traits that are transmitted from generation to generation. In more recent usage, the endophenotype might be *any* manifestation of the pathogenic process. A distinctive behavioral phenotype would characterize a recognizable, perhaps syndrome-specific, form of mental retardation; a behavioral *endo*phenotype would accomplish this and also be heritable.

### Recent History

Over the last decade, there has been an increasing effort to examine the behavioral phenotypes of individuals with identifiable developmental disorders (Broman & Grafman, 1994; Goldstein & Reynolds, 1999; Tager-Flusberg, 1999; Nelson & Luciana, 2001). Most of the behaviors described in this literature center on clinical, cognitive, and neuropsychological approaches.

### What Constitutes a Behavioral Phenotype?

In its most literal meaning, the term may be used whenever there are behavioral characteristics that define membership within a group. That definition can be quite broad. For example, the behavior phenotype associated with "mental retardation" can be accommodated within the functional definition provided by the AAMR. Indeed, one can view much of the history of mental retardation research as having been undertaken in the context of this broad phenotypical characterization of behavior.

Today, however, it is increasingly recognized that the more narrowly a given group or subgroup is defined, the more likely it will be that a truly characteristic and potentially informative phenotype can be delineated. However, arriving at a precise, highly specific, predictive behavioral phenotype is not as easy as it might seem. What follows will briefly present three important considerations to bear in mind while reading the current literature on behavioral phenotypes.

*1. It is a challenge to meet the criterion of a truly distinctive phenotype, since this characteristic may be shared among several conditions.*

Behavioral phenotypes cited in the literature to date can be found across a number of conditions, with varying etiologies (as we will illustrate below). The fact that similar behaviors describe the phenotype for separate etiologic conditions does not minimize their importance. On the contrary, this overlap may help to reveal the common pathways from physiology to behavior. Nevertheless, when evaluating statements concerning the behavioral phenotype of a given developmental disorder, it is important to know also about the uniqueness and degree of specificity of that phenotype, for example, when constituting comparison/contrast groups for research purposes.

*2. A seemingly narrowly-construed condition can still be subdivided into heterogeneous subgroups — some of which do not resemble each other phenotypically.*

This is true even for commonly accepted behavioral syndromes. This is particularly true for heritable conditions that derive not from single genes but from whole chains of genes within a chromosome *(contiguous gene disorders*; Punnett & Zakai, 1990). It is also the case for *in utero* toxins *(teratogens)*, that can produce dramatically different effects depending on the dosage and time of exposure (Schardein, 2000).

*3. A behavioral phenotype may be one of many manifestations of a genetic or environmental pathogen.*

In genetic terms, these varied appearances are termed *pleiotropic* (multiple forms), with seemingly unrelated phenotypes stemming from a single gene (Deutsch et al., 1990). Also, a host of genetic and environmental factors can modify the manifestation of a single gene. There is a gradation of severity and expression that depends on the presence of other etiologic factors *(epistasis)*, and randomness comes into play (Ozbudak et al., 2002).

## Behavioral Phenotypes In Specific Syndromes

This section is intended to provide a thumbnail sketch of many conditions and syndromes that have been characterized in the course of scientific study and clinical activity within the field of MR/DD research. The descriptions will be necessarily limited by space considerations to the essential features that are necessary to provide context for the present discussion. For readers interested in further details, we recommend the book-length treatments by Broman & Grafman (1994), Goldstein & Reynolds (1999), and Tager-Flusberg (1999).

### Lesch-Nyhan syndrome (LNS)

Textbook discussions of behavioral phenotypes typically cite the example of this rare X-linked recessive disorder (stemming from an enzyme deficiency). Perhaps this is because the behavioral phenotype for this single-gene disorder is so dramatic: a form of apparently involuntary, severe self-mutilation (Robey et al., 2003). (Also present are mental retardation and neurochemical alterations.) Thus, while self-injury is not uncommon among individuals with severe retardation, the nature and etiology of LNS is such that it commands attention as one of the best examples of behavior that is strongly determined by genetic endowment.

To what extent is the LNS behavioral phenotype truly distinctive, however? Actually, the associated behaviors are not unique to this condition, but rather are exhibited also in other conditions that produce mental retardation, including syndromes such as Smith-Magenis (Di Cicco et al., 2001). With these caveats acknowledged, LNS has a behavioral phenotype worthy of note that has been tied to defined pathophysiological processes that have in turn been tied to a specific gene disorder. Knowing that an individual has LNS will thus have certain implications for treatment that go beyond those that would be implied merely from a superficial evaluation of the behavioral manifestations of the disorder. For example, the clinician who is aware of the genetic determinants and pathophysiology of LNS would be in a better position to evaluate what types of intervention procedures would and would not be good choices.

## ARX Gene Mutations

Individuals with mutations in this single gene exhibit mental retardation, behaviors characteristic of autism, seizures, and atypical hand movements – all stemming from a single abnormal genetic locus (Turner et al., 2002). However, there is a remarkable range in severity of the associated mental retardation (ranging from mild to severe) and the type of manifestation, even in individuals with *identical* mutations. Why would this be the case? One possibility is that the expression of the gene is variable, due simply to random (*stochastic*) events (Ozbudak et al., 2002). Another possibility is that *epistatic* effects are at play, that is, other independent genes have a modifying effect (Wilkins, 1997). The ARX gene mutation disorder illustrates, therefore, a somewhat nonspecific, rather ill-defined behavioral phenotype even in the case of a very specific, very well-defined genetic association. Whereas knowing affected individual's genetic status/diagnosis could be of some help, the highly variable expression is such that characterizing the behavioral phenotype may be of only limited usefulness in informing clinicians and researchers.

## Down Syndrome

The behavioral phenotype in Down syndrome includes significant delay in nonverbal cognitive development, accompanied by additional specific deficits in speech, language production, and auditory short-term memory in infancy and childhood (Chapman & Hesketh, 2002). Yet these children have fewer adaptive behavior problems than individuals with other cognitive disabilities.

So far, little evidence has accrued to suggest that there are specific behavioral phenotypes in Down syndrome that are not seen in other forms of mental retardation (Sigman, 1999). Early educational intervention has provided an improvement in quality of life of these individuals (Roizen & Patterson, 2003).

In addition to the delays/deficits noted early in life (Sigman, 1999) there is also the phenomenon of Down syndrome dementia, with virtually every individual having neuropathologic changes characteristic of Alzheimer Disease by 40 years of age (Schupf et al., 1998). This overlap has prompted an investigation of neurochemical commonalities between the two conditions (Motonaga et al., 2002).

An extra chromosome 21 exposes the developing fetus to a host of disruptive influences. Given this fact, the level of intellectual functioning in Down syndrome is often maintained to a remarkable degree. What accounts for the variability in functional level from mild to severe MR? No doubt a multitude of factors comes into play, but a specific example can be seen among many cases of higher-functioning subjects who have a *mosaic* form of the trisomy, in which only a proportion of cells — sometimes a minority — have the abnormal complement of genes. The mean IQ of mosaic Down syndrome cases is significantly higher than simple trisomy 21 individuals, and many subjects with mosaicism show better verbal and visual-perceptual skills (Fishler & Koch, 1991).

Trisomy 21 does not always contain a complete triplicate set of genes. Sometimes only sections of the chromosome have the extra set of genes, and these natural variations have revealed critical regions for many of the phenotypes found in the syndrome, including mental retardation (Deutsch, 1990; Sago et al., 2000).

## Fragile-X Syndrome

This is the most common inherited condition associated with mental retardation, constituting half of the syndromes that have been located so far on the X chromosome. The critical area of damage appears to be the *fragile X MR 1 (FMR-1)* gene (Verkerk et al., 1991). This is characterized by a highly-repeated region of DNA, and the number of repeats can lengthen with each new generation, impacting upon the severity of the phenotype (Steyaert et al., 1996). Males who carry the full mutation have distinctive physical features, including a long face, prominent ears, and high-arched hard palates (Optiz et al., 1984). A connective-tissue disorder involving the protein elastin accounts for musculoskeletal manifestations frequently seen in the syndrome (e.g., lax joints, Davids et al., 1990; see also *Williams syndrome* below). In some cases, there is a marked increase in the volume of the brain, of the type seen in *Sotos syndrome* ("cerebral gigantism"; deVries et al., 1995).

The behavioral characteristics in Fragile-X syndrome are varied, including sterotypies, perseveration, hyperacute hearing and touch, and poor eye contact of the type that is frequently observed in many persons with autism; shyness is also frequently reported among individuals with Fragile-X syndrome, but they do not have the pronounced social impairments seen in many persons with autism (Hagerman & Cronister, 1996; Reiss & Freund, 1992). Surface behavioral characteristics are not limited to the autistic spectrum, but also can include behavior that is frequently associated with persons having ADHD diagnoses (Rogers et al., 2001). Dykens (1995) reported that the adaptive skills of persons with Fragile-X syndrome are generally consistent with their level of intellectual function, and language delay is common (Bailey et al., 1998), with a notable excess of language that is tangential to the situation (Sudhalter & Belser, 2001). Both the behavioral phenotype and physical features display a wide range of severity; it turns out that the extent of these

*Phenotypic Correlation Network for Fragile X Syndrome*
*The FMR1 gene produces multiple effects on proteins and phenotypes.*

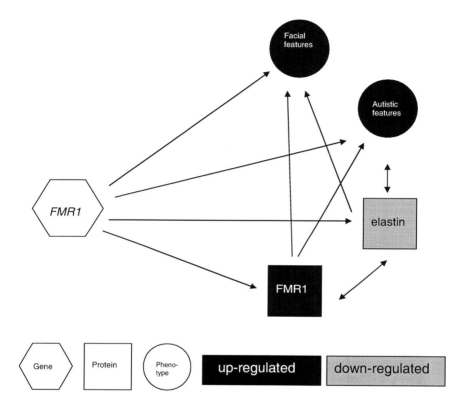

*Figure 2.1: Causal model relating genotype to phenotypes in Fragile X (FMR1).*

physical features correlates with the severity of the behavioral disorders exhibited (Fryns et al., 1986).

Thus, the *FMR-1* gene has multiple manifestations, that is, behaviors characteristic of persons with autism, physically dysmorphic features, and alterations of the FMR-1 and elastin proteins (see Figure 2.1). This network of phenotypes can also have interconnections, for instance, the impact of elastin on joint abnormalities in Fragile-X syndrome.

As the behavioral phenotype is refined, it will be interesting to determine the degree to which various behaviors cohere within individuals. This phenotypic correlation network drives home the point that common biological factors underlie

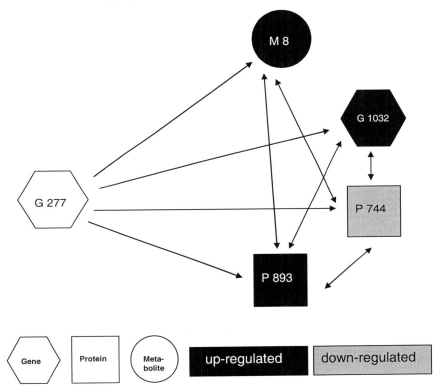

*Figure 2.2: Causal model within a biomolecular interaction network.*

these manifestations. This illustration resembles the networks of genes, proteins, and other phenotypes (e.g., biochemical metabolites) that are drawn for "biomolecular interaction networks" (Bader & Hogue, 2003). An example of one of these networks is given in Figure 2.2, showing how these various chemical species cluster together, presumably reflecting common regulatory of functional pathways. Perhaps this type of integrated Systems Biology approach will find application in behavioral phenotyping.

## Velo-cardio-facial Syndrome

This condition is caused by deletions of a region (q11) of Chromosome 22 (Shprintzen, 2000). It is a contiguous gene disorder, and there is variation in the length of deletion that is affected in this condition. Not surprisingly, many abnormalities have been observed in this syndrome – over 180 by Shprintzen's count. The behavioral phenotype has intrigued investigators, because it resembles some highly prevalent psychiatric disorders, but *which* disorders it resembles is a matter of some controversy. Similarities have been noted to the behaviors exhibited by persons with schizophrenia and bipolar disorders (Shprintzen, 2000; Murphy, 2002; Vogels et al., 2002). The circumscribed 22q11 region may well provide an opportunity to identify susceptibility genes for psychosis in the general population.

## Williams Syndrome

Like the preceding syndrome, this is also a contiguous gene disorder, this one caused by a small deletion of Chromosome 7 (7q11.23), a region that includes the *elastin (ELN)* and the *LIMK1* genes (Ewart et al., 1993; Mervis et al., 1999). It is characterized by a distinctive, dysmorphic facial appearance and a number of malformations related to connective tissue, including ones associated with cardio-vascular anatomy. It is noteworthy that the genetic locus of the elastin problems is different than that for *Fragile-X syndrome* described above. Mervis and her colleagues (1999) described the primary clinical profile, including distinctive facial appearance (present in 100% of cases), mental retardation or developmental delay (in 98%), hoarse voice (98%), and congenital heart disease (74%). These investigators also summarized the literature on behavioral phenotypes in the syndrome, concluding that these individuals have a characteristic cognitive profile. They tend to perform extremely poorly on visual-spatial construction tasks, although there may be improvement with age. For example, approximately 57% of individuals with the syndrome obtained the lowest possible score on a pattern construction test. In stark contrast are relative strengths in auditory rote memory and in language. Indeed, these individuals' verbal sophistication has been characterized as markedly greater than their overall level of functionally (Pearlman-Avnion & Eviatar, 2002).

It is noteworthy that the *LIMK1* gene appears to have greater correspondence to the behavioral phenotype than does *ELN*. Not all cases may have a deletion of the section of Chromosome 7 containing *LIMK1*, and those that do have a deletion of this gene seem to have the pronounced visual-spatial construction deficits. By contrast, the deletion of *ELN* does not seem to have this association – a fact that may be due to the fact that it is not much expressed in the central nervous system (Mervis et al., 1999).

As the field develops, one can envisage a "genetic dissection" of the behavioral phenotype of Williams syndrome such that the assortment of deleted regions can be correlated to functional deficits – much in the way investigators have done for *Down syndrome*.

## Prader-Willi syndrome

Yet another contiguous gene disorder, this syndrome results from a deletion of part of Chromosome 15 (15q11-13; Ledbetter et al., 1981). The most conspicuous behavioral phenotype in these individuals is an insatiable appetite; in fact, this syndrome is the most common form of obesity identified so far. Left to their own devices, individuals with Prader-Willi syndrome may eat to the point of stomach rupture (Thompson et al., 1999). These individuals are usually moderately to mildly mentally retarded, and have relative weaknesses in short-term memory, yet relative strengths in spatial-perceptual organization (e.g., block design and puzzle completion; Holm et al., 1993), a talent similar to that seen in autism (Deutsch, 1998). There are also behaviors that may be characterized as obsessive-compulsive and skin picking (Dykens & Shah, 2003).

One remarkable aspect of this condition is that its manifestation depends on the parental origin of the deletion. The mechanism by which parental origin imparts information has been termed *imprinting*. If the deletion is paternal in origin and the intact chromosome 15 is from the mother, Prader-Willi syndrome results. If the converse is true (with some exceptions), that is, the intact chromosome is from the father, a different syndrome, Angelman, results with a distinct set of phenotypes. Angelman syndrome is characterized by severe mental retardation, characteristic facial appearance, seizures, impaired speech and motor function, and inappropriate laughter (hence the commonly-used term "Happy Puppet Syndrome"; Clayton-Smith & Laan, 2003).

## Significance

As readers with various interests come to the end of this chapter, it is reasonable to expect questions such as, "Of what practical importance does behavioral phenotyping have for my specific interests?" To conclude, therefore, we will address the interests of three broadly defined constituencies.

## Behavioral Phenotypes In Biobehavioral/Genetic MR/DD Research

Behavioral phenotype analysis may find at least three applications within this general area:

1.  *A distinctive phenotype can help winnow down heterogeneity in a broadly defined condition.*

One good example of this is in the area of autism. Despite certain similarities in the behavior of persons who receive this diagnosis, there are also many individual differences. Thus, although autism is thought to be a heritable condition, heritability does not necessarily imply behavioral homogeneity within an affected group. Conversely, apparent behavioral homogeneity within such a group does not necessarily imply common pathophysiological process.

Efforts are needed to refine further the behavioral phenotypes associated within the autism spectrum, which are likely highly heterogeneous with respect to etiology. Indeed, perhaps autism is better thought of as a general behavioral syndrome rather than a single condition. Efforts to identify specific subtypes within autism may be aided by a search for unique constellations of behavioral and perhaps physical phenotypes. Such a search is likely to prove difficult, however. As we noted earlier, individuals with autism may display behaviors that are associated *Fragile-X syndrome*, and several other conditions do as well. These include *Hypomelanosis of Ito* (itself a heterogeneous collection of "genetic mosaics"), *Joubert syndrome, neurofibromatosis, Sotos syndrome* ("cerebral gigantism"), and *Cornelia deLange syndrome* (see reviews by A. Bailey et al., 1996; Deutsch, 1998; Gillberg & Coleman, 1992; Veenstra-Vanderweele et al., 2003). As specific subtypes of autism can be identified, however, they can be culled from samples to be analyzed for genetic linkage studies.

2.  *Behavioral phenotypes can also be related to biological correlates of conditions associated with MR/DD.*

This applies to the gamut of biobehavioral markers, from brain imaging to psychophysiology to biochemistry. These studies are helpful in defining how closely various measures intercorrelate and how they interact, rendering findings biologically interpretable. One example can be found in the MASA syndrome, an X-linked genetic condition characterized by mental retardation, aphasia, shuffling gait, and adducted thumbs. MRI studies suggest that there is marked hypoplasia (underformation) of the corpus callosum in this syndrome (Boyd et al., 1993). A contrast is the autosomal recessive disorder Cohen syndrome, characterized by psychomotor retardation, EEG abnormalities (low-voltage), motor clumsiness, microcephaly, dysmorphic features (e.g., prominent upper lip, small jaw, tapering fingers), hyperextensibility of the joints, and ophthalmologic findings of retinochoroidal dystrophy and myopia (Kivitie-Kallio & Norio, 2001). These individuals have *hyper*plasia of the corpus callosum. Conceivably, these neuroanatomic abnormalities of interhemispheric connections underlie some features of the behavioral phenotypes.

3.  *Behavioral phenotypes can help in studying MR/DD genetics.*

Differentiation of behavioral phenotypes could be employed in family and linkage studies, by reducing heterogeneity and thus increasing the power to detect genetic linkage. Another application of behavioral phenotypes in studies of MR/DD is the description of a range of pathologic effects on a continuum (*spectrum*). This is useful because the gene(s) for a disorder may have broader effects than just the conspicuous disease state, and confining analysis to the more extreme phenotype can hinder the power to detect linkage. The *spectrum* notion is not necessarily confined to the description of a graded continuum; it could include diverse behavioral phenotypes, stemming from different genes that conspire to produce the conspicuous disease state.

## Behavioral Phenotypes in Behavioral MR/DD Research

The impact of the current work on behavioral phenotyping has somewhat different implications depending on the interests of the researcher. To the extent that the researcher is interested in better defining the broader MR phenotype via large group studies, s/he must also take into account the implications of specific phenotypes within the planned sample. This is also true if the researcher is interested in better understanding behavioral processes of and/or developing broadly applicable intervention methods for "persons with mental retardation." For example, if the specific interest of the researcher was language processes, provisions would have to be made to control for the effects of the phenotypes associated with, for example, William Syndrome and/or Down syndrome.

One tactic that has been evolving to manage behavioral phenotype influence in large group studies has been merely to exclude all individuals with identifiable genetic syndromes. Groups are constituted with persons who have so-called undifferentiated mental retardation, that is, retardation that is not attributable to a specific etiology. It is not known for certain whether this procedure actually does increase the homogeneity of the samples. This is because most causes of mental retardation are not known or are not securely established (Batshaw, 2002). For example, a researcher constituting matched groups in the early 1980s would have likely lumped persons with Fragile-X syndrome into the "undifferentiated" group; the genetic causes was identified only later. To the extent that there was a great imbalance in Fragile-X participation in the two "undifferentiated" groups, the design could have been compromised.

As more and more causes of mental retardation are uncovered, it is likely that the undifferentiated MR group strategy will become increasingly less attractive. Individuals available for study will become increasingly fewer and the growing number of etiologically well-defined disorders and syndromes will increasingly present opportunities for potentially informative correlational studies.

The preceding points acknowledged, no one to our knowledge has as yet attempted to assess the degree to which failure to control behavioral phenotypes actually does constitute a threat to the traditional group designs. Many genetic disorders are quite rare, and the findings that have led to the definition of the current behavioral phenotypes have sometimes been fairly small statistical differences (i.e., relative strengths or weaknesses). Clearly needed in our opinion are studies that would assess directly the impact of behavior phenotypes on, for example, the cognitive processes involved in attention, memory, and executive functioning (cf. Lyon & Krasnegor, 1996). If it was shown, for example, that seemingly undesirable imbalances could be routinely controlled statistically, the need to pursue an undifferentiated-MR strategy might become less necessary. Also worthy of consideration may be what we may term *hybrid* designs in which individuals from phenotypically-defined groups are included with planned ongoing evaluation (similar to a power analysis) of whether the phenotypic status indeed introduces systematic bias that renders the individuals noncomparable to the rest of the sample; this strategy may be particularly useful in cases in which the phenotypically-defined disorder is very common (e.g., Fragile-X).

Until studies that address the critical issues directly are initiated, however, those interested in the broader MR phenotype have little recourse at present. It seems at best a provisional solution to a difficult problem that we may expect only to become more serious with time, as we have noted.

Regarding the researcher who employs small-N and or single-case design methods, the challenges introduced by the behavioral phenotyping phenomenon seem quite manageable. As noted, these methods compare individuals only to themselves, and the variables of interest are typically controlled procedurally rather than statistically as in applied behavior analysis. These facts acknowledged, however, it is also true that procedures that have strong, readily demonstrable effects with individual participants may not have the same effects with other, seemingly similar individuals. In our view, it is not enough to attribute such differences merely to "different histories" (e.g., of reinforcement). Rather, it seems appropriate for individual-oriented researchers also to become familiar with the etiological status of a potential research participant to the extent possible. Should atypical individual result from a given procedure, it might be useful to ask about the degree to which the atypical behavior is consistent with what is known concerning the participant's phenotypic status. Such information may not provide the entire account of the variable performance but it could prove to be a part of the analytical puzzle that allows a more informed individual analysis.

## Use of Behavioral Phenotyping in Intervention

Because intervention is typically made on a case-by-case basis, the clinician's task is similar to that of the researcher whose primary interest is the individual's behavior. By training, clinicians with backgrounds in medicine ought to be well-attuned to the implications of behavioral phenotypes. In medicine, differential diagnosis is at the heart of the activity, and treatment is often influenced greatly by the specifics of the diagnosis. In behavioral intervention for persons with disabilities, by contrast, the presence of a diagnosable disorder and an associated behavioral phenotype has not always been of major concern. As knowledge of the possible genetic contributions to behavior increases, however, so too do the behaviorally-oriented clinician's responsibilities. For the present, the main responsibilities appear to be (a) to acquaint oneself with the increasing efforts to define better the behavioral phenotypes, (b) to consider phenotypic expression in the design of intervention methods, (c) where logic and data indicate a probable need, to modify intervention methods in relation to behavioral phenotypes, and (d) where such modifications have proven beneficial, to contribute that information to the clinical literature.

## Footnote

Preparation of this chapter was supported by NICHD Grant HD25995 and by NIMH Grant MH20892. Communications concerning this manuscript may be addressed to either author at the UMMS Shriver Center, 200 Trapelo Road, Waltham, MA 02452. E-mail communications may be sent to william.mcilvane@umassmed.edu or curtis.deutsch@umassmed.edu.

## References

American Association on Mental Retardation. (2002). *Mental retardation: Definition, classification, and systems of supports* (10th Edition).

Bader, G. D., & Hogue, C. W. (2003). An automated method for finding molecular complexes in large protein interaction networks. *BMC Bioinformatics, 4*(1), 2.

Bailey, A., Phillips, W., & Rutter, M. (1996). Autism: Towards an integration of clinical, genetic, neuropsychological, and neurobiological perspectives. *Journal of Child Psychological Psychiatry, 37*(1), 89-126.

Bailey, D. B., Jr., Hatton, D. D., & Skinner, M. (1998). Early developmental trajectories of males with fragile X syndrome. *American Journal on Mental Retardation, 103*(1), 29-39.

Barlow, D. H., & Hersen, M. (1984). *Single case experimental designs.* New York: Pergamon.

Batshaw, M. L. (Ed.). (2002). *Children with disabilities.* Baltimore, MD: P. H. Brookes.

Boyd, E., Schwartz, C. E., Schroer, R. J., May, M. M., Shapiro, S. D., Arena, J. F., Lubs, H. A., & Stevenson, R. E. (1993). Agenesis of the corpus callosum associated with MASA syndrome. *Clinical Dysmorphology, 2*(4),332-41.

Broman, S. H., & Grafman, J. (Eds.). (1994). *Atypical cognitive deficits in developmental disorders: Implications for brain function.* Hillsdale, NJ: Lawrence Erlbaum Associates.

Chapman, R. S., & Hesketh, L. J. (2000). Behavioral phenotype of individuals with Down syndrome. *Mental Retardation and Developmental Disability Review, 6,* 84-95.

Clayton-Smith, J., & Laan, L. (2003). Angelman syndrome: A review of the clinical and genetic aspects. *Journal of Medical Genetics 40*(2), 87-95.

Davids, J. R, Hagerman, R. J., & Eilert, R. E. (1990). Orthopaedic aspects of fragile-X syndrome. *Journal of Bone Joint Surgery (American Volume), 72*(6), 889-896.

Deutsch, C. K. (1990). Down syndrome. In M. Buyse (Ed.), *Birth defects encyclopedia.* Cambridge, MA: Blackwell Scientific.

Deutsch, C. K. (1998). Emergent properties of brain function and development. In S. Soraci & W. J. McIlvane (Eds.), *Perspectives on fundamental processes in intellectual functioning: A Survey of Research Approaches*, volume 1. Stamford, CT: Ablex.

Deutsch, C. K., Matthysse, S., Swanson, J. M., & Farkas, L. G. (1990). Genetic latent structure analysis of dysmorphology in attention deficit disorder. *Journal of the American Academy of Child Adolescent Psychiatry , 29,* 189-94.

deVries, B. A., Robinson, H., Stolte-Dijkstra, I., Gi, C. V. T. P., Dijkstra, D. V., va Doom, J., Halley D. J. J., Oostra, B. A., Turner, G., & Niermeijer, M. F. (1995). General overgrowth in the fragile X syndrome: Variability in the phenotype expression of the *FMR1* gene mutation. *Journal of Medical Genetics, 32,* 764-769.

Di Cicco, M., Padoan, R., Felisati, G., Dilani, D., Moretti, E., Guerneri, S., & Selicorni, A. (2001). Otorhinolaringologic manifestation of Smith-Magenis syndrome. *International Journal of Pediatric Otorhinolaryngology, 59*(2), 147-150.

Dykens, E. M. (1995). Adaptive behavior in males with fragile X syndrome. *Mental Retardation and Developmental Disabilities Research Review, 1,* 281-285.

Dykens, E., & Shah, B. (2003). Psychiatric disorders in prader-willi syndrome: epidemiology and management. *CNS Drugs , 17*(3), 167-78.

Ellis, N. R. (1979). *Handbook of mental deficiency, psychological theory and research.* Hillsdale, NJ: Erlbaum.

Ellis, N. R., & Dulaney, C. L. (1991). Further evidence for cognitive inertia in persons with mental retardation. *American Journal on Mental Retardation, 95,* 613-621.

Ewart, A. K., Morris, C. A., Atkinson, D., Jin, W., Sternes, K., Spallone, P., Stock, A. D., Leppert, M., & Keating, M. T. (1993). Hemizygosity at the elastin locus in a developmental disorder, Williams syndrome. *Nature Genetics, 5,* 11-16.

Fishler, K., & Koch, R. (1991). Mental development in Down syndrome mosaicism. *American Journal on Mental Retardation, 96,* 345-351.

Fryns, J. P., Kleczkowska, A., Dereymaeker, A., Hoefnagels, M., Heremans, G., Marien, J., & van den Berghe, H. (1986). A genetic-diagnostic survey in an institutionalized population of 173 severely mentally retarded patients. *Clinical Genetics, 30*(4), 315-23.

Gillberg, C., & Coleman, M. (1992). *The Biology of the Autistic Syndromes* (2nd ed.). New York, NY: Mac Keith Press.

Goldstein, S., & Reynolds, C. (Eds.). (1999). *Handbook of neurodevelopmental and genetic disorders in children.* New York: Guilford.

Gottesman, I. I., & Gould, T. D. (2003). The endophenotype concept in psychiatry: Etymology and strategic intentions. *American Journal of Psychiatry, 160,* 1-10.

Hagerman, R. J., & Cronister, A. (1996). *Fragile X syndrome: Diagnosis, treatment, and research.* Baltimore, MD: John Hopkins University Press.

Holm, V. A., Cassidy, S. B., Butler, M. G., Hanchett, J. M., Greenswag, L. R., Whitman, B. Y., & Greenberg, F. (1993). Prader-Willi syndrome: consensus diagnostic criteria. *Pediatrics, 91*(2), 398-402.

Iwata, B. A., Dorsey, M. F., Slifer, K. J., Bauman, K. E., & Richman, G. S. (1994). Toward a functional analysis of self-injury. *Journal of Applied Behavior Analysis, 27,* 197-209.

John, B., & Lewis, K. (1966). Chromosome variability and geographic distribution in insects. *Science, 152,* 711–721.

Kivitie-Kallio, S., & Norio, R. (2001). Cohen syndrome: essential features, natural history, and heterogeneity. *American Journal of Medical Genetics, 102*(2), 125-135.

Ledbetter, D. H., Riccardi, V. M., Airhart, S. D., Strobel, R. J., Keenan, B. S., & Crawford, J. D. (1981). Deletions of chromosome 15 as a cause of the Prader-Willi syndrome. *New England Journal of Medicine, 304*(6), 325-9.

Lyon, G. R., & Krasnegor, N. A. (Eds.). (1996). *Attention, memory, and executive function.* Baltimore, MD: P. H. Brookes.

Maurice, C., Green, G., & Luce, S. (Eds.). (1996). *Behavioral intervention for young children with autism: A manual for parents and professionals.* Austin, TX: PRO-ED.

McIlvane, W. J., Bristol, M., & Alexander, D. (1998). Autism. *Mental Retardation and Developmental Disabilities Research Review, 4*(2), 61-64.

Mervis, C. B., Morris, C. A., Bertrand, J., & Robinson, B. F. (1999). Williams syndrome: Findings from an integrated program of research. In H. Tager-Flusberg (Ed.), *Neurodevelopmental Disorders.* Cambridge, MA: MIT Press.

Motonaga, K., Itoh, M., Becke, L. E., Goto, Y., & Takashima, S. (1992). Elevated expression of beta-site amyloid precursor protein cleaving enzyme 2 in brains of patients with Down syndrome. *Neuroscience Letters, 326,* 64-66.

Murphy, K. C. (2002). Schizophrenia and velo-cardio-facial syndrome. *Lancet, 359,* 426-430.

Nelson, C. A., & Luciana, M. (Eds.). (2001). *Handbook of developmental cognitive neuroscience.* Cambridge, MA: MIT Press.

Opitz, J. M., Westphal, J. M., & Daniel, A. (1984). Discovery of a connective tissue dysplasia in the Martin-Bell syndrome. *American Journal of Medical Genetics, 17*(1), 101-109.

Ozbudak, E. M., Thattai, M., Kurtser, I., Grossman, A. D., & van Oudenaarden, A. (2002). Regulation of noise in the expression of a single gene. *National Genetics, 31*(1), 69-73.

Pearlman-Avnion, S., & Eviatar, Z. (2002). Narrative analysis in developmental social and linguistic pathologies: dissociation between emotional and informational language use. *Brain & Cognition, 48*(2-3), 494-499.

Punnett, H. H., & Zakai, E. H. (1990). Old syndromes and new cytogenetics. *Developmental Medical Child Neurology, 32*(9), 824-831.

Reiss, A. L., & Freund, L. (1992). Behavioral phenotype of fragile X syndrome: DSM-III-R autistic behavior in male children. *American Journal of Medical Genetics, 43*(1-2), 35-46.

Robey, K. L., Reck, J. F., Giacomini, K. D., Barabas, G., & Eddey, G. E. (2003). Modes and patterns of self-mutilation in persons with Lesch-Nyhan disease. *Developmental Medical Child Neurology, 45*(3), 167-71.

Rogers, S. J., Jehner D. E, & Hagerman, R. J. (2001). The behavioral phenotype in fragile X: symptoms of autism in very young children with fragile X syndrome, idiopathic autism, and other developmental disorders. *Developmental Behavioral Pediatrics, 22,* 409-417.

Roid, G. H. (2003). *Stanford-Binet intelligence scales*-5th Edition. Itasca, IL: Riverside Publishing.

Roizen, N. J., & Patterson, D. (2003). Down's syndrome. *Lancet, 361,* 1281-1289.

Sago, H., Carlson, E. J., Smith, D. J., Rubin, E. M., Crnic, L. S., Huang, T. T., & Epstein, C. J. (2000). Genetic dissection of region associated with behavioral abnormalities in mouse models for Down syndrome. *Pediatric Research, 48*(5), 606-13.

Schardein, J. L. (2000). *Chemically induced birth defects.* New York: Marcel Dekker.

Schupf, N., Kapell, D., Nightingale, B., Rodriguez, A., Tycko, B., & Mayeux, R. (1998). Earlier onset of Alzheimer's disease in men with Down syndrome. *Neurology, 50,* 991-995.

Shprintzen, R. J. (2000). Velo-cardio-facial syndrome: a distinctive behavioral phenotype. *Mental Retardation and Developmental Disabilities Research Review, 6*(2), 142-147.

Sidman, M. (1960). *Tactics of scientific research*. New York: Basic Books: New York.

Sigman, M. (1999). Developmental deficits in children with Down syndrome. In H. Tager-Flusberg (Ed.), *Neurodevelopmental disorders*. Cambridge, MA: MIT Press.

Sparrow, S. S., Balla, D. A., & Cicchetti, D. V. (2001). *Vineland adaptive behavior scales*. Circle Pines, MN: AGS Publishing.

Steyaert, J., Borghgraef, M., Legius, E., & Fryns, J. P. (1996). Molecular-intelligence correlations in young fragile X males with a mild CGG repeat expansion in the FMR1 gene. *American Journal of Medical Genetics, 64*(2), 274-277.

Sudhalter, V., & Belser, R. C. (2001). Conversational characteristics of children with fragile X syndrome: tangential language. *American Journal of Mental Retardation, 106*(5), 389-400.

Symons, F. J., Butler, M. G., Sanders, M. D., Feurer, I. D., & Thompson, T. (1999). Self-injurious behavior and Prader-Willi syndrome: Behavioral forms and body locations. *American Journal on Mental Retardation, 104*, 260-269.

Tager-Flusberg, H. (Ed.). (1999). *Neurodevelopmental disorders*. Cambridge, MA: MIT Press.

Thompson, T., Butler, M., MacLean, W. E., Jr., Joseph, B., & Delaney, D. (1999). Cognition, behavior, neurochemistry, and genetics in Prader-Willi Syndrome. In H. Tager-Flusberg (Ed.), *Neurodevelopmental disorders*. Cambridge, MA: MIT Press.

Turner, G., Partington, M., Kerr, B., Mangelsdorf, M., & Gecz, J. (2002). Variable expression of mental retardation, autism, seizures, and dystonic hand movements in two families with an identical ARX gene mutation. *American Journal of Medical Genetics, 112*(4), 405-411.

Veenstra-Vanderweele, J., Cook, E., Jr., & Lombroso, P. J. (2003). Genetics of childhood disorders: XLVI. Autism, part 5: genetics of autism. *Journal of the American Academy of Child Adolescent Psychiatry, 42*(1), 116-118.

Verkerk, A. J., Pieretti, M., Sutcliffe, J. S., Fu, Y. H., Kuhl, D. P., Pizzuti, A., Reiner, O., Richards, S., Victoria, M. F., & Zhang, F. P. (1991). Identification of a gene (FMR-1) containing a CGG repeat coincident with a breakpoint cluster region exhibiting length variation in fragile X syndrome. *Cell, 65*(5), 905-914.

Vogels, A., Verhoeven, W. M., Tuinier, S., DeVriendt, K., Swillen, A., Curfs, L. M., & Frijns, J. P. (2002). The psychopathological phenotype of velo-cardio-facial syndrome. *Annals of Genetics, 45*(2), 89-95.

Wilkins, A. S. (1997). Canalization: A molecular genetic perspective. *Bioessays, 19*, 257-262.

# Chapter 3

# Recent Advances in Discrimination Learning with Individuals with Developmental Disabilities

### Richard W. Serna
*University of Massachusetts Medical School, Shriver Center*

Discrimination of stimuli and events in one's environment is fundamental to virtually every aspect of the daily lives of individuals with intellectual disabilities. Classroom teachers, therapists, parents and direct care staff often implement teaching programs as a means of establishing discrimination skills. From activity boards to verbal instructions to establishing the relations between communication symbols and their referents, instructors attempt to establish and maintain stimulus control over students' behaviors that occur in the presence of relevant stimuli. For many individuals with intellectual disabilities, relatively simple procedures like trial-and-error methods, are sufficient to establish discriminative stimulus control. However, for a substantial portion of students with intellectual disabilities, trial-and-error and traditional prompting methods, are not effective (Serna & Carlin, 2001).

To address this problem, our laboratory and others has sought to develop a true technology for teaching and evaluating individuals with substantial mental retardation, low mental ages (i.e., < 6 years), and limited language repertoires (McIlvane, Kledaras, Dube, Serna, & Hamad, 2000). The true technology of teaching we seek has the following defining characteristics: (1) Within its domain of application, all major steps of the teaching process must be specified, with objective measures determining whether or not teaching has been successful. (2) Teaching must reach all or virtually all individuals who meet the entry requirements. Branching options must be available to handle foreseeable individual differences in response to teaching. Where teaching fails, those outcomes must be explained in relation to missing behavioral prerequisites. (3) The technology must be principle-based and potentially applicable to a wide range of subject matter. (4) One must be able to reasonably anticipate that the technology can be used within the constraints of programs that provide exemplary behavioral evaluation or special education to our target population. It is unattractive, for example, to develop a technology that is so complex or expensive that it could not be used routinely by well-educated teachers in the schools.

Research having the above characteristics may be viewed as the natural outgrowth of behavior-analytically oriented research on procedures that might be used to teach people with disabilities more effectively. Within that research tradition, however, one may identify two major research styles. One focuses mainly on the development of effective intervention procedures; analyses of underlying behavioral processes are secondary to the goal of producing positive learning outcomes. The other style, by contrast, emphasizes analysis of basic processes, under the working assumption that one cannot fully manage processes that one does not fully understand. Our research program will be recognized as belonging to the latter category.

This chapter examines some recent advances in our theoretical and methodological foundations for understanding the stimulus control processes that underlie both successful and unsuccessful discrimination learning procedures, as we move closer to a true teaching technology.

## Stimulus-Control Shaping

The search for an effective means to establish stimulus control in individuals who fail to learn with standard methods has led mental retardation researchers and educators to use stimulus-control-shaping methods. *Stimulus-control shaping* is a generic term for a number of conceptually related methods that establish new discriminations through gradual stimulus changes in existing discriminations (McIlvane & Dube, 1992). The net result of these techniques is a transfer of stimulus control from current discriminative stimuli to new stimuli. In practice, the initial discrimination is typically one that is easily acquired, and the new discrimination is a more difficult one that would not be acquired without the transfer procedure. Although stimulus-control shaping techniques were developed originally to examine theoretical questions in discrimination learning (e.g., Terrace, 1963), early work by Sidman and Stoddard (1966, 1967), Touchette (1968), and others brought the methods to bear on the learning problems of individuals with developmental disabilities like mental retardation.

Sidman and Stoddard's (1966, 1967) circle/ellipse discrimination program illustrates transfer techniques. Individuals with severe mental retardation first learned to press a brightly lit white key bearing a black open circle (S+), and not to press plain dark keys (S-). Over a series of trials, the dark, plain keys were gradually illuminated until they were as bright as the key with the circle. Then, flat ellipses were introduced on the plain keys. At first, the ellipses were a very light shade of gray, much like the plain white key. Ellipse intensity was gradually increased through darker shades of gray until it was the same as the circle, completely black. Thus, initial stimulus control by the dimension of brightness (selecting a bright key and not a dark one) was transferred to the target dimension of form (selecting a circle and not an ellipse). This type of transfer, in which control changes across dimensions, is referred to as *interdimensional* transfer.

A follow-up study (Sidman & Stoddard, 1966) was designed to reverse the circle (S+) vs. ellipse (S-) discrimination, described above, so that participants would select the ellipse and not the circle. The reversal was accomplished by a program which gradually altered the physical features of the original forms. Four successive program phases altered one stimulus at a time: First, the circle was transformed into a square by gradually flattening the sides and adding corners; the result was a square vs. ellipse discrimination (S+ vs. S-). Second, the ellipse was changed into a circle (square vs. circle); third, the square became a flat rectangle (rectangle vs. circle); and finally, the rectangle became an ellipse (ellipse vs. circle). When given the final 41-step version of this program, children with mental retardation accomplished a complete discrimination reversal with few errors. We refer to this type of transfer, in which stimulus control was transferred within the dimension of form, as *intradimensional* transfer.

Since this early work, many studies have examined the potential for stimulus control shaping methods to teach individuals with intellectual disabilities (see Lancioni & Smeets, 1986, for a review). Much success has been realized in applications of these methods to a range of teaching problems. However, despite many impressive teaching successes, current methods are not always effective. A common finding in both the literature and in classroom teaching outcomes is low or intermediate accuracy scores (Dube, Iennaco, & McIlvane, 1993; Serna, Dube, & McIlvane, 1997).

## Theoretical Foundations and Empirical Evidence

### Stimulus Control Topography Coherence Theory

Findings of low and intermediate accuracy scores in discrimination tasks performed by individuals with intellectual disabilities have led to the development of "stimulus control topography coherence theory" (McIlvane & Dube, 2003; McIlvane, Serna, Dube, & Stromer, 2000). Coherence theory begins by proposing the concept of the stimulus control topography (SCT; McIlvane & Dube, 1992). An SCT is a direct conceptual parallel of response topography; just as response topography distinguishes among various forms of responses that produce the same measured outcome, SCT distinguishes among various forms of stimulus control that produce the same measured response. For example, in a two-choice simple-discrimination task involving S+ and S- form stimuli that appear equally often on the left and right portions of a display, at least two potential SCTs could control responding: (1) the form stimulus designated as "correct," and (2) the stimulus that appears on the left side of the stimulus display, regardless of its form. Selections made by the student on the basis of the form stimulus designated as correct are reinforced. Unfortunately, selections made on the basis of a stimulus appearing on the left side of the display will also be reinforced on some proportion of trials. If, for example, a student responds exclusively to stimuli appearing on the left side, session accuracy would average 50%. That percentage of reinforcement may be sufficient to maintain stimulus control by position rather than by the form stimulus designated the S+. In this example, the low accuracy score indicates there is a lack of coherence between the wanted (by the teacher or experimenter) and unwanted SCTs that were captured by the reinforcement contingencies. Intermediate scores typically result when both desirable and undesirable SCTs have been established and both occur with some frequency. Coherence theory assumes that only one stimulus control topography is expressed on any given discrimination trial. Across trials, however, accurate discrimination performance may incorporate more than one topography.

Multiple SCTs may become established when the experimental or teaching situation permits multiple bases for responding (e.g., stimulus form, size, position, etc.). This potential has long been acknowledged in discrimination learning, as in, for example, Harlow's (1950) proposal that learning requires the elimination of error factors, or statistical sampling theory (Estes, 1959). The SCT model differs from earlier formulations in that multiple topographies are seen to co-exist in the same baseline, occurring at different frequencies related to their associated schedules of reinforcement under certain conditions.

To demonstrate the presence of multiple SCTs, we have been investigating what we have termed the "delayed S+" method, which is designed to establish temporal separation of desired and undesired SCTs. The task involves discrimination between visual stimuli that are identical except for one feature. The difference is obvious to individuals without developmental limitations; a visual stimuli flash alternates with a gray field, or appears on a colored background (McIlvane, Kledaras, Dube, & Stoddard, 1989; McIlvane, Kledaras, Callahan, & Dube, 2002). Individuals with moderate and severe intellectual disabilities, however, often find the task very difficult.

Many participants show low, variable, or asymptotic intermediate accuracy. From the SCT perspective, such results challenge us to isolate the relevant SCT and to demonstrate that low or intermediate accuracy scores reflect the presence of and/or competition from other SCTs. What follows is a one illustrative example of our empirical work.

Initially, participants were exposed to displays of the type described above and to simple differential reinforcement contingencies: Selecting the S+ yielded a reinforcer and selecting the S- did not. S+ was differentiated from S- by a flashing cue. In Figure 3.1, the leftmost set of points for each participant shows low accuracy scores during such sessions. Our analysis asked whether the low accuracy resulted from competing SCTs involving positional stimuli and stimulus onset (i.e., so-called impulsive responding); such control could be captured and maintained by the contingencies because such responses were sometimes followed adventitiously by reinforcers. As an intervention, the contingencies were altered so that every trial began by presenting S- stimuli only in *both* stimulus locations. The appropriate response was to wait a few seconds until one stimulus became S+ (i.e., began to flash). Any failures to wait merely extended the delay. The results are shown in the right portion of each plot in Figure 3.1. The filled points show sudden jumps in accuracy for these participants; substantial control by the S+ stimulus became evident virtually immediately. The hollow points show the proportion of trials in which the participant responded prior to presentation of S+. Over sessions, this competing control by onset declined as it was extinguished. Data of this general type have been obtained on a variety of tasks in our laboratory, including both simple and conditional discriminations (McIlvane et al., 1989, 1991). Taken together, they strengthen the argument that certain apparent failures to learn occur when the teaching contingencies foster and maintain mixed topographies of stimulus control.

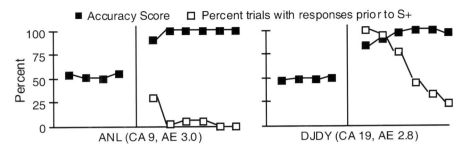

*Figure 3.1: Data from two participants illustrating the Delayed S+ procedure.*

## Challenges to Existing Accounts of Transfer Failures

Recent data of a different kind from our labs offer an account of failures of stimulus control transfer that is more consistent with coherence theory than other traditional accounts. As described earlier, new visual discriminations are often established via programs of graduated stimulus changes in existing discriminations. Consider the following interdimensional transfer-of-stimulus-control task: A student is presented first with a color discrimination. A red square is designated the S+ and a green square the S-. For many individuals with intellectual disabilities, this is a relatively easy task. We might now use the established stimulus control dimension (color) as a prompt to teach a form discrimination, on which the participant previously has demonstrated "chance" level performance. One way to begin is to superimpose the S+ form stimulus onto S+ color red and the S- form stimulus onto S- color green. Assuming that superimposition does not disrupt responding, we might then gradually fade out the color stimuli, maintaining high levels of accurate responding, until only the form stimuli remain. If accurate responding occurs to the form stimuli alone, it is said that a "transfer" of stimulus control from color to form has taken place. More accurately, stimulus control now exists by both the colors and forms included in the task. Decades of research have examined the potential for such stimulus control transfer methods to teach individuals with intellectual disabilities. Despite many teaching successes, such methods are not effective with all students. Sometimes, stimulus control shaping "breaks down" at some point in a graduated series of stimulus changes (Serna & Carlin, 2001). Often, stimulus control is maintained until the final program step in which the prompt (color, in the example above) is removed.

Failures of stimulus control transfer are often accounted for by the "blocking effect." (Fields, 1979; Solman, Singh, & Kehoe, 1992). Blocking occurs when previous conditioning to one stimulus dimension prevents or attenuates conditioning to a second stimulus dimension that is compounded with it (Kamin, 1969). A blocking account of failures of transfer procedure described above assumes that color blocked the development of stimulus control by the form stimuli. Our contention, however, is that stimulus control by the forms does in fact develop during the superimposition phase, but that such control may be exerted by features of the form stimuli that are not critical to making the final discrimination, that is, by an unwanted SCT.

To test this notion, we exposed four individuals with moderate to severe mental retardation to a simple discrimination task in which form stimuli were superimposed on color stimuli. The question was whether superimposition would result in any form of stimulus control with regard to the form stimuli. Each participant had demonstrated during pretesting high accuracy to a red vs. green color discrimination, but transfer failure to nonrepresentational forms when taught with superimposition and attenuation of the color prompts. Participants first were presented with several sessions with reinforcement in which two new form stimuli were superimposed onto the color stimuli. The form stimuli were very similar to one another, differing only in a single critical feature. Then, a series of unreinforced probe sessions presented various combinations of critical and non-critical features of the form stimuli with no color prompts.

Figure 3.2 shows representative results from a participant with mental retardation. Each quadrant of the figure shows the results of a different set of probe trials in percentages of responding, along with the percent of responding to the superimposition baseline. The first row of the upper left-hand quadrant shows that SPW responded 100% of trials to the red stimulus (previously reinforced color S+) with the superimposed pointed "anchor" form stimulus. The second and third rows of the quadrant show pairs of Type 1 form-stimulus probes. Type 1 probes presented the nominal form S+ and S- (pointed and curved anchors, respectively) paired with stimuli that had no bottoms to the anchor. Responding seemed to indicate that some stimulus control had developed during superimposition to the bottoms of the form stimulus. However, it is possible that SPW was merely responding *away from* relatively novel stimuli that had fewer strokes than the original. To test this notion, Type 2 probes (upper right-hand quadrant of Figure 3.2) were presented. Type 2 probes presented all stimuli with some type of bottom to the anchors. Again, responding was similar to that with Type 1 probes; control seemed to have developed to some aspect of original bottoms of the anchors. Type 3 probes (lower left-hand quadrant of Figure 3.2) – the form stimuli alone – suggested that SPW could not discriminate between the curved vs. pointed anchor bottoms. This was further confirmed during Type 4 probes. Other participants also showed stimulus control by some aspects of the forms, such as the upper "cross" portion of the stimulus, without demonstrating stimulus control by the entire form stimulus.

In sum, none of the participants acquired the form discrimination via superimposition. This would be predicted by a blocking account. However, probe trials demonstrated that stimulus control had in fact developed by the forms, but not to the critical, distinguishing features of the stimuli. These results suggest that color/form superimposition did not result in the blocking effect under the conditions of the present study. Further, the results suggest that the most effective stimulus control transfer methods would be those that ensured that the participant attends to, and comes to be controlled by, those features of a form stimulus deemed relevant by the teacher or experimenter.

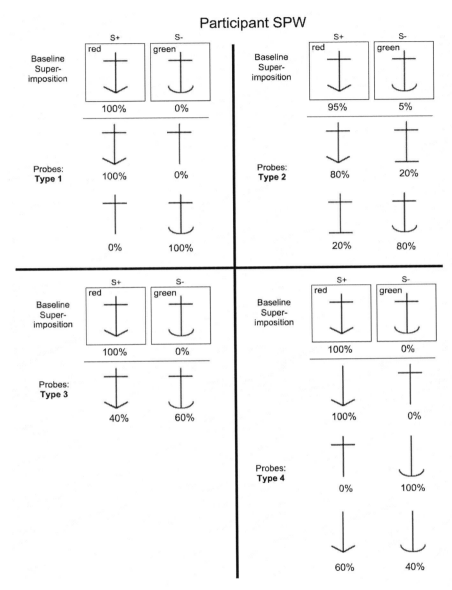

*Figure 3.2: Baseline and probe data for four probe types for Participant SPW.*

## Direct Tracking of Observing Behaviors

Work described thus far has shown that SCTs – wanted or unwanted – can be inferred through careful manipulation of training and testing conditions. Central to accounts of how such SCTs develop in the first place is the role that observing and attending behaviors play in shaping stimulus control. Dinsmoor (1985, 1995) emphasized the notion that observing behavior increases the likelihood that an individual will make contact with those aspects of the stimulus that are relevant (Dinsmoor, 1985). Thus, both observing behavior and a motor response are reinforced in the presence of an S+; during an S- presentation, neither are reinforced (Serna & Carlin, 2001). As has been known for many years, stimulus salience plays an important role in directing attending and observing (Lancioni & Smeets, 1986). More recently, work by Soraci and colleagues (see Serna & Carlin, 2001) has shown that the structure of stimulus displays can activate "pre-attentive" processes that can guide attention to relevant stimuli.

Guided by stimulus-control topography coherence theory, an analysis of observing and attending behaviors is important to determining how both wanted and unwanted SCTs might develop or be extinguished. How does one determine the topography of observing behavior? Recent work in the Shriver labs has made use of methods aimed at directly tracking a participant's eye movements. As detailed in Dube et al. (2003), such work makes use of an ISCAN Eyetracking System (ISCAN Corp., Burlington, MA). The ISCAN System produces a real-time video image of the participant's field of view, with a superimposed cursor indicating the point of gaze; it can also record the coordinates of the point-of-gaze and output a serial signal with those coordinates. The imaging components are mounted on a lightweight headband that is worn by the participant. The autocalibration system allows measurement of eyetracking with the effects of extraneous motion removed. This system affords the participant a free range of head movements and requires no stereotactic restriction. Further information, including photographs can be found at http://www.umassmed.edu/shriver/Research/Psychological/EyeTracking/.

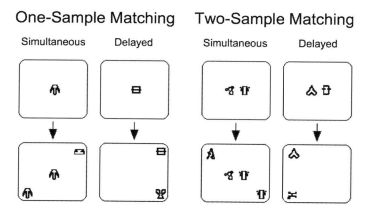

*Figure 3.3: One- and two-sample 0-delay matching tasks. The upper panels show the sample stimuli as they appear on a touch-sensitive computer screen; the lower panels show the corresponding comparison displays after a response as been made to the sample.*

Work by Dube and colleagues with the eye-tracking system has been reviewed elsewhere (Dube et al., 2003), and will be summarized briefly here. Much of the work has focused on the problem of stimulus overselectivity (Lovaas, Koegel, & Schreibman, 1979), also known as restricted stimulus control (Dube & McIlvane, 1997). Figure 3.3 illustrates a laboratory model of restricted stimulus control: the two-sample delayed matching-to-sample (2SDMTS) procedure. Participants' matching performance is first evaluated with standard simultaneous and delayed matching tasks with *one* sample stimulus. On the delayed matching-to-sample (DMTS) test (second column of Figure 3.3), the sample stimulus remains available for observation until the participant touches the sample display area, and then it disappears and the comparison stimuli are presented immediately (a 0-sec delay between sample offset and comparison onset). The comparisons are two individual stimuli, one of which is identical to the sample. Touching the identical comparison is a correct response. High accuracy (>90%) on 0-sec delayed one-sample matching verifies that the disappearance of sample stimuli did not disrupt performance. Next, participants are tested with two-sample matching tasks. Two samples are displayed on each trial, but only one of them appears as a comparison stimulus. High accuracy on this simultaneous two-sample matching task (third column of Figure 3.3) verifies that the participant can match the individual stimuli when they are presented in multi-stimulus sample arrays. During the sample observation period, the participant cannot predict which of the samples will appear as the correct comparison, and the contingencies thus require him/her to observe both, prior to responding, to maximize reinforcement. Intermediate accuracy scores (e.g., approximately 75% for a two-choice task) indicate overselectivity, typically due to failure to observe one of the sample stimuli (Dube et al., 2003); the participant is able to match only one of the two sample stimuli (the one s/he observed). On trials where that stimulus appears as a comparison (half of the trials in the session), the participant is usually correct. On the remaining trials, performance is at chance levels. The intermediate accuracy score for the entire session results from averaging scores from both types of trials.

Two findings using the model above are of note: First, using a three-choice 2SDMTS task, Dube et al. (2003) contrasted the observing behavior of an individual with mental retardation with that of a non-clinical adult, using eye-tracking measures. The primary finding was that the observing behavior patterns of the two participants differed significantly: Where the non-clinical adult routinely observed both samples in a left-right-left eye-movement sequence, the participant with mental retardation tended to observe only one of the samples. Further, the length of time observing a given stimulus was shorter than that for the non-clinical adult. These patterns of observing corresponded to accurate and inaccurate task performance for the non-clinical adult and participant with mental retardation, respectively. The second finding from this body of work concerns the modifiability of poor observing behavior. Data from studies by Dube and colleagues has shown that stimulus-control shaping and other types of intervention procedures can be used to improve observing behavior and reduce restricted stimulus control. The stimulus-control-shaping procedure uses within-stimulus prompts that may attract fixation with sudden changes in stimulus size and intensity. In many participants, however, overselectivity returns once the shaping procedures are withdrawn (Dube & McIlvane, 1997, 1999). Nevertheless, such studies provide an excellent foundation for the continued research in this area.

Using stimuli that differ only in one critical feature, as described earlier, Serna and Carlin (2001) reported two studies in which eye-tracking measures were used to determine which specific features of a stimulus a participant attended to during discrimination training. The first study asked (1) whether eye-tracking measures can distinguish observing behavior directed toward critical vs. common features of form stimuli, and (2) whether changes in such observation can be detected across sessions. An individual with mild mental retardation was presented with a simple discrimination using form stimuli similar to those in Figure 3.2. Initially, accuracy was at chance levels. Across several sessions, accuracy improved to near 100%. More importantly, however, is that the proportion of time that the participant spent observing the critical vs. non-critical features of the stimuli increased concomitantly with increases in accuracy. Thus, the two study questions were answered in the affirmative. A second study asked whether changes in patterns of observing behavior could be detected within a color/form transfer task. Again using form stimuli similar to those in Figure 3.2, an individual with moderate mental retardation initially showed both chance-level performance and low levels of observing the critical features of the S+ when the form stimuli were presented alone. In a second phase, in which the form stimuli were superimposed onto previously trained color stimuli, accuracy increased, as would be expected, given that color already controlled correct responding. However, observation of the critical features remained low initially. In the seventh and eighth superimposition session, however, the level of observing the critical features of the form stimuli increased dramatically. When the form stimuli were again presented alone, both accuracy and observation of the critical features remained high. What is noteworthy about this finding is that Serna and Carlin (2001) may have measured the moment during superimposition in which transfer took place. Such measurement would have been difficult if not impossible without the eye-tracking measurements.

In sum, eye-tracking data have and will likely continue to prove invaluable to the study of the role of observing and attending behavior in discrimination learning. Studies of this nature will also prove helpful in identifying sources of development for both wanted and unwanted SCTs. By understanding better the nature of stimulus control success and failures, we will be in a much better position to develop technological solutions for teaching individuals with intellectual disabilities.

## A Stimulus-Class Analysis of Intradimensional Transfer

Attempts in our lab to establish arbitrary matching-to-sample baselines with individuals with mental retardation using stimulus-control-shaping procedures have led us to examine more closely the behavioral processes that may be involved in such procedures. As is often the case, the methods we used (detailed below) were successful with many, but not all, of the participants. Issues raised during program revision, originally of applied significance, came to focus attention on more basic issues. In particular, we have begun to examine the role of stimulus classes in intradimensional transfer procedures.

## Sample Stimulus-Control Shaping

The analysis derives from attempts to teach arbitrary (symbolic) conditional relations to individuals who fail with standard teaching methods, such as trial-and-error, but who nevertheless are capable of reliable generalized identity matching to sample (IDMTS) performances. Taking advantage of the latter performance, individuals have been taught arbitrary matching to sample (arb MTS) via a procedure known as *sample stimulus-control shaping* (Maydak, Stromer, Mackay, & Stoddard, 1995; McIlvane, 1992; Zygmont, Lazar, Dube, & McIlvane, 1992). As shown in Figure 3.4, IDMTS performance is systematically transformed into arb MTS performance (upper portion of Figure 3.4) by gradual intradimensional alterations in the form of the sample stimulus across trials (an example graded series appears in the lower portion of Figure 3.4). For shorthand, this procedure will be referred to as sample shaping.

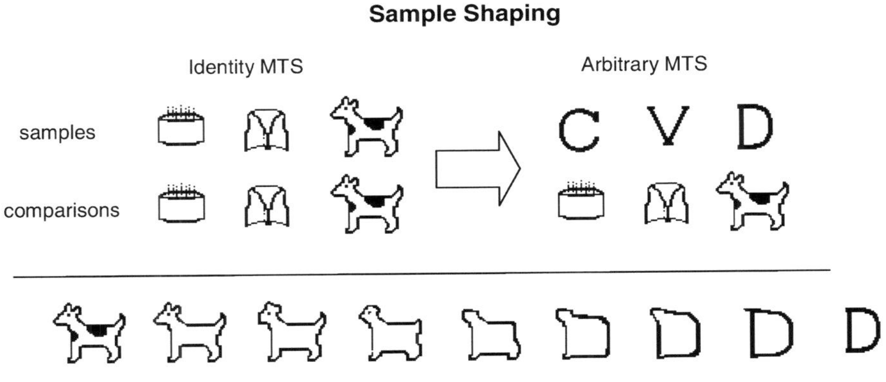

**Sample Shaping**

*Figure 3.4: Illustration of the sample (stimulus-control) shaping procedure. The lower panel shows a typical series of graded series for the Dog sample stimulus.*

Zygmont et al. (1992) developed a two-phase sample-shaping program to teach arb MTS to both typically developing preschoolers and adolescents, and to adults with mental retardation. In their program, participants first were taught two-choice simultaneous IDMTS, where stimuli B1 and B2 served as comparisons, and identical stimuli served as samples across trials to produced the following relations: B1-B1 and B2-B2. The target discrimination, arb MTS, was A1-B1 and A2-B2. The stimuli were nonrepresentational forms. In the first phase of the program, sample B1 was gradually transformed into sample A1 across several steps in a manner similar to that shown in Figure 3.4. These trials were interspersed among B2-B2 trials. In the second phase, sample B2 was gradually transformed into sample A2. All participants acquired arb MTS. Sample shaping programs have also been used successfully to establish arb MTS relations between numerals and nonrepresentational forms and between quantities of dots and corresponding numerals in individuals with mental retardation (Maydak et al., 1995).

Not all individuals complete sample-shaping programs as they are implemented initially. Performance sometimes "breaks down"; errors occur at some consistent point in the shaping series. Such was the case with one individual with mental retardation in Zygmont et al. (1992). Their participant showed breakdowns early and late in the sample shaping program. The assumption was that the breakdowns occurred because the degree of change in the physical characteristics of sample stimuli at adjacent steps of the program was too great to maintain stimulus control. In the Zygmont et al. (1992) study, the problem was overcome by adding stimuli between the steps presumed to be too great a change. In more recent attempts in our lab, however, adding stimuli to shaping series has not always been successful. It was these failures that prompted a closer examination of the stimulus processes involved in sample shaping.

## Existing Stimulus-Class Accounts of Intradimensional Transfer

Implicit in attempts to remediate sample-shaping errors, and in past analyses of errors (e.g., Sidman & Stoddard, 1966; Stoddard & Gerovac, 1981; Zygmont et al., 1992), is the notion that stimulus classes play a role in the successful transfer of stimulus control. Here, *stimulus class* refers to a set of stimuli that are functionally equivalent in their control of behavior (Goldiamond, 1966; McIlvane, Dube, Green, & Serna, 1993). The functional equivalence may result from commonalities in physical characteristics or from arbitrarily established stimulus functions. For example, in a literate English speaker, the visual stimuli VEK and *VEK* both control the same vocal response because of their similar physical characteristics (and, of course, the speaker's past learning about the phonology of our language); "TWO" and "2" do so for reasons other than common physical properties. Stimulus classes resulting from commonalities in physical characteristics have been termed *feature classes* (McIlvane et al., 1993; Serna, Wilkinson, & McIlvane, 1998).

What role might feature classes play in an intradimensional stimulus-control shaping program? The following sums up the working hypothesis inherent in much past work aimed at designing graded series of stimuli for use in such programs: The most effective and efficient series of graded stimuli for a successful shaping program is one in which the participant regards the stimuli from adjacent steps of a shaping series as members of the same feature class (Serna, Stoddard, & McIlvane, 1992; Stoddard, deRose, & McIlvane, 1986). Figure 3.5 illustrates the hypothesis. Each panel shows one of many types of logically possible feature-class relationships among stimuli in a graded series. For a given series of stimuli, we refer to the relationships as a *feature-class profile*. For example, consider the top panel of Figure 3.5. In this hypothetical example, the participant regards the stimuli in Steps 0 and 1 as feature-class members, as indicated by the ellipses enclosing them. The stimuli in Step 1 and 2 are also feature-class members, and so on. In the series shown in the upper panel of Figure 3.5, all the classes are overlapping, and consist of only two members. According to a feature-class hypothesis of intradimensional shaping, this would be an optimal series for accomplishing stimulus-control shaping.

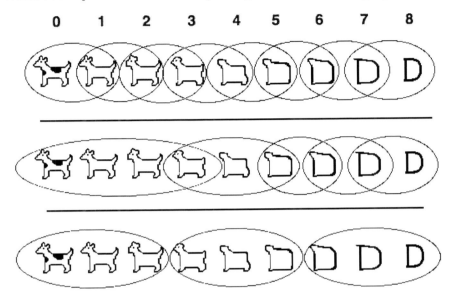

*Figure 3.5: Three hypothetical feature-class profiles. Feature classes are denoted by ellipses around groups of stimuli.*

An important assumption in the above analysis is that feature-class profiles are idiosyncratic across individuals and graded series of stimuli. Thus, it would be unusual for a feature-class profile to result in such neat, two-member-only classes. The profiles shown in the middle and lower panels of Figure 3.5 are more representative of the profile data obtained in the lab (e.g., Serna et al., 1998). For example, in the middle panel of Figure 3.5, a participant regards each of the first four stimuli in Steps 0, 1, 2, 3 as members of the same feature class. Other classes could be demonstrated as well: 3 to 5, 5 and 6, 6 and 7, and 7 and 8. If the series shown in the middle portion of Figure 3.5 were to be used in a stimulus-control transfer program, we would predict no errors during shaping because all five classes overlap with the class adjacent to it. However, this profile would not prove as efficient as that shown in the upper panel; Steps 1 and 2 would be superfluous to the series, as would be Step 4.

Finally, consider the profile shown in the lower portion of Figure 3.5. It illustrates three feature classes that have no overlapping class membership. A breakdown in performance would be predicted between Steps 2 and 3, the first "gap" that would be encountered. As was done by Zygmont et al. (1992), additional stimuli might be added to the series between Steps 2 and 3 and between Steps 5 and 6. The past success of adding intermediate steps or replacing stimuli, lends implicit support to the role of feature classes in stimulus-control shaping.

## A Revised Account of Intradimensional Transfer in Sample Shaping

Recent data from our lab suggests that the existing account of intradimensional transfer may not be adequate for predicting success in a sample-shaping program. For example, in an unpublished study by Wilkinson, it was found that modifications to series of graded stimuli, like those in Figure 3.5, were not successful with two of five participants with mental retardation in producing sample-shaping success, even when the modifications resulted in overlapping feature classes. These findings provided the impetus for a closer, more controlled investigation of the role of feature classes in sample shaping.

The first stage in the investigation was to develop solid assessment methodology for determining feature-class profiles of individuals with intellectual disabilities. This methodology is detailed in Serna et al. (1998), and will be briefly summarized here.

Because many of the participants in our studies are functionally non-verbal, it was important to develop selection-based procedures for asking participants whether two given stimuli are or are not members of a feature class. Thus, the feature-class assessment procedure is conducted in the context of a blank-comparison matching-to-sample (MTS) task. Figure 3.6 illustrates the procedure. Also illustrated are the non-representational forms used in the assessment. For control purposes, the stimuli are both vertically and horizontally symmetrical, and all are about 750 pixels in size. Using a touch-sensitive computer screen, blank-comparison MTS can be viewed as a "yes/no" procedure that asks the participant whether the sample and displayed comparison stimuli are related. If the participants judges the stimuli to be related, he/she makes a "yes" response by selecting the displayed stimulus (first and second rows of Figure 3.6); if not, he/she makes a "no" response by selecting a blank (blacked out) display (third and fourth rows of Figure 3.6). This procedure, and methods for training it, is well established in the literature (McIlvane, Kledaras, Lowrey, & Stoddard, 1992; Wilkinson & McIlvane, 1997).

The feature-class assessment protocol proceeds through three phases: In Phase 1, a baseline of zero-delay, similar-feature matching to sample (SFMTS) with the adjacent pairs of stimuli from two graded series of stimuli was established. In zero-delay matching, the sample disappears from view as soon as the comparison stimuli are displayed. (Because participants cannot look back and forth between the sample and displayed comparison, zero-delay results in a more general assessment of similarity, instead of one potentially based on careful comparison of minute differences between the sample and the displayed comparison.) In Phase 2, blank-comparison MTS is introduced, via a fading procedure, such that MTS trials are presented with a black mask over the S- on some trials, and over the S+ on others. Reinforcement rate is then dropped to 0% in preparation for the probe trials in Phase 3. In Phase 3, unreinforced blank-comparison probes are intermixed with the baseline trials. These probes test participants' judgments about the similarity of each stimulus to each other stimulus within new series of graded form stimuli.

## Blank-Comparison Matching to Sample

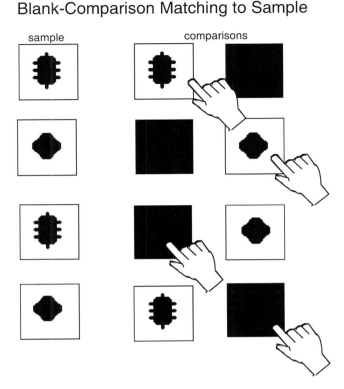

*Figure 3.6: Illustration of the blank-comparison matching to sample procedure. The pointing fingers indicate responses to various comparisons.*

For the assessment procedure to be a valid one, the following must hold true: (1) participants must maintain accurate performance on baseline trials, (2) participants must select the blank comparison on probe trials in which the sample is from one series and the displayed comparison is from the other (control trials); and (3) probe performance, regardless of judgments, must remain fairly consistent across multiple presentations of probes. This assessment procedure has been found to meet these criteria with several participants with intellectual disabilities (Serna et al., 1998).

Given a method by which individuals' feature-classes in series of graded stimuli can be assessed, we are in a better position to inquire about the role of stimulus classes in stimulus-control shaping. To that end, participant ALP, an individual with mental retardation (chronological age 16; estimated mental age 7.5) served in a follow-up study to Serna et al. (1998) designed to examine sample-shaping performance in the context of a feature-classes analysis. This study proceeded in three parts: (1) assess two new series of stimuli for feature-class membership, (2) use these series in a sample-shaping program, and (3) re-assess feature-class membership.

Two new series each consisting of eight stimuli were selected for feature-class assessment. The feature-class assessment protocol was virtually identical to that described above. ALP first received a review session of the SFMTS baseline in the context of the single-comparison procedure. In the next session, reinforcement was removed. ALP performed at 98% and 100% accuracy on these two sessions, respectively. Next, as in Phase 3 described earlier, probe trials were intermixed with the baseline trials to assess judgments about the similarity of stimuli from the two new series. The stimuli in the series and the results from the assessment are shown in the upper portion of Figure 3.7. As shown, the feature-class assessment revealed three broad, overlapping classes for both series of stimuli.

In the next part of the study, ALP was exposed to sample-shaping procedures, the goal of which was to transform IDMTS performance (sample-comparison relations E1-E1 and E2-E2) into arb MTS performance (sample-comparison relations F1-E1 and F2-E2). Because the feature-class assessment showed no gaps in either series, it was predicted that sample shaping would proceed smoothly. To keep the structure of the sample-shaping task as close as possible to that used during the assessment, the sample-shaping MTS task was conducted in zero-delay, blank-comparison format. The sample-shaping program began with an initial block of IDMTS, followed by six sample-shaping steps (as indicated by subscripts on the alpha-numeric stimulus label), in which samples changed while the comparisons remained the same. For example, following successful IDMTS performance (E1-E1 and E2-E2), the subsequent sample-shaping step presented $E1_1$ as the sample, with E1(+) and E2(-) as comparisons; likewise, $E2_1$ was presented as the sample with E1(-) and E2(+) as comparisons. The final performance step consisted of arb MTS, with F1 and F2 as samples. All responses to trials designated correct were reinforced; errors resulted in backup to the previous step.

The results of the four sample-shaping sessions are shown in the middle portion of Figure 3.7. The filled circles and the horizontal lines represent ALP's starting and ending points and his progression through the session, and correspond to the steps illustrated in the upper and lower portions of the figure. In the first session, ALP progressed from the first IDMTS block through Step 5, before the session ended. In the second session, ALP started on Step 4, completed Step 5, but consistently failed at Step 6; a similar pattern of performance was shown in the third session. In the final session, ALP began at Step 1, completed Step 3, but consistently failed Step 4; this performance represented a deterioration from the other sessions, thus no further sample-shaping sessions were conducted. In all sessions, failure occurred on stimuli from the E2-F2 series.

ALP's failure to complete the series runs counter to what was predicted. Given the three broad, overlapping feature classes, it was expected that ALP would complete sample shaping with few errors. More surprising was the fact that ALP's errors occurred between $E2_5$ and $E2_6$, stimuli in the middle of a feature-class consisting of $E2_3$, $E2_4$, $E2_5$, $E2_6$, and F2.

**Pre-Shaping Feature-Class Assessment**

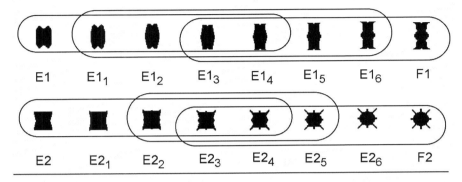

**Shaping**

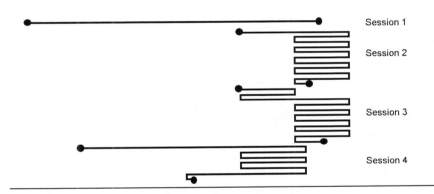

**POST-Shaping Feature-Class Assessment**

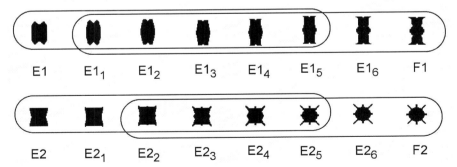

*Figure 3.7: Feature-class profiles and sample-shaping outcome data for Participant ALP.
The two shaping series in the upper and lower portions of the figure show the samples, E1
and E2, that were gradually transformed into the samples F1 and F2, via a shaping
program (e.g., $E1_1$ through $E1_6$).*

To complete the analysis, the feature-class assessment was re-administered under conditions identical to those used in the initial assessment. The results are shown in the lower portion of Figure 3.7. The most striking outcome is that the classes in both series expanded. In particular, the first class in each series expanded to include all stimuli with which ALP was successful in shaping.

What might account for ALP's failure to progress through sample shaping? Though not enough research has yet been conducted to provide definitive answers, ALP's second feature-class assessment suggests a few possibilities:

Most research on stimulus control shaping has been conducted in the context of simple discrimination (Lancioni & Smeets, 1986). The stimulus control requirements of simple discrimination allow for the relatively straightforward feature-class hypothesis described earlier. For example, in a simple simultaneous discrimination baseline, given a series of trials presenting stimuli X and Y, all selections of X (the S+) are reinforced and all other behavior is not. The individual need only discriminate X as different from Y (the S-), and all other stimuli in the environment, to meet the reinforcement contingencies. In a stimulus-control-shaping program conducted in this context (e.g., Stoddard & Sidman's circle/ellipse program), the initial discrimination is transformed into the target discrimination via a programmed series of gradual stimulus changes. The primary stimulus-control requirement for success is that control between the stimuli in adjacent program steps be maintained. With regard to feature classes, this means that only the adjacent steps in a graded series of stimuli would need to be members of the same class.

In contrast, the stimulus control requirements of conditional discrimination are more complex, as is the application of the feature-class hypothesis to stimulus-control shaping that occurs in this context. In a conditional discrimination baseline such as matching to sample, the positive and negative functions of comparison stimuli change from trial to trial conditionally upon the sample. Thus, selection of a given comparison is based on some relation between the comparison and the sample. In conditional identity matching, the sample and a comparison are related by physical similarity; in arbitrary matching, the relation is defined only by prior training contingencies.

The stimulus control requirements of conditional discrimination lead to unique requirements during sample shaping. As a participant progresses through a sample shaping program, two relational stimulus-control requirements must be maintained across successive program steps: (a) feature-class control between the adjacent, changing sample stimuli, and (b) arbitrary relational stimulus control between the sample and correct comparison. The implication of these requirements is that sample shaping can fail in two ways: First, if there is a feature-class gap between shaping series steps, performance will breakdown, just as it would in a simple discrimination. Note that there were no gaps in ALPs feature-class profile. Second, if, for example, the participant responds only on the basis of a feature-class relation between the sample and comparison, at some point when the similarity between the stimuli is no longer present, performance will break down. For ALP, that similarity likely ended after Step 5, as could be inferred from his post-shaping data (Figure 3.7) in which stimuli E2 through $E2_5$, and not $E2_6$ or F2 were members of a feature (similarity) class. Moreover, this is also the point at which his breakdown in performance occurred. In sum, while feature classes between sample stimuli almost certainly promote progression through a shaping series, feature classes between sample and comparison may hinder progression through a shaping series, once the boundary of the feature class is reached, unless that relation is an arbitrary one.

One reason that feature classes may exert a strong and undesirable influence on sample-comparison relations with individuals with intellectual disabilities is that response selection may be controlled by only a very limited portion of the individual stimulus. For example, a participant's comparison selections may be controlled only by a single distinct feature of the sample stimulus to the exclusion of all other features of the stimulus. Once the shaping series progresses to the point that the feature is gone, a performance breakdown occurs.

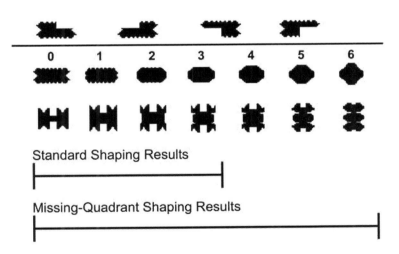

*Figure 3.8: Sample-shaping results for Participant STN. The upper portion of the figure shows four missing-quadrant stimuli from the first stimulus of the first series of graded form stimuli. Bars in the bottom of the figure illustrate the sample-shaping level reached with standard sample shaping vs. a sample shaping program using the missing quadrant method.*

Recently, a modification to the sample shaping procedure was instituted that may promote control by multiple aspects of the stimuli in sample shaping. Preliminary data collected with STN (chronological age 13; estimated age-equivalent 8.7) illustrate the procedure and findings. STN was initially given standard sample-shaping procedures, similar to those given to ALP. This resulted in a breakdown in performance between Steps 3 and 4, as summarized in the lower portion of Figure 3.8. Then, the "missing quadrant" method was instituted. In this method, each sample stimulus in the series was presented with one quadrant of the stimulus missing, as illustrated in the upper portion of Figure 3.8. To progress to the next step in the series, STN had to perform accurately with all four variations of a given sample stimulus. As shown in the lower portion of Figure 3.8, this procedure resulted in sample-shaping success. In addition, this procedure was replicated with another participant with intellectual disabilities using the sample-shaping task presented in Figure 3.4. Together, though preliminary, these data support the revised analysis of the role of feature classes presented above.

## Conclusions and Future Directions

Most of the work described in this chapter is aimed at achieving a better understanding of the behavioral processes involved in stimulus control transfer. As is so often the case in both the lab and in educational settings, transfer from prompts of various kinds is by no means automatic; in fact, with individuals with severe intellectual disabilities, transfer is particularly difficult. The research described in this chapter is part of a concerted effort to understand stimulus control as it applies to individuals with intellectual disabilities from both a basic and technological perspective. In our view, a complete understanding of basic processes in stimulus control will help tremendously in the development of the best technological teaching solutions to discrimination learning. Are we there yet? At this point, the answer is no, but much progress has been made, and the theoretical guidance from stimulus-control topography coherence theory will likely result in much future progress toward a true behavioral teaching technology.

Recall that the fourth characteristic of a true teaching technology is that it be readily usable by, for example, teachers in the classroom. A growing number of therapists and parents also conduct applied-behavior-analysis teaching sessions with individuals with autism and mental retardation in their homes. Thus, a true teaching technology must also reach these instructors. Given the theoretical and empirical work presented in this chapter, the reader might conclude that once basic processes have been fleshed out and appropriate methods developed, the complexity of the teaching solutions may be beyond the time and effort available to even the most dedicated teacher. In one sense, this notion may be true. Much of the basic research we have conducted has not only revealed the complexity of the discrimination problems but the complexity of the technological solutions that will be necessary to overcome them. A teacher having to translate basic and applied research found in journals into usable classroom solutions to fit individual student needs might be a daunting task.

One solution to the complexity problem lies in the use of computer technology. A current example comes from the body of research that addresses identity matching-to-sample skills. Serna et al. (1997) reviewed the identity matching literature and the various methods that have come from research aimed at understanding the basic processes involved in same/different judgments. Based on that research, a software company, Praxis, Inc., has recently developed and tested a complex identity matching curriculum that is presented and managed on a desktop computer. The product assesses current matching skills, then determines the most appropriate starting point among the various teaching components. Success within any one component leads to tests of generalized matching; failure results in training with a subsequent teaching component. The different training components are arranged from the least to most elaborate, in terms of time and effort required by the student. The curriculum is highly individualized, and decisions about which component to present to the student are made entirely by the software. Ultimately, it is envisioned that similar curricula will be developed for complex transfer-of-stimulus-control problems. Such curricula will take advantage of both the empirical developments in this area as well as increasingly powerful computer capabilities.

Finally, an important area for future research involves investigation of the role that schedules of reinforcement play in stimulus control. Recall that unwanted SCTs are often adventitiously reinforced, albeit at a schedule that is leaner than would be a wanted SCT. Using an example presented earlier, a simple discrimination problem, position preference (an unwanted SCT) would be inadvertently reinforced on a variable-ratio-2 (VR-2) schedule, whereas the wanted SCT of control by the form stimulus would be reinforced on a continuous reinforcement (CRF) schedule, if participants responded exclusively on the basis of one SCT or another. Though a CRF should support more responding than a VR-2, it is possible that individuals with intellectual disabilities are not sensitive to such differences. Put another way, such individuals may have difficulty discriminating relatively small schedule differences. A recently initiated program of research in our lab is designed to address this potential problem. The program is guided by Behavioral Detection Theory (McCarthy, 1991), a variation of Signal Detection Theory (Green & Swets, 1966) in which "hits" and "misses" equate well with wanted and unwanted SCTs. Some of the questions being addressed include: Can schedule-sensitivity assessment procedures be developed that predict success or failure in discrimination problems? Can sensitivity be increased? Will such increases in sensitivity lead to better discrimination learning? This focus on contingency discrimination is not meant to replace the focus on stimulus control factors in discrimination learning. Rather, it represents an expansion of our efforts to improve discrimination learning by recognizing the importance of all three of the terms (antecedents, behavior, and consequences) of a contingency (see Davison & Nevin, 1999). Of course, such an expansion of focus will likely increase even further the level of complexity of procedures designed to overcome discrimination problems. But again, taking advantage of powerful, yet available, computer technology may help bring complex solutions into widespread practice.

## References

Davison, M., & Nevin, J. A. (1999). Stimuli, reinforcers, and behavior: An integration. *Journal of the Experimental Analysis of Behavior, 71*, 439-482.

Dinsmoor, J. A. (1985). The role of observing and attention in establishing stimulus control. *Journal of the Experimental Analysis of Behavior, 43*, 365-382.

Dinsmoor, J. A. (1995). Stimulus control: Part I. *The Behavior Analyst, 18*, 51-68.

Dube, W. V., & McIlvane, W. J. (1997). Reinforcer frequency and restricted stimulus control. *Journal of the Experimental Analysis of Behavior, 68*, 303-316.

Dube, W. V., & McIlvane, W. J. (1999). Reduction of stimulus overselectivity with non-verbal differential observing responses. *Journal of Applied Behavior Analysis, 32*, 25-33.

Dube, W. V., Iennaco, F. M., & McIlvane, W. J. (1993). Generalized identity matching to sample of two-dimensional forms in individuals with intellectual disabilities. *Research in Developmental Disabilities, 14*, 457-477.

Dube, W. V., Lombard, K. M., Farren, K. M., Flusser, D. S., Balsamo, L. M., Fowler, T. R., & Tomanari, G. Y. (2003). Stimulus overselectivity and observing behavior in individuals with mental retardation. In R. Cook, K. Murata-Soraci, & S. Soraci (Eds.), *Perspectives on fundamental processes in intellectual functioning: Vol. 2. Visual information processing: Implications for understanding individual differences* (pp. 109-123). Stamford, CT: Ablex.

Estes, W. K. (1959). The statistical approach to learning theory. In S. Koch (Ed.), *Psychology: A study of a science* (Vol. 2, pp. 380-491). New York: McGraw-Hill.

Fields, L. (1979). Acquisition of stimulus control while introducing new stimuli in fading. *Journal of the Experimental Analysis of Behavior, 32*, 121-127.

Goldiamond, I. (1966). Perception, language, and conceptualization rules. In B. Kleinmuntz (Ed.), *Problem solving* (pp. 183-224). New York: Wiley.

Green, D. M., & Swets, J. W. (1966). *Signal detection theory and psychophysics.* New York: Wiley.

Harlow, H. F. (1950). Analysis of discrimination learning by monkeys. *Journal of Experimental Psychology, 40*, 26-39.

Kamin, L. J. (1969). Predictability, surprise, attention, and conditioning. In B. A. Campbell & R. M. Church (Eds.), *Punishment and aversive behavior.* New York: Appleton Century Crofts.

Lancioni, G. E., & Smeets, P. M. (1986). Procedures and parameters of errorless discrimination training with developmentally impaired individuals. In N. R. Ellis & N. W. Bray (Eds.), *International Review of Research in Mental Retardation* (Vol. 14, pp. 135-164). New York: Academic Press.

Lovaas, O. I., Koegel, R. L., & Schreibman, L. (1979). Stimulus overselectivity in autism: A review of research. *Psychological Bulletin, 86*, 1236-1254.

Maydak, M., R. Stromer, R., Mackay, H. A., & Stoddard, L. T. (1995). Stimulus classes in matching to sample and sequence production: The emergence of numeric relations. *Research in Developmental Disabilities, 16*, 179-204.

McCarthy, D. C. (1991). Behavioral detection theory: Some implications for applied human research. In M. L. Commons, J. A. Nevin, & M. C. Davison (Eds.), *Signal detection: Mechanisms, models and applications* (pp. 239-255). Hillsdale, NJ: Erlbaum.

McIlvane, W. J. (1992). Stimulus control analysis and nonverbal instructional technology for people with mental handicaps. In N. R. Bray (Ed.), *International review of research in mental retardation* (Vol. 18, pp. 55-109). New York: Academic Press.

McIlvane, W. J., & Dube, W. V. (1992). Stimulus control shaping and stimulus control topographies. *The Behavior Analyst, 15,* 89-94.

McIlvane, W. J. & Dube, W. V. (2003). Stimulus control topography coherence theory: Foundations and extensions. *The Behavior Analyst, 26,* 195-213.

McIlvane, W. J., Dube, W. V., Green, G., & Serna, R. W. (1993). Programming conceptual and communication skill development: A methodological stimulus class analysis. In A. P. Kaiser & D. B. Gray (Eds.), *Enhancing childrens' communication* (Vol. 2, 242-285). Baltimore, MD: Paul H. Brookes.

McIlvane, W. J., Kledaras, J. B., Callahan, T. C., & Dube, W. V. (2002). High probability stimulus control topographies with delayed S+ onset in a simultaneous discrimination procedure. *Journal of the Experimental Analysis of Behavior, 77,* 189-198.

McIlvane, W. J., Kledaras, J. B., Dube, W. V., Serna, R. W. & Hamad, C. (2000). Developing a true behavioral technology for teaching pre-academic skills to people with mental retardation. *Journal of Intellectual Disabilities, 44,* 388.

McIlvane, W. J., Kledaras, J. B., Dube, W. V., & Stoddard, L. T. (1989). Automated instruction of severely and profoundly retarded individuals. In J. Mulick & R. Antonak (Eds.), *Transitions in Mental Retardation: Vol. 4. Applications and Implications of Technology* (pp. 15-76). Norwood, NJ: Ablex.

McIlvane, W. J., Kledaras, J. B., Lowry, M. W., & Stoddard, L. T. (1992). Studies of exclusion in individuals with severe mental retardation. *Research in Developmental Disabilities, 13,* 509-532.

McIlvane, W. J., Kledaras, J. B., White, M. J., & Stoddard, L. T. (1991). Acquisition of spoken word: object relation in people with severe mental retardation: The role of novelty in learning by exclusion. *Proceedings of the 24th Annual Gatlinburg Conference on Research and Theory in Mental Retardation and Developmental Disabilities,* 90.

McIlvane, W. J., Serna, R. W., Dube, W. V., & Stromer, R. (2000). Stimulus control topography coherence and stimulus equivalence: Reconciling test outcomes with theory. In J. Leslie & D. E. Blackman (Eds.), *Experimental and applied analyses of human behavior* (pp. 85-110). Reno, NV: Context Press.

Serna, R. W., & Carlin, M. T. (2001). Guiding visual attention in individuals with mental retardation. In L. M. Glidden (Ed.), *International review of research in mental retardation* (Vol. 24, pp. 321-357). New York: Academic Press.

Serna, R. W., Dube, W. V., & McIlvane, W. J. (1997). Assessing same/different judgements in individuals with severe intellectual disabilities: A status report. *Research in Developmental Disabilities, 18,* 343-368.

Serna, R. W., Stoddard, L. T., & McIlvane, W. J. (1992). Developing auditory stimulus control: A note on methodology. *Journal of Behavioral Education, 2,* 391-403.

Serna, R. W., Wilkinson, K. M., & McIlvane, W. J. (1998). Blank-comparison assessment of stimulus-stimulus relations in individuals with mental retardation. *American Journal on Mental Retardation, 103*, 60-74.

Sidman, M., & Stoddard, L. T. (1966). Programming perception and learning for retarded children. In N. R. Ellis (Ed.), *International Review of Research in Mental Retardation* (Vol. 2, pp. 151-208). New York: Academic Press.

Sidman, M., & Stoddard, L. T. (1967). The effectiveness of fading in programming a simultaneous form discrimination for retarded children. *Journal of the Experimental Analysis of Behavior, 10*, 3-15.

Solman, R. T, Singh, N., & Kehoe, E. J. (1992). Pictures block the learning of sightwords. *Educational Psychology, 12*, 143-153.

Stoddard, L. T., & Gerovac, B. J. (1981). A stimulus shaping method for teaching complex motor performance to severely and profoundly retarded individuals. *Applied Research in Mental Retardation, 2*, 281-295.

Stoddard, L. T., de Rose, J. C., & McIlvane, W. J. (1986). Observacoes curiosas acerca do desempenho deficiente apos a ocorrencia de erros. [Curious observations on defective performance following errors]. *Psicologia, 12*, 1-18.

Terrace, H. S. (1963). Discrimination learning with and without "errors". *Journal of the Experimental Analysis of Behavior, 6*, 1-27.

Touchette, P. E. (1968). The effects of graduated stimulus change on the acquisition of a simple discrimination in severely retarded boys. *Journal of the Experimental Analysis of Behavior, 11*, 39-48.

Wilkinson, K. M., & McIlvane, W. J. (1997). Blank comparison analysis of emergent symbolic mapping by young children. *Journal of Experimental Child Psychology, 67*, 115-130.

Zygmont, D. M., Lazar, R. M., Dube, W. V., & McIlvane, W. J. (1992). Teaching arbitrary matching via sample stimulus control shaping to young children and mentally retarded individuals: A methodological note. *Journal of the Experimental Analysis of Behavior, 57*, 109-117.

## Acknowledgments

Manuscript preparation and the research described in this chapter received support from the National Institute of Child Health and Human Development, Grants HD 25995, HD 32049, and HD 37663. I gratefully acknowledge William J. McIlvane and William V. Dube for generous support and guidance during the preparation of this chapter. In addition, I would like to thank Brooks Thompson and Jason Krienke for help conducting some of the research described in this chapter.

# Chapter 4

# Pharmaceutical Interventions and Developmental Disabilities

**Alan Poling, Sean Laraway, Kristal Ehrhardt,
Lanai Jennings, and Lynne Turner**
*Western Michigan University*

Psychotropic drugs are medications prescribed with the intent of improving an individual's mood, cognition, or overt behavior. For nearly 50 years, these drugs have been widely prescribed to treat behavior disorders in people with developmental disabilities. As used in this chapter, the term *behavior disorders* refers to conditions in which individuals cause problems for themselves or for others by engaging in unacceptable behavior or by failing to engage in appropriate or functional behavior (cf. Poling, Gadow, & Cleary, 1991, p. 2). Such conditions might involve one or two discrete responses or a broad range of signs and symptoms, in which case the individual characteristically would receive a psychiatric diagnosis. In most cases, the appearance of a behavior disorder provides the rationale for pharmaceutical intervention.

Successful drug treatment changes behavior in a way that substantially improves the functioning and quality of life of the individual being treated. In most cases, the successful use of a psychotropic drug also improves the quality of life of other persons directly affected by the behavior disorder (e.g., parents, caregivers, direct service staff). Whether or not use of psychotropic drugs produces clinically significant behavior change depends on features of the behavior disorder in question and the drug(s) and dose(s) prescribed. Whether such change is detected depends, in part, on the assessment procedures used to evaluate the drug treatment. The primary purpose of this chapter is to overview the use of psychotropic drugs in persons with developmental disabilities.

## Historical Overview

Perhaps the best-known antipsychotic drug, chlorpromazine, was developed in France in 1950 and was marketed as Thorazine in the United States in 1955 (McKim, 2003). Chlorpromazine successfully reduced many of the symptoms (e.g., hallucinations, thought disorders, and delusions) associated with psychotic disorders, and physicians soon began prescribing the drug for people with developmental disabilities (Gadow & Poling, 1988). Today, physicians have several dozen psychotropic medications at their disposal, and these drugs collectively account for approximately 10-15% of all prescriptions written in the United States (Baldessarini, 1996). Although most of these prescriptions are not written for persons with developmental disabilities, the use of psychotropic drugs is especially prevalent in these individuals. Since the introduction of chlorpromazine, the use of psychotropic drugs in this population has become common. Several researchers estimate that approximately 25-50% of adults living in institutions, and 25-40% of those living in the community, receive some kind of psychotropic medication (Aman & Singh, 1988; Gadow & Poling, 1988; Reiss, 1998).

From the time that psychotropic drugs were first prescribed for people with developmental disabilities, researchers have expressed concern over the inappropriate use of such drugs in this population (e.g., Greiner, 1958). Concern became more pervasive during the late 1960s and early 1970s, as researchers began reporting startling prescription practices for the management of behavioral disorders in persons with developmental disabilities. For example, patients often received doses that surpassed the suggested therapeutic range, received drugs for very long periods of time (e.g., 4 years) without periodic evaluations or adjustments, and received multiple psychotropic medications to treat the same behavior (i.e., *polypharmacy*; Findholt & Emmett, 1990; Rinck, 1998).

Despite the widespread use of psychotropic drugs in institutions, few empirically verified the therapeutic effects of those medications (Rinck, Guidry, & Calkins, 1989). Moreover, most studies of therapeutic effectiveness that did appear were suspect in light of poor methods of evaluation (Kalachnik et al., 1998; Poling, Picker, & Wallace, 1983). Few studies were concerned with side effects, but some evidence of serious adverse effects did emerge (Rinck et al., 1989).

By 1970, it became apparent that psychotropic drugs were frequently used to the detriment of institutionalized people with developmental disabilities. Fostered in large part by litigation brought forth on behalf of residents with developmental disabilities, two reform initiatives were initiated (Gadow, 1993; Kalachnick, 1988, Lepler, Hodas, & Cotter-Mack, 1993). The basis for these initiatives was a series of court cases, legislative acts, and regulations that are considered in detail elsewhere (Sprague, 1982; Sprague & Galliher, 1988).

The first reform initiative came in the form of best practice guidelines. In 1971, the Accreditation Council on Services for Facilities for the Mentally Retarded (ACMR) released standards for psychotropic drug use in institutions. The standards deemed unnecessarily high doses inappropriate, especially when used for punitive purposes, for care provider convenience, or in place of educational programming (AMCR, 1971).

Several associations issued guidelines after the ACMR did so in 1971. For example, in 1977 the Accreditation Council for Services for Mentally Retarded and Other Developmentally Disabled Persons (ACMRDD) released comprehensive and influential standards (Kalachnick, 1988; Kalachnick et al., 1998; Lepler et al., 1993). The ACMRDD guidelines outlined the essential steps for psychotropic drug prescription and monitoring for individuals with developmental disabilities. Initial steps involve obtaining informed consent and having an interdisciplinary team assess the need for medication. The ACMRDD guidelines also emphasized the need to specify target behaviors for the purposes of evaluating drug effects. Other steps include practitioners working toward a "minimal effective" dosage, while incorporating behavioral and educational interventions to reduce inappropriate behaviors (Kalachnick, 1988). The final step requires data-driven evaluations of therapeutic and side effects. Although these guidelines failed to specify precisely how each step should be accomplished, they did provide valuable insight as to what objectives should be pursued (Kalachnick, 1988).

The second reform effort involved both litigation and federal legislation. The landmark case of *Wyatt v. Stickney* (1972) was one of the earliest and most influential lawsuits regarding the use of psychotropic medications with institutionalized persons. The lawsuit stemmed from staff cutbacks in institutions for the mentally ill and/or disabled in Alabama. The main conflict involved an institutionalized person's "right to treatment" (MacMillan, 1982). In his decision on *Wyatt v. Stickney*, Judge Frank Johnson, overseer of the United States District Court, made the following ruling:

> Residents shall have a right to be free from unnecessary or excessive medication. The resident's records shall state the effects of psychoactive medication on the resident. When dosages of such are changed or other psychoactive mediations are prescribed, a notation shall be made in the resident's record concerning the effect of the new medication or new dosages and the behavior changes, if any, which occur (cited in Sprague, 1982, p. 380-381).

In accordance with the 1971 ACMR guidelines, Judge Frank Johnson also ruled that medication is not an acceptable replacement for habilitation nor should it be used for punitive purposes or for staff benefit (Sprague, 1982).

The *Wyatt v. Stickney* case served as the impetus for congressional action (Sprague & Galliher, 1988). In 1980, the United States Congress passed Public Law 96-247, the Civil Rights of Institutionalized Persons Act. This law permitted the federal government to bring civil actions lawsuits against state governments in the event that institutions disenfranchised individuals with disabilities. (Sprague & Galliher, 1988). After legislators enacted Public Law 96-247, several suits (e.g., *U.S. v. Indiana*, 1984; *U.S. v. South Carolina*, 1986; *U.S. v. Colorado*, 1986) were brought against state governments concerning the inappropriate use of psychotropic medications.

Legislation, litigation, and professional guidelines placed considerable pressure on institutional personnel to use drugs cautiously and to monitor their positive and adverse effects carefully. Administrators and other care providers responded to this pressure by making systematic attempts to reduce unwarranted psychotropic drug use among institutionalized individuals. For example, Hancock, Weber, Kaxa, and Her (1991) tracked antipsychotic drug use for residents at a state care facility between 1979 and 1988. Antipsychotic medication use was eliminated for nearly 75% of individuals who received such drugs at the onset of this period. Similarly dramatic reductions in the prevalence of psychotropic drug use occurred in other institutions. In two 8-year investigations, for instance, Findholt and Emmett (1990) and Briggs, Hamad, Garrard, and Wills (1984) documented 53% and 37% declines, respectively, in the use of psychotropic medications.

## Provisions Resulting from Litigation, Legislation, and Regulations

In addition to increasing the likelihood that clients with developmental disabilities would be free of inappropriate medications, provisions established as a result of litigation, legislation, and regulations made it more likely that medications would be used appropriately with those who received them. The essence of these provisions is as follows (Kalachnik, 1988):

1. Specific target behaviors that are to improve as a function of drug treatment should be delineated.
2. An interdisciplinary team should evaluate the need for medication.
3. Written informed consent should be obtained from the parent or guardian of the client before drug treatment is initiated.
4. The minimal effective dose should be used.
5. Periodic attempts at drug reduction should be scheduled.
6. Drug treatment should be integrated with behavioral and educational interventions.
7. Periodic data-based evaluations of drug efficacy should be arranged.
8. Evaluations of drug efficacy should include monitoring for side effects (especially tardive dyskinesia if antipsychotics are prescribed).

These are eminently reasonably provisions; following them goes far in ensuring that clients benefit from the medications that they receive. We have suggested elsewhere (e.g., Poling, 1994; Poling & Ehrhardt, 1999) that the essence of appropriate use of psychotropic drugs entails:

1. Ensuring that the goals of treatment are clear and in the client's best interest.
2. Ensuring that treatment decisions are made on the basis of real drug effects.
3. Ensuring that drug therapy is flexible and integrated with non-pharmacological interventions.

Caregivers who adhere closely to the provisions established as a result of litigation, legislation, and regulations do these things automatically.

Unfortunately, however, many of the federal laws that prompted the aforementioned changes in how psychotropic drugs are used with people who reside in institutions do not apply directly to persons with developmental disabilities who live in the community. Moreover, fewer state regulations exist controlling psychotropic drug use and monitoring in community settings, as compared to institutional settings (Rinck et al., 1989). For example, whereas nine states mandate *drug holidays* (i.e., drug-free periods) in institutions, only five states require drug holidays in community settings. Eighty-two percent of the states prohibit physicians from prescribing a psychotropic medication indefinitely to an institutionalized person. In contrast, only 54% of the states prohibit physicians from doing so in community settings. State regulations also differentially tolerate polypharmacy. Whereas 43% of the states regulate polypharmacy in institutions, only 16% of the states do so in community placements (Rinck et al., 1989).

Put simply, the rigorous procedural safeguards that regulate psychotropic drug usage in institutions do not necessarily or typically apply to most people with developmental disabilities, because they live in community placements. For example, from 1975 (Hobbs, 1975) to the present, over 95% of people with mental retardation live outside institutions. With such individuals, drug usage often is governed by general standards of medical practice alone. Surprisingly little is known regarding how psychotropic medications are used outside institutions.

Two factors contribute to the paucity of knowledge concerning the effectiveness of psychotropic drugs in people with mental retardation (Schroeder et al., 1998). One is that practical and ethical constraints make it difficult to study such populations. The other is that little funding has been available for studies of the psychopharmacology of developmental disabilities. For these and perhaps other reasons, the literature concerning pharmaceutical interventions for people with developmental disabilities leaves much to be desired. The following section summarizes that literature.

## The Literature

Publications describing the results of well-controlled experiments provide the best information regarding the effectiveness of drug therapies. Indeed, for physicians and other concerned parties to make informed decisions regarding the many treatment alternatives, they must have access to data from empirical investigations of drug effectiveness. To appraise currently available information regarding drug treatment for people with developmental disabilities, we conducted a limited review of relevant publications. This review entailed searches (December, 2002) of English-language publications listed in the MEDLINE database. Each search combined (using a Boolean AND) the subject term *drug therapy* with one of the following subject terms: *autistic disorder, mental retardation,* or *developmental disabilities.* No effort was made to identify duplicate publications across searches; therefore, individual searches likely include some of the same publications. It should be noted that this review was not exhaustive; other searches using different criteria or different databases might yield dissimilar results. Nevertheless, our review gives some indication of the number and kind of publications available to those involved in making treatment decisions

One purpose of this review was simply to identify trends over time in the number of publications matching the specified search criteria. Figure 4.1 depicts the

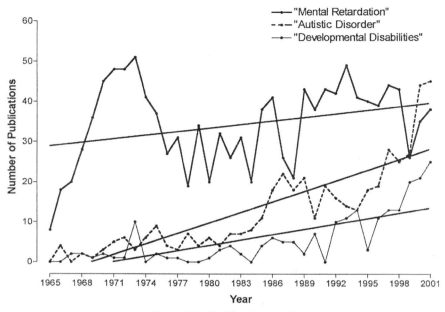

*Figure 4.1: Publication trends.*

number of publications meeting each combination of search criteria. For each set of data, best-fit regression lines were computed via the least squares method. As this table shows, since the mid-1960s there has been an increasing trend in the number of publications related to the use of drugs in people with autism, mental retardation, and other developmental disabilities. Moreover, in the last 5 years there have been sharp increases in the number of articles related to the terms *autism* and *developmental disabilities*. These increases probably reflect, at least in part, changes in the popularity of diagnostic categories.

Given that recent publications should provide the most current information regarding the effects of psychotropic drug therapies, we evaluated the characteristics of publications that appeared in the last 5 years (i.e., 1997-2001). We determined whether or not these recent publications empirically assessed psychotropic drugs in treating behavioral and cognitive problems. Table 4.1 shows the percentage of total publications that were empirical studies of drug efficacy for each set of search criteria, while Table 4.2 lists the drugs investigated in those studies. As Table 4.1 shows, most of the publications disclosed by our MEDLINE search were not empirical drug evaluations. Nonetheless, a sizeable number of different drugs have been evaluated. Most, however, have been examined in a single study. No attempt was made to evaluate the methodological quality of those studies, but other authors have done so (e.g., Brylewski & Duggan, 1999; Matson et al., 2000). Their general conclusion was that most studies concerning the effects of psychotropic drugs in people with developmental disabilities are not well controlled. For example, they lack placebo controls or double blinds, do not involve random selection or assignment of participants, or fail to distinguish non-selective suppression of behavior from selective effects on target responses. In summarizing what is probably the most comprehensive recent review of psychopharmacology and mental retardation, Matson et al. (2000) concluded:

> Our findings were startling and consistent with Baumeister and Sevin's findings in 1990. Professionals continue to medicate individuals in their

| Search Criteria | Year | Empirical Studies/ Total Publications | Percentage |
|---|---|---|---|
| su= "Drug Therapy" and su= "Autistic Disorder" | 1997 | 10/28 | 36% |
| | 1998 | 5/25 | 20% |
| | 1999 | 7/27 | 26% |
| | 2000 | 8/44 | 18% |
| | 2001 | 21/45 | 47% |
| su= "Drug Therapy" and su="Developmental Disabilities" | 1997 | 0/13 | 0% |
| | 1998 | 0/13 | 0% |
| | 1999 | 3/20 | 15% |
| | 2000 | 0/21 | 0% |
| | 2001 | 1/25 | 4% |
| su= "Drug Therapy" and su= "Mental Retardation" | 1997 | 6/44 | 14% |
| | 1998 | 1/43 | 2% |
| | 1999 | 0/26 | 0% |
| | 2000 | 4/35 | 11% |
| | 2001 | 12/38 | 32% |

*Table 4.1: Trends in publications meeting MEDLINE search criteria. Percent Empirical Studies Published 1997-2001.*

| Search Criteria | Drugs |
| --- | --- |
| su= "Drug Therapy" and su= "Autistic Disorder" | secretin (11), risperidone (10), naltrexone (3), clomipramine (3), haloperidol (3), mirtazepine (2), sertraline (2), fluoxetine (2), dimethylglycine (2), famotidine, lamotrigine, olanzapine, clonazepam, propanolol, divalproex, amantadine, flumazenil, methylphenidate, vancomycin, prednisone, venlafaxine, vigabatrin, niaprazine, quetiapine, paroxetine, pyridoxine, magnexium, buspirone, tetrahydrobiopterin, inositol |
| su= "Drug Therapy" and su= "Developmental Disabilities" | amantadine, methylphenidate, carbimazole, clonidine |
| su= "Drug Therapy" and su= "Mental Retardation" | risperidone (8), olanzapine (2), paroxetine (2), zuclopenthixol, clonidine, naltrexone, gabapentin, piracetam, citalopram, clozapine, sertraline, clomipramine, allopurinol, lithium, haloperidol, fenfluramine, methylphenidate |

*Table 4.2: Drugs Evaluated in Articles Published 1997-2001 Meeting Search Criteria. Note: Numbers in parentheses indicate the number of publications that studied that particular drug.*

care despite a lack of a sound research base to support their treatment decisions. While a small amount of research does exist, it is seriously flawed from a research design perspective. The studies routinely lack appropriate experimental control, and lack reliable measures of drug effect, collateral behaviors, and side effects. Methodological controls are far short of psychological treatment in the field with little improvement over precious decades. This trend is extremely disappointing given the dangerous and restrictive nature of these treatment options. (p. 291)

Matson et al. (2000) are not alone in their skepticism. For example, in reviewing studies examining the effects of antipsychotic medications for challenging behavior in people with intellectual disorder (ID), Brylewski and Duggan (1999) reported that they could find only three studies that could be classified as randomized controlled trials. "These trials provided no evidence as to whether antipsychotic medication does or does not help adults with ID and challenging behavior" (Brylewski & Duggan, 1999, p. 360).

Similar results have been found for persons receiving a dual diagnoses of intellectual disability (ID) and schizophrenia. In a review of studies that examined the effectiveness of antipsychotic medication in people diagnosed with ID and schizophrenia, Duggan and Brylewski (1999) found only one relevant randomized controlled trial, which was published over 40 years ago (i.e., Foote, 1958). These authors found that there is no empirical evidence that antipsychotic medications are, or are not, effective in individuals with developmental disabilities and schizophrenia. Until methodologically sound trials are conducted, practitioners will have to rely on personal experience as well as extrapolations from studies with individuals with schizophrenia and "normal" intelligence. These extrapolations may or may not be valid (Duggan & Brylewski, 1999).

Many studies of drug effects in people with autism also lack methodological rigor. For instance, a panel of experts convened by the New York State Department of Health (Clinical Practice Guideline, 1999) evaluated the use of psychoactive medications in young children (0-3 years of age) with autism/pervasive developmental disorders. They found a total of 99 relevant articles, 12 of which met the group's criteria for providing adequate evidence of efficacy. Four of those studies examined haloperidol, five examined naltrexone, and three examined fenfluramine. When these and other studies (e.g., those conducted with older children or weaker methods) were considered, the panel concluded that drugs may be beneficial in reducing maladaptive autistic or associated behavioral problems for which other interventions have not been effective. Nonetheless, they noted that the short- and long-term efficacy and safety of most drugs have not been adequately evaluated, that side effects are often serious in young children, and that non-pharmacological alternatives are often available.

It is distressingly easy to find other authors who have lamented the deficiencies of the empirical literature concerning the psychopharmacology of developmental disabilities (e.g., Gadow & Poling, 1988; Kennedy & Meyer, 1998; Lewis, Aman, Gadow, Schroeder, & Thompson, 1996; Schroeder et al., 1998; Singh & Beale, 1986). In fairness, however, empirical studies have yielded some very important findings regarding the effects of psychotropic drugs in people with developmental disabilities. A striking case in point concerns the effects of secretin in the treatment of people with autism (or autistic spectrum disorder).

Secretin is a peptide hormone that stimulates the production of pepsin and bile and the release of digestive fluids from the pancreas. It had generated no interest as a psychotropic medication prior to 1996, when it was administered to Parker Beck, a boy diagnosed with autism, who was having problems with diarrhea and vomiting. Parker received an endoscopy at the University of Maryland, and was given secretin as part of a procedure to evaluate functioning of the pancreas. Following the treatment, his gastrointestinal problems reportedly disappeared and, moreover, his verbal behavior and overall deportment dramatically improved. Parker's parents attributed his improvement to the secretin that he received, and his case was described on the popular television show, "Dateline." Soon thereafter, secretin became a popular, although expensive, treatment for people with autism.

The value of the drug supposedly was confirmed in a poorly controlled study in which Parker Beck and two other children participated (Horvath et al., 1998). Positive results were not, however, produced in several subsequent and better-controlled studies (reviewed by Posey & McDougle, 2000), and it appears that secretin is not a generally effective psychotropic medication for people with autism or pervasive developmental disorders. Nonetheless, enthusiasm for secretin continues in some quarters, in part because Bernard Rimland has argued vigorously that parental impression and the results of uncontrolled investigations are more revealing than objective data collected in double-blind studies using generally accepted research design. For example, in August, 2000 Rimland wrote on the website of the Autistic Research Institute, that:

> The double-blind study is considered to be the 'gold standard.' But the gold is tarnished…The medical community looks with a jaundiced eye at reports that do not involve the use of placebo-controlled blind studies, dismissing them as merely anecdotal. I believe that the medical community should be looking with an equally jaundiced eye at controlled studies.

Replication of results across well-controlled studies is the only legitimate scientific proof of the effectiveness (or ineffectiveness) of a particular treatment for a given behavior disorder. Although other sorts of evidence, including testimonials and the results of uncontrolled or poorly-controlled studies may *suggest* whether or not a treatment is useful, and be valuable in that sense, placing too much faith in such evidence is ill-advised. Accepting as effective, and therefore using, treatments that have not been empirically validated may make well-intentioned care givers feel good – they have faith in the interventions and implement them in the hope and expectation of a positive result – and such treatments may even benefit certain people with developmental disabilities. It is, however, essential that the benefit actually is documented, not simply assumed. In cases where the preponderance of evidence from controlled studies suggests that the treatment is unlikely to be effective, for instance, in the case of using secretin to treat people with autism, particular care should be taken to document treatment effects adequately, as well as to consider whether alternative, apparently more effective, treatment alternatives are available. A healthy dose of skepticism is appropriate with respect to *all* proposed treatments for people with developmental disabilities, and the size of the dose should be inversely proportional to the size of the data base that supports the effectiveness of the treatment. With respect to pharmaceutical interventions, there are several areas where a larger data base is badly needed and a strong dose of skepticism is most appropriate.

## Areas for Future Research

For decades, authors have suggested areas for future research concerning pharmaceutical interventions for people with developmental disabilities. Nine areas that we consider to be particularly important are considered here, in no particular order.

## Effects of Commonly Used but Rarely Studied Medications

Some drugs that are widely used to treat behavior disorders in people with developmental disabilities, such as propranolol (Inderal) and valproic acid (Depakote), have received little or no attention from researchers. This poses obvious difficulties for physicians who are considering the use of those drugs.

## Studies of Developmental Psychopharmacology

The effects of psychotropic drugs may vary as a function of the age of the person who takes them (Brown & Sawyer, 1998; Taylor, 1994), therefore, studies of people of different ages are important in evaluating the utility of a given medication. Of particular concern are drug effects in children and elderly people with developmental disabilities, both groups that have received little research attention. It is disheartening that the rationale for prescribing psychotropic drugs to children with developmental disabilities often involves the findings of clinical trials involving adults with no developmental disabilities.

## Effects of Long-Term Drug Treatments

People with developmental disabilities frequently receive psychotropic drugs for many years, sometimes literally from cradle to grave. Most drug studies, however, comprise a few months at most. There is need for studies that examine drug effects over long periods, perhaps by intermittently collecting follow-up data years after an initial, intensive study documenting efficacy has ended. Including such data in the initial report of drug effects would slow publication sufficiently to be untenable in many cases, but such data might form the basis of short subsequent reports that are evaluated in consideration of the inevitable problems posed by long-term data collection (e.g., participant attrition).

## Predictors of Responsiveness to Drug Treatments

Even when their behavior disorders seem very similar, people with developmental disabilities frequently differ in their responsiveness to a given psychotropic medication. Why they do so is unknown. It may be possible to isolate predictors of responsiveness at the behavioral, genetic, or physiological level, and work at each level is justified.

## Effects of Drug Combinations

It is not unusual for people with developmental disabilities to receive two or more psychotropic medications. For instance, of the 21 participants in an ongoing study that we are conducting to examine how drug effects are assessed in students with autism or mental retardation, 16 (76%) are receiving more than one psychotropic medication. One person is receiving seven medications; two are receiving six. Whether those medications interactive positively, negatively, or not at all is unknown. There are no published data to support or refute the use of so many psychotropic medications and such data are badly needed.

## Studies Using Single-Case Research Methods

Practical and ethical restrictions make it very difficult to conduct traditional randomized-group, placebo-controlled studies involving people with developmental disabilities. Although such studies understandably are held as the "gold standard" in clinical psychopharmacology, other experimental arrangements also may yield valuable data. Several authors have proposed that the strategies and tactics characteristic of applied behavior analysis are valuable in clinical psychopharmacology and should be more widely used in that area (e.g., Kennedy & Meyer, 1998; Poling & Ehrhardt, 1999; Schroeder, 1985; Singh & Beale, 1986). Meaningful studies using this approach can be conducted with a small number of participants and the potential of such studies for isolating useful interventions is evident in the applied behavior analysis literature. This approach is, however, foreign to most medical personnel and a strong political and educational campaign will be required before it is accepted by them.

## Studies of Behavioral Mechanisms of Drug Action

Studying how psychotropic drugs alter interactions between behavior and environmental events may help to understand and predict the effects of these agents. For example, there is evidence that methylphenidate alters the relative reinforcing effectiveness of food and social interaction in young people diagnosed with attention deficit hyperactivity disorder (ADHD) (Northup, Fusilier, Swanson, Roane, & Borrero, 1997). In behavior-analytic terms, the drug acts as an establishing operation for social interaction and as an abolishing operation for food. This general action could potentially account for many different specific effects of the drug. It appears to be worth investigating other types of behavioral mechanisms of drug action, and other drugs that may have these actions.

## Research Examining the Appropriateness of Drug Use

Bates, Smeltzer, and Arnoczky (1986) examined the drugs that were prescribed for 242 institutionalized adults with mental retardation in light of their psychiatric diagnoses. They reported that "at least 39.1% and possibly as many as 54.6% of the medication regimens seemed inappropriate for the conditions diagnosed" (p. 368). Sixteen years later, Young and Hawkins (2002) published the results of a similar analysis based on 71 adults with mental retardation who received services from a community mental health and mental retardation agency. A total of 145 psychotropic medications were prescribed. Young and Hawkins reported that 85 medications (59%) were prescribed for appropriate diagnoses or disorders, whereas 20% were not prescribed for appropriate reasons. According to them:

> This study provides some evidence of what has been suspected within the field all along. Prescribing practices for people with mental retardation may not always be legitimate and may not follow standard prescribing practices dictated by the FDA and current research. (p. 139)

Whether the same is true with prescribing practices for people with developmental disabilities who are not mentally retarded is of interest. Also of interest are the variables that contribute to the inappropriate and appropriate use of medications, including physicians' knowledge of developmental disabilities and the relevant psychopharmacological literature.

Another topic that merits investigation concerns physicians' understanding of non-pharmacological (e.g., behavior-analytic) interventions for dealing with behavioral problems common in people with developmental disabilities and their willingness to work with other professionals to arrange those interventions. As Sovner (1989) points out, psychotropic drugs often are used to treat specific behaviors, such as physical assault or self-injury. In many cases, these behaviors are operant responses that are sensitive to environmental manipulations, and it is both unnecessary and inappropriate to treat them with drugs. Determining the conditions under which physicians refer clients to psychologists or other professionals, instead of prescribing a medication, might suggest strategies for reducing such inappropriate use.

## Studies Examining Procedures to Facilitate Data-Based Treatment Decisions

As discussed in the next section, because prescribing physicians can almost never be certain that a particular psychotropic medication will produce the desired effect in a person with a developmental disability, careful monitoring of drug effects is required to ensure appropriate treatment of the patient. Although some relevant research concerning monitoring drug effects in people with ADHD has appeared, few studies have examined how data should be collected and reported to physicians to facilitate data-based treatment decisions. More work in this area, including studies examining a team approach to evaluating drug effects outside institutional settings, should prove valuable.

### Clinical Drug Assessment

At present, there is simply no way to predict accurately how a given person with a developmental disability will react to a particular psychotropic medication. Therefore, it is essential that medication effects be monitored carefully. Relative to other medications, psychotropic drugs are unique in that they are used to treat disorders that are defined by, measured in terms of, and best understood at the level of overt behavior. Although the neuropharmacological effects of a psychotropic drug may be known, the relationship between the neurochemical mechanism of actions of these drugs and problem behaviors has not been clearly established, so clinical effectiveness cannot be assessed at the neurochemical level of analysis. Rather, clinical evaluations of psychotropic drugs must ascertain whether medication substantially improves some targeted aspect of the client's behavior without producing intolerable adverse reactions (side effects). To determine the effectiveness of a pharmacological treatment for a behavior disorder, three questions must be answered (Kollins, Ehrhardt, & Poling, 2000): (a) What were the desired effects of the medication? (b) Were those effects obtained? and (c) Were there any significant adverse reactions? Although these questions seem relatively straightforward, answering them can be complex, especially in the context of everyday drug evaluations. At minimum, assessment of the therapeutic efficacy of a drug requires well-defined treatment goals and objectively measured behavioral outcomes.

Effective systematic monitoring may be accomplished in several ways. Direct observation is particularly useful. In some cases, meaningful data also can be produced through the use of structured interviews, rating scales, and measures of performance, achievement, and activity (Brown & Sawyer, 1998). Unfortunately, decisions to prescribe psychotropic medications or change dosage levels typically are based on informal global assessments provided by parents or teachers (Brown & Sawyer, 1998; Fredericks & Hayes, 1995; Gadow, 1982, 1983; Singh & Winton, 1984). The patient's actual behavior may have little influence on these decisions. Singh and Winton (1984), for example, examined the correlation between behavioral observations of the target symptoms and a physician's decision to change a patient's medication. Naturalistic observations were made of a 15-year-old boy with profound mental retardation while he received medications to treat his self-injurious behavior. The results suggested that the physician's decisions to change medication dosages were often not based on related changes in the target behavior, but rather on the global impressions of the ward staff. Interestingly, such physician practices appear not to have changed in 11 years, as these exact findings were replicated in another, more recent study (Fredericks & Hayes, 1995).

Two studies by Gadow (1982, 1983) found that school personnel characteristically fail to play an important role in monitoring the effects of psychotropic medications in students with mental retardation or other developmental disabilities. Teachers in early childhood special education programs and in classrooms for students diagnosed with mental retardation who had at least one student receiving medication for a behavior or a learning disorder were surveyed. The results indicated that teachers were often not involved in referral, diagnosis, or the withdrawal of medication. Furthermore, 60% of the teachers reported drug effects even though there were no systematic monitoring procedures in place and standardized evaluation instruments were rarely used.

Although teachers and other school personnel are in a good position to collect data relevant to desired and adverse effects of pharmacological treatments, that information typically is not systematically shared with physicians (Brown & Sawyer, 1998; Gadow, 1982, 1983). The ADHD literature suggests that treatment decisions regarding the use of psychotropic medications in schools are based primarily on physician's reactions to reports from parents, who may have little opportunity to observe a child's behavior at school, where the problems that define ADHD are particularly likely to occur (Brown & Sawyer, 1998). Sleator and Sprague (1978) note the importance of this issue and recommend that monitoring of drug effects must include reports from the teacher. They further recommend that medical professionals should play an active role in facilitating communication between physicians and school personnel. It appears, however, that this has not occurred during the 24 years since their recommendation appeared. In discussing medication monitoring in students with mental retardation, Gadow (1997) noted that "there was little evidence of interdisciplinary collaboration or the use of standardized instruments to assess therapeutic or untoward drug effects" (p. 225). No studies have followed up on the findings of Gadow (1982, 1983), and in a 1997 article he lamented: "Unfortunately, there remains little information on current practices in treatment evaluation for children with mental retardation" (p. 225). As noted previously, research examining such practices is needed. Development and widespread use of practical and accurate procedures for monitoring drug effects in people with developmental disabilities would go far in ensuring that the proper people receive medication and that their medication regimen is appropriate.

## Concluding Comments

The use of pharmaceutical interventions to treat behavior disorders in people with developmental disabilities has been widespread for nearly 50 years. Over that time, much has changed. An ever-increasing array of psychotropic drugs has become available and has been prescribed for this population. Today, scores of different drugs are at least occasionally prescribed for people with developmental disabilities. Interest in the psychopharmacology of developmental disabilities has grown, and a recent conference was devoted entirely to the topic (see Reiss & Aman, 1998). Nonetheless, much remains the same. In concluding a 1983 review of pharmacological interventions for people with mental retardation, Aman and Singh wrote:

> We have now witnessed three decades of research and several hundred studies since the synthetic antipsychotic drugs were introduced to treat behavior problems in retarded persons. Despite this fact, there is a remarkable lack of information regarding any of the drug groups commonly used in mental retardation. Standards and expectations regarding drug research have risen dramatically in the last five or so years. It is hoped that we can now look forward to an era of discovery and consolidation, so that the true value of these agents is known. Only in this way can pharmacotherapy genuinely contribute to the well-being of those receiving such treatment. (p. 332)

The era of discovery and consolidation to which Aman and Singh and many others looked forward has not yet arrived. Few, if any, psychotropic drugs have been adequately evaluated in people with developmental disabilities, despite repeated calls for further research. In that regard, much remains the same. As in years past, further research is needed to produce data that will guide physicians in accurately matching drugs to patients. Unfortunately, there are substantial obstacles to conducing the needed work, including a lack of funding and difficulty in gaining access to participants. The use of single-case research methods may make it easier to conduct research, although these methods have been used infrequently in clinical psychopharmacology.

In some cases, results of studies involving people without developmental disabilities may provide a rationale for the use of psychotropic medications in people with developmental disabilities. The presence of a developmental disability may, however, make it difficult to diagnose conditions for which medications have proven effective. For example, many of the symptoms of schizophrenia (e.g., hallucinations, thought disorders, delusions, impoverished speech) involve verbal behavior, which may be absent or severely impoverished in people with mental retardation. Therefore, accurate diagnosis of schizophrenia in people with mental retardation can be especially difficult.

At present, because of the absence of relevant outcome data, it is almost impossible to know *a priori* whether a given medication will positively affect the behavior of a person with a developmental disability. Therefore, drug effects should be carefully monitored in any such person who received a psychotropic medication. Unfortunately, however, this appears to occur rarely. The result is that many people with developmental disabilities receive medications that affect them in unknown ways. Given that medications are relatively restrictive interventions, this is unfortunate. Enhanced monitoring of drug effects is an essential step in improving the pharmaceutical treatment of behavior disorders in people with developmental disabilities. Despite arguments to the contrary, such drugs are not "bad" or "good." Some people with developmental disabilities derive benefits from drug treatment that cannot be produced by other kinds of interventions. Other people, however, are exposed to unnecessary and even harmful drug regimens. Appropriate drug treatment requires that the right people receive medication, and that their medication regimen be managed to produce optimal benefit. Careful drug monitoring helps to achieve both ends. At present, our best advice for anyone concerned with the pharmaceutical treatment of behavior disorders in people with developmental disabilities is simple: Be skeptical and collect data.

## References

Accreditation Council for Facilities for the Mentally Retarded (ACMR). (1971). *Standards for residential facilities for the mentally retarded.* Chicago: Joint Commission on Accreditation of Hospitals.

Accreditation Council for Services for Mentally Retarded and Other Developmentally Disabled Persons (ACMRDD). (1983). *Standards for services for developmentally disabled individuals.* Washington, DC: Author

Aman, M. G., & Singh, N. N. (1983). Pharmacological interventions. In J. L. Matson & J. A. Mulick (Eds.), *Handbook of mental retardation* (pp. 317-337). New York: Pergamon.

Aman, M. G., & Singh, N. N. (1988). *Psychopharmacology of the developmental disabilities.* New York: Springer-Verlag.

Baldessarini, R. J. (1996). Drugs and the treatment of psychiatric disorders: Psychosis and anxiety. In J. G. Hardmann, L. E. Limbird, P. B. Molinoff, R. W. Ruddon, & A. G. Gilman (Eds.), *The pharmacological basis of therapeutics* (pp. 399-430). New York: McGraw-Hill.

Bates, W. J., Smeltzer, D. J., & Arnoczky, S. M. (1986). Appropriate and inappropriate use of psychotherapeutic medications for institutionalized mentally retarded persons. *American Journal of Mental Deficiency, 90*, 363-370

Baumeister, A. A., & Sein, J. A. (1990). Pharmacological control of aberrant behavior in the mentally retarded: Towards a more rational approach. *Neuroscience & Biobehavioral Reviews, 14*, 253-262.

Briggs, R., Hamad, C., Garrard, S., & Willis, F. (1984). A model for evaluating psychoactive medication use with the mentally retarded. In J. Mulick & B. Mallory (Eds.), *Transitions in mental retardation: Advocacy, technology, and science* (pp. 229-248). Norwood, NJ: Ablex.

Brown, R. T., & Sawyer, M. G. (1998). *Medications for school-age children: Effects on learning and behavior.* New York: The Guilford Press.

Brylewski, J., & Duggan, L. (1999). Antipsychotic medication for challenging behaviour in people with intellectual disability: A systematic review of randomized controlled trials. *Journal of Intellectual Disability Research, 43*, 360-371.

Civil Rights of Institutionalized Persons Act. *Public Law 96-247*, 1980; 42 U.S.C., 1982.

Clinical Practice Guideline. (1999). *Report of the recommendations autism/pervasive developmental disorders assessment and intervention for young children (age 0-3 years).* Albany, NY: New York State Department of Health.

Duggan, L., & Brylewski, J. (1999). Effectiveness of antipsychotic medication in people with intellectual disability and schizophrenia: A systematic review. *Journal of Intellectual Disability Research, 43*, 94-104.

Findholt, N. E., & Emmett, C. G. (1990). Impact of interdisciplinary team review on psychotropic drug use with persons who have mental retardation. *Mental Retardation, 28*, 41-46.

Foote, E. S. (1958). Combined chlorpromazine and reserpine in the treatment of chronic psychotics. *Journal of Mental Science, 58*, 201-205.

Fredericks, D. W., & Hayes, L. J. (1995). Effects of drug changes and physician prescribing practices on the behavior of persons with mental retardation. *Journal of Developmental and Physical Disabilities, 7*, 105-122.

Gadow, K. D. (1982). School involvement in pharmacotherapy for behavior disorders. *The Journal of Special Education, 16*, 385-399.

Gadow, K. D. (1983). Pharmacotherapy for behavior disorders: Typical treatment practices. *Clinical Pediatrics, 22*, 48-53.

Gadow, K. D. (1993). Prevalence of drug therapy. In J. S. Werry & M. G. Aman (Eds.), *Practitioner's guide to psychoactive drugs for children and adolescents* (pp. 57-74). New York: Plenum Press.

Gadow, K. D. (1997). An overview of three decades of research in pediatric psychopharmacoepidemiology. *Journal of Child and Adolescent Psychopharmacology, 7*, 219-236.

Gadow, K. D., & Poling, A. (1988). *Psychopharmacotherapy and mental retardation.* Austin, TX: Pro-Ed.

Gadow, K. D., Pomeroy, J. C.,& Nolan, E. E. (1992). A procedure for monitoring stimulant medication in hyperactive mentally retarded school children. *Journal of Child and Adolescent Psychopharmacology, 2*, 131-143.

Greiner, T. (1958). Problem of methodology in research with drugs. *American Journal of Mental Deficiency, 64,* 346-352.

Hancock, R. D., Weber, S. L., Kaza, R., & Her, K. S. (1991). Changes in psychotropic drug use in ling-term residents of an ICR/MR facility. *American Journal on Mental Retardation, 96,* 137-141.

Hobbs, N. (1975). *The futures of children.* San Francisco: Jossey-Bass.

Horvath, K., Stefanatos, G., Sololski, K. N., Wachtel, R., Nabors, L., & Tildon, J. T. (1998). Improved social and language skills after secretin administration in patients with autistic spectrum disorders. *Journal of the Association for Academic Minority Physicians, 9,* 9-15.

Kalachnik, J. E. (1988). Medication monitoring procedures. In K. D. Gadow, & A. Poling (Eds.), *Pharmacology and mental retardation* (pp. 231-268). Boston: College-Hill Press.

Kalacknick, J. E., Leventahl, B. L., James, D. H., Sovner, R., Kastner, T. A., Walsh, K., Weisblatt, S. A., & Klitzke, M. G. (1998). Guidelines for the use of psychotropic medication. In S. Reiss & M. G. Aman (Eds.), *Psychotropic medication and developmental disabilities: The international consensus handbook* (pp. 45-72). Columbus: Ohio State University Nisonger Center.

Kennedy, C. H., & Meyer, K. A., (1998). The use of psychotropic medication for people with severe disabilities and challenging behavior: Current status and future directions. *Journal of the Association for Persons with Severe Handicaps, 23,* 83-97.

Kollins, S. H., Ehrhardt, K., & Poling, A. (2000). Clinical drug assessment. In A. Poling & T. Byrne (Eds.), *Behavioral pharmacology* (pp. 191-218). Reno, NV: Context Press.

Lepler, S., Hodas, A., & Cotter-Mack, A. (1993). Implementation of an interdisciplinary psychotropic drug review process for community-based facilities. *Mental Retardation, 31,* 3076-315.

Lewis, M. H., Aman, M. G., Gadow, K. D., Schroeder, S. R., & Thompson, T. (1996). Psychopharmacology. In J. W. Jacobson & J. A. Mulick (Eds.), *Manual of diagnosis and professional practice in mental retardation* (pp. 323-340). Washington, DC: American Psychological Association.

MacMillan, D. L. (1982). *Mental retardation in school and society* (2nd Edition). Boston: Little, Brown, & Company.

Matson, J. L., Bamburg, J. W., Mayville, E. A., Pinkston, J., Bielecki, J., Kuhn, D., Smalls, Y., & Logan. J. R. (2000). Psychopharmacology and mental retardation: A 10 year review (1990-1999). *Research in Developmental Disabilities, 21,* 263-296.

McKim, W. A. (2003). *Drugs and behavior.* Upper Saddle River, NJ: PrenticeHall.

Northup, J., Fusilier, I., Swanson, V., Roane, H., & Borrero, J. (1997). An evaluation of methylphenidate as a potential establishing operation for some common classroom reinforcers. *Journal of Applied Behavior Analysis, 30,* 615-625.

Poling, A. (1994). Pharmacological treatment of behavioral problems in people with mental retardation: Some ethical considerations. In L. J. Hayes, G. J. Hayes, S. C. Moore, & P. M. Ghezzi (Eds.), *Ethical issues in developmental disabilities* (pp. 149-177). Reno, Nevada: Context Press.

Poling, A., & Ehrhardt, K. (1999). Applied behavior analysis, social validation, and the psychopharmacology of mental retardation. *Mental Retardation and Developmental Disabilities Research Reviews, 5,* 342-347.

Poling, A., Gadow, K. D., & Cleary, J. (1991). *Drug therapy for behavior disorders: an introduction.* New York: Pergamon.

Poling, A., Picker, M., & Wallace, S. (1983). Some methodological characteristics of psychopharmacological research with the mentally retarded. *Mental Retardation and Developmental Disability Bulletin, 11,* 110-121.

Posey, D. J., & McDougle, C. J. (2000). The pharmacotherapy of target symptoms associated with autistic disorder and other pervasive disorders. *Harvard Review of Psychiatry, 8,* 45-63.

Reiss, S. (1998). Preface. In S. Reiss & M. G. Aman (Eds.), *Psychotropic medications and developmental disabilities: The international consensus handbook* (pp. 1-2). Columbus, OH: The Ohio State University Nisonger Center.

Reiss, S., & Aman, M. G. (1998). (Eds.). *Psychotropic medications and developmental disabilities: The international consensus handbook* (pp. 1-2). Columbus, OH: The Ohio State University Nisonger Center.

Rimland, B. (2000). Secretin update: A negative placebo effect? Available on-line: http://www.autism.com/ari/secretin2.html

Rinck, C. (1998). Epidemiology and psychoactive medication. In S. Reiss & M. G. Aman (Eds.), *Psychotropic medications and developmental disabilities: The international consensus handbook* (pp. 31-44). Columbus, OH: The Ohio State University Nisonger Center.

Rinck, C., Guidry, J., & Calkins, C. (1989). Review of states' practices on the use of psychotropic medication. *American Journal on Mental Retardation, 93,* 657-668.

Schroeder, S. R. (1985). Issues and future directions of psychopharmacology in mental retardation. *Psychopharmacology Bulletin, 21,* 323-326.

Schroeder, S. R., Bouras, N., Ellis, C. R., Reid, A. H., Sandman, C., Werry, J. S., & Wisniewski, H. (1998). Past research on psychopharmacology of people with mental retardation and developmental disabilities. In S. Reiss & M.G. Aman (Eds.), *Psychotropic medication and developmental disabilities: The international consensus handbook* (pp. 19-29). Columbus: Ohio State University Nisonger Center.

Singh, N. N., Ellis, C. R., & Wechsler, H. (1997). Psychopharmacoepidemiology of mental retardation: 1966 to 1995. *Journal of Child and Adolescent Psychopharmacology, 7,* 255-266.

Singh, N. N., Guernsey, T. F., & Ellis, C. R. (1992). Drug therapy for persons with developmental disabilities: Legislation and litigation. *Clinical Psychology Review, 12,* 663-679.

Singh, N. N., & Winton, A. S. W. (1984). Behavioral monitoring of pharmacological interventions for self-injury. *Applied Research in Mental Retardation, 5,* 161-170.

Sovner, R. (1989). Treating mentally retarded adults with psychotropic drugs: A clinical perspective. In R. Fletcher & F. J. Menolascino (Eds.), *Mental retardation and mental illness* (pp. 157-183). Boston: Lexington Books.

Sprague, R. L. (1982). Litigation, legislation, and regulations. In S. E. Breuning & A. Poling (Eds.), *Drugs and mental retardation* (pp. 377-414). Springfield, IL: Charles C. Thomas.

Sprague, R. L., & Galliher, L. (1988). Litigation about psychotropic medication. In K. D. Gadow & A. Poling (Eds.), *Pharmacotherapy and mental retardation* (pp. 297-312). Austin, TX: Pro-Ed.

Taylor, E. (1994). Physical treatments. In M. Rutter, E. Taylor, & L. Herson (Eds.), *Child and psychiatry: Modern approaches* (pp. 880-899). Melbourne, Australia: Blackwell.

*U.S. v. Colorado,* (Consent dec. July 24, 1986).

*U.S. v. Indiana,* (Consent dec. April 6, 1984).

*U.S. v. South Carolina,* (Consent dec. June 24, 1986).

*Wyatt v. Stickney,* 325 F. Supp. 387 (filed 1972)

Young, A. T., & Hawkins, J. (2002). Psychotropic medication prescriptions: An analysis of the reasons people with mental retardation are prescribed psychotropic medication. *Journal of Developmental and Physical Disabilities, 14,* 129-142.

# Chapter 5

# Innovation in Functional Behavioral Assessment

## Michele D. Wallace, Amy Kenzer, and Becky Penrod
*University of Nevada, Reno*

Research over the last 30 years on behavioral disorders such as aggression, noncompliance, property destruction, disruption, and self-injurious behavior (SIB) has indicated that these responses are learned performances. As such, best practice in treating these disorders is to conduct a functional behavioral assessment (i.e., identify the function of the behavior) prior to developing an intervention. Current approaches to functional behavioral assessments include three general categories: Indirect assessments, descriptive assessments, and functional analyses (See Iwata, Kahng, Wallace, & Lindberg, 2000 for a review). Although these approaches have had a long history, current research has demonstrated improved techniques for conducting functional behavioral assessments. This chapter will provide a review of the innovations that have been developed in recent years on indirect assessments, descriptive assessments, and functional analysis methodology.

## Indirect Assessment

Indirect assessments are based upon informal observations of behavior and are designed to identify circumstances under which behavior occurs. A clinician solicits verbal reports from significant others regarding an individual's behavior. Typically, parents, teachers, and caregivers may be asked to rate the likelihood that a particular behavior will occur under various conditions. Two indirect assessments that are typically used are the Motivation Analysis Rating Scale (MARS; Wieseler, Hanson, Chamberlain, & Thompson, 1985) and the Motivation Assessment Scale (MAS; Durand & Crimmins, 1988). In these assessments, the clinician summarizes the point values to specific questions to determine the conditions under which problem behavior is most likely to occur and then develops a hypothesis regarding the function of the target behavior.

Another assessment, which is commonly used, is the Stimulus Control Checklist (SCC; Rolider & Van Houten, 1993). It is similar to the MARS and MAS, however, the responses do not yield numerical values and, the clinician, in a manner consistent with an interview, must interpret results. A more detailed format for conducting an indirect assessment can be obtained by using the Functional Analysis Interview Form (FAIF; O'Neill, Horner, Albin, Storey, & Sprague, 1990). This assessment includes a variety of questions designed to assess the relative influence of several variables on the target behavior, including social-positive reinforcement, social-negative reinforcement, automatic reinforcement, physiological factors, and daily schedules, to name a few.

## Innovative Uses of Indirect Assessment

Indirect assessments have historically been conducted with individuals with severe disabilities and, thus, include interviewing, or otherwise obtaining information from a significant other (i.e., family member, teacher, etc.) regarding an individual's problem behavior. Data collected with indirect assessments, thus, consist of verbal reports of persons other than those engaging in the problem behavior of focus. Some recent applications of indirect assessment methodology, however, have included interviewing children who engage in problem behavior rather than their significant others. Lauterback (1990) interviewed typically developing children who engaged in thumb sucking. The assessment consisted of presenting the children with several hypothetical situations hypothesized to be neutral, stimulating, or boring and allowing the children to choose from several potential responses, including thumb sucking. Results indicated that most of the children reported they were more likely to suck their thumb when in a stimulating situation and when there was little chance that another person would see them.

Kern, Dunlap, Clarke, and Childs (1994) also interviewed students regarding their appropriate and inappropriate behaviors. The functional assessment interview was administered to students with emotional and/or behavioral disorders who engaged in inappropriate classroom behavior. The interview contained several questions specifically about curricular, academic and environmental variables that can be manipulated in school settings. Results indicated that children were capable of completing the interview, though younger children were more likely to provide inconsistent or vague responses.

Lewis, Scott, and Sugai (1994) developed the problem behavior questionnaire to be implemented with children in regular education settings. Additionally, the assessment is a teacher-based instrument in which the teacher conducts the interview with children in their classes.

## New Indirect Assessment Methodologies

Related to the routine use of significant others as the source of information, is the focus on social-attention as a consequence and possible maintaining variable for problem behavior. Social attention is typically addressed with respect to adult caregivers or other adults close to the individual. However, social-attention from other sources may also be related to the occurrence of problem behavior. In particular, peers may respond to problem behavior in a way that reinforces or punishes the individual's behavior. The problem behavior questionnaire (Lewis et al., 1994) attempts to assess the effects of peer attention on the child's problem behavior. The assessment includes ranking the likelihood that problem behavior would occur in the presence or absence of peer attention. The case study presented indicated that peer attention was correlated with a higher likelihood of problem behavior in the classroom for that child.

Indirect assessments typically consist of ranking the likelihood of problem behavior under a variety of situations and circumstances, interview questions designed to assess the relative influence of several variables on the target behavior, or a combination of both. In contrast, Lauterback (1990) utilized an indirect assessment in which specific responses were provided for the participants to select from when given a hypothetical situation and asked what he/she were likely to do in those circumstances.

Despite these innovations it should be noted that these assessments rely on highly subjective data, have questionable reliability and validity, and are generally considered to be insufficient for treatment development. However, despite these limitations indirect assessments can be an efficient preliminary guide to structure both descriptive assessments and functional analyses. Future research in this area needs to address the questionable reliability and validity that these assessments afford.

## Descriptive Assessments

Descriptive assessments consist of direct observation of circumstances under which behavior occurs. These observations are typically conducted under naturalistic conditions and in contexts relevant to the target behavior, such as during math class in the child's school. There are three types of descriptive analysis including continuous observation, A-B-C (antecedent-behavior-consequence), and scatter plot analyses. Continuous observation, consisting of continuous observation and recording of behavior as well as stimulus and response events, is the most common form of descriptive analysis currently conducted. Recording may consist of a frequency count, interval, or time-sample recording. The frequency of occurrence of the target behavior is used to make a hypothesis regarding the function of target behaviors. With continuous observation, conditional probabilities may also be calculated in which a ratio is calculated based on the frequency of the target behavior occurring in close temporal proximity to a particular antecedent or consequence divided by the total frequency of the target behavior.

ABC narrative recording involves collecting data on occurrence of the target behavior under natural conditions. For each occurrence of the target behavior, the events immediately preceding and following the behavior are also recorded in the sequence in which they occurred. An ABC analysis may be either open-ended or structured. In the open-ended ABC, observers are free to record any number of events (or non-events) as antecedent or consequent to the target behavior. It is very subjective and allows for the situation in which an observer could record for example, the removal of a preferred item or "feeling frustrated" as the antecedent to a target behavior. The structured ABC provides several possible antecedents and consequences for observers to select from when recording data. Thus, attempting to eliminate the subjectivity found in the open-ended assessment.

Scatter plot, a third type of descriptive assessment, consists of recording on a grid the actual or relative (none, few, many) frequency of the target behavior during specified periods of time (e.g., 1/2 hour) throughout the day (Touchette, MacDonald,

& Langer, 1985). The grid is then visually assessed to identify patterns of responding that may reveal potential variables associated with the occurrence of the target behavior. Thus, if the pattern of responding reveals consistently higher frequency of the target behavior between one o'clock p.m. and two o'clock p.m. every Monday through Friday, which is when the individual attends physical therapy, further analyses may be conducted to determine which variables correlated with physical therapy may be maintaining the target behavior. Conversely, time periods without target behavior occurrence may also reveal important environmental variables.

## Innovative Uses of Descriptive Assessments

Descriptive assessments have primarily been employed for the purpose of identifying correlational relationships such that subsequent evaluations may be conducted and/or treatments developed. More recently, however, the descriptive assessment technology has been utilized to assess the ecological validity of analogue functional analyses. Thompson and Iwata (2001) used a descriptive assessment to determine whether access to attention, escape, or tangible items – those consequences typically manipulated during functional analyses - are frequently observed as a consequence of problem behavior under naturalistic conditions. The conditional probabilities of the consequences described above were recorded for 27 adults with developmental disabilities whose target behaviors included SIB, aggression, and disruption using a 10 s partial interval recording method. Results indicated that attention was the most common consequence for all behaviors and that aggression was most likely to produce social consequences than other types of problem behavior. Additionally, tangible consequences were rarely observed under naturalistic conditions, lending support to the notion that a tangible condition should only be included in a functional analysis if caregiver reports or descriptive assessments indicate tangibles are typically provided following problem behavior.

Conroy, Fox, Crain, Jenkins, and Belcher (1996) also used a descriptive assessment to evaluate the ecological validity of analog assessment procedures by comparing the motivational variable(s) identified by direct observation and analogue assessment. Following the completion of an analogue functional analysis, direct observations were conduced in which continuous, sequential recording was used to measure the frequency of stereotypy, SIB, and noncompliance for four children with developmental disabilities. Observers also recorded the frequency of antecedent and consequent teacher behaviors such as providing demands, attention, escape, and tangibles. Conditional probabilities were then calculated. Similar to the findings obtained by Thompson and Iwata (2001), results indicated attention to be the most likely consequence for problem behavior in the natural environment. A comparison of motivational variables identified by the descriptive and experimental assessments indicated that the same function was identified for only one of the four participants. However, these results must be addressed with caution due to limitations of the analogue assessment utilized and the possibility of multiple control of target behaviors.

Cunningham and O'Neil (2000) conducted indirect, descriptive, and experimental assessments on the problem behaviors of three children diagnosed with autism. An event recording (ABC recording) method was conducted to record each occurrence of the target behavior, immediate antecedent, and perceived function (e.g., escape, attention, tangible, or automatic) in the descriptive assessment. An experimental functional analysis was also conducted to assess the effects of contingent attention, escape, access to tangibles, and no consequences on the occurrence of target behaviors. The relative influence of each possible function as identified by each of the assessment methods was then ranked and compared. Results indicated exact agreement between all methods on the rank order of motivating variables for two of the three participants. For the third participant, the same two functions were ranked as first or second for all assessments, though exact agreement was not achieved.

## New Descriptive Assessment Methods

Descriptive assessments, as opposed to experimental assessments, typically consist of passively observing the individual in his/her natural environment with no manipulation of environmental variables (other than the presence of an observer). Observers simply record the occurrence of events as they happen. One disadvantage of descriptive assessments is a direct result of this passivity, such that an observer must wait for the target behavior to occur naturally. In the absence of particular antecedents (e.g., difficult tasks), the target behavior may occur infrequently or not at all, thus rendering the assessment ineffectual. The structured descriptive assessment, however, attempts to avoid this disadvantage by manipulating antecedent events while allowing the target behavior and consequences to occur naturally.

Freeman, Anderson, and Scotti (2000) compared the results obtained from an unstructured descriptive assessment, a structured descriptive assessment, and an experimental analysis in identifying the maintaining variables of "challenging behavior" for two participants. The unstructured descriptive assessment included observing the child in his/her natural environment across an entire day. No variables were manipulated experimentally. The structured descriptive assessment included observations at various times across the day in which antecedent manipulations were made and the target behavior was thus observed in that "condition." Attempts were made to manipulate antecedent conditions at a time of day when it would coincide with the typical routine of the child. The functional analysis was conducted in an analogue setting with four rotations of each experimental condition in which both antecedent and consequent variables were manipulated. Results demonstrated that the structured descriptive assessment resulted in a greater frequency of targeted environmental events occurring than in the unstructured descriptive assessment. Furthermore, results of the structural descriptive assessment when comparable to results of the functional analysis were similar.

Anderson and Long (2002) also compared a structured descriptive assessment with the results of an analogue functional analysis. Conditional probabilities were calculated for both antecedent and consequent events and then compared to the rates of responding observed during the experimental analysis. Results indicated that the structured descriptive assessment identified the same maintaining variable for each participant as was identified in the analogue functional analysis. The results of these two studies, though preliminary, support the idea of conducting more rigorous analyses in the naturalistic setting and manipulating antecedent variables to increase the efficiency of descriptive assessments.

Despite these advances in descriptive analyses, it should be noted that the information obtained may be only correlational in nature, in that consequent events are not manipulated to specify maintaining functions of behavior. Thus, a thorough FBA should include manipulations of the suspecting variables to demonstrate a functional rather than a correlational relationship.

## Functional Analyses

Iwata, Dorsey, Slifer, Bauman, and Richman (1982/1994) proposed a general model for conducting a functional analysis, in which several environmental contingencies, possibly responsible for the maintenance of problem behavior, can be tested concurrently. Three test conditions (attention, demand, and alone), each containing a discriminative stimulus (Sd), an establishing operation (EO), and a consequence, were developed, as well as a fourth condition (play) which was included as a control. During the attention condition, attention is delivered contingent only on the occurrence of the problem behavior. During the demand condition, demand trials are continuously presented and demands are removed for a brief period of time contingent upon occurrence of the problem behavior. During the alone condition, the participant is observed by him/herself in a room containing few stimuli to determine if the problem behavior occurs in the absence of any social contingencies. During the play condition, no demands are placed on the participant, attention is frequently delivered, and leisure items are continuously present. Each condition is 15-min in length and conditions are arranged in a multielement design. This general paradigm was tested with 9 individuals, who engaged in SIB and was demonstrated to be useful for identifying various environmental contingencies responsible for the maintenance of SIB. This general paradigm has since been replicated and extended several times and advancements in the following areas have been made: basic paradigms and interpretation; methodological changes; procedural changes; variations; and miscellaneous innovations.

## Advances in Basic Paradigm and Interpretation

Worsdell, Iwata, Conners, Kahng, and Thompson (2000) conducted a study, which advanced the basic functional analysis paradigm in terms of the design of test and control conditions. They examined the separate and combined effects of antecedent and consequent events on the maintenance of attention-maintained SIB. Functional analysis conditions were designed to determine whether SIB would be maintained in the presence and absence of an EO when reinforcement for SIB was either available or not available. Participants were exposed to multielement functional analyses prior to the study, in order to determine whether or not they engaged in SIB to gain access to social positive reinforcement. Participants were then exposed to a second functional analysis, identical to the first, with the exception of one added condition designed to evaluate the effects of reinforcement in the absence of an EO. Results showed that for two out of the six participants, SIB occurred only in the ignore/fixed ratio (FR) 1 condition (EO present/contingency present), while for four out of the six participants, SIB occurred in both the ignore/FR 1 (EO present/contingency present) and the fixed-time (FT)/FR 1 (EO absent/contingency present) conditions. However, the rate of SIB per minute was slightly higher in the ignore/FR 1 condition. This study contributes to the literature in that it contains implications for the design of functional analysis test and control conditions. Findings obtained during the ignore/FR 1 condition lend support to previous studies based on the antecedent-behavior-consequence model of functional analyses, indicating that a response maintained by a particular reinforcer is most likely to occur when both an EO is present and contingent reinforcement is available. Hence, this study confirms that the ignore/FR 1 condition is an ideal test condition. In addition, the finding that all participants engaged in low rates of SIB during the FT/ignore condition suggests that this condition is the most appropriate control condition, in contrast to other studies that have used this condition as a test condition (e.g., Durand & Carr, 1987).

In addition to advancements with respect to the basic functional analysis paradigm, advancements have been made with respect to how functional analysis outcomes are interpreted. The way in which the results of functional analyses are typically interpreted is by visual inspection of the data. Because individuals may interpret the same results in different ways, Hagopian, Fisher, Thompson, Owen-DeSchryver, Iwata, and Wacker (1997) developed a set of structured criteria for visually inspecting functional analysis data, which was demonstrated to increase interobserver agreement and result in interpretations consistent with those made by experts in behavior analysis. In the first study, 3 psychology interns were asked to interpret functional analysis graphs using traditional visual inspection procedures. Interpretations of the functional analysis graphs across the 3 participants varied, indicating that visual inspection was not a reliable method. In the second study, interpretations of a set of 64 functional analysis graphs were obtained from experts, in an effort to operationalize the way in which functional analysis graphs are visually inspected and interpreted. Finally, in the third study, the psychology interns were asked to use the structured criteria developed in the second study to interpret functional analysis graphs to assess whether their interpretations would be similar to those made by experts. Results indicated that interobserver agreement improved due to the application of operationally defined decision-making rules.

## Advances in Methodology

Advancements in functional analysis methodology have been made with respect to the length of time needed to conduct an accurate assessment. In a typical functional analysis, observation sessions last 10- or 15-min. Because of the length of these observation sessions, functional analyses have been argued to be too time consuming (e.g., Durrand & Crimmins, 1988). Wallace and Iwata (1999) explored the utility of a more brief assessment by examining the extent to which brief exposure to assessment conditions would produce similar results to those produced from assessments in which exposure to assessment conditions were longer. Outcomes from 15-, 10-, and 5-min functional analyses were compared. Data sets of 5- and 10-min were generated from 46 functional analyses based on 15-min sessions by subtracting the last 5-min and the last 10-min from each session. Results indicated that interpretations based on 15- and 10-min sessions were identical and there were only 3 disagreements based on 15-min and 5-min sessions, suggesting that brief repeated exposure to session conditions may be adequate for the identification of environmental variables maintaining problem behavior.

Wallace and Knights (2003) further examined the utility of brief functional analyses by comparing their results to the results of more extended functional analyses. During the brief functional analysis, a modified pair-wise design was used, wherein each session was 2-min in length, the first minute serving as the test condition and the second minute serving as the control condition. Conditions were conducted in the following order: Attention-Control, Demand-Control, and Ignore-Control. During the extended functional analysis, sessions were 10-min in length, and Attention, Demand, Ignore, and Control conditions were alternated. Results indicated that brief functional analyses can be effective for identifying the function of behavior for some individuals.

The development of brief functional analyses is an important advancement, in that most clinicians operate under time constraints, which may prevent them from conducting a functional analysis test. However, there are cases in which behavior occurs at a very low rate, precluding even a typical functional analysis test (lasting 10- to 15-min) from being conducted. Kahng, Abt, and Schonbachler (2001) addressed this issue by evaluating whether extended periods of observation would increase the probability that low-rate problem behavior would be observed. They first conducted a functional analysis, during which sessions were 10-min in length. When no behavior occurred, the functional analysis was modified, such that one condition was conducted in a given observation session lasting from 9:00 a.m. to 4:00 p.m. Results showed that the functional analysis during which observation sessions were longer was successful in identifying the function maintaining low-rate problem behavior.

Another advancement to functional analysis methodology is the analysis of within-session response patterns. Within-session analyses are useful when results of functional analyses are undifferentiated. A popular analysis of within-session data has been the minute-by-minute analysis, in which data, yielded from interval or event recording, is plotted for each minute of the session (Vollmer, Iwata, Zarcone, Smith, & Mazaleski, 1993). However, minute-by-minute analyses are technically compromised when the data being plotted are obtained from interval recording. That is, exact relationships between stimuli and responses cannot be obtained, in that interval-recording methods are discontinuous (Rapp, Carr, Miltenberger, Dozier, & Kellum, 2001). Rapp et al. addressed this problem by conducting an analysis of a real time recording (RTR) method, in which target behaviors and other events are recorded second-by-second, enabling the exact time of onset and offset of the events to be determined, thus, avoiding the problems associated with within-session analyses based on interval recording methods.

## Procedural Advances

Procedural advancements have been made with respect to the order in which functional analysis conditions are conducted. Berg et al. (2000) conducted a study designed to show that the order of assessment conditions could affect the results and interpretations of assessment. They conducted 3 behavioral assessments for attention as a reinforcer, in which they manipulated the sequence of assessment conditions. In experiment 1, when a contingent attention condition, as described by Iwata et al. (1982/1994), was preceded by frequent delivery of attention versus contingent escape, problem behavior occurred less frequently. In experiment 2, when an ignore condition was preceded by noncontingent attention versus an alone condition, problem behavior was less likely to occur. Finally, in experiment 3, the participant was given a choice to play with their mother or play alone and preference seemed to vary depending on the condition that immediately preceded the choice assessment. All of these experiments suggest that the order of conditions can influence assessment results. This evaluation indicates the importance of controlling pre-session conditions.

Another procedural advancement is related to antecedent stimuli that are included during assessment. Functional analysis results may be unclear if the antecedent stimuli used are not the same as those that are in close temporal proximity to problem behavior that occur in the natural environment (Ringdahl & Sellers, 2000). Ringdahl and Sellers examined this possibility by comparing the results of a functional analysis, where the child's caregiver acted as therapist, to the results of a functional analysis where a clinic staff acted as therapist. Results indicated that problem behavior occurred more frequently when the functional analysis was conducted by the child's caregiver versus a clinic staff, suggesting that certain individuals may be an Sd for problem behavior or that novel individuals may alter EOs. This investigation points to the importance of careful consideration of what antecedent stimuli should be included in assessment.

Finally, procedural advancements have been made with respect to how functional analysis conditions are arranged. Typically, functional analysis conditions are arranged in a multielement design, so as to quickly compare the effects of several environmental contingencies on behavior and, further, to reduce the likelihood of multiple treatment interference resulting from historical effects related to extended exposure to a particular condition. However, as a result of using a multielement design, another type of multiple treatment interference can occur. That is, contrast effects, resulting from rapidly changing conditions (Conners, Iwata, Kahng, Hanley, Worsdell, & Thompson, 2000). In an effort to prevent this type of multiple treatment interference, Conners et al. evaluated the extent to which Sds, included during assessment, improved differential responding during multielement functional analyses. Participants were exposed to two functional analyses; one, during which each condition was conducted in a different colored room with a different therapist and the other, during which each condition was conducted in the same room with the same therapist. Results suggested that by including Sds, the efficiency of functional analyses, as well as the likelihood of obtaining clear findings, may increase. This is especially important when conducting brief functional analyses, as there is not as much time within each session for participants to discriminate which contingencies are in effect.

## Variations

One variation of the way in which functional analyses are typically conducted has been to conduct a functional analysis on more than one problem behavior exhibited by the same individual, and then graph the data in such a way that separate response topographies can be analyzed. Typically, functional analyses are conducted on only one behavior, however, when an individual presents with several different topographies of problem behavior, it is usually not feasible to conduct a separate functional analysis on each topography (Derby, Hagopian, Fisher, Richman, Augustine, Fahs, & Thompson, 2000). As a result, Derby et al. determined the degree to which assessment results varied with respect to different topographies by examining the results for several clients using the procedures described by Derby, Wacker, Peck, Sasso, DeRaad, Berg, Asmus, and Ulrich (1994), in which functional analysis data were analyzed when graphed aggregately and as separate response topographies. Results suggested that different topographies of problem behavior observed in the same individual may have different functions; hence, it may be useful to analyze functional analysis data for separate topographies when functional analyses of more than one problem behavior are conducted.

Another variation has been the extension of functional analysis methodology to the assessment of SIB evoked by transitions (McCord, Thompson, & Iwata, 2001). McCord et al. defined transitions as "the termination or initiation of an activity, with or without a change in location (p. 206)." Initially, they conducted preference assessments to identify both preferred and nonpreferred activities, which were then followed by a functional analysis, in which various combinations of activities were manipulated, while the effects of these manipulations on SIB were observed. Results for one participant showed that his SIB was maintained by avoidance of having to change locations, while results for the other participant showed the same function, as well as escape from and avoidance of tasks. This investigation extends functional analysis research in that it is one of the only studies that have determined the function of problem behavior that occurs during transitions by isolating the different components of a transition.

Another variation has been to place functional analysis contingencies on behaviors that occur immediately prior to the target behavior of interest, due to the potential danger of placing functional analysis contingencies on the target behavior itself. Smith and Churchill (2002) conducted a study comparing the outcomes of standard functional analyses of problem behavior to outcomes of functional analyses of precursor behavior to determine whether: a) a common maintaining contingency was identified by both; and b) target problem behaviors occurred less frequently during functional analyses of precursor behavior. Precursor behaviors were identified via reports from caregivers and direct observations. Participants were first exposed to a standard functional analysis, as described by Iwata et al. (1982/94). Following the standard functional analysis, experimental contingencies were placed on precursor behaviors instead of problem behaviors. Results showed that outcomes of both functional analyses of problem behaviors and precursor behaviors identified common maintaining contingencies for all participants. In addition, less problem behavior was observed during functional analyses of precursor behaviors. This study contributes to the literature in that it attempts to evaluate an experimental analysis designed to reduce risk to participants and/or caregivers. The alternative to standard functional analyses provided by the authors promotes a more active role be taken by those who are less experienced in conducting functional analyses, such as teachers and parents. Moreover, functional analyses of precursor behaviors not only provides an alternative to conducting functional analyses of dangerous behaviors, but an alternative to conducting functional analyses of behaviors that are not easily observed or cannot be observed, such as not eating, for example.

A final variation has been to include protective equipment (which does not prevent the target behavior from occurring) during functional analyses. One such study was conducted by Borrero, Vollmer, Wright, Lerman, and Kelly (2002), during which they compared functional analyses without protective equipment to functional analyses with protective equipment, to evaluate trichotillomania (hair pulling). Results indicated that the use of protective equipment resulted in suppression or elimination of trichotillomania, suggesting that the use of protective equipment during functional analyses may hinder one from obtaining clear results.

## Miscellaneous Innovations

Innovations to functional analysis test methodology have been made with respect to assessing behaviors maintained by automatic reinforcement. Behavior maintained by automatic reinforcement is difficult to treat in that the nature of the reinforcement is unknown. In addition, automatic reinforcers cannot be directly manipulated or controlled. Piazza, Adelinis, Hanley, Goh, and Delia (2000) extended previous studies that evaluated the effects of providing matched stimuli (similar to the stimulation produced by the aberrant behavior) on the occurrence of automatically reinforced behaviors (determined by pretreatment functional analyses). Preference assessments were conducted to identify both items that matched and did not match hypothesized sensory consequences of problem behavior, following which, sensory match and preference were evaluated by providing noncontingent access to either highly preferred matched or highly preferred unmatched stimuli. Results indicated that providing access to matched stimuli was more effective in reducing automatically maintained problem behavior.

Patel, Carr, Kim, Robles, and Eastridge (2000) developed a package for assessing problem behavior maintained by automatic reinforcement. They first conducted a functional analysis test, according to the procedures described by Iwata et al. (1982/ 1994). Following the functional analysis test, they conducted an antecedent assessment to identify the specific components of the sensory stimuli correlated with the problem behaviors. In the third phase, stimuli were chosen based on the results of the antecedent assessment and a stimulus preference assessment was conducted. Finally, treatment was implemented. The assessment package was validated due to the success of treatment based on its results. This study advances functional analysis research in that it develops a method for systematically evaluating specific components of sensory stimuli correlated with automatically maintained problem behavior.

In addition to innovations made with respect to assessing automatically reinforced behaviors, innovations have been made with respect to assessing problem behavior correlated with idiosyncratic variables. Idiosyncratic variables, independent of the environmental events typically manipulated in a functional analysis, can influence assessment results (Van Camp, Lerman, Kelley, Roane, Contrucci, & Vorndran, 2000). Van Camp et al. identified idiosyncratic stimuli (i.e., a particular toy and social interaction) associated with problem behavior in an initial functional analysis and then evaluated these stimuli in a second functional analysis to determine if they had a functional relationship to the problem behavior. Finally, specific aspects of the stimuli that were directly related to problem behavior were identified, in order to develop successful treatments. Results of the functional analyses (for both participants) identified antecedents not typically associated with problem behavior that occurs in the absence of social contingencies. That is, low levels of problem behavior occurred in the alone condition because the alone condition did not contain the relevant antecedents for the participants' behavior. Moreover, in the first functional analysis, problem behavior occurred most frequently in the play condition because idiosyncratic sources of stimulation were evoking behavior.

McCord, Iwata, Galensky, Ellingson, and Thompson (2001) evaluated how the idiosyncratic variable of noise influenced assessment results. They first conducted a noise avoidance assessment, in which participants were exposed to several noises at different decibel levels to determine if they were hypersensitive to particular noises. Following this assessment, problem behavior was examined under test (noise) and control (no noise) conditions. Results showed that both participants' problem behaviors were maintained by escape from noise.

These studies point to the importance of determining idiosyncratic environmental variables that may evoke problem behavior prior to conducting functional analyses, in that such variables may influence assessment results.

Although conducting functional analyses is directly tied to developing effective function based treatments for individuals who engage in severe behavior problems, this methodology is not without its limitations. Moreover, despite the innovations that have been made with respect to functional analysis methodology and its implementation, there is a need for more empirical work in this area. Specifically, more efficient methodologies, as well as an increase in the practicality of implementation within various settings (e.g., schools, after school programs, vocational programs, etc.) and across different populations (e.g., pediatrics, older adults, individuals without disabilities, etc.) need to be addressed.

Finally, the ways in which we assess and treat various behavioral disorders needs to be evaluated. Innovations from this area could be obtained across all three-assessment methodologies. For example, eating disorders (anorexia, binge eating, etc.) are likely to be maintained by social components. Thus, assessing these variables may identify social contingencies that may be altered to promote therapeutic effects. These assessments may initially be composed of indirect assessments, which may yield insight into how to conduct descriptive assessments and functional analyses, as well as lead to effective interventions. Moreover, innovations with respect to assessing and treating various psychiatric disorders may benefit from a functional behavioral assessment approach.

## References

Anderson, C. M., & Long, E. S. (2002). Use of structured descriptive assessment methodology to identify variables affecting problem behavior. *Journal of Applied Behavior Analysis, 35*, 137-154.

Berg, W. K., Peck, S., Wacker, D. P., Harding, J., McComas, J., Richman, D., & Brown, K. (2000). The effects of presession exposure to attention on the results of assessments of attention as a reinforcer. *Journal of Applied Behavior Analysis, 33*, 463-477.

Borrero, J. C., Vollmer, T. R., Wright, C. S., Lerman, D. C., & Kelley, M. E. (2002). Further evaluation of the role of protective equipment in the functional analysis of self-injurious behavior. *Journal of Applied Behavior Analysis, 35*, 69-72.

Conners, J. Iwata, B. A. Kahng, S., Hanley, G. P., Worsdell, A. S., & Thompson, R. H. (2000). Differential responding in the presence and absence of discriminative stimuli during multielement functional analyses. *Journal of Applied Behavior Analysis, 33*, 299-308.

Conroy, M., Fox, J., Crain, L., Jenkins, A., & Belcher, K. (1996). Evaluating the social and ecological validity of analog assessment procedures for challenging behaviors in young children. *Education and Treatment of Children, 19*, 233-256.

Cunningham, E., & O'Neil, R. E. (2000). Comparison of results of functional assessment and analysis methods with young children with autism. *Education and Training in Mental Retardation and Developmental Disabilities, 35*, 406-414.

Derby, K. M., Hagopian, L., Fisher, W. W., Richman, D., Augustine, M., Fahs, A., & Thompson, R. (2000). Functional analysis of aberrant behavior through measurement of separate response topographies. *Journal of Applied Behavior Analysis, 33*, 113-117.

Derby, K. M., Wacker, D. P., Peck, S., Sasso, G., DeRaad, A., Berg, W., Asmus, J., & Ulrich, S. (1994). Functional analysis of separate topographies of aberrant behavior. *Journal of Applied Behavior Analysis, 27*, 267-278.

Durand, V. M., & Carr, E. G. (1987). Social influences on "self-stimulatory" behavior: Analysis and treatment application. *Journal of Applied Behavior Analysis, 20,* 119-132.

Durand, V. M., & Crimmins, D. B. (1988). Identifying the variables maintaining self-injurious behavior. *Journal of Autism and Developmental Disorders, 18,* 99-117.

Freeman, K. A., Anderson, C. M., & Scotti, J. R. (2000). A structured descriptive methodology: Increasing agreement between descriptive and experimental analyses. *Education and Training in Mental Retardation and Developmental Disabilities, 35,* 406-414.

Hagopian, L. P., Fisher, W. W., Thompson, R. H., Owen-DeSchryver, J., Iwata, B. A., & Wacker, D. P. (1997). Toward the development of structured criteria for interpretation of functional analysis data. *Journal of Applied Behavior Analysis, 30,* 313-326.

Iwata, B. A., Dorsey, M. F., Slifer, K. J., Bauman, K. E., & Richman, G. S. (1982/1994). Toward a functional analysis of self-injury. *Journal of Applied Behavior Analysis, 27,* 197-209. Reprinted from *Analysis and Intervention in Developmental Disabilities, 2,* 3-20.

Iwata, B. A., Kahng, S., Wallace, M. D., & Lindberg, J. S. (2000). The functional analysis model of behavioral assessment. In J. Austin & J. E. Carr (Eds.), *Handbook of applied behavior analysis* (pp. 61-90). Reno, NV: Context Press.

Kahng, S., Abt, K. A., & Schonbachler, H. E. (2001). Assessment and treatment of low-rate high-intensity problem behavior. *Journal of Applied Behavior Analysis, 34,* 225-228.

Kern, L., Dunlap, G., Clarke, S., & Childs, K. E. (1994). Student-assisted functional assessment interview. *Diagnostique, 19,* 29-39.

Lauterback, W. (1990). Situation-response (S-R) questions for identifying the function of problem behavior: The example of thumb sucking. *British Journal of Clinical Psychology, 29,* 51-57.

Lewis, T., J., Scott, T. M., & Sugai, G. (1994). The problem behavior questionnaire: A teacher-based instrument to develop functional hypotheses of problem behavior in general education classrooms. *Diagnostique, 19,* 103-115.

McCord, B. E., Iwata, B. A., Galensky, T. L., Ellingson, S. A., & Thomson, R. J. (2001). Functional analysis and treatment of problem behavior evoked by noise. *Journal of Applied Behavior Analysis, 34,* 447-462.

McCord, B. E., Thomson, R. J., & Iwata, B. A. (2001). Functional analysis and treatment of self-injury associated with transitions. *Journal of Applied Behavior Analysis, 34,* 195-210.

O'Neill, R. E., Horner, R. H., Albin, R. W., Storey, K., & Sprague, J. R. (1990). *Functional analysis of problem behavior: A practical guide.* Sycamore, IL: Sycamore.

Patel, M. R., Carr, J. E., Kim, C., Robles, A., & Eastridge, D. (2000). Functional analysis of aberrant behavior maintained by automatic reinforcement: Assessments of specific sensory reinforcement. *Research in Developmental Disabilities, 21,* 393-407.

Piazza, C. C., Adelinis, J. D., Hanley, G. P., Goh, H., & Delia, M. D. (2000). An evaluation of the effects of matched stimuli on behaviors maintained by automatic reinforcement. *Journal of Applied Behavior Analysis, 33,* 13-27.

Rapp, J. T., Carr, J. E., Miltenberger, R. G., Dozier, C. L., & Kellum, K. K. (2001). Using real-time recording to enhance the analysis of within-session functional analysis data. *Behavior Modification, 25,* 79-93.

Ringdahl, J. E., & Sellers, J. A. (2000). The effects of different adults as therapist during functional analyses. *Journal of Applied Behavior Analysis, 33,* 247-250.

Rolider, A., & Van Houten, R. (1993). The interpersonal treatment model. In R. Van Houten & S. Axelrod (Eds.), *Behavior analysis and treatment* (pp. 127-168). New York: Plenum.

Smith, R. G., & Churchill, R. M. (2002). Identification of environmental determinants of behavior disorders through functional analysis of precursor behaviors. *Journal of Applied Behavior Analysis, 35,* 125-136.

Thompson, R. H., & Iwata, B. A. (2001). A descriptive analysis of social consequences following problem behavior. *Journal of Applied Behavior Analysis, 34,* 169-178.

Touchette, P. E., MacDonald, R. F., & Langer, S. N. (1985). A scatter plot for identifying stimulus control of problem behavior. *Journal of Applied Behavior Analysis, 18,* 343-351.

VanCamp, C. M., Lerman, D. C., Kelley, M. E., Roane, H. S., Contrucci, S. A., & Vorndran, C. M. (2000). Further analysis of idiosyncratic antecedent influences during the assessment and treatment of problem behavior. *Journal of Applied Behavior Analysis, 33,* 207-221.

Vollmer, T. R., Iwata, B. A., Duncan, B. A., & Lerman, D. C. (1993). Within-session patterns of self-injury as indicators of behavioral function. *Research in Developmental Disabilities, 14,* 479-492.

Vollmer, T. R., Iwata, B. A., Zarcone, J. R., Smith, R. G., & Mazaleski, J. L. (1993). Within-session patterns of self-injury as indicators of behavior function. *Research in Developmental Disabilities, 14,* 479-492.

Wallace, M. D., & Iwata, B. A. (1999). Effects of session duration on functional analysis outcomes. *Journal of Applied Behavior Analysis, 32,* 175-183.

Wallace, M. D., & Knights, D. J. (2003). An evaluation of a brief functional analysis format within a vocational setting. *Journal of Applied Behavior Analysis, 36,* 125-128.

Wiesler, N. A., Hanson, R. H., Chamberlain, T. P., & Thompson, T. (1985). Functional taxonomy of stereotypic and self-injurious behavior. *Mental Retardation, 23,* 230-234.

Worsdell, A. S., Iwata, B. A., Conners, J., Kahng, S., & Thompson, R. H. (2000). Relative influences of establishing operations and reinforcement contingencies on self-injurious behavior during functional analyses. *Journal of Applied Behavior Analysis, 33,* 451-461.

# Chapter 6

# Assessment and Treatment of Tics and Repetitive Movement Disorders

**Raymond G. Miltenberger and Ethan S. Long**
*North Dakota State University*
*and Association of University Centers on Disabilities*

This chapter focuses on two categories of problem behaviors experienced by some individuals diagnosed with mental retardation; tic disorders and repetitive movement disorders. Tic disorders, as described in the Diagnostic and Statistical Manual of Mental Disorders (APA, 1994), consist of motor tics, vocal tics, or some combination. Repetitive movement disorders refers to a category of problem behaviors consisting of body-focused repetitive movements such as hair pulling, nail biting, finger sucking, skin picking, and oral habits such as mouth biting or bruxism. These behavior problems have been described in the literature as habit disorders (Azrin & Nunn, 1973; Miltenberger, Fuqua, & Woods, 1998) or body-focused repetitive behavior disorders (Teng, Woods, Twohig, & Marcks, 2002). For the purposes of this chapter, repetitive movement disorders will exclude behaviors commonly referred to as stereotypy or self-stimulatory behavior, a large class of repetitive movements common in some individuals diagnosed with mental retardation and autism. In this chapter, we provide a description of tic disorders and repetitive movement disorders, information on prevalence and etiology, and a review of behavioral approaches to assessment and treatment.

## Defining Tic Disorders and Repetitive Movement Disorders

In the DSM-IV, a tic is defined as a "sudden, rapid, recurrent nonrhythmic stereotyped motor movement or vocalization." Motor and vocal tics are classified as either simple or complex. Simple tics are generally described as more rapid and appear to occur without purpose. Simple motor tics are composed of repetitive and rapid contractions of functionally similar muscle groups (e.g., eye blinking, facial grimacing, shoulder shrugging), whereas simple vocal tics involve repetitive sounds (e.g., grunting, throat clearing, snorting). Complex tics are generally described as occurring more slowly and appearing to be more purposeful than simple tics. Common complex motor tics include grooming behaviors, the smelling of objects, and touching behaviors. Complex vocal tics include repeating word out of context, coprolalia (the use of obscene words or phrases), and echolalia (the repetition of the last-heard words of others).

Three tic disorders are discussed in the DSM IV. All three have an onset before the age of 18 and cause marked distressed or significant impairment in social, occupational and other important areas of functioning. Transient tic disorders are diagnosed when motor and/or vocal tics occur numerous times a day for a minimum of 4 weeks, but for no longer than 12 consecutive months. Chronic motor or vocal tic disorders occur when either motor tics or vocal tics, but not both, occur for a period of more than 12 months. Tourette's disorder consists of multiple motor tics and one or more vocal tics that occur many times a day for more than 12 months. During this time, there is never a tic-free period of more than 3 consecutive months. Tic disorders may be experienced by individuals with or without developmental disabilities. Treatment may be sought for individuals with tic disorders because tics can be associated with negative physical consequences (e.g., tissue damage) and negative social consequences (e.g., decreased social acceptability and stigma) for the individual (e.g., Woods, Friman, & Teng, 2001; Woods, Koch, & Miltenberger, 2003).

In addition to tic disorders, a variety of other problematic habitual behaviors can produce negative physical and social consequences for individuals with and without disabilities (e.g., Long, Woods, Miltenberger, Fuqua, & Boudjouk, 1999). These repetitive movement disorders consist of hand-to-head behaviors such as trichotillomania (or chronic hair pulling), nail biting, and finger sucking; hand-to-body behaviors such as skin picking; and repetitive oral movements such as bruxism or mouth biting. Chronic hair pulling that results in noticeable hair loss is the cardinal feature of the DSM-IV diagnosis of trichotillomania. According to the DSM-IV, trichotillomania is diagnosed when the individual experiences a sense of tension prior to pulling hair and a sense of gratification or relief after the hair has been pulled, and the hair pulling results in significant distress or impairment in important areas of functioning.

Bruxism refers to the nonfunctional grinding of teeth (Glaros & Rao, 1977). Bruxism may include the clenching, gnashing, and tapping of teeth and can occur diurnally or nocturnally. Chronic bruxism has been associated with severe physical damage including abnormal wear of the teeth, damaged gum and bone structures surrounding the teeth, facial pain, and tooth sensitivity (Glaros & Rao, 1977).

Nail biting, finger sucking and skin picking are examples of behaviors that, if exhibited excessively, may qualify as repetitive movement disorders. The physical or social concerns associated with these repetitive movement disorders may not be as apparent as some of the other habit disorders. However, each of these behaviors has the potential to cause physical and social concerns. Excessive nail biting can lead to not only disfigured finger nails and finger tips, but also a number of skin infections (Leonard, Lenane, Swedo, Rettew, & Rapoport, 1991) and dental problems (Odenrick & Brattstrom, 1985). Nail biting can also cause gingival injuries, microfractures of the teeth, and an increased risk of infections in the oral cavity (Creath, Steinmetz, & Roebuck, 1995). Finger sucking, including thumb sucking, has been associated with a number of secondary medical conditions including digital deformities (Reid & Price, 1984), dental complications, and increased risk of poisoning (Josell, 1995).

Likewise, repetitive skin picking has been associated with minor sores, permanent scars, and various skin infections (Wilhelm et al., 1999).

## Prevalence and Etiology of Tic Disorders and Repetitive Movement Disorders

Tic disorders have been reported in individuals diagnosed with mental retardation (Crews, Bonaventura, Hay, Steele, & Rowe, 1993; Sverd, 1988), autism (Burd, Fisher, Kerbeshian, & Arnold, 1987; Kerbeshian, Burd, & Martsolf, 1984) and Down's Syndrome (Collacott & Ismail, 1988; Karlinsky, Sandor, Berg, Moldofsky, & Crawford, 1986). Long, Miltenberger, and Rapp (1998) surveyed direct care staff and found that 17% of 259 individuals diagnosed with mental retardation living in community residences exhibited a motor and/or vocal tic.

There are numerous genetic, neurobiological, and environmental theories about the etiology of tic disorders. Genetic explanations of tic disorders result from studies demonstrating a higher incidence of tic disorders in biological relatives of individuals diagnosed with Tourette's disorder. Data from a number of family studies have shown that for a family member of a person diagnosed with Tourette's disorder, the risk for developing Tourette's disorder is 10-11% and chronic tics is 15% (Pauls, Alsobrook, Gelernter, & Leckman, 1999). It is unlikely that a single gene is responsible for Tourette's and other tic disorders, and is more likely that there are several genes that have some moderate effect of the susceptibility to Tourette's and other tic disorders (Findley, 2001). Biological variables hypothesized to contribute to tic disorders include various regions of brain circuitry (Peterson et al., 1999), biochemical dysfunction (Anderson, Leckman, & Cohen, 1999; Synder, Taylor, Coyle, & Meyerhoff, 1970), and neurological defects (Golden, 1977). Evidence suggests the involvement of cortico-striatal-thalamo-cortical (CSTC) circuits in tic disorders. Finally, the contribution of environmental variables has focused on the effects of perinatal risks, stress, infection, and stimulant exposure (Findley, 2001).

Estimates of the prevalence of hair pulling exhibited by individuals diagnosed with mental retardation and disabilities are limited. Dimoski and Duricic (1991) (cited in Christenson & Mansueto, 1999) found that 3.1% of 457 children and adolescents diagnosed with mental retardation they examined had trichotillomania. Likewise, Long et al. (1998) found that 5% of 259 individuals living in group homes reportedly engaged in hair pulling resulting in noticeable hair loss.

Etiologic theories on the development and maintenance of trichotillomania include operant variables, genetic predisposition, and biological factors. Operant variables suspected in the maintenance of trichotillomania include self-reports of hair pulling in response to experiencing negative affect (e.g., sadness, anxiety, frustration, and tension) or when engaged in sedentary activities (e.g., doing homework, reading, or getting reading for bed) (Christenson & Mansueto, 1999; Christenson, Ristvedt, & Mackenzie, 1993). In the few studies that have systematically manipulated environmental conditions, investigators found that hair pulling was more probable in an anxiety-provoking situation (Woods & Miltenberger, 1996) and when left alone (Miltenberger, Long, Rapp, Lumley, & Elliot, 1998; Rapp ,

Miltenberger, Galensky, Ellingson, & Long, 1999). Taken together, these investigations suggest that hair pulling may be maintained due to the behavior producing some form of stimulation (automatic positive reinforcement) or reducing antecedent levels of anxiety or negative affect (automatic negative reinforcement).

Support for genetic variables and biological factors that may contribute to hair pulling include reports of first-degree relatives within a hair puller's family that also exhibit hair pulling and other psychiatric disorders (Cohen, Stein, Simeon, Spadaccini, Rosen, Aronowitz, & Hollander, 1995; Schlosser, Black, Blum, & Goldstein, 1994). However, these correlational studies are only suggestive of a genetic link. Likewise, some investigators have suggested that higher pain thresholds may predispose certain individuals to pull their hair (Christenson, Raymond, Faris, McAllister, Crow, Howard, & Mitchell, 1994). However, at least one study has failed to support this assertion (Christenson et al., 1994).

The reports of prevalence rates for bruxism vary dramatically probably due to disparities in defining the behavior. Prevalence rates for adults and children without disabilities vary widely, with adult estimates ranging from 5-20% and child estimates ranging from 7 to 88%. A number of researchers have noted higher incidences of bruxism in children diagnosed with mental retardation, especially those diagnosed with Down's Syndrome (Perlstein & Barnett, 1952) and severe cerebral palsy (Brown, 1970; Lindquvist & Heijbel, 1974), than in children without disabilities. In addition, Swallow (1972) found that children diagnosed with mental retardation had more extensive dental wear (dental wear is one measure used to determine the extent of bruxism) than did children without mental retardation. Richmond, Rugh, Dolfi, and Wasilewsky (1984) assessed bruxism in 358 institutionalized individuals diagnosed with mental retardation by questioning direct-care staff familiar with each resident and conducting oral examinations of each resident. Results of the staff survey suggested that 41% of the population exhibited bruxism whereas examinations of tooth wear found 58% of the population exhibited bruxism. Long et al. (1998) found that 13.1% of individuals diagnosed with mental retardation in community residences exhibited some form of bruxism behavior according to staff reports.

Etiological explanations for the development and maintenance of bruxism include occlusal abnormalities, psychological factors; such as stress and subsequent nervous tension from other environmental sources (Glaros & Rao, 1977), and neurophysiological factors; such as neurological dysfunction, heredity, and endocrine disorders (Glaros & Rao, 1977; Brown, 1970).

There are few reports of prevalence rates for individuals diagnosed with mental retardation exhibiting the repetitive movement disorders of nail biting, finger sucking, and skin picking. The few reports of the prevalence of nail biting exhibited by individuals diagnosed with mental retardation have been similar to the prevalence rates reported in the general population (23% - 41%; Leonard et al., 1991). For example, Ballinger (1970) compared the prevalence of nail biting exhibited by 832 individuals in the general community to 631 individuals diagnosed with mental retardation living in an institution, and 598 individuals in a psychiatric hospital.

Results demonstrated that the rates of nail biting were similar in all three populations across age groups. Likewise, Clark (1970) compared 452 individuals diagnosed with mental retardation living in a hospital to 104 school children without mental retardation and found fairly equivalent prevalence rates between the groups. However, in the survey by Long et al. (1998), staff reported that 14% of individuals diagnosed with mental retardation in community residences bit their nails. Further research is necessary to develop estimates of the prevalence of nail biting, finger sucking and skin picking exhibited by individuals diagnosed with mental retardation. Moreover, research on the etiological variables that contribute to these repetitive movement disorders exhibited by individuals diagnosed with mental retardation is needed.

## Assessment of Tics and Repetitive Movement Disorders

Assessment of tics and repetitive movement disorders in individuals diagnosed with developmental disabilities typically takes two forms; direct observation of the behavior and product measures of the behavior or damage caused by the behaviors (e. g., Carr & Rapp, 2001). Indirect measures such as interviews, questionnaires, and rating scales are less applicable for individuals diagnosed with disabilities because such measures require retrospective reporting from memory or reports of subjective experiences that may be difficult for individuals diagnosed with intellectual impairments. Indirect measures may be more useful when a significant other who has regular contact with the person with a disability (parent, teacher, staff) serves as an informant (e.g., Miltenberger et al., 1998).

### Direct Observation

To use direct observation procedures to assess tics or repetitive movements in individuals with disabilities, the assessor must (a) define the target behaviors, (b) choose the dimension of the behavior to be measured (frequency or duration), (c) decide on event recording or interval or time sample measures, and (d) choose a representative observation period.

To define the target behavior, the assessor must identify the movements involved in the behavior and determine the onset and offset of the behavior. This may be a challenging task for some tics as they can occur rapidly with numerous or changing topographies (Meidinger, Miltenberger, Himle, Omvig, Trainer, & Crosby, in press). If it is difficult to identify the onset and offset of each instance of the behavior, then time sample or interval recording may be most appropriate.

The dimension chosen for measurement will be determined by the most relevant features of the target behavior. For tics, a frequency measure will probably be most appropriate because the behaviors occur quickly and counting their occurrence will provide the best indication of the behavior. For target behaviors such as finger sucking, a duration measure may best capture the behavior because each instance of the behavior occurs for a long period of time. For hair pulling, nail biting, bruxism, or skin picking, frequency or duration may be most appropriate depending on the characteristics of the behavior under observation.

When the onset and offset of each instance of the target behavior can be identified, an event recording procedure will be most appropriate because event recording provides a true measure of the behavior. Interval and time sample recording on the other hand produce estimates of the true occurrence of the behavior as they indicate the percentage of observation intervals in which the behavior occurred. Interval or time sample recording are appropriate when the onset and offset of each instance of the target behavior are difficult to discriminate, making event recording unreliable (e.g., Meidinger et al., in press).

The observation period and setting for a particular individual should be chosen to produce representative samples of the target behavior. As such, the observations should occur in the places and at the times when the target behaviors are most likely to occur. Observations in natural settings or analogues to natural settings will typically produce the most representative samples of the behavior. For example, Long, Miltenberger, Ellingson, and Ott, (1999) recorded the thumb sucking of an individual diagnosed with mental retardation through an observation window as the individual watched television in an interview room at the university. This analogue setting was chosen because staff reported that the individual frequently sucked his thumb in his room at the group home while watching television. To choose the appropriate observation periods and settings, it is helpful to interview parents, staff, teachers, and the client him/herself to determine when and where the target behavior is most likely to occur. Some behaviors such as tics, may occur across environments and time periods making it easier to choose convenient observation periods. Other behaviors such as hair pulling, finger sucking, and skin picking may be more likely to occur when the individual is alone, possible due to a history of punishment by significant others (Rapp, Miltenberger, Galensky, Roberts, & Ellingson, 1999). To record such behaviors, it is often necessary to observe surreptitiously through an observation window (e.g., Long, Miltenberger, et al., 1999) or with a video camera placed in the environment in advance of the observation period (e.g., Rapp, Miltenberger, & Long, 1998).

## Product Measures

Product measures can be used as an adjunct to direct observation or, is some cases, in lieu of direct observation. Product measures will be useful for those behaviors such as hair pulling, skin picking, or nail biting that produce some physical damage to the person. For hair pulling, product measures may include measurement of size of the bald areas produced by hair pulling, a rating of the amount of hair growth or density of hair in the affected area (Rapp et al., 1998; Romaniuk, Miltenberger, & Deaver, 2003), and a count of the hairs collected from the location where the individual sat or lied down while pulling his/her hair (Altman, Grahs, & Friman, 1982). For nail biting, a product measure would consist of measurement of nail length (Twohig & Woods, 2001a) or a rating of damage to the nail, cuticle, or skin surrounding the nail. For skin picking, a rating of the physical damage to the skin may be used as a product measure (Twohig & Woods, 2001b).

An advantage of product measures is that they provide an index of the damage caused by the behavior or the severity of the behavior. Furthermore, the use of product measures does not require the assessor to be present to observe the actual occurrence of the target behavior. The disadvantage of product measures is that some repetitive behaviors may not produce physical damage and some types of physical damage may be produced by behaviors other than the target behavior. Therefore the product measure may not accurately reflect the occurrence of the target behavior.

## Functional Analyses of Tics and Repetitive Movement Disorders

Since the development of functional analysis methodologies in the early 1980s (Carr & Durand, 1985; Iwata Dorsey, Slifer, Bauman, & Richman, 1982), a functional approach to treatment of problem behaviors exhibited by individuals diagnosed with mental retardation has been established as best practice (Iwata, Pace, Cowdery, & Miltenberger, 1994; Iwata Vollmer, Zarcone, & Rodgers, 1993; O'Neill et al., 1997). In the functional approach, the clinician first conducts a functional assessment of the targeted behavior to identify the antecedents and consequences that are functionally related to the behavior. Functional assessment procedures can involve indirect approaches (behavioral interviews or questionnaires), direct observation of the antecedents and consequences of the behavior, or experimental (functional analysis) procedures in which possible antecedents and consequences are manipulated to demonstrate their effects on the behavior (e.g., Miltenberger, 1999). Once the antecedents and consequences are identified, treatment involves manipulating the relevant antecedents and consequences to decrease the problem behavior (through extinction and antecedent control procedures) and increase desirable replacement behaviors (through differential reinforcement procedures). In a functional approach to treatment, punishment procedures are used as a last resort only if extinction, antecedent control, and differential reinforcement procedures have not produced the desired changes in the behavior (Miltenberger, 2001).

Unfortunately, the functional approach has rarely been employed in the assessment and treatment of tics and repetitive movement disorders exhibited by individuals diagnosed with developmental disabilities. Most of the treatments utilized for these disorders have involved some form of punishment (Long & Miltenberger, 1998). Only in recent years has a functional approach been evaluated for the assessment of tics and repetitive movement disorders in individuals with disabilities (Carr, Taylor, Wallander, & Reiss, 1996; Miltenberger, Long, et al., 1998; Rapp, Miltenberger, Galensky, Ellingson, & Long, 1999; Scotti, Schulman, & Hojnacki, 1994).

## Functional Analysis of Hair Pulling

Two studies evaluated a functional analysis methodology for assessing the reinforcing consequences of hair pulling exhibited by individuals diagnosed with disabilities. Miltenberger, Long, et al. (1998) evaluated hair pulling and hair manipulation exhibited by a woman diagnosed with moderate mental retardation in three experimental conditions. In one condition, the researchers provided social disapproval to see whether attention maintained the behavior. In another condition, the researchers provided escape from tasks contingent on hair pulling to see if escape was maintaining hair pulling. Finally the client was observed while alone in a room to see if hair pulling persisted in the absence of social reinforcement. The results showed that hair pulling occurred primarily while she was alone suggesting that the behavior was maintained by automatic reinforcement. In this case, the authors speculated that the sensory stimulation resulting from twirling the pulled hair between her fingers maintained the hair pulling and hair manipulation.

In a second study evaluating the function of hair pulling in a 19 year old woman diagnosed with severe mental retardation, Rapp, Miltenberger, Galensky, Ellingson, et al. (1999) showed that hair pulling occurred primarily while the woman was alone and that it was not maintained by attention or escape. Rapp et al. then conducted further analyses and showed that hair pulling ceased when the woman wore a latex glove, thus masking the sensory stimulation the resulted from manipulating the hair. In the final analysis, Rapp et al. showed that she manipulated hairs that were placed in her reach, demonstrating that hair manipulation was the reinforcing consequence for hair pulling.

## Functional Analysis of Tics

Two studies evaluated functional analysis procedures for tics experienced by individuals diagnosed with developmental disabilities. Scotti et al. (1994) conducted a functional analysis of motor and vocal tics exhibited by a man diagnosed with profound mental retardation. The conditions included two forms of attention for tics (approval and social disapproval), escape for tics, access to a rocking chair, and an alone condition. The participant's tics occurred across all conditions but were slightly higher in the escape condition and slightly lower in the social disapproval condition. When escape extinction and social disapproval were implemented as treatment, the tics did not decrease, suggesting that the tics were not influenced to any great extent by social factors.

In another study evaluating functional analysis procedures with a vocal tic exhibited by an 11 year old boy diagnosed with learning disabilities and language deficits, Carr et al. (1996) implemented conditions involving attention for tics, escape for tics, high sensory stimulation, free play with a peer, and being alone in a room. Although the tic was slightly higher in escape and attention conditions, it occurred across all experimental conditions leading the authors to conclude that it was not maintained by social reinforcement.

In both studies evaluating functional analysis procedures applied to tics, the authors concluded that the tics had a biological or neurological basis because they occurred in the absence of social consequences when the individuals were alone. Such an explanation is not inconsistent with an automatic reinforcement hypothesis, especially automatic negative reinforcement. The person may experience aversive sensory stimulation (e.g., an itch, tickle, burning sensation, or muscle tension) that is biological in origin and the occurrence of the tic provides fleeting relief from the sensations (e.g., Evers & Van de Wetering, 1994; Findley, 2001).

Although such sensory experiences are reported by individuals without mental retardation who experience tics, these sensory phenomena would be difficult to verify in individuals with significant intellectual impairments who experience tics. Thus, such an explanation is implied by default when common forms of social reinforcement are ruled out as the maintaining variables for the tics.

## Behavioral Treatment of Tics and Repetitive Movement Disorders

In this section we review the existing research evaluating behavioral treatments for tics and repetitive movement disorders in individuals with disabilities.

### Tic Disorders

Reports in the literature describing behavioral treatments for tics exhibited by individuals with disabilities are limited. Zarkowska, Crawley, and Locke (1989) attempted to use interruption and behavioral relaxation procedures to reduce tics associated with Tourettes Disorder exhibited by a 13-year-old diagnosed with severe mental retardation. Intensive relaxation training decreased the participant's tics during session, however the frequency of the tics increased to baseline levels outside of training sessions. Ultimately, pharmacological treatment consisting of pimozide was necessary to reduce the participant's tics.

Scotti et al. (1994) implemented treatment involving escape extinction (tasks were continued to completion when tics occurred) and social disapproval (a firm reprimand) for tics exhibited by a man diagnosed with profound mental retardation. The treatment was based on functional analysis results showing that the rate of tics was highest in the escape condition and lowest in the social disapproval condition. However, the treatment did not produce reductions in the man's tics, suggesting that social reinforcement or punishment did not play a role in the occurrence of the tics.

### Trichotillomania

Treatments for hair pulling exhibited by individuals diagnosed with mental retardation have included a number of punishment procedures including electric shock, aromatic ammonia, facial screening, overcorrection, contingent noise, and brief restraint. Corte, Wolf, and Locke (1971) reduced hair pulling exhibited by an adolescent with profound mental retardation by administering a mild electric shock contingent on hand movements involved in hair pulling. Although the contingent shock reduced the hair pulling to zero in the initial setting in which it was implemented, the shock needed to be administered in a variety of settings by different individuals to promote generalization.

Altman, Haavik, and Cook (1978) used contingent aromatic ammonia and differential reinforcement for the absence of hair pulling (DRO) to treat hair pulling exhibited by a 4-year-old diagnosed with cerebral palsy and severe mental retardation. The treatment consisted of placing an ammonia capsule under the nose of the individual contingent upon hair pulling. Treatment was applied in four different settings and reduced hair pulling to near zero rates.

Barmann and Vitali (1982) used a facial screening procedure to reduce hair pulling exhibited by three children with developmental delays. The authors hypothesized that the participants were pulling their hair in order to manipulate and look at the hair after it was pulled. As a result, the authors trained the children's parents or caregivers to pull a terrycloth bib over the eyes of the participant for 5 s contingent upon hair pulling. Hair pulling was immediately decreased and appropriate interactions with the participants' family and caregivers increased.

Likewise, Gross, Farrar, and Liner (1982) used a facial screening procedure and DRO procedures to reduce hair pulling exhibited by a 4-year-old diagnosed with moderate mental retardation and cerebral palsy. After failing to reduce hair pulling with overcorrection and DRO procedures, the authors lifted a bib over the participant's face for 15 s contingent on hair pulling.

Response prevention procedures to decrease hair pulling have been described in at least two studies. Maguire, Piersel, and Hansen (1995) hypothesized that for a 46-year-old woman with profound mental retardation hair pulling served a self-stimulatory function. As a result, the authors implemented a response prevention procedure in which padded mittens were placed on the participant's hands contingent on hair pulling. Ratings of hair growth from photographs revealed a steady increase in hair growth over the course of 3 years. Similarly, Barrett and Shapiro (1980) had parents shave the head of their 7-year-old girl diagnosed with severe mental retardation to decrease hair pulling. Hair pulling decreased while the girl's hair was short, but increased as her hair grew back. Ultimately, the authors employed a verbal warning and an overcorrection procedure, in which the participant was required to brush her hair for 2 min contingent upon each incident of hair pulling, to reduce hair pulling to near zero rates. Treatment effects were maintained at 1 year follow-up.

Matson, Stephens, and Smith (1978) employed a similar positive practice overcorrection procedure to reduce hair pulling exhibited by a 57-year-old diagnosed with profound mental retardation. Contingent on hair pulling the participant was required to brush her hair for 10 min. Treatment resulted in reductions in hair pulling to near zero levels.

Rapp et al. (1998) evaluated the effectiveness of habit reversal to treat hair pulling exhibited by a woman diagnosed with moderate mental retardation. In the habit reversal procedure, the authors taught the individual to become aware of each instance of hair pulling and to use a competing response (crossing her arms across her chest) each time she started to pull her hair. Although she used the procedure correctly in the presence of the researchers and stopped pulling her hair, she continued to pull her hair while alone. The researchers then evaluated an Awareness Enhancement Device (AED) consisting of a small electronic unit worn on the wrist and a small unit worn on her shirt collar. When she raised her hand to pull her hair, the unit on her wrist came in proximity of the unit on her collar and sounded an alarm, which only stopped when she pulled her hand away from her head. Her hair pulling was eliminated with the use of the AED.

Rapp et al. (2000) used a combination of procedures to decrease hair pulling by a 19 year old woman diagnosed with severe mental retardation. Assessment showed that she pulled her hair while watching television alone in the living room and while in bed. The researchers used a response interruption and DRO procedure in the living room and a response prevention procedure at night. They observed her while she watched television and provided periodic praise for the absence of the behavior while interrupting her attempts to pull hair and holding her hand at her side for 30 s. This procedure was effective when implemented by the researchers and by the individual's mother. At bed time, she wore a splint that prevented her from being able to grasp hair. Hair pulling was also eliminated at bedtime as well.

## Bruxism

Similar to the research on treatment of hair pulling, behavioral treatments for bruxism in individuals with developmental disabilities have included various punishment techniques, such as reprimands, pressure on the jaw, contingent icing, overcorrection, and firm massage. Kramer (1981) successfully treated bruxism exhibited by an 8-year-old boy with mental retardation whose teeth grinding was damaging his teeth and gums and distracting his classmates. During treatment, the boy's teacher delivered the verbal prompt "No" and firmly pressed on the boy's jaw for 2-3 s after each audible occurrence of bruxism. The child's bruxing was substantially reduced from baseline levels in approximately 3 weeks.

Blount, Drabman, Wilson, and Stewart (1982) treated diurnal bruxism exhibited by two individuals diagnosed with profound mental retardation with the contingent application of ice. A cube of ice was applied to the facial area for 6-8 s contingent on each instance of bruxing. Substantial reductions in bruxism occurred during treatment sessions (94% and 95% reductions from baseline for each respective participant), however treatments gains failed to maintain during generalization sessions.

Gross and Isaac (1983) treated bruxism in two 4-year-olds diagnosed with mild to moderate mental retardations using differential reinforcement of other behavior (DRO) and overcorrection procedures. The classroom teacher and aides were trained to provide the boys with social praise following every 10-s period without bruxism (the DRO component). Upon hearing an occurrence of bruxism, the boys were made to cover their mouths for 10 s and then to keep their arms perpendicular to their body for an additional 10 s (the overcorrection component). Treatment procedures resulted in substantial reductions in the behavior and treatment effects were maintained at 3 months follow-up.

In a procedure that technically can be described as a punishment procedure, Rudrud and Halaszyn (1981) used contingent massage to treat bruxism exhibited by a 43-year-old woman diagnosed with severe mental retardation. The authors trained the vocational staff at the community-based training program where the woman worked to firmly massage the woman's masseter muscles for one minute contingent upon each instance of bruxism. With the implementation of the contingent massage throughout the day, the woman's bruxism was not totally eliminated, but substantially reduced from baseline levels. The author's speculated that the contingent massage may have functioned as a mildly aversive punishment procedure or served to reduce masseter muscle tension, which in turn, reduced bruxism.

Bebko and Lennox (1988) used a reprimand and cueing procedure based on Azrin and Nunn's (1977) habit reversal procedure to treat diurnal bruxism exhibited by a 10-year-old and an 11-year-old male both diagnosed with autism and severe developmental delays. Contingent on hearing the bruxing, a verbal cue, "No grinding" was given and the therapist gently touched the child's chin with an index finger, prompting the child to open his mouth for 10 s. The child was then redirected backed to a previous activity and praised intermittently for being on-task or waiting without bruxing when appropriate. The implementation of the cueing procedure resulted in immediate decreases in the frequency of the behavior, however treatment procedures did not generalize to additional settings. Only with the implementation of the cueing procedure in the additional setting did treatment effects occur. Follow-up data for each boy at 2 years demonstrated that the rate of bruxing remained relatively lower than baseline levels for both children, with one child exhibiting no incidents of bruxism.

None of the studies evaluating treatment for hair pulling or bruxism used nonaversive interventions based on results derived from functional analyses. In fact, no functional analyses were conducted in these studies. All of the studies involved some form of punishment to reduce hair pulling or bruxism. It is questionable whether these types of punishment procedures would be employed today considering the aversiveness of the procedures and the lack of acceptability. For example, the use of shock, contingent icing, or aromatic ammonia would not be acceptable in most treatment settings. As a result, the severity of damage resulting from hair pulling or bruxism would need to be weighed against the acceptability of using punishment procedures when considering treatment options.

## Nail Biting and Thumb Sucking

There are few published studies employing behavioral treatments for nail biting or thumb sucking exhibited by individuals with disabilities. Mulick, Hoyt, Rojahn, and Schroeder (1978) decreased nail biting and skin picking exhibited by a 22-year-old with profound mental retardation. The authors restructured the environment to increase access to his toys and then systematically trained the participant to exchange old toys for new toys. Treatment resulted in near zero levels of nail biting and skin picking.

Barmann (1979) described the use of positive practice and restitutional overcorrection procedures to reduce severe nail biting exhibited by a 9-year-old girl diagnosed with moderate mental retardation. Positive practice consisted of the repeated practice of bringing her hands up to her mouth (but not placing them in her mouth) and then folding her hands at her sides. Restitutional overcorrection consisted of requiring the girl to repair and paint not only her nails but also her mother's nails contingent on nail biting. The treatment reduced the nail biting entirely and increased nail growth.

Long, Miltenberger et al. (1999) used simplified habit reversal procedures to treat nail biting, skin picking, and thumb sucking exhibited by four adults diagnosed with mental retardation. Simplified habit reversal consisted of awareness training (the individuals simulated the behavior in session to increase awareness), competing response training (the use of incompatible responses contingent on the target behavior), and social support procedures (involving staff prompts to use the competing response and praise from staff for the absence of the behavior or use of the competing response). Although simplified habit reversal has been shown to be an effective procedure for similar habit behaviors in numerous studies with persons without disabilities (e.g., Miltenberger, Fuqua, & Woods, 1998) the procedure produced little change in the target behaviors for these individuals until additional contingencies were added. Additional prompting for one individual lead to decreases in thumb sucking and the addition of DRO and response cost procedures resulted in decreases in nail biting and thumb/finger sucking for two other individuals. In all three cases the individuals were observed surreptitiously while alone and the prompts and consequences were delivered in that context. Finally, when differential reinforcement of nail growth was implemented, nail biting decreased for the fourth individual. His nails were measured weekly and a monetary reward was given is nail length increased.

## Conclusions

A number of conclusions can be drawn from research on the assessment and treatment of tics and repetitive movement disorders in individuals diagnosed with developmental disabilities. First, very little research has been conducted evaluating functional analysis procedures for understanding the variables maintaining these behaviors. Two studies reported the results of functional analyses with tics (Carr et al., 1996; Scotti et al., 1994) and two studies reported functional analyses with hair pulling exhibited by individuals with disabilities (Miltenberger, Long, et al., 1998; Rapp, Miltenberger, Galensky, Ellingson, et al., 1999). These four studies suggest that, in the individuals studied, tics and hair pulling were not maintained by any form of social reinforcement and instead were automatically reinforced. Only Rapp, Miltenberger, Galensky, Ellingson, et al. (1999) conducted further analyses to identify the nature of the sensory reinforcement maintaining hair pulling in one individual and found that tactile stimulation resulting from hair manipulation was maintaining the behavior.

There is a need for future research to utilize functional analysis methodologies to better understand the antecedents and consequences of tics and repetitive movement disorders. If these behaviors are maintained through automatic reinforcement, future research should seek to establish the nature of the reinforcing consequences maintaining the behavior. Although Rapp, Miltenberger, Galensky, Ellingson, et al. (1999) showed that automatic positive reinforcement in the form of tactile stimulation from hair twirling maintained hair pulling for one individual, it is quite possible that other forms of sensory stimulation maintain repetitive behaviors and that automatic negative reinforcement plays a role as well. If tics or repetitive behaviors function to bring momentary relief from aversive stimulation experienced by the individual (e.g., Findley, 2001; Miltenberger, Rapp, & Long,

2001) then creative functional analysis methodologies will be needed to document these automatically negatively reinforcing consequences.

Given the paucity of functional analysis research with tics and repetitive movement disorders in persons with developmental disabilities, it is not surprising that scant research has been conducted evaluating functional procedures for addressing these behaviors. Instead punishment procedures have largely been used in the treatment of repetitive movement disorders, sometimes in combination with differential reinforcement procedures. Although punishment procedures have been shown to be effective, such procedures are seen as less acceptable than functional approaches and they may be less effective in the long run because they do not address the function of the behavior. Therefore future research is needed evaluating functional approaches to the treatment of repetitive movement disorders in persons diagnosed with developmental disabilities. Such approaches would involve sensory extinction to eliminate or attenuate the reinforcing consequences for the behavior (e.g., Rapp, Miltenberger, Galensky, Ellingson, et al., 1999), antecedent control procedures to alter establishing operations for the behavior, and differential reinforcement to promote functionally equivalent desirable behaviors to replace the problem behaviors. Of course, these proposed procedures would go hand in hand with the expanded use of functional analysis methodologies to better understand the antecedents and consequences responsible for the occurrence of the behaviors.

## References

Altman, K., Haavik, S., & Cook, J. W. (1978). Punishment of self-injurious behavior in natural settings using contingent aromatic ammonia. *Behaviour Research and Therapy, 16,* 85-96.

Altman, K., Grahs, C., & Friman, P. (1982). Treatment of unobserved trichotillomania by attention-reflection and punishment of an apparent covariant. *Journal of Behavior Therapy and Experimental Psychiatry, 13,* 337-340.

American Psychiatric Association. (1994). *Diagnostic and statistical manual of mental disorders* (4th ed.). Washington, D.C.: Author.

Anderson, G. M., Leckman, J. F., & Cohen, D. J. (1999). Neurochemical and neuropeptide systems. In J. F. Leckman & D. J. Cohen (Eds.), *Tourette's syndrome: Tics, obsessions, compulsions: Developmental psychopathology and clinical care* (pp. 262-280). New York: John Wiley.

Azrin, N. H., & Nunn, R. G. (1973). Habit Reversal: A method of eliminating nervous habits and tics. *Behaviour Research and Therapy, 11,* 619-628.

Azrin, N. H., & Nunn, R. G. (1977). *Habit control in a day.* New York: Simon and Schuster.

Ballinger, B. R. (1970). The prevalence of nail-biting in normal and abnormal populations. *British Journal of Psychiatry, 117,* 445-446.

Barmann, B. C. (1979). The use of overcorrection with artificial nails in the treatment of chronic fingernail biting. *Mental Retardation, 17,* 309-311.

Barmann, B. C., & Vitali, D. L. (1982). Facial screening to eliminate trichotillomania in developmentally disabled persons. *Behavior Therapy, 13,* 735-742.

Barrett, R. P., & Shapiro, E. S. (1980). Treatment of stereotyped hair pulling with overcorrection: A case study with long term follow-up. *Journal of Behavior Therapy and Experimental Psychiatry, 11,* 317-320.

Bebko, J. M., & Lennox, C. (1988). Teaching the control of diurnal bruxism to two children with autism using a simple cueing procedure. *Behavior Therapy, 19,* 249-255.

Blount, R. L., Drabman, R. S., Wilson, N., & Stewart, D. (1982). Reducing severe diurnal bruxism in two profoundly retarded females. *Journal of Applied Behavior Analysis, 15,* 565-571.

Brown, R. H. (1970). Traumatic bruxism in a mentally retarded child. *New Zealand Dental Journal, 66,* 67-70.

Burd, L., Fisher, W. W., Kerbeshian, J., & Arnold, M. E. (1987). Is the development of Tourette disorder a marker for improvement in patients with autism and other pervasive developmental disorders? *Journal of the American Academy of Child and Adolescent Psychiatry, 26,* 162-165.

Carr, E. G., & Durand, V. M. (1985). Reducing behavior problems through functional communication training. *Journal of Applied Behavior Analysis, 18,* 111-126.

Carr, J. E., & Rapp, J. T. (2001). Assessment of repetitive behavior disorders. In D. W. Woods & R. G. Miltenberger (Eds.), *Tic disorders, trichotillomania, and other repetitive behavior disorders: Behavioral approaches to analysis and treatment* (pp. 9-31). Boston: Kluwer.

Carr, J. E., Taylor, C. C., Wallander, R. J., & Reiss, M. L. (1996). A functional-analytic approach to the diagnosis of a transient tic disorder. *Journal of Behavior Therapy & Experimental Psychiatry, 27,* 291-297.

Christenson, G. A., & Mansueto, C. (1999). Trichotillomania: Descriptive characteristics and phenomenology. In M. B. Stein, G. A. Christenson, & E. Hollander (Eds.), *Trichotillomania* (pp. 1-41). Washington, DC: American Psychiatric Press.

Christenson, G. A., Raymond, N. C., Faris, P. L., McAllister, R. D., Crow, S. J., Howard, L. A., & Mitchell, J. E. (1994). Pain thresholds are not elevated in trichotillomania. *Biological Psychiatry, 36,* 347-349.

Christenson, G. A., Ristvedt, S. L., & Mackenzie, T. B. (1993). Identification of trichotillomania cue profiles. *Behavior Research and Therapy, 31,* 315-320.

Clark, D. F. (1970). Nail-biting in subnormals. *British Journal of Medical Psychology, 43,* 69-81.

Cohen, L. J., Stein, D. J., Simeon, D., Spadaccini, E., Rosen, J., Aronowitz, B., & Hollander, E. (1995). Clinical profile, comorbidity, and treatment history in 123 hair pullers: A survey study. *Journal of Clinical Psychiatry, 56,* 319-326.

Collacott, R. A., & Ismail, I. A. (1988). Tourettism in a patient with Down's syndrome. *Journal of Mental Deficiency Research, 32,* 163-166.

Corte, H. E., Wolf, M. M., & Locke, B. J. (1971). A comparison of procedures for eliminating self-injurious behavior of retarded adolescents. *Journal of Applied Behavior Analysis, 4,* 201-213.

Creath, C. J., Steinmetz, S., & Roebuck, R. (1995). Gingival swelling due to a fingernail biting habit. *Journal of the American Dental Association, 126,* 1019-1021.

Crews, W. D., Jr., Bonaventura, S., Hay, C. L., Steele, W. K., & Rowe, F. B. (1993). Gilles de la Tourette disorder among individuals with severe or profound mental retardation. *Mental Retardation, 3,* 25-28.

Evers, R. A. F., & Van de Wetering, B. J. M. (1994). A treatment model for motor tics based on a specific tension-reduction technique. *Journal of Behavior Therapy and Experimental Psychiatry, 25,* 255-260.

Findley, D. B. (2001). Characteristics of tic disorders. In D. W. Woods & R. G. Miltenberger (Eds.), *Tic Disorders, trichotillomania, and other repetitive behavior disorders: Behavioral approaches to analysis and treatment* (pp. 53-71). Boston: Kluwer.

Glaros, A. G., & Rao, S. M. (1977). Bruxism: A critical review. *Psychological Bulletin, 84,* 767-781.

Golden, G. S. (1977). Tourette syndrome: The pediatric perspective. *American Journal of Disabled Children, 13,* 531-534.

Gross, A. M., Farrar, M. J., & Liner, D. (1982). Positive reinforcement and punishment in the treatment of childhood trichotillomania. *Journal of Behavior Therapy and Experimental Psychiatry, 5,* 133-140.

Gross, A. M., & Isaac, L. (1983). Forced arm exercise and DRO in the treatment of bruxism in cerebral palsied children. *Child and Family Behavior Therapy, 4,* 175-181.

Iwata, B. A., Dorsey, M., Slifer, K., Bauman, K., & Richman, G. (1982). Toward a functional analysis of self-injury. *Analysis and Intervention in Developmental Disabilities, 2,* 3-20.

Iwata, B. A., Pace, G. M., Cowdery, G. E., & Miltenberger, R. G. (1994). What makes extinction work: An analysis of procedural form and function. *Journal of Applied Behavior Analysis, 27,* 131-144.

Iwata, B. A., Vollmer, T. R., Zarcone, J. R., & Rodgers, T. A. (1993). Treatment classification and selection based on behavioral function. In R. Van Houten & S. Axelrod (Eds.), *Behavior analysis and treatment* (pp. 101-125). New York: Plenum.

Josell, S. D. (1995). Habits affecting dental and maxillofacial growth and development. *Dental Clinics of North America, 39,* 851-860.

Karlinsky, H., Sandor, P., Berg, J. M., Moldofsky, H., & Crawford, E. (1986). Gilles de la Tourette's syndrome in Down's syndrome: A case report. *British Journal of Psychiatry, 148,* 601-604.

Kerbeshian, J., Burd, L., & Martsolf, J. T. (1984). A family with fragile-X syndrome. *The Journal of Nervous and Mental Disease, 172,* 549-551.

Kramer, J. J. (1981). Aversive control of bruxism in a mentally retarded child: A case study. *Psychological Reports, 49,* 815-818.

Leonard, H. L., Lenane, M. C., Swedo, S. E., Rettew, D. C., & Rapoport, J. L. (1991). A double-blind comparison of clomipramine and desipramine treatment of severe onychophagia (nail biting). *Archives of General Psychiatry, 48*, 821-827.

Lindquvist, B., & Heijbel, J. (1974). Bruxism in children with brain damage. *Acta Odontologica Scandinavica, 32*, 313-319.

Long, E. S., & Miltenberger, R. G. (1998). A review of behavioral and pharmacological treatments for habit disorders in individuals with mental retardation. *Journal of Behavior Therapy and Experimental Psychiatry, 29*, 143-156.

Long, E. S., Miltenberger, R. G., Ellingson, S. A., & Ott, S. (1999). Augmenting simplified habit reversal in the treatment of oral-digital habits exhibited by individuals with mental retardation. *Journal of Applied Behavior Analysis, 32*, 353-365.

Long, E. S., Miltenberger, R. G., & Rapp, J. T. (1998). Survey of habit behaviors exhibited by individuals with mental retardation. *Behavioral Interventions, 13*, 79-89.

Long, E. S., Woods, D. W., Miltenberger, R. G., Fuqua, R. W., & Boudjouk, P. (1999). Examining the social effects of habit behaviors exhibited by individuals with mental retardation. *Journal of Developmental and Physical Disabilities, 11*, 295-312.

Maguire, K. B., Piersel, W. C., & Hauser, B. G. (1995). The long-term treatment of trichotillomania: A case study of a woman with profound mental retardation living in an applied setting. *Journal of Developmental and Physical Disabilities, 7*, 185-202.

Matson, J. L., Stevens, R. M., & Smith, C. (1978). Treatment of self-injurious behavior with overcorrection. *Journal of Mental Deficiency Research, 22*, 175-178.

Meidinger, A. L., Miltenberger, R. G., Himle, M., Omvig, M., Trainer, C., & Crosby, R. (in press). An investigation of tic suppression and the rebound effect in Tourette syndrome. *Behavior Modification.*

Miltenberger, R. G. (1999). Understanding problem behavior through functional assessment. In N. Wieseler & R. Hanson (Eds.), *Challenging behaviors in persons with mental health disorders and developmental disabilities* (pp. 215-235). Washington, DC: AAMR.

Miltenberger, R. G., (2001). *Behavior modification: Principles and procedures* (2nd ed). Pacific Grove, CA: Wadsworth Publishing Company.

Miltenberger, R. G., Fuqua, R. W., & Woods, D. W. (1998). Applying behavior analysis to clinical problems: Review and analysis of habit reversal. *Journal of Applied Behavior Analysis, 31*, 447-469.

Miltenberger, R. G., Rapp, J. T., & Long, E. S. (2001). Characteristics of trichotillomania. In D. W. Woods & R. G. Miltenberger (Eds.), *Tic disorders, trichotillomania, and other repetitive behavior disorders* (pp. 133-150). Boston: Kluwer.

Miltenberger, R. G., Long, E. S., Rapp, J. T., Lumley, V. A., & Elliott, A. J. (1998). Evaluation the function of hair pulling: A preliminary investigation. *Behavior Therapy, 29*, 211-219.

Mulick, J. A., Hoyt, P., Rojahn, J., & Schroeder, S. R. (1978). Reduction of a "nervous habit" in a profoundly retarded youth by increasing toy play. *Journal of Behavior Therapy and Experimental Psychiatry, 9,* 381-385.

Odenrick, L., & Brattstrom, V. (1985). Nail biting: Frequency and association with root resorption during orthodontic treatment. *British Journal of Orthodontics, 12,* 78-81.

O'Neill, R. E., Horner, R. H., Albin, R. W., Sprague, J. R., Storey, K., & Newton, J. S. (1997). *Functional assessment and program development for problem behavior: A practical guide.* Pacific Grove, CA: Brooks/Cole.

Pauls, D. L., Alsobrook, J. P., Gelernter, J., & Leckman, J. F. (1999). Genetic vulnerability. In J. F. Leckman & D. J. Cohen (Eds.), *Tourette's syndrome: Tics, obsessions, compulsions: Developmental psychopathology and clinical care* (pp. 194-211). New York: John Wiley.

Perlstein, M. A., & Barnett, H. E. (1952). Nature and recognition of cerebral palsy in infancy. *Journal of the American Medical Association, 148,* 1389-1397.

Peterson, B. S., Leckman, J. F., Arnsten, A., Anderson, G. M., Staib, L. H., Gore, J. C., Bronen, R. A., Malison, R., Scahill, L., & Cohen, D. J., (1999). Neuroanatomical circuitry. In J. F. Leckman & D. J. Cohen (Eds.), *Tourette's syndrome: Tics, obsessions, compulsions: Developmental psychopathology and clinical care* (pp. 230-259). New York: John Wiley.

Rapp, J. T., Miltenberger, R. G., Galensky, T. L., Ellingson, S. A., & Long, E. S. (1999). A functional analysis of hair pulling. *Journal of Applied Behavior Analysis, 32,* 329-337.

Rapp, J. T., Miltenberger, R. G., Galensky, T. L., Ellingson, S. A., Stricker, J., Garlinghouse, M., & Long, E. S. (2000). Treatment of hair pulling and hair manipulation maintained by digital-tactile stimulation. *Behavior Therapy, 31,* 381-393.

Rapp, J. T., Miltenberger, R. G., Galensky, T. L., Roberts, J., & Ellingson, S. A. (1999). Brief functional analysis and simplified habit reversal treatment of thumb sucking in fraternal twin brothers. *Child and Family Behavior Therapy, 21(2),* 1-17.

Rapp, J. T., Miltenberger, R. G., & Long, E. S. (1998). Augmenting simplified habit reversal with an awareness enhancement device: Preliminary findings. *Journal of Applied Behavior Analysis, 31,* 655-668.

Reid, D., & Price, A. (1984). Digital deformities and dental malocclusion due to finger sucking. *British Journal of Plastic Surgery, 37,* 445-452.

Richmond, G., Rugh, J. D., Dolfi, R., & Wasilewsky, J. W. (1984). Survey of bruxism in an institutionalized mentally retarded population. *American Journal of Mental Deficiency, 88,* 418-421.

Romaniuk, C., Miltenberger, R., & Deaver, C. (2003). Long term maintenance following habit reversal and adjunct treatment for trichotillomania. *Child and Family Behavior Therapy, 25(2),* 45-59.

Rudrud, E., & Halaszyn, J. (1981). Reduction of bruxism by contingent massage. *Special Care in Dentistry, 1,* 122-124.

Scotti, J. R., Schulman, D. E., & Hojnacki, R. M. (1994). Functional analysis and unsuccessful treatment of Tourette's Syndrome in a man with profound mental retardation. *Behavior Therapy, 25,* 721-738.

Schlosser, S., Black, D. W., Blum, N., & Goldstein, R. B. (1994). The demography, phenomenology, and family history of 22 persons with compulsive hair pulling. *Annals of Clinical Psychiatry, 6,* 147-152.

Synder, S. H., Taylor, K. M., Coyle, J. T., & Meyerhoff, J. L. (1970). The role of brain dopamine in behavioral regulation and the actions of psychotropic drugs. *American Journal of Psychiatry, 127,* 199-207.

Sverd, J. (1988). Tourette syndrome associated with pervasive developmental disorder: Is there an etiological relationship? *Journal of the Multihandicapped Person, 1,* 281-291.

Swallow, J. N. (1972). Dental disease in handicapped children: An epidemiological study. *Israel Journal of Dental Medicine, 21,* 41-51.

Teng, E. J., Woods, D. W., Twohig, M. P., & Marcks, B. A. (2002). Body focused repetitive behavior problems: Prevalence in a nonreferred population and differences in perceived somatic activity. *Behavior Modification, 26,* 340-360.

Twohig M. P., & Woods, D. W. (2001a). Evaluating the duration of the competing response in habit reversal: A parametric analysis. *Journal of Applied Behavior Analysis, 34,* 517-520.

Twohig, M. P., & Woods, D. W. (2001b). Habit reversal as a treatment for chronic skin picking in typically developing adult male siblings. *Journal of Applied Behavior Analysis, 34,* 217-220.

Wilhelm S., Keuthen, N. J., Deckersbach, T., Engelhard, I. M., Forker, A. E., Baer, L., O'Sullivan, R. L., & Jenike, M. A. (1999). Self-injurious skin picking: Clinical characteristics and comorbidity. *Journal of Clinical Psychiatry, 60,* 454-459.

Woods, D. W., & Miltenberger, R. G. (1996). Are people with nervous habits nervous? A preliminary examination of habit function in a nonreferred population. *Journal of Applied Behavior Analysis, 29,* 259-261.

Woods, D. W., Friman, P. C., & Teng, E. J. (2001). Physical and social impairments in persons with repetitive behavior disorders. In D. W. Woods & R. G. Miltenberger (Eds.), *Tic disorders, trichotillomania, and other repetitive behavior disorders: Behavioral approaches to analysis and treatment* (pp. 33-52). Boston: Kluwer.

Woods, D. W., Koch, M., & Miltenberger, R. G. (2003). The impact of tic severity on the effects of peer education about Tourette syndrome. *Journal of Developmental and Physical Disabilities, 15,* 67-78.

Zarkowska, E., Crawley, B., & Locke, J. (1989). A behavioural intervention for Gilles de la Tourette syndrome in a severely mentally handicapped girl. *Journal of Mental Deficiency Research, 33,* 245-253.

# Chapter 7

# Assessment of Basic Learning Abilities Test: Recent Research and Future Directions

**Garry L. Martin, C. T. Yu, and Tricia Vause**
*University of Manitoba and St. Amant Centre*

Teachers and rehabilitation staff who work with individuals with intellectual disabilities often observe the ease with which some persons are able to perform some tasks, but struggle to learn other tasks that seem very similar. For example, an adolescent with severe intellectual disability is able to pass the pepper when salt and pepper shakers remain in fixed positions on the table, but is unable to do so when their positions are changed. As another example, an adult with severe intellectual disability is able to restock all types of paper at a copy shop, but when asked for a package of lined paper versus clear paper, is not able to retrieve the appropriate package. After observing these types of problems, Nancy Kerr and Lee Meyerson realized that they were often due to deficiencies in the ability to make position, visual, and auditory discriminations that are prerequisite to the learning of basic self-care, academic, prevocational, and vocational skills. They further observed that global measures of assessment that were often used to evaluate an individual's skills were insufficient in determining the required discriminations. To address this problem, Kerr, Meyerson, and Flora (1977) developed an assessment tool named the *Assessment of Basic Learning Abilities* (ABLA) test. Early research on the ABLA (Yu, Martin, & Williams, 1989) indicated that it is useful for selecting and sequencing training tasks to ensure optimal learning for individuals with moderate, severe, and profound intellectual disabilities. In addition, researchers use the ABLA test as a screening tool for determining appropriate intervention procedures (e.g., Conyers, Martin, Yu, & Vause, 2000; Yu & Martin, 1986). This chapter outlines past and recent research findings concerning the ABLA test, as well as potential directions for future research. Conference presentations and unpublished theses are not included in this paper.

*Table 7.1: A Description of the ABLA Levels, Discriminations Required, and Sample Everyday Behaviors Requiring the Discriminations.*

| ABLA Levels | Discriminations | Sample Behaviors |
|---|---|---|
| **Level 1**: Imitation. A tester puts an object into a container and asks the testee to do likewise. | A simple imitation. | Children playing Follow-the-Leader. |
| **Level 2**: Position Discrimination. When a red box or a yellow can are presented in a fixed position, a testee is required to consistently place a piece of beige foam in the container on the left when the tester says, "Put it in." | A simultaneous visual discrimination with position, color, shape, and size as relevant visual cues. | Turning on the cold (vs. the hot) water tap. |
| **Level 3**: Visual Discrimination. When a red box and a yellow can are randomly presented in left-right positions, a testee is required to consistently place a piece of beige foam in the yellow can when the tester says, "Put it in." | A simultaneous visual discrimination with color, shape, and size as relevant visual cues. | Locating one's coat from among other coats hung in a closet, with the coats in no fixed positions. |
| **Level 4**: Match-to-Sample. When a yellow can and a red box are presented in random left-right positions and a testee is presented with a yellow cylinder or a red cube, he/she consistently places the cylinder in the yellow can and the cube in the red box. | A conditional visual-visual quasi-identity discrimination with color, shape, and size as relevant visual cues. | Sorting socks into pairs. |
| **Level 5**: Auditory Discrimination. When presented with a yellow can and a red box (in fixed positions), a testee is required to consistently place a piece of foam in the appropriate container when the tester randomly says, "red box" (in a high-pitched rapid fashion) or "yellow can" (in a low-pitched drawn-out fashion). | A conditional auditory-visual nonidentity discrimination, with pitch, pronunciation, and duration as relevant auditory cues, and with position, color, shape, and size as relevant visual cues. | Responding to instructions to go left or right, to go to different rooms, or to open different drawers. |
| **Level 6**: Auditory-Visual Combined. The same as Level 5, except that the right-left position of the containers is randomly alternated. | A conditional auditory-visual nonidentity discrimination, with the same auditory cues as Level 5, and with only color, shape, and size as relevant visual cues. | Responding appropriately to requests such as, "pass the salt" vs. "pass the pepper" when the salt and pepper shakers are in different places on the table from meal to meal. |

## The ABLA Test

### A Learning-to-Learn Test

When administering the ABLA test, a tester attempts to teach to a testee the following six learning tasks: a simple visual imitation, a position discrimination, a visual discrimination, a visual match-to-sample discrimination, an auditory discrimination, and an auditory-visual combined discrimination. A brief description of each task, and the types of discriminations required is presented in Table 7.1.

As mentioned previously, Kerr et al. (1977) chose these particular discriminations because one or more of them appeared to be required for a person to readily learn a large number of self-care, academic, prevocational, and vocational tasks in programs at facilities for individuals with intellectual disabilities. To examine this contention, DeWiele and Martin (1996) assessed the basic discriminations required to perform 194 tasks, which were randomly selected from a total of 500 tasks that were taught to individuals in a residential training facility. These tasks were selected from various habilitative service departments including vocational training, recreation, communication, physiotherapy, and by staff in the home residence of each of the individuals. Experts on the ABLA test rated each task to determine whether it could be classified within the levels included in the ABLA test. The experts agreed that 69% of the tasks involved discriminations assessed by the ABLA test.

The materials for the ABLA test include a yellow can, approximately 15 cm in diameter and 17 cm in height; a red box approximately 14 cm X 14 cm X 10 cm; a yellow wooden cylinder, approximately 4 cm in diameter, 9 cm in height; a red wooden cube with approximate dimensions of 5 cm X 5 cm X 5 cm; and a piece of irregularly shaped beige foam, approximately 5 cm in diameter. There were several considerations that influenced Kerr et al. (1977) to choose the test materials listed above. First, red and yellow are primary colors, and are usually among the first taught to children. Also, the materials required are inexpensive, readily available, and easy to make. Third, the box and can are extremely common shapes; teaching two-choice discriminations involving these objects is likely to have practical value in everyday life. Kerr et al. (1977) used containers as comparison stimuli in order to more easily determine whether a correct response was made. Containers minimized the likelihood of subjective judgments on the part of the tester (e.g., if pointing counted as a response, it may be difficult to distinguish between a testee pointing to a container vs. pointing between the containers), and they reduced the possibility of a participant being able to switch his or her initial response.

### Testing Procedures

The six levels of the ABLA (refer to Table 7.1) can be administered to a testee in approximately 30 minutes. During assessment sessions, the testee is seated directly across from the tester. Prior to testing each level, the testee is provided with a demonstration, a guided trial, and an opportunity to respond independently. Testing and recording begins on a task after an individual is able to demonstrate an independent correct response on all sample-comparison relations included in the task. Throughout all testing sessions, a continuous reinforcement schedule (CRF) is used whereby each correct response is immediately followed by verbal praise and an edible. Errors are followed by a correction procedure that involves a demonstration, a guided trial, and an opportunity to respond independently. Testing continues on each task until either eight consecutive correct responses (passing criterion) or eight cumulative errors (failing criterion) occur.

## Substantiated Generalizations on the ABLA Test

### The Test has High Test-Retest and Intertester Reliability

Martin, Yu, Quinn, & Patterson (1983) tested 42 individuals on the ABLA and then retested them three months later. Results indicated that there were no changes in the pass/fail performance pattern from the first to the second testing for all testees. Also, because several different testers administered the tests during the two assessments, the study demonstrated very high intertester reliability. During the retest, testers were not informed of the results of the first test.

### Test Levels are Hierarchically Ordered in Difficulty

Research indicates that the six ABLA levels are hierarchically ordered in level of difficulty in the order listed in Table 1. For example, Kerr et al. (1977) found that 111 out of a total of 117 participants who passed a given level on the ABLA test were able to pass at lower levels in the hierarchy, but failed at higher levels. Similarly, of a total of 135 individuals assessed by Martin et al. (1983), only 2 deviated from the hierarchical pattern. Casey and Kerr (1977) demonstrated the hierarchical order of acquisition with typically developing children, with ABLA Level 4 developing at approximately 17 to 18 months of age, and ABLA Levels 5 and 6 (auditory discriminations) developing at 27 to 32 months of age. The latter finding corresponds with the age at which children typically experience a rapid growth in speech production. Lastly, Kerr and Meyerson (1977) and Wacker (1981) confirmed the hierarchy with individuals who were hearing impaired, and had multiple handicaps. The tests were administered in the same format, with the exception that signs replaced the verbal requests that are presented at ABLA Levels 5 and 6.

### Failed Levels are Difficult to Teach

Typically, individuals pass or fail a given level on the ABLA test in fewer than 30 test trials (Kerr et al., 1977). Research indicates that failed levels are difficult to teach using standard reinforcement and prompting procedures which usually consist of the following components: a reinforcer preference assessment to determine preferred items; a demonstration, a guided trial, and a practice trial with sample-comparison relations prior to the beginning of each session; extra-stimulus prompt-fading; positive reinforcement (praise and edibles) contingent upon correct responses; and the implementation of a correction procedure (a demonstration, a guided trial, and an opportunity to respond independently) following an error. Research suggests that, after 100 to 900 training trials, using standard prompting and reinforcement procedures, individuals typically are not able to perform a failed level (e.g., Meyerson, 1977; Witt & Wacker, 1981; Yu & Martin, 1986). However, several studies (e.g., Conyers et al., 2000; Hazen, Szendrei, & Martin, 1989; Yu & Martin, 1986) have shown that failed ABLA levels and other tasks requiring similar discriminations can be rapidly taught using a training package that consists of components such as reinforcer preference testing, within-stimulus prompt-fading, error interruption, and direct-response reinforcement.

## The ABLA Has Predictive Validity for Performance on Other Tasks

Research findings suggest that the ABLA test is highly predictive of the ease or difficulty with which an individual is able to perform academic, prevocational, and vocational tasks (e.g., Stubbings & Martin, 1995, 1998; Tharinger, Schallert, & Kerr, 1977; Wacker, Kerr, & Carroll, 1983; Wacker, Steil, & Greenbaum, 1983; Witt & Wacker, 1981). Tharinger et al. (1977) tested 11 children, 4 to 11 years of age, on the ABLA test and on a series of educational training tasks. Results indicated that in 83% of cases, children passed only those training tasks that required a discrimination level that was passed on the ABLA assessment. Likewise, Wacker, Kerr, et al. examined whether the ABLA test predicted participants' abilities to perform two-choice and four-choice vocational tasks. Results on the ABLA predicted performance on the analogue tasks for 11 of 12 participants.

## The ABLA Is a Better Predictor of Individuals' Learning Performance Than Experienced Staff with Direct Knowledge of The Individuals

When the ABLA test is recommended to direct-care staff as a tool to assess an individual's ability to perform different tasks, a question is often raised. Considering that it takes approximately 30 minutes to administer the ABLA, do the results add anything to what an experienced teacher or rehabilitation worker would have learned after multiple interactions during training sessions with an individual? Stubbings and Martin (1998) attempted to address this question. They compared three sets of predictions concerning the ability of 18 individuals with severe or moderate developmental disabilities to learn 12 training tasks. Predictions were made by: (a) experienced qualified instructors who had worked with the individuals for at least eight months; (b) experienced qualified instructors who did not know the individuals personally, but were able to interact with them for 30 minutes; and (c) predictions based on the ABLA test. Using standard reinforcement and prompting procedures, individuals were tested on each of the 12 tasks, until the ABLA passing or failing criterion occurred. The ABLA test was statistically significantly more accurate at predicting individual performance than either group of experienced staff.

## The ABLA Has Concurrent Validity with Language and Reading Assessments

Research indicates that an individual's performance on the ABLA test is related to his or her receptive and expressive language skills. For example, Casey and Kerr (1977) showed that 42 typically developing children (aged 13 to 35 months), within age-matched groups (5-month blocks) who passed up to ABLA Level 6 had significantly higher scores on a vocabulary sample, mean length of utterance, and longest utterance, than age-matched children who were not able to pass Level 6. Meyerson (1977) found that 52 children with developmental disabilities who failed ABLA Levels 5 and 6 also failed the Distar Reading Readiness test; whereas, those individuals who passed these levels were able to pass the reading test. Ward and Yu (2000) reported that individuals with developmental disabilities who were unable to pass Levels 5 and 6 of the ABLA were identified as communicating with single words or less; whereas, individuals who passed these auditory levels were able to combine two or more words in phrases and sentences. In a similar vein, Barker-Collo, Jamieson, and Boo (1995) assessed 40 individuals with developmental disabilities on the ABLA test, the communication portion of the Vineland Adaptive Behavior Scales (Sparrow, Balla, & Cicchetti, 1984) and the Communication Status Survey (Barker-Collo et al., 1995). Results indicated that the ABLA was significantly correlated with Vineland scores of receptive and expressive communication, and aspects of communication as measured by the Communication Status Survey. Results of Barker-Collo et al. were essentially replicated by Vause, Martin, and Yu (2000). Recently, Richards, Williams, and Follette (2002) also reported significant positive correlations between the ABLA test and Vineland communication, daily living, and social skills subdomains (Sparrow et al., 1984). Moreover, they found that the Vineland and the WAIS-R failed to differentiate individuals below ABLA Level 6 in that participants who scored below ABLA Level 6 were untestable on the WAIS-R and showed low age equivalent scores with limited range on the Vineland.

## Mismatching of ABLA Test Level of Participants to ABLA Difficulty of Training Tasks Causes Aberrant Behavior

As indicated previously, attempting to teach an individual a task using standard reinforcement and prompting procedures that is above his or her ABLA level will likely result in unproductive training time, as 100 or more trials are likely to be implemented with the individual showing little or no progress (Stubbings & Martin, 1998). An additional concern is the possibility that mismatching the learning abilities of participants to the difficulty level of training tasks could result in aberrant behavior on the part of the participant. Vause, Martin, and Yu (1999) employed a single-subject alternating treatments design to study aberrant behavior (e.g., repetitive movements, inattentiveness, grabbing task materials, etc.) of 3 individuals with developmental disabilities when they were presented with: (a) tasks at their highest passed ABLA level, (b) tasks above their highest passed ABLA level, and (c) tasks below their highest passed ABLA level. Results indicated that, for all participants, there was a higher frequency of aberrant responses, during one-to-one training sessions, when training tasks were above or below their highest passed level, as compared to when tasks were at their highest passed level. In addition, aberrant behaviors generalized to a second training setting. Similarly, a second study, conducted by Vause, Martin, Cornick, et al. (2000) indicated that 9 out of 13 participants with developmental disabilities, in a group training setting, had higher frequencies of aberrant behavior when tasks were mismatched to their ABLA levels.

## Direct-Care Staff with No Knowledge of the ABLA Test Often Mismatch the ABLA Test Level of Individuals and the ABLA Difficulty Level of Training Tasks

Considering that research indicates that mismatching tasks to the learning ability of individuals results in more aberrant behavior, an important question to ask is: How often does this occur by direct-care staff who have no knowledge of the ABLA test? DeWiele and Martin (1996) studied 54 individuals who were randomly selected from 540 residents at a large residential training facility for persons with intellectual disabilities. Of those individuals who were testable, 40% passed ABLA Level 6. However, 85% of the 133 training tasks typically presented to these individuals required only an ABLA Level 3 discrimination. In another study, Vause, Martin, Cornick, et al. (2000) monitored the training tasks that were presented to 13 individuals with intellectual disabilities in three adult training classrooms at a training facility (different from the one in DeWiele and Martin's study). Across 10 training sessions, 83% of tasks were mismatched to participants' ABLA levels. Similar to the findings of DeWiele and Martin, of the tasks that were mismatched, 87% required only a discrimination level that was below the highest passed ABLA level of participants.

## Recent Research and Future Directions

### Can the ABLA Test Be Used for Selecting the Optimal Stimulus Modality for Presenting Choices?

There is increasing recognition that the opportunity to make choices is important for improving the quality of life of persons with intellectual disabilities (Wehmeyer & Schwartz, 1998) and there is ample research to show that persons with severe disabilities can express their preferences through direct systematic assessment (e.g., Green, Reid, Canipe, & Gardner, 1991; Lohrman-O'Rourke & Browder, 1998; Wacker, Berg, Wiggins, Muldoon, & Cavanaugh, 1985). A number of studies have compared the sensitivity and efficiency of multiple versus single stimulus presentation methods (DeLeon & Iwata, 1996; Fisher et al., 1992; Fisher, Thompson, Piazza, Crosland, & Gotjen, 1997; Pace, Ivancic, Edwards, Iwata, & Page, 1985), but there is little research on optimal stimulus modalities for presenting choices. Some individuals may be able to reliably choose preferred items after hearing a spoken description of the options, some may need to view pictures of the options in order to make a meaningful choice, and others may make reliable choices only when the actual options are presented. Is there a way to reliably predict which choice presentation method (actual options, pictures of options, vocal description of options) would be most appropriate for individuals based on an assessment of their discrimination skills? We recently addressed this question.

We first identified 9 individuals with intellectual disabilities, 3 who had passed ABLA Level 3 and failed higher levels, 3 who had passed ABLA Level 4 and failed higher levels, and 3 who had passed ABLA Level 6. Choices between a high preference item and a low preference item were then presented to participants using a two-choice format (Fisher et al., 1992). Each pair of items, selected based on a prior preference assessment, was presented to each participant in three conditions (actual items, pictures of the items, and spoken name presentation) using a reversal design. The evaluation was conducted using food items, and was then repeated using non-food items. We predicted that participants who functioned at ABLA Level 3 would reliably select their preferred items consistently only when the actual objects were used as choice options, that participants who passed ABLA Level 4 would reliably select their preferred items in the object and picture phases, but not when spoken cues were used, and that participants who passed ABLA Level 6 would reliably select their preferred items consistently under all three conditions. Ninety-four percent of our predictions were confirmed and the results could not have been predicted by the participant's levels of mental retardation (Conyers et al., 2002). These findings were replicated in a study of preferences for food items by Schwartzman, Yu, and Martin (2003). The results suggest that the ABLA test is a useful tool to help determine the appropriate stimulus modality in preference assessment or choice presentation for persons with profound, severe and moderate mental retardation.

*Future directions.* While providing an individual with a choice of two stimuli is an effective method for assessing preferences for stimuli that can be easily presented (such as specific food items), that method may not be practical for comparing preferences between less manipulable objects (e.g., a television set versus a treadmill), nor between protracted leisure activities (e.g., going for a walk versus bowling). Can the ABLA test predict the optimal choice presentation method for preference assessments of protracted activities? Future research needs to address this question.

## Should a New Level Be Added to the ABLA Test to Replace Level 5?

Kerr et al. (1977) originally included Level 5, an auditory discrimination, in the ABLA test. However, in six studies (DeWiele & Martin, 1996; Kerr et al., 1977; Lin, Martin, & Collo, 1995; Martin et al., 1983; Stubbings & Martin, 1998; Walker, Lin, & Martin, 1994) involving 197 participants who passed Level 5, 96% of those participants also passed Level 6. Is there another task that might be more informative than, and therefore replace, Level 5? We recently addressed this question.

ABLA Level 4 is a visual-visual quasi-identity matching task. We recently examined a prototype visual-visual nonidentity matching (VVNM) task for its relationship to the ABLA test (Sakko, Martin, Vause, Martin, & Yu, in press). The task used the two containers of the ABLA test. It required a participant to match a silver colored piece of wood that was shaped into the word, "BOX", in capital letters, to the red box, and match a purple colored piece of wood that was shaped into the word, "Can", in upper case and lower case letters, to the yellow can. This task was administered in the same manner as the ABLA tasks to 23 participants with intellectual disabilities. Because, as indicated above, ABLA Level 5 was not considered informative, it was not assessed. The results suggest that VVNM is positioned in the ABLA hierarchy above Level 4, visual-visual quasi-identity matching, and below Level 6, an auditory-visual discrimination. Performance on the prototype VVNM task also demonstrated high predictive validity for performance on other VVNM tasks, and high test-retest reliability.

*Future directions.* Because of the small sample size, future research is needed with more participants to confirm the test-retest reliability and that VVNM falls between ABLA Levels 4 and 6. If the VVNM is to be added to the ABLA test, future research should also assess whether, like failed ABLA levels, a failed VVNM task is difficult to teach using standard prompting and reinforcement procedures.

## Are Additional Matching Discriminations Worthwhile Additions to the ABLA Test?

Are there additional tasks (i.e., levels) that are beyond Level 6, that might make the ABLA test useful for a greater number of individuals with intellectual disabilities? We recently addressed this question.

Considering that the ability to imitate sounds is one of the first expressive language skills that children acquire, and considering that the ability to recognize that two sounds are the same is a part of accurate vocal imitation, we examined two prototype auditory matching tasks for their relationship to each other and to the ABLA levels. An auditory-auditory identity matching (AAIM) prototype task requires a tester to say a word (e.g., "pen") on some trials and a different word (e.g., "block") on other trials, while one assistant says "pen" and a second assistant says "block". The assistants randomly alternate as to who says which word, and who speaks first. The participant must learn to point to the assistant who spoke the word that matched that of the tester. An auditory-auditory nonidentity matching (AANM) prototype task requires a tester to say "ball" on some trials and "ice" on other trials. Two assistants say either "field" or "rink". The participant must learn to point to the assistant who says "rink" when the tester says "ice" and to point to the assistant who says "field" when the tester says "ball". Our research (Harapiak, Martin, & Yu, 1999; Vause, Harapiak, Martin, & Yu, 2003; Vause, Martin, & Yu, 2000) indicates that: (a) AAIM is more difficult than ABLA Level 6, (b) AANM is more difficult than AAIM, and (c) performance on the AAIM and AANM prototype tasks has good predictive validity for performance on similar tasks.

Does the addition of the auditory matching tasks to the ABLA test increase its correlation with communication ability? Our research indicates that the answer is yes. In one of our studies, 40 persons with intellectual disabilities were assessed on the ABLA test, the auditory matching tasks, the Communication Status Survey (Barker-Collo et al., 1995), and the receptive and expressive subdomains of the Vineland (Sparrow et al., 1984). Using a forward-multiple regression analysis for individuals classified at or above ABLA Level 4, the addition of the AAIM and AANM tasks to the ABLA test significantly differentiated individual communicative ability to a greater extent than did the ABLA test alone (Vause, Martin, & Yu, 2000). These results suggest that the tests of auditory matching may be worthwhile additions to the ABLA test.

*Future directions.* Future research should examine if failed AAIM and AANM tasks, like failed ABLA levels, are difficult to teach using standard prompting and reinforcement procedures. In addition, additional research is needed to assess the test-retest reliability of these discriminations.

## Are ABLA Level 6 and the Auditory Matching Tasks Bridging Tasks for Echoics, Tacts, and Mands?

As indicated previously, research has demonstrated that performances on ABLA Level 6 and the auditory matching tasks are correlated with global measures of communication ability, such as scores of receptive and expressive communication of the Vineland Adaptive Behavior Scales (Sparrow et al., 1984). But what about the relationship between performance on the ABLA test and the auditory matching tasks and the ability to perform specific verbal operants (Skinner, 1957)? One of our studies addressed that topic (Marion et al., 2003). First, we developed a test of echoics, tacts, and mands. Next, we examined the performance of 38 persons with intellectual disabilities on the ABLA test, the prototype tests for AAIM and AANM, and the test of verbal operants. Our sample included: (a) 14 participants who passed up to and including either ABLA Levels 3 or 4, but failed ABLA Levels 5 and 6, AAIM, and AANM (referred to as the visual group); (b) 13 participants who passed up to and including ABLA Level 6, but failed AAIM and AANM (referred to as the auditory-visual group); and (c) 11 participants who passed all ABLA levels and the auditory matching tasks (referred to as the auditory-auditory group). It was found that: (a) discrimination skill (visual, auditory-visual, and auditory-auditory) was a better predictor of performance on the verbal operant assessments than level of functioning based on diagnosis; (b) individuals who passed the two auditory matching tasks performed better on the test of three verbal operants than those unable to pass the auditory matching tasks; and (c) individuals who passed ABLA Level 6 performed better on the test of the three verbal operants than those unable to perform this discrimination. The results also showed high test-retest reliability for the test of verbal operants. Finally, no hierarchical relationship was found among the three verbal operants.

*Future directions.* Future research might proceed in several directions. First, only 2% of the verbal assessments were passed by participants who failed ABLA Level 6, while 36% of the verbal assessments were passed by individuals who passed ABLA Level 6. Thus, further research is warranted to evaluate ABLA Level 6 as a possible bridging task for teaching echoics, tacts, and mands, to persons with intellectual disabilities.

Second, performance on the test of the three verbal operants may be different for participants who pass both AAIM and AANM than for participants who pass only AAIM. In the current study, 2 of the 11 participants in the auditory-auditory group passed AAIM and failed AANM, while the other 9 participants passed both auditory matching tasks. The 2 participants who passed only AAIM had lower scores on the test of verbal operants than the 9 participants who passed both AAIM and AANM. Is performance on the AAIM and AANM tasks differentially related to performance on the tests of verbal operants? Might the AAIM prototype task serve as a bridging task for teaching echoics, tacts, and mands? Future research is needed to assess these possibilities.

## Is ABLA Level 6 a Bridging Task for Learning Stimulus Equivalence?

A controversy exists in the literature as to whether individuals with minimal verbal repertoires are capable of demonstrating stimulus equivalence (e.g., compare Horne & Lowe, 1996 to Sidman, 2000). Studies that have examined whether individuals with minimal verbal repertoires are able to learn stimulus equivalence have used global measures of "minimal verbal repertoires" (e.g., see Carr, Wilkinson, Blackman, & McIlvane, 2000). In an attempt to more clearly specify the characteristics of "minimal verbal repertoire", we recently studied 5 participants with intellectual disabilities who failed the test of echoics, tacts, and mands mentioned previously (see Marion et al, 2003). Three of the five individuals passed ABLA Level 4, but failed ABLA Level 6 and the VVNM prototype task. Two of the five individuals passed ABLA Level 6 and the VVNM prototype task, but failed the AAIM and AANM prototype tasks. Thus, all individuals had minimal verbal repertoires and were fairly closely matched except for the measurement of discrimination skills specified previously. After approximately 2000 training trials, the 3 participants who passed only up to ABLA Level 4 were not able to learn the first taught relation, AB, that was prerequisite for stimulus equivalence. In contrast, the other 2 participants, who passed ABLA Level 6 and VVNM, learned the AB relation in approximately two thirds of the amount of training trials of the other participants, learned the BC relation, and demonstrated positive outcomes on equivalence tests comparable to those reported by Carr et al. (Vause, Martin, Yu, Marion & Sakko, in press).

*Future directions.* The results of the Vause, Martin, et al. (in press) study have several implications for future research. First, replication is needed with additional participants to convincingly demonstrate that performance on ABLA Level 6 and VVNM may be prerequisite to the learning of the arbitrary relations that are necessary to test for stimulus equivalence. Second, future studies concerned with the importance of "minimal verbal repertoires" for learning stimulus equivalence might capitalize on the test of echoics, tacts, and mands in order to more precisely describe the language repertoire of participants. Third, use of the ABLA test and the prototype tasks for VVNM, AAIM, and AANM as screening tools in future studies of stimulus equivalence with persons with intellectual disabilities might enable researchers to account for various discrepant findings, and to increase the generality of effects both within and across participants.

## Are the ABLA Test Results Applicable for Children with Autism Spectrum Disorders?

To date, only two published studies on the ABLA test have been conducted with children with autism spectrum disorders. Ward and Yu (2000) found that children with autism spectrum disorders showed consistent hierarchical relations among the ABLA discriminations, similar to that found with adults with intellectual disabilities, and their ability to make auditory discriminations was positively correlated with expressive communication. Cummings and Williams (2000) successfully taught 5 children with autism or PDD to perform identity matching involving three-dimensional objects (a Level 4 task on the ABLA test), matching pictures to objects, and then pictures to pictures. While 2 of the 5 children passed ABLA Level 4 at the beginning of training, the other 3 passed only up to ABLA Level 2. The training results are encouraging in that the children with autism and PDD readily learned the new discriminations, but also surprising for the 3 Level 2 children given the difficulty in teaching failed ABLA discriminations with persons with intellectual disabilities.

*Future directions.* Considering the paucity of ABLA studies for this population and the potential applicability of the ABLA test for training, future ABLA research with children with autism spectrum disorders is warranted.

## Does the ABLA Test Have Relevance for the Functional Assessment and Treatment of Noncompliance?

In a group study, Laforce and Feldman (2000) showed that discrimination ability as measured by the ABLA test interacted with instructional prompts to influence compliance. Specifically, they found that persons who showed auditory discriminations (Levels 5 and 6) responded to over 90% of instructions with or without visual prompts, whereas persons who showed visual discriminations (up to ABLA Level 4) responded to approximately 85% of instructions with visual prompts, but only 65% of the instructions without visual prompts. The prompt by discrimination ability interaction was statistically significant and could not have been explained by level of functioning alone. In addition to antecedents and consequences, the authors suggest that discrimination ability needs to be taken into account in conceptualizing cooperation.

*Future directions.* Research is needed to replicate the finding of LaForce and Feldman (2000). In addition, research is needed to investigate the functional relations between the characteristics of instructions and discrimination ability. Such research could have important implications for the functional assessment and treatment of noncompliance.

## Are the ABLA Test Results Applicable to Three-Choice Discriminations?

All of the ABLA tasks involve two-choice discriminations. In the study of stimulus equivalence, researchers have recommended the use of three-choice discriminations in order to yield unambiguous outcomes (e.g., Carrigan & Sidman, 1992; Sidman, 1987). Boelens (2002), however, argued that two-choice discriminations could yield meaningful results not available in a three-choice equivalence test.

*Future directions.* Regardless of the above debate, considering that many functional skills involve simultaneous discriminations among more than two stimuli, increasing the number of choice stimuli in ABLA research should add to our understanding of the relationship between two-choice discriminations, such as those represented by the ABLA tasks, and three-choice discriminations.

## Conclusions

Theoretically, it is possible to analyze all complex skills into a series of discriminations or stimulus control relations between task stimuli and responses. The ABLA test, including VVNM, AAIM, and AANM, represents only a few of these discriminations. Yet, the discriminations assessed by these prototype tasks have been shown to have considerable practical application for the assessment and training of persons with profound, severe, and moderate intellectual disabilities. Future research is likely to make an expanded ABLA test even more useful for researchers and practitioners.

## References

Barker-Collo, S., Jamieson, J., & Boo, F. (1995). Assessment of Basic Learning Abilities test: Prediction of communication ability in persons with developmental disabilities. *International Journal of Practical Approaches to Disability, 19*, 23-28.

Boelens, H. (2002). Studying stimulus equivalence: Defense of the two-choice procedure. *The Psychological Record, 52*, 305-314.

Carr, D., Wilkinson, K. M., Blackman, D., & McIlvane, W. J. (2000). Equivalence classes in individuals with minimal verbal repertoires. *Journal of the Experimental Analysis of Behavior, 74*, 101-114.

Carrigan, P. F., Jr., & Sidman, M. (1992). Conditional discrimination and equivalence relations: A theoretical analysis of control by negative stimuli. *Journal of the Experimental Analysis of Behavior, 58*, 183-204.

Casey, L., & Kerr, N. (1977). Auditory-visual discrimination and language prediction. *Rehabilitation Psychology, 24 (Monograph Issue)*, 137-155.

Conyers, C., Doole, A., Vause, T., Harapiak, S., Yu, D. C. T., & Martin, G. L. (2002). Predicting the relative efficacy of three presentation methods for assessing preferences of persons with developmental disabilities. *Journal of Applied Behavior Analysis, 35*, 49-58.

Conyers, C. J., Martin, G. L., Yu, D. C. T., & Vause, T. (2000). Rapid teaching of a two-choice auditory-visual discrimination to persons with developmental disabilities. *Journal on Developmental Disabilities, 7*(2), 84-92.

Cummings, A. R., & Williams, W. L. (2000). Visual identity matching and vocal imitation training with children with autism: A surprising finding. *Journal on Developmental Disabilities, 7(2)*, 109-122.

DeLeon, I. G., & Iwata, B. A. (1996). Evaluation of a multiple-stimulus presentation format for assessing reinforcer preferences. *Journal of Applied Behavior Analysis, 29*, 519-533.

DeWiele, L. A., & Martin, G. L. (1996). Can the ABLA test help staff match training tasks to the abilities of developmentally disabled trainees? *International Journal of Practical Approaches to Disability, 20*, 7-11.

Fisher, W. W., Piazza, C. C., Bowman, L. G., Hagopian, L. P., Owens, J. C., & Slevin, I. (1992). A comparison of two approaches for identifying reinforcers for persons with severe and profound disabilities. *Journal of Applied Behavior Analysis, 25*, 491-498.

Fisher, W. W., Thompson, R. H., Piazza, C. C., Crosland, K., & Gotjen, D. (1997). On the relative reinforcing effects of choice and differential consequence. *Journal of Applied Behavior Analysis, 30,* 423- 438.

Green, C. W., Reid, D. H., Canipe, V. S., & Gardner, S. M. (1991). A comprehensive evaluation of reinforcer identification processes for persons with profound multiple handicaps. *Journal of Applied Behavior Analysis, 24,* 537-552.

Harapiak, S., Martin, G. L., & Yu, D. (1999). Hierarchical ordering of auditory discriminations and the Assessment of Basic Learning Abilities test. *Journal on Developmental Disabilities, 6,* 32-50.

Hazen, A., Szendrei, V., & Martin, G. L. (1989). The AVC discrimination test: A valuable tool for teachers of developmentally disabled persons. *Journal of Practical Approaches to Developmental Handicap, 13*(1), 7-13.

Horne, P. J., & Lowe, C. F. (1996). On the origins of naming and symbolic behavior. *Journal of the Experimental Analysis of Behavior, 65,* 185-241.

Kerr, N. & Meyerson, L. (1977). Further evidence on ordering, generalization, and prediction from the AVC scales: AVC skills in deaf retarded adults. *Rehabilitation Psychology, 24* (Monograph Issue), 127-131.

Kerr, N., Meyerson, L., & Flora, J. A. (1977). The measurement of motor, visual, and auditory discrimination skills. *Rehabilitation Psychology, 24* (Monograph issue), 95-112.

Laforce, J. C., & Feldman, M. A. (2000). Role of discriminations ability in the cooperative behaviour of persons with developmental disabilities. *Journal on Developmental Disabilities, 7*(2), 156-170.

Lin, Y. H., Martin, G. L., & Collo, S. (1995). Prediction of auditory matching performance of developmentally handicapped individuals. *Developmental Disabilities Bulletin, 23,* 1-15.

Lohrmann-O'Rouke, S., & Browder, D. M. (1998). Empirically based methods to assess preferences of individuals with severe disabilities. *American Journal on Mental Retardation, 103,* 146-161.

Marion, C., Vause, T., Harapiak, S., Martin, G. L., Yu, C. T., Sakko, G., & Walters, K. (2003). The hierarchical relationship between several visual and auditory discriminations and three verbal operants among individuals with developmental disabilities. *The Analysis of Verbal Behavior, 19,* 91-105.

Martin, G. L., Yu, D., Quinn, G., & Patterson, S. (1983). Measurement and training of AVC discrimination skills: Independent confirmation and extension. *Rehabilitation Psychology, 28,* 231-237.

Meyerson, L. (1977). AVC behavior and attempts to modify it. *Rehabilitation Psychology, 24* (Monograph Issue), 119-122.

Pace, G. M., Ivancic, M. T., Edwards, G. L., Iwata, B. A., & Page, T. J. (1985). Assessment of stimulus preference and reinforcer value with profoundly retarded individuals. *Journal of Applied Behavior Analysis, 18,* 249-255.

Richards, D. F., Williams, W. L., & Follette, W. C. (2002). Two new empirically derived reasons to use the Assessment of Basic Learning Abilities. *American Journal on Mental Retardation, 107,* 329-339.

Sakko, G., Martin, T. L., Vause, T., Martin, G. L., & Yu, C. T. (in press). A visual-visual nonidentity matching assessment is a worthwhile addition to the Assessment of Basic Learning Abilities test. *American Journal on Mental Retardation.*

Schwartzman, L., Yu, D. C. T., & Martin, G. L. (2003). Choice responding as a function of choice presentation method and level of preference in persons with developmental disabilities. *International Journal of Disability, Community, and Rehabilitation, 1*(3), 1-7.

Sidman, M. (1987). Two choices are not enough. *Behavior Analysis, 22,* 11-18.

Sidman, M. (2000). Equivalence relations and the reinforcement contingency. *Journal of the Experimental Analysis of Behavior, 74,* 127-146.

Skinner, B. F. (1957). *Verbal behavior.* Englewood Cliffs, NJ: Prentice-Hall.

Sparrow, S., Balla, D., & Ceccetti, D. (1984). *Vineland adaptive behavior scales.* Circle Pines, MN: American Guidance Service.

Stubbings, V., & Martin, G. L. (1995). The ABLA test for predicting performance of developmentally disabled persons on prevocational training tasks. *International Journal of Practical Approaches to Disability, 19,* 12-17.

Stubbings, V., & Martin, G. L. (1998). Matching training tasks to abilities of people with mental retardation: A learning test versus experienced staff. *American Journal on Mental Retardation, 102,* 473-484.

Tharinger, D., Schallert, D., & Kerr, N. (1977). Use of AVC tasks to predict classroom learning in mentally retarded children. *Rehabilitation Psychology, 24,* 113-118.

Vause, T., Harapiak, S., Martin, G. L., & Yu, C. T. (2003). Assessment of the predictive validity of prototype auditory matching tasks. *Journal on Developmental Disabilities, 10,* 21-34.

Vause, T., Martin, G. L., Cornick, A., Harapiak, S., Chong, I., Yu, D. C. T., & Garinger, J. (2000). Training task assignments and aberrant behavior of persons with developmental disabilities. *Journal on Developmental Disabilities, 7*(2), 37-53.

Vause, T., Martin, G. L., & Yu, D. (1999). Aberrant behavior of persons with developmental disabilities as a function of the characteristics of training tasks. *International Journal of Rehabilitation Research, 22,* 321-325.

Vause, T., Martin, G. L., & Yu, D. (2000). ABLA test performance, auditory matching, and communication ability. *Journal on Developmental Disabilities, 7(2),* 123-141.

Vause, T., Martin, G. L., Yu, D., Marion, C., & Sakko, G. (in press). Teaching equivalence relations to individuals with minimal verbal repertoires: Are visual and auditory-visual discriminations predictive of stimulus equivalence? *The Psychological Record.*

Wacker, D. P. (1981). Applicability of a discrimination assessment procedure with hearing impaired mentally handicapped clients. *Journal of the Association for the Severely Handicapped, 6,* 51-58.

Wacker, D. P., Berg, W. K., Wiggins, B., Muldoon, M., & Cavanaugh, J. (1985). Evaluation of reinforcer preferences for profoundly handicapped students. *Journal of Applied Behavior Analysis, 18,* 173-178.

Wacker, D. P., Kerr, N. J., & Carroll, J. L. (1983). Discrimination skill as a predictor of prevocational performance of institutionalized mentally retarded children. *Rehabilitation Psychology, 28,* 45-59.

Wacker, D. P., Steil, D. A., & Greenebaum, F. T. (1983). Assessment of discrimination skills of multiply-handicapped preschoolers and prediction of classroom task performance. *Journal of the Association for the Severely Handicapped, 8,* 65-78.

Walker, J. G., Lin, Y. H., & Martin, G. L. (1994). Auditory matching skills and the Assessment of Basic Learning Abilities test: Where do they fit? *Developmental Disabilities Bulletin, 22,* 16-26.

Ward, R., & Yu, D. C. T. (2000). Bridging the gap between visual and auditory discrimination learning in children with autism and severe developmental disabilities. *Journal on Developmental Disabilities, 7*(2), 142-155.

Wehmeyer, M., & Schwartz, M. (1998). The relationship between self-determination and quality of life for individuals with mental retardation. *Education and Training in Mental Retardation and Developmental Disabilities, 33,* 3-12.

Witt, J. C., & Wacker, D. P. (1981). Teaching children to respond to auditory directives: An evaluation of two procedures. *Behavior Research of Severe Developmental Disabilities, 2,* 175-189.

Yu, D., & Martin, G. L. (1986). Comparison of two procedures to teach visual discriminations to severely handicapped persons. *Journal of Practical Approaches to Developmental Handicap, 10,* 7-12.

Yu, D., Martin, G. L., & Williams, L. (1989). Expanded assessment of discrimination learning with the developmentally handicapped: A practical strategy for research and training. *American Journal on Mental Retardation, 94,* 161-169.

## Footnotes

Research described in this chapter was supported by grants MOP6353 and MOP36433 from the Canadian Institutes of Health Research. The St. Amant Centre Research Program is supported by the St. Amant Foundation, St. Boniface General Hospital Research Centre, and the Faculty of Nursing, University of Manitoba. For reprints, write to Dr. Garry L. Martin, University of Manitoba, 129 St. Paul's College, 70 Dysart Road, Winnipeg, Manitoba, Canada R3T 2M6, e-mail: gmartin@cc.umanitoba.ca; or Dr. C. T. Yu, Director of Research, St. Amant Centre, 440 River Road, Winnipeg, Manitoba R2M 3Z8, e-mail: yu@stamant.mb.ca.

# Chapter 8

# Autism

### Ruth Anne Rehfeldt and Anthony J. Cuvo
*Southern Illinois University*

Twenty years ago the word autism had a very different meaning among the common public than it does today. Many laypersons were unfamiliar with the term. For those who were familiar, the word often inspired images of once normal children who became deeply disturbed emotionally and retreated deep within the depths of their own body to avoid the overwhelming stimulation of the world around them. Indeed, professionals often regarded autism with the same mystery and intrigue with which they approached schizophrenia and other perplexing psychotic disorders, often attributing a child's bizarre behaviors to a cold and uncaring mother. Fortunately, the reality of the disorder is clearer to laypersons and professionals today. Earlier conceptualizations of disturbed children trapped within malfunctioning bodies have subsided.

Although the conceptualization of autism has become more apparent, many unanswered questions concerning its etiology persist. Likewise, many controversies surrounding effective treatment plague parents and professionals alike. Fortunately, the past decade has seen the expenditure of tremendous efforts toward the identification of causal variables. Well researched diagnostic instruments are now widely used that can detect autism at relatively young ages. Accumulating evidence suggests that applied behavior analysis is effective in overcoming deficits associated with the disorder, and evidence confirming that some other treatments are not effective is also mounting. Thus, much progress has been made within a relatively short time period toward a realization of the cause, course, assessment, and treatment, of the disorder.

The purposes of this chapter are to (a) define autism and its associated characteristics, (b) describe recent advances in etiological research, (c) discuss the diagnosis and assessment of the disorder, (d) illustrate effective treatment for the disorder, and (e) depict efforts in assessment and intervention that are currently underway in southern Illinois.

## Definition and Classification

### Primary Characteristics

Autism is one of five disorders categorized as a Pervasive Developmental Disorder in the *Diagnostic and Statistical Manual of Mental Disorder* (DSM-IV-TR) (American Psychiatric Association, 2000). All pervasive developmental disorders are characterized by deficits in language and communication and impaired social functioning. Autism is considered to be the most common pervasive developmental disorder, with anywhere from 2-6 individuals per 1,000 individuals having it (Centers for Disease Control and Prevention, 2001). Pervasive developmental disorders including autism are conceptualized as developmental disabilities, meaning that the condition is chronic and an individual with the disorder will have a lifelong need for supports.

The characteristics of autistic disorder, as outlined by the American Psychiatric Association (2000), are as follows: (a) Impaired social interactions. An individual with autism may display deficits in the use of nonverbal behavior such as eye contact, facial expression, and posture. They may also fail to establish developmentally appropriate peer relationships, and show a lack of emotional reciprocity. (b) Impaired communication abilities. This may include a delay in or a complete lack of development of expressive speech, difficulties sustaining or initiating conversation with others, stereotyped or repetitive use of language, or a lack of developmentally appropriate play. (c) Stereotyped interests and activities. An individual with autism may be unusually preoccupied with one or more areas of interest, they may adhere to nonfunctional rituals or routines or display repetitive motor movements such as hand-flapping. The DSM-IV-TR further specifies that the deficits in language and communication, social skills, and imaginative play must have their onset prior to age three. Autism and the other pervasive developmental disorders are considered to be spectrum disorders, because the characteristics can be mild to severe and can appear in a variety of combinations. Some children with autism are educated alongside their peers without disabilities and may achieve independent living and employment as adults. Other children with autism are educated in special education classrooms and require extensive residential services as adults.

## Associated Characteristics

There are a number of secondary characteristics associated with autism that may or may not all be present in a given individual and that may range from being mild to severe. Common associated characteristics include an adherence to a specific routine or schedule; strong visual-motor skills that often surpass the individual's overall intellectual functioning; challenging behaviors such as self-stimulation, self-injury, aggression, or noncompliance; savant skills, or skills that are advanced relative to the individual's overall level of intellectual functioning; and distractibility (Smith, Belcher, & Juhrs, 1995). Many children with autism also experience sleep difficulties, food preferences and aversions, and gastrointestinal ailments.

## Course

The diagnostic criteria for autism states that deficits in either language and communication, social skills, or imaginative play must have their onset prior to the age of three. Some parents report that their child underwent a "regression," or a period of seemingly normal development followed by a deterioration of skills. The symptoms of autism change with age and developmental level. Children often make gains in social skills during childhood and adolescence. Lord (1984) suggested that as children with autism develop, they transition from being "aloof" to becoming "passive but responsive," and to ultimately becoming "active but odd" (see also Wing & Gould, 1979). Some individuals develop challenging behaviors that may worsen during the adolescent years. Thirty percent of all individuals with autism show evidence of increased aggression during adolescence, which may or may not continue into adulthood (Gillberg, 1984). Increased aggression during adolescence may be due to the development of seizures during this period, as well as to the development of comorbid psychiatric conditions such as depression and anxiety. Despite the growing availability of specialized supports (see Rehfeldt, in press), only a small percentage of individuals with autism live and work independently in adulthood. One third of all individuals achieve partial independence (American Psychiatric Association, 2000).

## Comorbid Conditions

Approximately 70% of all individuals with autism also meet the criteria for the condition of mental retardation, typically in the moderate range (Sigman, Ungerer, Mundy, & Sherman, 1987). Several other medical and psychological conditions have been reported to occur comorbidly: Twenty-five percent of individuals with autism experience some sort of seizure disorder (Volkmar, Klin, & Cohen, 1997), while smaller proportions (8.1%) experience other medical conditions, including fragile X syndrome, bilateral deafness, cerebral palsy, multiple congenital abnormalities, and other chromosomal abnormalities (Dykens & Volkmar, 1997; Rutter, Bailey, Bolton, & Le Couteur, 1993). Tuberous sclerosis occurs at a rate of between 0.4% and 2.8%, a frequency higher than that of the general population (Dykens & Volkmar, 1997; see also Smalley, Tanguay, Smith, & Gutierrez, 1992).

Because the characteristics of autism overlap with those of other disorders, it is not surprising to find that some individuals with autism have been dually diagnosed with Tourette's syndrome, obsessive-compulsive disorder, or Attention Deficit and Hyperactivity Disorder. Affective disorders such as depression and anxiety are also relatively common (see Wing, 1992). Depression is particularly common among more cognitively-able adults, who have experienced years of failed relationships and social rejection. Psychotic disorders such as schizophrenia are less common. It is important that individuals with autism be treated for their primary condition, and that professionals carefully consider the advantages of a second diagnosis.

## Epidemiology

The prevalence of autism has increased in recent years, to the point where concern is sometimes expressed that the disorder is becoming an epidemic. Epidemiological studies conducted in the United States have shown prevalence estimates to be at least twice as high in the past ten years as those reported for previous decades (Bryson, 1997). Prior to 1985, the estimated prevalence was 4-5 per 10,000, but today the estimated prevalence is in the range of 10-12 per 10,000. Various states have conducted epidemiological studies of their own. Eighteen percent of children diagnosed with mental retardation born between 1983-1985 and 1993-1995 in

California also displayed characteristics of autism (Report to the Legislature, M.I.N.D. Institute, 2002). Thirty-four children per 10,000 were recently found to have autism spectrum disorders in metropolitan Atlanta (Yeargin-Allsopp et al., 2003). In Rhode Island, the number of school-age children with autism has increased by 1,115% between 1994 and 2002 (Yazbak, 2002). Autism appears to be more common in males, but the ratio of males to females differs depending on how autism is defined: The ratio of males to females is 4:1 for classic cases of autism (50-70 IQ range), but 2:1 for those functioning intellectually in the lower extreme, and greater than 4:1 for those functioning intellectually in the higher extreme (see Bryson, 1997).

The increase in prevalence estimates has been speculatively attributed to increases in population growth and in-migration. It seems more plausible that the higher prevalence estimates reflect changes in diagnostic criteria and definition. Classic autism was originally defined by an IQ range of 50-70, but today the definition has been broadened to include individuals functioning at the lower and higher extremes. It is possible that more cognitively impaired and cognitively able individuals were not included in earlier estimates. In addition, improved methods for identifying individuals with autism have become more available (see Fombonne, 2003).

## Etiology

The occurrence of autism is not correlated with a particular parenting style, socioeconomic status, race, or cultural background. Research efforts are largely focused upon the identification of an underlying neurological or genetic abnormality. In addition, much controversy has been generated by the supposition that the measles, mumps, and rubella vaccination and candida infection cause autism.

## CNS Dysfunction

It is generally accepted that some sort of neurological abnormality underlies autism, but a consensus has yet to be reached as to what that abnormality is. Some studies have shown that individuals with autism show right-hemisphere dominance, particularly during motor imitation and language tasks (Dawson, Warrenburg, & Fuller, 1982, 1983). People with autism show evoked potentials in response to novel stimuli but further processing of those stimuli has been reported to be deficient (Dawson & Lewey, 1989). A number of studies have identified elevated peripheral levels of serotonin (see Volkmar & Anderson, 1989).

## Genetic Mechanisms

Without a doubt genes contribute to the expression of autism, but their effects are not entirely understood to date. Small numbers of individuals with autism have also been shown to have certain genetic diseases such as Fragile X syndrome, tuberous sclerosis, and phenylketonuria, suggesting a genetic link. Siblings of individuals with autism have an approximately 3% chance of having autism themselves, a risk that is 50 times greater than the risk for the general population (Herbert, Sharp, & Gaudiano, 2002). If one member of a monozygotic twin has autism, however, the other member has only a 36% chance of developing the disorder (100% concordance would be expected if genetic factors were acting alone) (Trottier, Srivastava, & Walker, 1999). Research is currently examining the role of a gene known as HOXA1, which resides on chromosome 7. Variant alleles of this gene are present in 20% of individuals without autism and 40% of individuals with autism (Rodier, 2000). Thus, the presence of this gene doubles the likelihood that an individual will display characteristics of autism.

Certain teratogens have been shown to increase the likelihood of autism, including maternal rubella and exposure to ethanol and thalidomide (Rodier, 2000). At present, this body of findings suggest that genes may give rise to a susceptibility to insult by some environmental factor.

## MMR Vaccination

Recently there has been much debate that the measles portion of the measles, mumps, and rubella vaccine causes autism, in light of the fact that the vaccine is given during the first few years of life when the symptoms of autism typically occur. A widescale study conducted in Denmark that assessed all children born between January of 1991 through December of 1998 showed that children who received the vaccine were not at any greater risk for developing autism than were children who did not receive the vaccine. In addition, no relationships were observed between the onset of autism and the child's age at the time of vaccination, the time elapsed since the vaccination, or the date of vaccination (Madsen et al., 2002).

## Candida Infection

Candida is a fungus that occurs naturally in the body. Infection occurs when the fungus is overproduced. Case studies showed that children with candida infection later developed autism, and, moreover, showed improved skill functioning when treated for the infection (Rimland, 1988). To date, any evidence suggesting a link between the yeast infection and autism is merely anecdotal and stems largely from parental reports.

## Assessment and Diagnosis

A reliable diagnosis of autism can be made at approximately 30 months, and the disorder can be screened as early as 18 months (Gillberg & Ehlers, 1996). The average age of diagnosis is currently four. It is important that a reliable diagnosis be obtained at an early age so that effective treatment can be implemented as soon possible. Research has also shown that early diagnoses are correlated with better outcomes. A number of issues often complicate the assessment process. First, many assessment instruments involve tasks that require the use of receptive and expressive language, making it difficult for many children with autism to perform the required tasks. Second, diagnostic instruments have historically been most accurate in detecting the disorder in individuals with mild-to-moderate mental retardation; findings are more difficult to interpret in individuals falling outside of this range (Lord & Rutter, 1994). Third, characteristics of autism are similar to characteristics of other disorders, such as mental retardation and hearing impairments. These barriers have led Lord (1991) to call for more standardized protocols designed exclusively for individuals with autism. Lord (1997) also suggests that diagnostic instruments that rely on direct observations and parent or teacher ratings are ideal.

The assessment process is usually initiated by a child's pediatrician, who conducts a thorough developmental screening. If the child has not reached certain developmental milestones, the pediatrician is likely to refer the child and his or her family to a multidisciplinary team of professionals for further evaluation. Other medical tests may be ordered to rule out other conditions. Because the pediatrician is often the first step, it is crucial that he or she be familiar with autism symptomatology. Some reports suggest that medical professionals are not well-trained in the characteristics of the disorder. Shah (2001) showed that first-year and fourth-year medical students were similarly deficient in their abilities to recognize possible causes, IQ profiles, prognosis, and treatments for autism. Likewise, Stone (1988) found that professionals from several disciplines including pediatrics had a number of misconceptions regarding the social, emotional, and cognitive aspects of the disorder. These findings suggest that the diagnosis and treatment of autism warrants greater emphasis in medical school curricula.

A multidisciplinary team typically consists of professionals from such disciplines as neurology, pediatrics, speech-language pathology, physical and occupational therapy, psychology, audiology, and social work. Multidisciplinary team assessment often includes evaluations of cognitive functioning, adaptive behavior, communication skills, motor skills, play and leisure skills, and challenging behaviors. It is important that parents have an active role in the assessment process. It is also important that the clinicians involved in the assessment be well-trained in evaluating children with cognitive deficits and language delays. The clinician should have prior knowledge of effective reinforcers for a particular child, so that the child can be reinforced for attention and compliance during the evaluation. The test session should be characterized by a smooth transition from one task to the next, and challenging tasks should be interspersed within easier tasks so as to sustain the child's interest and prevent frustration (Sparrow et al., 1997).

## Checklists and Rating Scales

A number of questionnaires, checklists, and rating scales are widely used in the assessment and diagnosis of autism. Such instruments, often to be completed by parents or teachers, can also be conveniently used as screening instruments. The Childhood Autism Rating Scale (CARS) (Schopler, Reichler, & Renner, 1988) and the Autism Behavior Checklist (ABC) (Krug, Arick, & Almond, 1993) are two popular instruments. The CARS is a 15-item rating scale that distinguishes children with autism from children with other developmental disabilities. A total score is computed by summing the individual ratings on each of the 15 items. The CARS is easy and convenient to use but some prior knowledge of typical child development is necessary. Several studies have shown the CARS to have good internal consistency (e.g., Schopler et al., 1988; Sturmey, Matson, & Sevin, 1992), and it has been shown to reliably discriminate between children with and without autism (DeLalla & Rogers, 1994).

The ABC is a checklist of non-adaptive behaviors which is completed by circling the numerals following the characteristics that accurately describe the person being rated. A total score is computed by summing the numerals corresponding to each behavior. The ABC breaks a child's score down into five areas. These include sensory, relating, body and object use, language, social, and self-help. The ABC appears to be a useful screening instrument, but its value as a diagnostic instrument has been questioned, due to its failure to detect high functioning individuals with autism (Volkmar, 1988). The CARS was shown to be superior to the ABC in identifying individuals diagnosed with autism (Eaves & Milner, 1993).

## Diagnostic Instruments

A number of instruments completed by different members of the multidisciplinary team aid in the diagnosis of autism. An evaluation of the individual's intellectual functioning is typically included, as an intelligence test provides a valid picture of the individual's strengths and deficits. The language requirements and the timed tasks involved in intelligence testing may pose concerns for individuals with autism. The Kaufman-Assessment Battery (K-ABC) for Children (Kaufman & Kaufman, 1983) is recommended for use with this population due to its reduced emphasis on verbal abilities (Sparrow et al., 1997). Adaptive behavior, or an individual's adjustment to the demands of everyday life, is also typically examined. The Vineland Adaptive Behavior Scales (Sparrow, Balla, & Cicchetti, 1984a; 1984b; 1985) are the most widely used instruments for assessing adaptive behavior. The Adaptive Behavior Scale is available in three editions: a survey form, an expanded form for use in the specification of learning goals and objectives, and a classroom edition to be used by teachers. Adaptive behavior of individuals with autism is often much lower than their overall intellectual functioning. Sparrow et al. (1997) recommend use of the expanded form for this reason. It is advised that social emotional functioning be included in the assessment, but traditional projective instruments typically used with other populations are unlikely to be useful. Observations of structured and unstructured play may provide more valuable information.

There are also instruments that have been specifically designed for the assessment of autism. One example is the Autism Diagnostic Observation Scale (ADOS) (Lord, Rutter, & DiLavore, 1996), which is used to evaluate the social and communicative behaviors of children suspected of having a pervasive developmental disorder. The ADOS is a standardized protocol for observing social and communicative behavior. It includes structured and semi-structured observations. The ADOS resolves some of the barriers inherent in assessing children with autism that were noted previously, because it is designed for use specifically with children with pervasive developmental disorders and follows a standardized protocol. In the state of Illinois, efforts are currently underway to provide training on the ADOS to professionals affiliated with the northern, central, and southern Autism Centers for

Excellence. (For more information on the ADOS, the reader is referred to Lord et al., 1989). Several other instruments for assessing language, communication, and social skills are routinely used by speech-language pathologists (see Sparrow et al., 1997).

## Functional Assessment

Functional assessment procedures are now widely used to determine the variables controlling the challenging behaviors exhibited by individuals with autism. Conducting a functional assessment involves identifying the target behavior, determining controlling antecedent and consequent stimuli, developing and implementing an intervention, and evaluating the effects of that intervention (see Powers, 1997; Wallace et al., this volume). Functional analysis methodology (Iwata, Dorsey, Slifer, Bauman, & Richman, 1982; 1994) more specifically involves experimentally manipulating the environmental variables of which a challenging behavior is hypothesized to be a function. Functional analysis procedures have proven useful in identifying the environmental variables controlling self-injury (e.g., Healey, Ahearn, Graff, & Libby, 2001), aggression (e.g., Mueller, Wilczynski, Moore, Fusilier, & Trahant, 2001), psychotic speech (Durand & Crimmins, 1987) and perseverative speech (Rehfeldt & Chambers, 2003) demonstrated by individuals with autism.

## Intervention

## Pharmacological

A number of pharmacological agents have been used with varying success in the treatment of autism. Low-dose, high-potency neuroleptic medications such as haloperidol, a dopamine receptor antagonist, have been widely researched. Haloperidol has been shown to reduce aggression and stereotypies, and was shown to be superior to placebo in establishing word-imitation skills in children with autism when used in conjunction with behavior therapy (Campbell, Anderson, Perry, Green, & Kaplan, 1982). Haloperidol may cause sedation and tardive dyskinesia. Risperidone, a neuroleptic agent often prescribed for persons with schizophrenia, has been shown to have similar desirable effects with fewer adverse side effects (Purdon, Lit, Labelle, & Jones, 1994).

Opiate antagonists have also been used in the treatment of autism, the rationale being that certain characteristics of the disorder, such as pain insensitivity, repetitive motor behaviors, and lack of social interest are similar to opiate addiction (see Holm & Varley, 1987). Naltrexone is an opiate antagonist that has been correlated with decreases in noncompliance and stereotypies (Campbell et al., 1988). Borghese et al. (1991) showed improved scores on the CARS for subjects who took naltrexone when compared to placebo controls, with no improvements in eye contact or social interaction skills. Naltrexone also produces sedation, so it is possible that the desirable effects reported were not due to the drug, but were merely the result of sedation.

Because autism has been linked to elevated serotonin levels, selective serotonin reuptake inhibitors (SSRIs) and nonselective serotonin reuptake inhibitors such as clomipramine are frequently prescribed. Fenfluramine hydrochloride is an SSRI traditionally used to treat obesity in adults. Some studies have shown that fenfluramine was effective in reducing serotonin levels in individuals with autism, as well as decreasing stereotypies and improving social, self-help, and communication skills (Ritvo, Freeman, Geller, & Yuwiler, 1983). Similarly, clomipramine has been associated with improvements in obsessive-compulsive symptoms and reduced aggression and self-injury (Gordon, 2000). Side effects include hyperactivity and/or insomnia, and children with autism appear to be more sensitive to these effects than other populations (Gordon, 2000).

## Behavioral

Applied behavior analysis is the only scientifically verified intervention for autism. Efforts to extend behavioral principles to the treatment of children with autism were pioneered by Lovaas and colleagues, who developed a highly structured teaching approach that today is often referred to as discrete trial training. Early reports suggested that children who received intensive one-on-one behavior therapy (typically for 40 hours a week) showed reductions in echolalia and self-stimulatory behavior, and showed increases in appropriate speech, play, and social interaction skills (Lovaas, Koegel, Simmons, & Long, 1973). Importantly, behavior change generalized to novel settings and stimuli. These initial results have been replicated and extended. Smith, Eikeseth, Klevstrand, and Lovaas (1997) compared the mean IQ of a group of children who received intensive behavioral intervention to that of a comparison group who received only minimal treatment. At intake the groups had similar mean IQs, but at follow-up, the treatment group had a higher mean IQ. Expressive language was also shown to be superior for children in the treatment group. Eikeseth, Smith, Jahr, and Eldevik (2002) reported large gains on standardized tests for children who received intensive behavioral intervention relative to children who received more eclectic treatment. Despite the significance of these results, this body of research has been criticized on grounds that children were not randomly assigned to treatment and control groups, and that comparisons were not made on the same pre- and post-test measures for all children (see Sallows & Graupner, 1999).

Other varieties of behavioral intervention have also emerged. While discrete trial training is typically conducted in a specific and structured manner, naturalistic or incidental teaching is conducted in a less structured format and focuses upon the learner's interests and activities. During discrete trial training, the instructor presents the instructions for some targeted skill and reinforces correct responses with an edible or desired activity. Trials for a particular skill are often presented until mastery. With naturalistic teaching, response requirements are based upon the learner's ongoing interests and consequences are related to those interests (see Sundberg, this volume; Sundberg & Partington, 1999). Naturalistic and incidental teaching approaches have been shown to be effective in improving upon some of the deficits associated with autism, including speech intelligibility (e.g., Koegel, Camarata, Koegel, Ben-Tall, & Smith, 1998), imitative utterances (Koegel, O'Dell, & Koegel, 1987), and social responsiveness (see McGee, Morrier, & Daly, 1999), as well as maintaining high motivation levels during instruction (Koegel & Mentis, 1985).

Other instructional techniques based on applied behavior analysis have also been successful with individuals with autism. One example is activity schedules. Activity schedules (McClannahan & Krantz, 1999) consist of a sequence of pictures, words, or symbols that occasion a chain of activities. Activity schedules often take the form of placards or in notebooks, but can also be presented via computer (Rehfeldt, Kinney, Root, & Stromer, in press). A proficient schedule user is an individual whose completion of and transition between activities is occasioned by the visual cues presented in his or her schedule, rather than by the instructions of an adult (e.g., MacDuff, Krantz, & McClannahan, 1993; Rehfeldt, 2002). Activity schedules have been shown to be effective in teaching social, leisure, and communication skills to children (e.g., Krantz & McClannahan 1993) and vocational and domestic tasks to adults (McClannahan, MacDuff, & Krantz, 2002). Similarly, the Picture Exchange Communication System, or P.E.C.S. (Bondy & Frost, 1993; Bondy & Frost, 1994) is an alternative form of communication designed to establish mand repertoires in children with autism. P.E.C.S. teaching is based heavily on applied behavior analysis. Individuals learn to mand (Skinner, 1957) using P.E.C.S. by handing a picture of a desired item to a caregiver in exchange for the desired item itself. Pictures of preferred items are often contained in a three-ring binder that the individual keeps on his or her person. The rationale behind P.E.C.S is that the picture exchange approximates the communicative exchange that takes place in typical everyday conversation (Bondy & Frost, 1993; Bondy & Frost, 1994). Much evidence supports the effectiveness of teaching children with autism to mand using P.E.C.S. (e.g., Bondy & Battaglini, 1992; Bondy & Frost, 1993; see also Chambers & Rehfeldt, in press). Increased eye contact and spontaneous vocalizations have also been established via P.E.C.S. training (Charlop-Christy, Carpenter, Loc, LeBlanc, & Keller, 2002).

## Invalidated Treatments

Several biological agents are currently popular in the treatment of autism, but claims about such treatments have been unsubstantiated. Secretin, a hormone that regulates digestion, is one such example. Secretin gained attention when parents reported enhanced language and social skills in children prescribed with a single dose of its synthetic form. However, placebo-controlled trials revealed that secretin is not correlated with such improvements (Sandler et al., 1999), and its effects did not covary with cognitive level, gastrointestinal symptoms, or a history of regression (Roberts et al., 2001). Similar claims can be made for gluten- and casein-free diets and for the use of vitamin B6 and magnesium. Although some studies report improvements following such treatments, such studies are fraught with methodological weaknesses. Any evidence for the effectiveness of secretin, gluton- and casein-free diets, and vitamin therapy in the treatment of autism stems from anecdotal parental reports only.

## Lifelong Supports

Although intensive early behavioral intervention is correlated with better outcomes, many individuals with autism have a lifelong need for supports. A small proportion of children with autism will achieve complete independence in adulthood, but many, with the right supports, will achieve partial independence in living and employment. Individuals may require thorough preparation for entering the work-force and intensive supports once employed. Social skills training may be necessary to ensure an individual's success in work-place and community activities. Supports in the form of job coaches, leisure coaches, or life-skill coaches may be necessary. (For a description of best practices in adult services for individuals with autism, the reader is referred to McClannahan et al., 2002, and Mesibov, 1992).

## The Center for Autism Spectrum Disorders at Southern Illinois University: The Preschool Program

The preschool program is one of the components of the Center for Autism Spectrum Disorders at Southern Illinois University. The program is administered jointly by the Behavior Analysis and Therapy and Communication Disorders and Sciences graduate programs, both in the Rehabilitation Institute. The preschool program's mission is to develop and disseminate evidence-based practice about children with autism by teaching, service, and research. The implementation of these goals includes the joint training and supervision of graduate students in the behavior analysis and speech therapy disciplines, including classroom coursework and clinical activities, the implementation of community services based on evidence based best practices for children with autism and their families, and the conduct of research and program evaluation to develop additional evidence based practices. The therapy activities of the preschool program principally address the core deficits of autism: impairments in communication and reciprocal social interaction, as well as a restricted repertoire of activities and interests. The program structures and processes are consistent with the common elements of effective early intervention (Dawson & Osterling, 1997).

At referral, children either may already have an autism spectrum disorder diagnosis or their parents may request an evaluation for their concerns (e.g., speech delay, overall developmental delay). Subsequent to evaluation and acceptance for therapy, children and their families enter one or more of the therapy programs described below.

## Preschool Program Structure

*Individual Therapy.* Initially, most children enter an individual therapy program either as their only form of therapy or as an adjunct to one of the groups described below. Children who receive individual therapy sessions generally are 2-3 years old. The length of sessions is tailored to the individual child, but they are 50 minutes when possible. The goals of individual therapy typically include reinforcer identification, and the training of instructional control, vocal, verbal, and motor imitation, manding to the therapist, receptive and basic expressive language, and simple visual discriminations. In addition, individual therapy may be used for traditional speech therapy, as well as to supplement acquisition, fluency, maintenance, and stimulus and response class expansion training trials for responses taught in group activities described below. Individual sessions also are used to prime activities prior to undertaking them in a group. In addition, problem behaviors encountered in the home or individual clinic sessions are addressed based on a functional assessment. Generally, after 3 months of individual therapy the child progresses to the Lab to Promote Social Interaction.

*Lab to Promote Social Interaction.* Most children in this group are 3 years old, and participate for 6-15 months. These children have shown progress on the individual therapy activities cited previously, and now have as an additional goal learning to interact socially with other children. In addition to the social goals, effort is directed toward the continued development of the children's communication repertoire; however, these communication goals are addressed in the context of group social activities. The emphasis is placed on language in a social context. Examples of children's goals are tolerating physical proximity and touch, engaging in parallel play with toys in close physical proximity, imitating peer motor behavior, initiating and reciprocating social bids by peers, taking turns, playing cooperatively, and manding to clinicians. These goals are addressed by a sequence of age appropriate social activities throughout sessions, which have ranged from 1-3 hours during various years. For longer sessions, in particular, the time is divided between group and individual therapy activities.

*Lab to Support Full Inclusion.* This Lab, which is the most advanced preschool component, is dedicated to teach children to function as independently as possible in either a community school or daycare program. Children typically are 4-6 years old and may already be either in a school program or will be within 1 year. These children typically have made considerable progress in the Lab to Promote Social Interaction and have acquired the basic language and social skills taught there. In this Lab, clinicians continue to work on developing the children's language and social behavior repertoires in the context of age appropriate social activities. Individual training may be interspersed with group activities either to accomplish individual speech goals or to provide additional training trials. As an example of a more advanced pragmatic language skill, manding is now directed toward other children in the group and not the therapists. Conversation among the children is also a goal, as is teaching pronouns, prepositions, the function-features-and class of objects, asking and answering questions, and increasing the mean language utterance, including speaking in sentences.

*School Consultation and Intervention.* Therapists who work with the children in the Lab to Support Full Inclusion go to the children's schools to observe them. At school, children's goals for training in the Lab are identified, the therapists consult with teachers to help insure consistent Lab and school implementation of behavioral programs, and the clinicians and teachers discuss intervention strategies. In addition, therapists may intervene directly with the child in the classroom to assist with learning activities or control problem behavior. Therapists may also help promote social interaction between children with autism and their typically developing classmates, both in their classroom and playground.

*Home Consultation and Parent Training.* Parent training occurs continuously while children are in individual or group therapy. Parents observe sessions and staff explain the rationale and techniques of the intervention the children are receiving. Parents may also be trained to implement programs in the Lab and be supported implementing the procedures at home. In addition, therapists may go to the family home to observe children's behavior there, and develop a home-based program for parents to implement, when appropriate. Likewise, Center staff may consult with home -based therapists hired by families.

## Preschool Program Processes

*Hybrid Analog-Natural Environment Model.* The instructional model involves both analog and natural environment aspects. Individual therapy is structured around tabletop and floor discrete trial training. Group therapy involves discrete trial training in a group format with children taking turns. These trials occur in the context of indoor and outdoor activities that are on a written plan based on the instructional model presented below. In addition, there may be incidental teaching by structuring the environment and anticipating that the opportunity will arise to provide training trials. In addition, we follow the child's lead and incidentally embed training trials consistent with a child's goals in activities that the child initiates.

Within these contexts, interactions between children and clinicians may occur in several ways. Children engage in programmed reciprocal functional interactions with each other in a discrete trial format with clinician instruction. This child-to-child interaction occurs in the context of age appropriate natural activities. Children also may interact with each other in a free operant manner. In addition, children interact individually with one or more clinicians in a free operant manner.

*Instructional Model.* The following is an outline for the instruction of each activity during a session. Each of the numbered and lettered items in the outline is developed in detail for each activity for the entire session.

I. Instructional Goal & Justification
II. Instructional Objective
III. Target Responses
IV. Materials Needed
V. Testing Procedures
VI. Acquisition and Fluency Training Procedures
    A. Task presentation
    B. Mand (instruction) to student
    C. Prompting & transfer of stimulus control procedures.
    D. Response consequences
    E. Data collection
VII. Extending Stimulus and Response Classes
VIII. Promoting Response Maintenance

Several of the components of the instructional model will be discussed below.

*Goal Selection.* The instructional goals are derived, in the first instance, from the current and future behavioral requirements in children's natural environments. Center staff observe children in school and identify performance discrepancies. If they are a result of a skill deficit, that skill could be trained either in the Lab or in individual therapy sessions. In addition, children are prepared for typical classroom routines that they will encounter in the near future and have not yet experienced. For younger children who are not in or about to enter another educational program, goals are principally derived from standardized assessment instruments, observed deficits in the Lab and individual therapy, and developmental norms. For all children, parent concerns are seriously considered for goal identification.

*Instructional and Reinforcing Stimuli Selection and Use.* Efforts are made to select age appropriate instructional stimuli from the natural environment that would reinforce children's task attention and engagement. To that end, parents periodically complete a Preferred Child Activities Questionnaire. In addition, reinforcer preference assessments (De Leon & Iwata, 1996) are also administered from time to time to determine stimuli that might serve as response reinforcers. Parents also complete a sensory checklist to assess the types of sensory stimuli that might be both reinforcing and aversive. These assessments help identify stimuli that could be either used therapeutically or avoided during instruction. Based on this assessment information, personalized boxes of stimuli are created for each child.

*Use of Establishing Operations.* Establishing operations are taken into consideration in several ways. Parents complete a questionnaire prior to each session that asks a series of questions pertaining to the possibility that establishing operations might be affecting their child during the session. In addition, parents are asked to withhold food and preferred activity reinforcers immediately prior to sessions. During therapy sessions themselves, reinforcing stimuli are limited and withheld to create more opportunities for responding.

*Expanding Stimulus and Response Classes; Maintaining Responses.* All training is aimed at producing and maintaining appropriate classes of stimuli and responses. Consideration is given to relevant stimulus class members initially when instructional goals are determined, and then continuously over time as children acquire and generalize responses. The intended members of a stimulus class are identified, and instruction is directed at transferring those initially neutral antecedents to function as discriminative stimuli and evoke response class members. For example, we vary the irrelevant cues of training stimuli, location where training occurs, and clinician that trains the response class members. Such variation occurs both within and between sessions. In addition, incidental teaching is used to expand stimulus and response classes. Parent training and sibling models, as discussed below, also help extend responding to the home setting.

In addition to expanding stimulus classes, instruction is aimed at building functional response classes. When the behavior component of an instructional objective is written, both the expected and acceptable variation in responding is considered. That variation may be verbally instructed and modeled, and responses that demonstrate that variation are contingently reinforced. Teaching appropriately expansive verbal response classes, for example, is especially important for children with autism who may tend to use unvaried stereotypical verbal statements in the context of a stimulus class.

Programming for response maintenance occurs in several ways consistent with best practices (e.g., Sulzer-Azaroff & Mayer, 1990). We use a stringent acquisition criterion and progress over trials toward intermittent reinforcement. We also intersperse training on responses that have met an acquisition and fluency criterion with responses undergoing acquisition training. To promote response maintenance and class expansion, parents have a homework assignment each week. They are given a printed form that specifies two responses to teach, as well as their teaching procedures. Parents are asked to conduct 10 training trials at home and score each one as unprompted, prompted, or not emitted.

*Peer/Sibling Models.* Chronological age peers and siblings have been incorporated into group training sessions. Peers and siblings can be effective models if they are similar in age to the children, competent, and have had previous interactions with the children (Sulzer-Azaroff & Mayer, 1990). There is a formal training program for peers and siblings that includes instruction prior to participation and in-vivo instruction in the Lab. Initial instruction includes a verbal description of training activities, verbal instructions and rationales regarding how to model, clinician modeling for the peer, role play with or without scripts, prompts, corrective feedback, and praise as a response contingent consequence. Subsequently, additional instruction occurs in the Lab during actual training activities where peers may use scripts and receive prompts as necessary. Peers and siblings have been used throughout entire sessions in the Lab to Support Full Inclusion. They have been effective models, for example, for how to mand to peers, initiate and sustain a conversation, and make choices. Peers and siblings could also be used in individual therapy to prime responding to activities that occur in the group. For example, a peer model and client could work together to practice initiating conversation and responding appropriately.

## Conclusion

With the passage of time, misapprehensions regarding the nature and causes of autism have gradually diminished. The possibility of the identification of neurophysiological or genetic mechanisms underlying the disorder in the coming years appears promising. Knowledge of applied behavior analysis as a treatment for autism is now widely distributed among the general public, and a number of colleges and universities provide clinical services for children and their families that also serve as graduate training opportunities for students. It is crucial that these efforts continue so as to meet the needs of the growing number of children diagnosed with the disorder. It is also imperative that professionals in other disciplines become well-versed in recognizing the characteristics of autism and in making treatment recommendations. Finally, the necessity of evidence-based claims about etiology and treatment must be underscored, and the general public must recognize this requisite.

# References

American Psychiatric Association. (2000). *Diagnostic and statistical manual of mental disorders* (4th ed., text revision). Washington, DC: Author.

Bondy, A. S., & Battaglini, K. (1992). A public school for students with autism and severe handicaps. In S. Christenson & J. C. Conoley (Eds.), *Home-school collaboration: Enhancing children's academic and social competence* (pp. 223-242). Silver Spring, MD: NASP.

Bondy, A. S., & Frost, L. A. (1993). Mands across the water: A report on the application of the picture exchange communication system in Peru. *The Behavior Analyst, 16,* 123-128.

Bondy, A. S., & Frost, L. A. (1994). The picture exchange communication system. *Focus on Autistic Behavior, 9,* 1-17.

Borghese, I. F., Herman, B. H., Asleson, G. S., Chatoor, I., Benoit, M. B., Papero, P., & McNulty, G. (1991). Effects of acutely administered naltrexone on social behavior of autistic children. *Society for Neuroscience Abstracts, 17,* 1252.

Bryson, S. E. (1997). Epidemiology of autism: Overview and issues outstanding. In D. J. Cohen & F. R. Volkmar (Eds.), *Handbook of autism and pervasive developmental disorders* (pp. 41-46). New York: Wiley.

Campbell, M., Anderson, L. T., Perry, R., Green, W. H., & Kaplan, R. (1982). The effects of haloperidol on learning and behavior in autistic children. *Journal of Autism and Developmental Disorders, 12,* 167-175.

Campbell, M., Overall, J. E., Small, A. M., Sokol, M. S., Spencer, E. L., Adams, P., Foltz, R. L., Monti, K. M., Perry, R., Nobler, M., & Roberts, E. (1989). Naltrexone in autistic children: An acute open dose range tolerance trial. *Journal of the American Academy of Child and Adolescent Psychiatry, 28,* 200-206.

Chambers, M., & Rehfeldt, R. A. (2003). Assessing the acquisition and generalization of two mand forms with adults with severe developmental disabilities. *Research in Developmental Disabilities, 24,* 265-280.

Charlop-Christy, M. H., Carpenter, M. L., Loc, L., LeBlanc, L., & Keller, K. (2002). Using the picture exchange communication system (PECS) with children with autism: Assessment of PECS acquisition, speech, social-communicative behavior, and problem behavior. *Journal of Applied Behavior Analysis, 35,* 213-231.

Dawson, G., & Osterling, J. (1997). Early intervention in autism. In M. J. Guralnick (Ed.), *The effectiveness of early intervention* (pp. 307-326). Baltimore: Paul H. Brookes.

Dawson, G., Warrenburg, S., & Fuller, P. (1982). Cerebral lateralization in individuals diagnosed as autistic in early childhood. *Brain and Language, 15,* 353-368.

Dawson, G., Warrenburg, S., & Fuller, P. (1983). Hemisphere functioning and motor imitation in autistic persons. *Brain and Cognition, 2,* 346-354.

De Leon, I. G., & Iwata, B. A. (1996). Evaluation of a multiple-stimulus presentation format for assessing reinforcer preferences. *Journal of Applied Behavior Analysis, 29,* 519-533.

DiLalla, D. L., & Rogers, S. J. (1994). Domains of the Childhood Autism Rating Scale: Relevance for diagnosis and treatment. *Journal of Autism and Developmental Disorders,* 115-128.

Durand, V. M., & Crimmins, D. B. (1987). Assessment and treatment of psychotic speech in an autistic child. *Journal of Autism and Developmental Disorders, 17,* 17-28.

Dykens, E. M., & Volkmar, F. R. (1997). Medical conditions associated with autism. In D. J. Cohen & F. R. Volkmar (Eds.), *Handbook of autism and pervasive developmental disorders* (pp. 388-407). New York: Wiley.

Eaves, R. C., & Milner, B. (1993). The criterion-related validity of the Childhood Autism Rating Scale and the Autism Behavior Checklist. *Journal of Abnormal Child Psychology, 21,* 481-491.

Eikeseth, S., Smith, T., Jahr, E., & Eldevik, S. (2002). Intensive behavioral treatment at school for 4- to 7-year old children with autism: A 1-year comparison controlled study. *Behavior Modification, 26,* 49-68.

Fombonne, E. (2003). The prevalence of autism. *Journal of the American Medical Association, 289,* 1-3.

Gillberg, C. (1984). Autistic children growing up: Problems during puberty and adolescence. *Developmental Medicine and Child Neurology, 26,* 122-129.

Gillberg, C., Nordin, V., & Ehlers, S. (1996). Early detection of autism. Diagnostic instruments for clinicians. *European Child and Adolescent Psychiatry, 5,* 67-74.

Gordon, C. T. (2000). Commentary: Considerations on the pharmacological treatment of compulsions and stereotypies with serotonin reuptake inhibitors in pervasive developmental disorders. *Journal of Autism and Developmental Disorders, 30,* 437-438.

Healey, J. J., Ahearn, W. H., Graff, R. B., & Libby, M. E. (2001). Extended analysis and treatment of self-injurious behavior. *Behavioral Interventions, 16,* 181-195.

Herbert, J. D., Sharp, I. R., & Gaudiano, B. A. (2002). Separating fact from fiction in the etiology and treatment of autism. *Scientific Mental Health, 11,* 1-23.

Holm, V. A., & Varley, C. K. (1989). Pharmacological treatment of autistic children. Neurochemical perspectives on infantile autism. In G. Dawson (Ed.), *Autism: nature, diagnosis, and treatment* (pp. 386-404). New York: Guilford Press.

Kaufman, A. S., & Kaufman, N. L. (1983). K-ABC: Kaufman-Assessment Battery for Children. Circle Pines, MN: American Guidance Service

Koegel, R. L., Camarata, S., Koegel, L. K., Ben-Tall, A., & Smith, A. (1998). Increasing speech intelligibility in children with autism. *Journal of Autism and Developmental Disorders, 28,* 241-251.

Koegel, R. L., & Mentis, M. (1986). Motivation in childhood autism: Can they or won't they? *Journal of Child Psychological Psychiatry, 26,* 185-194.

Koegel, R. L., O'Dell, M. C., & Koegel, L. K. (1987). A natural language teaching paradigm for nonverbal autistic children. *Journal of Autism and Developmental Disorders, 17,* 187-200.

Krantz, P. J., & McClannahan, L. E. (1993). Teaching children with autism to initiate to peers: Effects of a script-fading procedure. *Journal of Applied Behavior Analysis, 26,*121-132.

Krantz, P. J., MacDuff, M. T., & McClannahan, L. E. (1993). Programming participation in activities for children with autism: Parents' use of photographic activity schedules. *Journal of Applied Behavior Analysis, 26,* 137-138.

Krug, D. A., Arick, J., & Almond, P. (1980). Behavior checklist for identifying severely handicapped individuals with high levels of autistic behavior. *Journal of Child Psychology and Psychiatry, 21,* 221-229.

Iwata, B. A., Dorsey, M. F., Slifer, K. J., Bauman, K. E., & Richman, G. S. (1994). Toward a functional analysis of self-injury. *Journal of Applied Behavior Analysis, 27,* 197-209. (Reprinted from *Analysis and Intervention in Developmental Disabilities, 2,* 3-20, 1982).

Lord, C. (1984). Development of peer relations in children with autism. In F. Morrison, C. Lord, & D. Keating (Eds.), *Applied developmental psychology* (Vol. 1, 166-230). New York: Academic Press.

Lord, C., Rutter, M., Goode, S., Heemsbergen, J., Jordan, H., Mawhood, L., & Schopler, E. (1989). Autism Diagnostic Observation Schedule: A standardized observation of communicative and social behavior. *Journal of Autism and Developmental Disorders, 19,* 185-212.

Lord, C. (1991). Methods and measures of behavior in the diagnosis of autism and related disorders. *Psychiatric Clinics of North America, 14,* 69-80.

Lord, C., Rutter, M., & DiLavore, P. (1996). *Autism Diagnostic Observation Schedule – Generic (ADOS-G).* Unpublished manuscript, University of Chicago.

Lord, C. (1997). Diagnostic instruments in autism spectrum disorders. In D. J. Cohen & F. R. Volkmar (Eds.), *Handbook of autism and pervasive developmental disorders* (pp. 460-483). New York: Wiley.

Lord, C., & Rutter, M. (1994). Autism and pervasive developmental disorders. In M. Rutter, L. Hersov, & E. Taylor (Eds.), *Child and adolescent psychiatry: Modern approaches* (3rd ed.) (pp. 569-593). Oxford, England: Blackwell.

Lovaas, O. I., Koegel, R., Simmons, J. Q., & Long, J. (1973). Some generalization and follow-up measures on autistic children in behavior therapy. *Journal of Applied Behavior Analysis, 6,* 131-166.

Madsen, K. M., Hviid, A., Verstergaard, M., Schendel, D., Wohlfhrt, J., Thorsen, P., Olsen, J., & Melbye, M. (2002). A population-based study of measles, mumps, and rubella vaccination and autism. *The New England Journal of Medicine, 347,* 1477-1482.

McClannahan, L. E., MacDuff, G. S., & Krantz, P. J. (2002). Behavior analysis and intervention for adults with autism. *Behavior Modification, 26,* 9-27.

McClannahan, L. E., & Krantz, P. J. (1999). *Activity schedules for children with autism: Teaching independent behavior.* Bethesda, MD: Woodbine House.

MacDuff, G. S., Krantz, P. J., & McClannahan, L. E. (1993). Teaching children with autism to use photographic activity schedules: Maintenance and generalization of complex response chains. *Journal of Applied Behavior Analysis, 26,* 89-97.

McGee, G. G., Morrier, M. J., & Daly, T. (1999). An incidental teaching approach to early intervention for toddlers with autism. *Journal of Severe Handicaps, 24,* 133-146.

Mesibov, G. B. (1992). Treatment issues with high-functioning adolescents and adults with autism. In E. Schopler & G. B. Mesibov (Eds.), *High-functioning individuals with autism* (pp. 143-155). New York: Plenum Press.

M.I.N.D. Institute (October 17, 2002). Report to the legislature on the principal findings from the epidemiology of autism in California. University of California, Davis.

Mueller, M. M., Wilczynski, S. M., Moore, J. W., Fusilier, I., & Trahant, D. (2001). Antecedent manipulations in a tangible condition: Effects of stimulus preference on aggression. *Journal of Applied Behavior Analysis, 34,* 237-240.

Purdon, S. E., Lit, W., LaBelle, A., & Jones, D. W. (1994). Risperidone in the treatment of Pervasive Developmental Disorder. *Canadian Journal of Psychiatry, 39,* 400-405.

Rehfeldt, R. A. (in press). Supported employment for adults with high functioning autism and Asperger syndrome. *Australian Journal of Rehabilitation Counseling.*

Rehfeldt, R. A. (2002). A Review of *Activity schedules for children with autism: Teaching independent behavior,* by McClannahan & Krantz, (1999): Toward independence and inclusion. *The Behavior Analyst, 25,* 103-108.

Rehfeldt, R. A., & Chambers, M. R. (2003). Functional analysis and treatment of verbal perseverations for an adult with autism. *Journal of Applied Behavior Analysis, 36,* 259-261.

Rehfeldt, R. A., Kinney, E. M., Root, S., & Stromer, R. (in press). Creating Activity Schedules Using Microsoft PowerPoint. *Journal of Applied Behavior Analysis.*

Rimland, B. (1988). Candida-caused autism? *Autism Research Review International Newsletter.* www.autism.com/ari/editorials/candida.

Ritvo, E. R., Yuwiler, A., Geller, E., Ornitz, E. M., Saeger, K., & Plotkin, S. (1980). Increased blood serotonin and platelets in early infantile autism. *Archives of General Psychiatry, 23,* 566-572.

Robert, W., Weaver, L., Brian, J., Bryson, S., Emelianova, S., Griffiths, A., MacKinnon, B., Yim, C., Wolpin, J., & Koren, G. (2001). Repeated doses of porcine secretin in the treatment of autism: A randomized, placebo-controlled trial. *Pediatrics, 107,* 1-5.

Rodier, P. (2000). The early origins of autism. *Scientific American, 282,* 56-63.

Rutter, M., Bailey, A., Bolton, P., & Le Couteur, A. (1993). Autism: Syndrome of definition and possible genetic mechanisms. In R. Plomin & G. E. McLearn

(Eds.), *Nature, nurture and psychology*. Washington, DC: American Psychological Association Press.

Sallows, G. O., & Graupner, T. D. (1999). *Replicating Lovaas' treatment and findings: Preliminary results*. Paper presented at the PEACH conference, London, England.

Sandler, A. D., Sutton, K. A., DeWeese, J., Girardi, M. A., Sheppard, V., & Bodfish, J. W. (1999). Lack of benefit of a single dose of synthetic human secretin in the treatment of autism and pervasive developmental disorder. *The New England Journal of Medicine, 341,* 1801-1806.

Schopler, E., Reichler, R. J., & Renner, B. R. (1988). *The childhood autism rating scale*. Los Angeles: Western Psychological Services.

Smith, T., Eikeseth, S., Klevstrand, M., & Lovaas, I. (1997). Intensive behavioral treatment for preschoolers with severe mental retardation and pervasive developmental disorder. *American Journal on Mental Retardation, 102,* 238-249.

Sparrow, S., Balla, D., & Cicchetti, D. (1984a). *Vineland adaptive behavior scales* (Survey ed.). Circle Pines, MN: American Guidance Service.

Sparrow, S., Balla, D., & Cicchetti, D. (1984b). *Vineland adaptive behavior scales* (Expanded ed.). Circle Pines, MN: American Guidance Service.

Sparrow, S., Balla, D., & Cicchetti, D. (1985). *Vineland adaptive behavior scales* (Classroom ed.). Circle Pines, MN: American Guidance Service.

Sparrow, S., Marans, W., Klin, A., Carter, A., Volkmar, F. R., & Cohen, D. J. (1997). Developmentally based assessments. In D. J. Cohen & F. R. Volkmar (Eds.), *Handbook of autism and pervasive developmental disorders* (pp. 411-447). New York: Wiley.

Sturmey, P., Matson, J. L., & Sevin, J. A. (1992). Brief report: Analysis of the internal consistency of three autism scales. *Journal of Autism and Developmental Disorders, 22,* 321-328.

Shah, K. (2001). What do medical students know about autism? *Autism, 5,* 127-133.

Sigman, M., Ungerer, J. A., Mundy, P., & Sherman, T. (1987). Cognition in autistic children. In D. J. Cohen, A. M. Donnellan, & R. Paul (Eds.), *Handbook of autism and pervasive developmental disorders* (pp. 103-120). New York: Wiley.

Smalley, S. L., Tanguay, P. E., Smith, M., & Gutierrez, G. (1992). Autism and tuberous sclerosis. *Journal of Autism and Developmental Disorders, 22,* 339-335.

Smith, M. D., Belcher, R. G., & Juhrs, P. D. (2000). *A Guide to Successful Employment for Individuals with Autism*. Baltimore: Paul H. Brookes.

Stone, W. L. (1988). Cross-disciplinary perspectives on autism. *Journal of Pediatric Psychology, 12,* 615-630.

Sulzer-Azaroff, B., & Mayer, G. R. (1991). *Behavior analysis for lasting change*. Orlando: Holt, Rinehart, & Winston.

Trottier, G., Srivastava, L., & Walker, C. D. (1999). Etiology of infantile autism: A review of recent advancements in genetic and neurobiological research. *Journal of Psychiatry and Neuroscience, 24,* 103-115.

Volkmar, F. R. (1988). An evaluation of the Autism Behavior Checklist. *Journal of Autism and Developmental Disabilities, 18,* 81-97.

Volkmar, F. R., & Anderson, G. M. (1989). Neurochemical perspectives on infantile autism. In G. Dawson (Ed.), *Autism: Nature, diagnosis, and treatment* (pp. 208-224). New York: Guilford Press.

Volkmar, F. R., Klin, A., & Cohen, D. J. (1997). Diagnosis and classification of autism and related conditions: Consensus and issues. In D. J. Cohen & F. R. Volkmar (Eds.), *Handbook of Autism and Pervasive Developmental Disorders* (pp. 5-40). New York: Wiley.

Yazbak, F. E. (2002). *Autism in Rhode Island.* www.Autismautoimunityproject.org

Yeargin-Allsopp, M., Rice, C., Karapurkar, T., Doernberg, N., Boyle, C., & Murphy, C. (2003). Prevalence of autism in a US metropolitan area. *Journal of the American Medical Association, 289,* 49-55.

Wing, L., & Gould, J. (1979). Severe impairments of social interaction and associated abnormalities in children: Epidemiology and classification. *Journal of Autism and Childhood Schizophrenia, 9,* 11-29.

Wing, L. (1992). Manifestations of social problems in high-functioning autistic people. In E. Schopler & G. B. Mesibov (Eds.), *High-functioning individuals with autism* (pp. 129-142). New York: Plenum Press.

# Chapter 9

# A Behavioral Analysis of Motivation and its Relation to Mand Training

## Mark L. Sundberg
### *Behavior Analysts, Inc./STARS School*

The field of behavior analysis has a long-standing, but confusing and conflicting treatment of motivation as a source of behavioral control. In many behavioral textbooks motivation is not considered as an independent variable, nor given its own chapter along with the other behavioral principles and major concepts (e.g., reinforcement, extinction, stimulus control, generalization). However, in all of Skinner's early books on behavior analysis (1938, 1953, 1957), and in the first generation of textbooks on behavior analysis (Holland & Skinner, 1961; Keller & Schoenfeld, 1950; Millenson, 1967) motivation was presented as a basic principle of behavior. The primary purpose of the current chapter is to examine the behavioral analysis of motivation and its relation to mand training for persons with language delays. First however, a brief review of the history of a behavioral analysis of motivation will be provided

In *Behavior of Organisms* (1938) Skinner devoted two chapters to the treatment of motivation; Chapter 9 titled "Drive" and Chapter 10 titled "Drive and Conditioning: The Interaction of Two Variables." In Chapter 9, he presented his arguments against the term "drive" and the treatment of motivation common at that time. "The 'drive' is a hypothetical state interpolated between operation and behavior and is not actually required in a descriptive system" (p. 368). Skinner argued against the common practice of viewing drive as an internal causal variable, and proposed that environmental variables be the focus of the analysis. In the analysis of hunger for example, rather than talking about a "hunger drive" he proposed that the relation between food deprivation and its evocative effect on behavior be the focus of the analysis. Skinner argued, "The degree of hunger developed during the fast is, of course, increased, and the rate at which the rat begins to eat is therefore increased as well" (p. 350). Following his analysis of hunger, Skinner went on to suggest, "The formulation applied to hunger in the preceding pages may be extended to other drives" (p. 358). He also made it clear in the section titled "Drive Not a Stimulus" (pp. 374-376) that the type of antecedent control over behavior that occurs with motivation is not the same as the type of antecedent control exerted by discriminative, unconditioned, or conditioned stimuli.

The next significant development in the behavioral treatment of motivation occurred with the publication of Keller and Schoenfeld's book *Principles of Psychology* (1950). Chapter 9 was titled "Motivation" and contained several refinements of the behavioral analysis of motivation. In this chapter Keller and Schoenfeld further developed the relation between deprivation and satiation, and response strength. These authors stated, "depriving an animal of food is a way of increasing the strength of a conditioned reflex like bar-pressing...with sufficient intake of food (*satiation*), these reflexes drop in strength to zero" (p. 264). They also provided a detailed analysis of how aversive stimuli can function as motivative variables (pp. 303-316), and supported this analysis with experimental data (e.g., Keller, 1941).

Keller and Schoenfeld further developed Skinner's point, "A drive is not a stimulus" (p. 276), and suggested, "It is because responses can be controlled in other ways than by reinforcement, that a new descriptive term is called for and a new behavioral concept emerges" (p. 264). The authors spent several interesting pages attempting to identify an appropriate term for this different behavioral effect, and gradually worked their way to the term "establishing operation." They first suggested, "We shall, then, henceforth use expressions like 'establishing a drive' 'reducing a drive' and others, because they are neat" (271). However, the term "drive" was still problematic because of its etymological sanctions, and the authors went on to say, "The discovery, classification, measurement, and the study of any drive are inextricably related to the identification of (and, hopefully, mastery over) its establishing operations" (p. 272). Ultimately, the authors concluded that the term "establishing operation" was a more precise term than drive, and that "The establishing operation is our independent variable, the behavior our dependent variable; the former is specifiable as to kind and degree, the latter is measured for extent of change. The concomitant variation of the two gives rise to, and defines, the concept and problem of motivation" (p. 273). It is here that we see clearly the suggestion that the "establishing operation" be considered as a separate independent variable in behavior analysis, and a call for the experimental analysis of this variable.

## The Application of Establishing Operations Emerge

In *Science and Human Behavior* (1953) Skinner devoted three chapters to motivation as an independent variable; Chapter 9: "Deprivation and Satiation," Chapter 10: "Emotion," and Chapter 11: "Aversion, Avoidance, Anxiety." Although he does not use the term establishing operation (EO), his definition of motivative variables still consisted of a functional relation between (1) the level of deprivation, satiation, and aversive stimulation and (2) its evocative effect on behavior. Skinner also expanded on his analysis of motivational variables in several ways in these 3 chapters. For example, he made it clear that a single motivational variable can affect a large class of behaviors when he stated, "A given act of deprivation usually increases the strength of many kinds of behavior simultaneously...when an adult goes without water for a long time, a large group of operants are strengthened" (p. 143). He also further elaborated on his original point, "A drive is not a stimulus" (p. 144), rather it is a separate type of antecedent control.

In addition, he provided a full chapter (Chapter 10) on the treatment of aversive stimuli as motivational variables. Skinner concluded that the evocative effects of aversive stimulation were more like those of deprivation and satiation, than those of stimulus control. He wrote "When we present an aversive stimulus, any behavior which has previously been conditioned by the withdrawal of the stimulus immediately follows....The presentation of the aversive stimulus therefore resembles a sudden increase in deprivation" (p. 172).

Given the general theme of the book *Science and Human Behavior* as the application of behavioral principles to the analysis of human behavior, Skinner provided several examples of how motivation affects human behavior. For example, "*Deprivation* is put to practical use when a child is made more likely to drink milk by restriction of his water intake" (p. 146). Thus, by increasing the level of deprivation it may be possible to evoke a specific behavior or class of behaviors that is related to a history of reinforcement relevant to that deprivation variable. The opposite is also possible with reduced deprivation levels where "*Satiation* is put to practical use when...an abundance of hors d'oeuvres is use to conceal the scantiness of the dinner which follows" (p. 147). Hence, deprivation and satiation can be used as independent variables to evoke or suppress operant behavior.

In *Verbal Behavior* (1957) Skinner provided a comprehensive analysis of how motivational variables play a significant role in a human's initial acquisition of language, as well as in later verbal functions. In Chapter 2 he identifies the independent variables in the analysis of language and suggested that motivation and emotion (pp. 31-32), as well as aversive control (p. 33) are separate from the other behavioral principles. For example, "By reinforcing with candy we strengthen the response *Candy*! but the response will be emitted only when the child is, as we say, hungry for candy. Subsequently we control the response, not by further reinforcement, but by depriving or satiating the child with candy" (p. 31). These motivational variables can evoke verbal or nonverbal behaviors. For example, "Whether a door is opened with a 'twist-and-push' or with an *Out!* we make the response more or less likely by altering the deprivation associated with the reinforcement of getting through the door" (p. 31).

In Chapter 3 he introduced the concept of the mand. "A 'mand' then may be defined as a verbal operant in which the response is reinforced by a characteristic consequence and is therefore under the functional control of relevant conditions of deprivation or aversive stimulation" (pp. 35-36). Skinner proposed that the mand was separate from the other types of language (i.e., echoic, tact, intraverbal, textual, and transcriptive) because of its control by motivational variables, rather than discriminative stimuli that control the other types of verbal behavior. He identified several different types of mands, and explained how deprivation, satiation, and aversive stimulation controlled these mands, as well as other types of nonverbal behavior (p. 31). Skinner also described how motivational variables could be controlled and manipulated to evoke verbal behaviors. For example "The response *Quiet!* is reinforced through the reduction of an aversive condition, and we can increase the probability of its occurrence by creating such a condition–that is, by making noise" (p. 35). Many other examples of the use of motivational variables as independent variables can be found throughout the book.

## Holland and Skinner (1961) and Millenson (1967)

The programmed text by Holland and Skinner (1961) covered the basic concepts of behavior analysis as presented in *Science and Human Behavior* (Skinner, 1953), and some of the resulting research and developments from the emerging field of behavior analysis. The book contained four chapters relevant to Skinner's analysis of motivation. Chapters 7 ("Deprivation"), 8 ("Emotion I"), 9 ("Avoidance and Escape Behavior)" and 10 ("Emotion II"). They presented a behavioral analysis of motivation as involving a functional relation between variables determining the momentary value of events functioning as reinforcement or punishment, and the current frequency of behavior that has been so reinforced or punished.

Millenson's *Principles of Behavioral Analysis* (1967), contained four chapters relevant to motivation and presented an excellent summary of the relevant empirical research. Chapters 15 and 16 were titled "Motivation I," and "Motivation II," Chapter 17 was titled "Aversive Contingencies," and Chapter 18 was titled "Emotional Behavior." Skinner (1938) had pointed out several years earlier that the next step in the development of an environmental analysis of motivation was to quantify the relation. "Some measure of the strength of the behavior must be obtained, and the relation between that strength and the various operations that affect it then determined" (p. 358). In the section titled "Measurement of drives" (pp. 372-384), Millenson summarized the existing research as "showing that behavior of several sorts varies in an orderly fashion with changes in deprivation, satiation, and allied operations. There appears to exist a set of behavioral measures which, within limits, covary with deprivation of the reinforcer" (p. 383).

A number of empirical studies are described in this section, such as Clark's (1958) demonstration that various degrees of food deprivation had differential effects on stabilized VI response rates in rats. And Broadhurst's (1957) research with rats in an underwater Y maze that showed "the longer the deprivation time for air, the more efficient was the acquisition performance" (p. 378). This section concluded with a call for a new term; "The systematic covariation in a number of independent behavioral measures in relation to a single operation (for example deprivation) provides grounds for the introduction of a concept which will summarize and stand for this covariance....The actual concept of drive...remains a relation between a reinforcement-establishing operation and the reinforcing value of a class of stimuli" (p. 383). (It should be noted that while no mention was made of Keller and Schoenfeld's (1950) use of the term "establishing operation" in this section, or anywhere in the chapters on motivational variables, Millenson credited Schoenfeld in the Preface of the book saying that to him (and Francis Mechner) "must go credit for whatever of any original value is to be found within.") A second edition of Millenson's book, coauthored by Millenson and Leslie was published in 1979, and although a number of details were added to the earlier treatment, there seem to be no major changes.

There are at least three alternatives to Skinner's analysis of motivation that are behaviorally based and should be mentioned: Kantor's (1959) analysis of setting events, Goldiamond's concept of potentiating variables (Goldiamond & Dyrud, 1967), and Premack's (1971) work on manipulations that change reinforcing properties. While all have their merit, it is beyond the scope of the current paper to compare and contrast these different points of view. It appears that the conceptualization of motivation following Skinner's original analysis has survived the test of time, and has led to a productive line of research and applications (see below).

## What Happened to the Behavioral Analysis of Motivation?

The topic of motivation was for the most part dropped from the behavioral textbooks that followed Millenson's book (e.g., Fantino & Logan, 1979; Martin & Pear, 1978; Powers & Osborne, 1976; Whaley & Malott, 1971). None had a full chapter on motivation like all the earlier textbooks, or considered Skinner (1938, 1953, 1957) and Keller and Schoenfeld's (1950) position that deprivation, satiation, and aversive stimulation (EOs) constituted a separate behavioral principle. The topic was simply not mentioned in many of the books, nor was it incorporated into the behavioral analyses provided in these textbooks. In addition, motivation as a topic of research was absent from the behavioral journals. For example, *The Journal of Applied Behavior Analysis* which began publication in 1968, contained no entries of "establishing operations" in the cumulative indexes (1978, 1988) covering the first 20 years of publication. However, there were 5 entries on "motivation," but they all involved the use of motivation as a consequence rather than as an antecedent variable (see below).

In explaining what happened to the analysis of motivation in behavior analysis, Michael (1993) pointed out, "In applied behavior analysis or behavior modification, the concept of reinforcement seems to have taken over much of the subject matter that was once considered a part of the topic of motivation" (p. 191). Michael (1982, 1988, 1993) argued that this was an inadequate solution to the issue of motivation and that the topic continues to deserve special treatment and consideration as a separate antecedent principle of behavior. As a result of Michael's persistent efforts, motivational variables began to appear more frequently in the behavioral literature. For example, Martin and Pear's (1988) 3rd Edition of *Behavior Modification* contained a two page extended note on EOs, and their 4th, 5th, and 6th Editions contained even more detailed treatments with each new edition. Cooper, Heron, & Heward's (1987) book *Applied Behavior Analysis* contained several sections on the EO. Catania's, (1994) 3rd Edition of *Learning* contained not only the basic definition of the EO, but it was incorporated throughout the book in the analysis of many aspects of behavior. The 3rd Edition of *Elementary Principles of Behavior* by Malott, Whaley, and Malott (1997) contained a full chapter on the EO.

Research on the EO also began to appear in the behavioral journals. *The Analysis of Verbal Behavior* contained several studies on the EO as an independent variable (e.g., Carroll & Hesse, 1987; Hall & Sundberg, 1987; Sundberg, San Juan, Dawdy,

& Arguelles, 1990). The *Journal of the Experimental Analysis of Behavior* also contained a line of basic research on the EO (e.g., Lamarre & Holland, 1985; McPherson & Osborne, 1988; Pierce, Epling, & Boer, 1986). Papers on the EO have also been published in *The Behavior Analyst* (e.g., Leigland, 1984), and in 1993 a special section of that journal was devoted to the EO (Catania, 1993; Hesse, 1993; McDevitt & Fantino, 1993; Michael, 1993; Schlinger, 1993; Sundberg, 1993). The *Journal of Applied Behavior Analysis* saw a rapid expansion of EO research in the 1990s and early 2000s (e.g., Gottschalk, Libby, & Graff, 2000; McGill, 1999; Smith & Iwata, 1997; Vollmer & Iwata, 1991), and in 2000 dedicated much of a single issue to papers on the EO (e.g., Iwata, Smith, & Michael, 2000, McComas, Hoch, Paone, & El-Roy, 2000; Michael, 2000). In addition, other behavioral journals have shown an increase in papers relevant to EOs such as *Research in Developmental Disabilities* (e.g., Fisher, Thompson, DeLeon, Piazza, Kuhn, Rodriguez-Catter, & Adelinis, 1999), *Behavior Modification* (e.g., Sundberg & Michael, 2001), and *Behavioral Interventions* (e.g., Wilder & Carr, 1998). Thus, it appears that the EO and the behavior analysis of motivation have worked their way back into mainstream behavior analysis.

## Michael's Refinement and Extension of the Establishing Operation

In a series of papers Michael (1982, 1988, 1993, 2000) elaborated on Skinner's analysis of motivation, while adopting Keller and Schoenfeld's (1950) term "establishing operation." Michael's definition of the EO was essentially the same as Skinner's (1938, 1953, 1957) definition of the behavioral effects of deprivation, satiation, and aversive stimulation. However, Michael, like Keller and Schoenfeld, felt that a special term was needed for the different types of variables that fit Skinner's definition. "The term 'deprivation' has generally been used...but does not adequately characterize....Salt ingestion, perspiration, and blood loss...likewise temperature changes...emotional operations...and fear....A general term is needed for operations having these two effects on behavior" (Michael, 1982, p. 150). Perhaps the most significant aspect of Michael's work was an extension of the basic EO concept from innate physiological motivative variables to learned motivative variables. A brief overview of Michael's definition of the EO and his classification of the different types of EOs will be presented.

Michael (1993) defined the EO as "an environmental event...that affects an organism by momentarily altering (a) the reinforcing effectiveness (*value*) of other events, and (b) the frequency of occurrence of that part of the organism's repertoire relevant to those events as consequences" (p. 192). For example, food deprivation (a) increases the momentary effectiveness of food as a reinforcer, and (b) increases the frequency of any behavior that has been followed by food. For a child, food deprivation will (a) make food effective as reinforcement and (b) evoke behavior such as going to the place where food has been found, or possibly evoke a mand such as, "eat," or "popcorn," if this verbal behavior has been followed by the receipt of food in the past. "The first effect can be called *reinforcer establishing* and the second *evocative*" (Michael, 1993, p. 192). These two effects will be presented in detail later as the key elements to mand training for individuals with delayed or defective mand repertoires.

EOs not only increase the value of reinforcers, but they also decrease the value of reinforcers (e.g., satiation). Michael (1993) points out, "it is more accurate to think of motivative variables as establishing or abolishing operations and to think of their evocative effect as an increase or a decrease in the momentary or current frequency of the relevant kind of behavior" (p. 193). In a recent paper, the term "abative" has been suggested for this reduction effect (Laraway, Snycerski, Michael, & Poling, 2002).

Michael (1993) distinguished between two main types of EOs, unconditioned establishing operations (UEOs) and conditioned establishing operations (CEOs). Unconditioned EOs are related to unlearned forms of motivation (those frequently discussed in psychology textbooks as "innate drives" or "physiological motives"), such as deprivation of food, water, sleep, activity and oxygen; temperature regulation such as too hot or too cold; variables related to sexual reinforcement; and painful stimulation. The reinforcer-establishing effect of the UEO is innate, however, the behavior that is evoked by the UEO is learned. For example, food deprivation increases the effectiveness of food as reinforcement as an unlearned or innate effect, but the behavior of searching for food or asking for (manding) food is learned. The change in value is innate, but the change in behavior depends on the organism's learning history.

Conditioned EOs are related to learned forms of motivation (those frequently discussed in psychology textbooks as "acquired drives" or "social motives") such as those responsible for social attention, toys, and money functioning as reinforcement. The reinforcer establishing effect in the CEO is learned, and the behavior that is evoked by the change in the value of certain consequences is also learned. For example, when video taping an important event, such as a child's first birthday, the "end of tape" icon flashes on the screen. This stimulus change alters the value of a new tape (the reinforcer-establishing effect) and evokes behavior that has been followed by obtaining new videotapes in the past. As with UEOs, this behavior can be nonverbal such as searching in a drawer that often contains new tapes, or verbal such as the mand "Honey, can you get me a new tape?" The increase in the value of the tape is a learned relation, as is the behavior relating to obtaining a new tape. We are not born needing videotapes, nor do we inherit the behavior of looking or manding for them.

Michael (1993) identified three types of CEOs: transitive, reflexive, and surrogate. The transitive CEO consists of a stimulus condition that makes *some other stimulus condition* effective as a form of conditioned reinforcement, and evokes behavior that has obtained that item in the past. The example above with the videotape represents this type of CEO. The flashing icon is a stimulus condition that makes the other stimulus conditions (a new tape) reinforcing, and evokes the behavior of searching or manding. Transitive CEOs occur frequently throughout a person's day. Common activities such as self-care, cooking, cleaning, shopping, social interaction, schoolwork, and employment all involve transitive CEOs as a source of motivation.

The reflexive CEO involves an aversive stimulus condition that is a warning of some form of further worsening. This warning stimulus increases the current frequency of responses that have terminated the warning stimulus. For example, while eating lunch you drip tomato sauce on your tie. This stimulus change is probably an aversive stimulus, especially if you will be meeting with an important client after lunch. Thus, the soiled tie is a warning stimulus that more bad things are about to come (this is the reinforcer-establishing effect of the EO, in this case a clean tie is the reinforcer). The warning stimulus will evoke behavior that has resulted in the termination of the aversive stimulus. The person may begin to look for a napkin and water, if none are available he may mand to a waiter for them. Or, the person may mand for advice from others at the table as to the best method of removing tomato sauce from a tie. Reflexive CEOs occur frequently throughout a person's day. Many daily activities can involve aversive stimuli that need to be terminated (e.g., the water boiling over, smoke coming from the vacuum, not enough money in your wallet). Reflexive CEOs can be a main source of stress in one's life, especially if they do not evoke effective terminating behavior.

The surrogate CEO is a stimulus that is paired with some other effective EO, and can have the same effects as that EO. Beginning with the work of Pavlov (1927) on respondent conditioning, it became clear that a neutral stimulus can be paired with another effective stimulus and acquire some of the evocative effects of the original stimulus. Skinner (1938) extended this concept of stimulus-stimulus pairing to operant conditioning by demonstrating that previously neutral stimuli could acquire reinforcing or punishing properties by being paired with established forms of reinforcement or punishment (i.e., the behavioral principles of conditioned reinforcement and conditioned punishment). Michael (1993) suggested that similar effects are possible with EOs. While acknowledging that there are, as of yet, no data to support this extension of behavioral concepts, Michael suggested that the surrogate CEO is a different type of CEO because of the way it acquires its reinforcer-establishing and evocative effect. The concept also parallels the way other neutral stimuli acquire functional control in relation to other behavioral principles.

For example, say a person is food deprived (UEO) and a friend takes him to Krispy Kreme™ donuts to buy him a donut. While in line, the Krispy Kreme logo may be paired with food deprivation and acquire some of its reinforcer-establishing and evocative effects. This could only be observed on a future occasion when say, the person drives by a Krispy Kreme shop and finds he suddenly wants a donut, even though he previously was not hungry. The sign may have established donuts as a form of reinforcement and evoked the behavior of pulling into the parking lot and going into the shop and buying a donut. Michael (1993) also suggested that the operant components of some several types of emotional behavior may be more parsimoniously analyzed as surrogate CEOs, but the complexity of the analysis exceeds the purpose of the present chapter. For a more detailed analysis of EOs and emotion see Dougher and Hackbert, 2000.

## Multiple Effects

A single stimulus change may have several effects on behavior (Michael, 1985). In the example above, the sight of the Krispy Kreme logo could also function as a conditioned stimulus and elicit salivation (or an increased heart rate, perspiration, etc., if it was paired with the breakup). It also could function as a conditioned reinforcer (or punisher) and strengthen (or weaken) any behavior that preceded the presentation of the logo, such as singing a certain song in the car. The logo could also function as a discriminative stimulus, evoking verbal behavior such as the textual response "Krispy Kreme." In addition to all these effects, the EO effect may be most obvious when a mand occurs such as "I want a Krispy Kreme donut now!"

## Application of the EO to Language Training

EOs play a significant role in the early language acquisition of typical children (Bijou & Baer, 1965; Skinner, 1957). They are also an essential part of the training procedures used with nonverbal developmentally disabled individuals. In addition, they are directly relevant to a wide variety of more complex mands in advanced verbal behavior, and they often share control with verbal and nonverbal discriminative stimuli in other verbal operants. The definition of the mand and the EO, and the types of EOs identified by Michael (1993), can serve as a guide for the application of the EO as an independent variable in language training (Sundberg, 1993; Sundberg & Michael, 2001; Sundberg & Partington, 1998). However, the type of antecedent control for the mand, the EO, is often not as conspicuous as a discriminative stimulus, and may be overlooked as an essential part of the verbal functional relation.

Effective application of the EO, like the effective application of the other behavioral principles and concepts, requires special training. For example, the use of reinforcement as a teaching tool requires that the teacher be able to identify what functions as reinforcement, deliver it immediately and contingently on successive approximations of the target behavior, ultimately thin out the reinforcement schedule, and so on. The application of the EO to language instruction similarly requires specific skills on the part of the behavior analyst or practitioner to maximize its effectiveness as an independent variable.

## The Difference Between EOs and $S^D$s

In order to successfully use the EO as an independent variable, it is critical to be able to distinguish an EO from an $S^D$. Both antecedent variables evoke behavior, often the same behavior, but for different reasons. For example, a child may say "Juice" because he wants juice (a mand), or he may say "Juice" because he sees a juice box (a tact), or because the word "juice" is heard (an echoic), or a combination of these variables (multiple control). Michael (1982, 1993) states the difference as follows, "Discriminative variables are related to the differential *availability* of an effective form of reinforcement given a particular type of behavior; motivative variables are related to the differential *reinforcing effectiveness* of environmental events" (1993, p. 193). Availability means that a consequence for a particular response is more likely to occur in the presence of the stimulus than in its absence. For example, a greeting response to a passerby (e.g., "Good morning") is likely to be reinforced in the presence, but not the absence, of the person. Thus, passers-by become discriminative stimuli for greeting responses because of their relation to various forms of generalized conditioned reinforcement. Reinforcer-effectiveness is related to momentary value of those consequences. If a person is not reinforced by stranger attention at that moment, or is currently affected by some other EO, such as those related to a recent mugging, then the greeting response is less likely to occur, even though the reinforcement might be available.

Skinner's (1957) distinction between the mand and the tact provides a good example of the difference between the two forms of control. Mands are evoked when the value of what functions as reinforcement becomes strong, and the consequences for manding are specifically related to that form of reinforcement. Juice will be effective as reinforcement only when the child is thirsty. If the child is satiated with juice, then juice is not effective as reinforcement and the mand is less likely to occur. "Juice" as a tact is not related to the momentary value of juice, but rather to the availability of other forms of generalized conditioned reinforcement, such as praise or attention. Tacting juice does not result in receiving juice, but some other form of reinforcement (e.g., "Right!"). This is why what is often recorded as a correct response on a data sheet, may actually be an incorrect response if the data sheet is focusing on mand development, rather than tact development.

## Tacting the Presence and Strength of an EO

All mands are controlled by EOs, thus in order to teach a child to mand there must be an EO in effect during training. If there is not an EO controlling the response, then the response is not a mand. For example, when asked, "What toy do you want?" a child may respond "slinky," but when presented with the slinky he refuses the toy. The response "slinky" could be under the intraverbal control of the verbal stimulus "toy." It could be under tact control if a slinky is present, or echoic control if someone previously said "slinky," or textual control if he saw and could read the word "slinky." The point is, the defining feature of a mand is that the verbal response is primarily under the functional control of an EO. Other types of stimulus control are often present (i.e., verbal, nonverbal, audience), but the form of the response is controlled by an EO.

In order to use the EO as an independent variable in day-to-day language instruction, the trainer must be able to tact the presence and strength of an EO. When conducting mand training, as previously stated, an EO must be in effect or one cannot do mand training. If a child does not want bubbles at a particular time, a mand for bubbles cannot be taught at that time. Thus, it is critical that the trainer be able to tact the presence of an EO. Does the child want a particular item? Reinforcement surveys may tell you what the child liked at some time or another, but they will not tell you if a child wants that particular item at that particular moment. One must determine what functions as an effective form of reinforcement at that moment. Observation of a child's behavior in a natural setting can tell you some of what a child wants. Choice procedures can also be effective in determining the relative value of various forms of reinforcement (e.g., DeLeon & Iwata, 1996).

EOs vary in strength across time, and may be related to other EOs or the demands placed on a child. Therefore, teachers conducting mand training must be constantly aware of the relative strength of EOs at any given point in time. EOs also compete with each other. For example, a child may first want a specific toy, but when another child has a better toy, the first toy is dropped in preference for the second. Satiation will also affect the value of the EO. For example, popcorn may function as reinforcement for the first 50 kernels, but as the child satiates, the value of the reinforcer decreases. Thus, a language trainer must be aware of the fact that mands may not occur, or if a response does occur, it might not be a mand, but rather some other type of verbal behavior.

EOs may have an instant or gradual onset or offset. Food deprivation may build up slowly, but decrease quickly. The value of a particular toy may increase quickly and decrease quickly. For example, if a child is given a Magna Doodle® writing board, but no magnetic pen, the value of the pen might be strong immediately. Following a few minutes of drawing, the child might drop the pen and board and move on to another activity. A language trainer must be aware of all of these varying aspects of the EO. Otherwise mand training becomes much more difficult, if not impossible to conduct.

## Delivering Specific Reinforcement

The mand is strengthened by a type of reinforcement that is unique to the mand relation. Skinner (1957) terms this consequence "specific reinforcement" (p. 38). Specific reinforcement is directly related to the relevant EO, and may increase the future frequency of several different response forms if several different response forms have been reinforced. For example, if there is an EO for water, the effective consequence that is established is water. The response form may occur in several topographical variations, such as pointing to one's throat or a glass of water, or saying "Water," "I'm thirsty," "Can I have a drink?" and so on. However, the response form alone is insufficient for the classification of verbal behavior. It is the functional relation between antecedents, behavior, and consequence that is the unit of analysis (Skinner, 1957).

A thematic line of research has demonstrated that specific reinforcement has behavioral effects that are different from nonspecific reinforcement. The results have shown that specific reinforcement produces a higher percentage of correct responses (Sanders & Sailor, 1979); shorter response latencies, and subject preference for specific reinforcement conditions (Stafford, Sundberg, & Braam, 1988); better generalization, and the emergence of untrained receptive language (Braam & Sundberg, 1991).

## Capturing and Contriving EOs

There are several ways to capture or contrive EOs for purposes of language instruction. Michael's (1993) classification of the different types of EOs provides a useful guide for such applications. UEOs such as thirst and hunger are perhaps the simplest to use, since it is the passage of time that increases the momentary effectiveness of these consequences. These sources of control can be easily captured and manipulated in the natural environment simply by waiting until the EO is strong (a similar procedure could be used to remove an aversive stimulus occurring in the natural environment). UEOs can also be contrived by, for example, giving someone salty crackers to increase the value of liquids, or decreasing the temperature in a room to increase the value of warmth.

The three types of CEOs described by Michael (1993), transitive, reflexive and surrogate, can be captured or contrived, and used for behavioral assessments and interventions. Capturing a transitive CEO in the natural environment, for example, involves capitalizing on a situation where one stimulus increases the value of a second stimulus. For example, a nonverbal child who likes fire trucks sees a fire truck parked outside the window. This stimulus increases the value of a second stimulus, an unlocked door, and will evoke behavior that has resulted in doors opening in the past. A skilled trainer would be watchful for these events and would be quick to conduct a mand trial for the word "Open" or "Out." Since the EO is strong, this is the time to conduct mand training. The work of Hart and Risley (1975) and their incidental teaching model exemplifies this teaching strategy.

Transitive CEOs can also be contrived in order to conduct mand training (e.g., Carroll & Hesse, 1987; Hall & Sundberg, 1987; Sigafoos, Doss, & Reichele, 1989; Sundberg, Loeb, Hale, & Eigenheer, 2002; Sundberg & Partington, 1998). For example, in using this type of CEO procedure Hall and Sundberg (1987) presented a stimulus that increased the value of another stimulus, such as instant coffee without hot water. The coffee altered the value of hot water and thereby evoked behavior that had been followed by that form of reinforcement in the past. Appropriate mands were easy to teach when this EO was in effect. In fact, a number of mands were taught by using this procedure, and often the procedure led to the emission of untrained mands.

There are several possible applications of the reflexive CEO. For example, many individuals diagnosed with developmentally disabilities have acquired strong repertoires of escape and avoidance behavior (e.g., aggression, self-injurious behaviors). These behaviors often occur when attempts are made to teach language and other skills. Verbal stimuli presented to the individual may function like a reflexive CEO in that these stimuli are warning stimuli indicating that more bad things are coming, and behaviors that have terminated similar stimuli in the past occur immediately. The offset of the warning stimulus (e.g., the removal of the demand) will immediately reinforce any behavior that precedes such offset. Reducing these behaviors requires extinguishing the behaviors by not terminating the teaching situation, and by teaching an alternative mand that involves a more acceptable response form (e.g., Wilder & Carr, 1998).

The surrogate CEO, where a stimulus is correlated with a UEO, is relevant to analyses of emotional behavior. Specifically, neutral stimuli correlated with aversive stimuli may evoke emotional behavior as a CEO rather than as an S$^D$ or conditioned eliciting stimulus. For example, a child may engage in a high rate of crying upon entering a dentist's office because that particular room has been previously paired with painful stimuli. The previously neutral stimulus (the room) now may evoke behavior (tantrums) that has terminated such stimuli (the child is removed from the room). There could be many other negative behaviors that are caused, in part, by the surrogate CEO such as shyness or other emotional behaviors (Dougher & Hackbert, 2000). Reducing such negative behavior requires extinction of the behavior, and teaching the individual to remove the CEO by manding with a more acceptable response form.

It is not enough to be able to identify, capture, or contrive an EO. Once the value of a form of reinforcement is strong, the trainer must then be able to shape the appropriate verbal response. Effective shaping requires that a trainer be able to differentially reinforce successive approximations to the target behavior when the EO is strong. For example, the moment a child expresses interest in bubbles, the delivery of echoic prompts and the fading of those prompts is necessary to establish the verbal response "bubbles." In addition, the trainer must be assured that the response is truly free from other types of stimulus control, such as the presence of the bottle of bubbles, or the wand.

## Language Assessment

Most standardized language assessments test a child's language skills under the control of discriminative stimuli (e.g., pictures, words, questions, etc.). However, a substantial percentage of a typical child's verbal behavior is under the functional control of EOs. Manding is a dominating type of verbal behavior, yet rarely is this repertoire assessed in standardized testing. It is quite common to observe children diagnosed with autism or other developmental disabilities who are unable to mand, or have defective mand repertoires. Negative behavior may serve the mand function, or the response that is assumed to be a mand is actually controlled by discriminative stimuli rather than by EOs. If a language assessment fails to identify delayed or defective language skills that are related to EO control, an appropriate intervention program may be difficult to establish. A complete language assessment should determine the strength of verbal responses under not only discriminative stimuli, but also under the control of EOs (e.g., Partington & Sundberg, 1998; Sundberg, 1983; Sundberg & Partington, 1998).

## EOs and Mand Training

Mands are the first type of verbal behavior acquired by a human child (Bijou & Baer, 1965; Skinner, 1957). These mands typically occur in the form of differential crying when a child is hungry, tired, in pain, afraid, etc. Mands are very important to early language learners. They allow a child to control not only the delivery of conditioned and unconditioned reinforcers, but they begin to establish the speaker and listener roles that are essential to further verbal development. Mands are also the most likely type of verbal behavior to be emitted spontaneously, and generalization may occur quickly because of the unique effects of the EO. The data are quite clear that manding does not emerge from tact and receptive training for severely language delayed children (for a review see Shafer, 1994). Controlling and manipulating EOs can be more complex than presenting S^Ds, but if one is familiar with the methods of contriving and capturing EOs, the procedures are relatively straightforward. In addition, it is frequently reported by parents and trainers that mand training is more enjoyable for both parties, negative behavior occurs less, and children are more willing to participate in language training activities.

The best place to start mand training is with mands for reinforcers that have high EO values (e.g., food, outside, music, books, toys, tickles, juice, swing). Typically there is no need to contrive the EO for these strong motivators. The focus is on development of an acceptable response form under the control of the relevant EO. Other types of stimulus control (e.g., imitative prompts) can be used to develop EO control, but ultimately the mand should be free of verbal, nonverbal, echoic, or imitative stimulus control (e.g., see the "quick transfer procedure" described by Sundberg & Partington, 1998). Following the acquisition of mands related to EOs that are typically strong, the language trainer must often look to procedures that involve contriving EOs in order to establish the targeted mand. Below are a number of important mand repertoires that involve contriving EOs.

## Mands for Missing Items

The value of the mand to a speaker is that it has obtained objects and actions, or has brought about conditions that are not present. This means that to be optimally useful a mand should occur in the absence of the object or condition that is the reinforcement for the mand; it should occur primarily under the control of the EO. A common problem faced by many children diagnosed with autism or other developmental disabilities is that they are unable to mand for items that are not physically present. For example, a child may be able to ask for a specific toy when that toy is present, but if the toy is missing the child may be unable to tell anyone what is desired. The child may engage in generalized mand behavior such as pulling at the adult, or crying. Thus, many parents find themselves playing a guessing game by presenting several toys or objects or actions in order to satisfy the child.

Mand training may consist largely of presenting an object that is assumed to be effective as a reinforcer, and asking, "What do you want?" The "correct" answer to the question is then the same response form that has been appropriate as a tact, and the social reinforcement for making the response as a tact may be as important to the child as receiving the object. This procedure results in a functional relation that is part tact and part mand, and the mand relation may be the smaller part. The result may be no strong tendency to make the same response in the absence of the object (when the tact stimulus is not present) even when it would be effective as a form of reinforcement. The target repertoire for mand training is a response that is primarily under the control of an EO, even though additional contextual variables such as a specific setting or audience may be important. Training on these verbal skills is typically necessary and must occur when the EO is strong by either capturing an existing EO, or contriving a new EO (Hall & Sundberg, 1987; Sundberg, 1993; Sundberg, Loeb, Hale, & Eigenheer, 2002; Sundberg & Partington, 1998).

## Mands Involving the Different Parts of Speech

Perhaps one of the most significant aspects of Skinner's analysis of verbal behavior is the point that the same response form can occur in different verbal operants. For example, the response "red" can occur as an echoic, a tact, mand, intraverbal, or textual response. The controlling variables are different, but the form of the response is the same. Therefore, an important aspect of language training is to establish all of these different types of control for the different vocabulary words a person may emit. The traditional classification of nouns, verbs, adjectives, prepositions, etc. is a classification based somewhat on the form of the response (in addition to its function), however, it is still quite relevant to a behavioral analysis of language. The important point is to be sure to establish each of these different parts of speech in each of the elementary verbal operants. Perhaps the most elusive of these tasks is the establishment of these responses as mands, because they require that the functional source of control be an EO rather than a discriminative stimulus. Below are several examples of contriving or capturing the relevant EOs for teaching mands involving different parts of speech.

*Verbs: Mands controlled by an EO for movement.* For example, if watching things roll down an incline functions as reinforcement for a student, the trainer should hold the item at the top of the incline and prompt and differentially reinforce the mand "Roll."

*Adjectives: Mands controlled by an EO for specific properties of objects.* For example, if a student is reinforced by objects of a certain color, the trainer should prompt and differentially reinforce a mand involving that color (e.g., "Red candy").

*Prepositions: Mands controlled by an EO for specific positions.* For example, if a student is reinforced by playing games such as hide and seek, the trainer should prompt and differentially reinforce mands for movement to certain hiding places (e.g., "Behind the door").

*Adverbs: Mands controlled by an EO involving the properties of movement.* For example, if a student is reinforced by the song "Head, shoulders, knees and toes" sung at different paces, the trainer should prompt and differentially reinforce the responses "Go fast," or "Go slow."

## Mands for Information

According to Skinner (1957), "A question is a mand which specifies verbal action" (p. 39). The relevant EOs for asking questions are variables that result in an increase in the value of specific verbal information as a form of conditioned reinforcement and that evoke behavior that has been followed by such information. Questions are important for verbal development because they allow a speaker to react more precisely to the environment and to acquire additional verbal behavior. When an EO relevant to a mother's location becomes strong the relevant information would function as reinforcement for any response that preceded receiving such information and responses such as "Where's Mommy" will be strong. In this example, the relevant consequences involve the listener providing the child with verbal information regarding his mother's location (e.g., "She went to the store").

Part of the reason that language delayed children may have difficulty acquiring question-asking behavior is that for many of these children verbal information does not function as a form of conditioned reinforcement. Any procedure that attempts to teach this behavior without a relevant EO that makes information valuable must rely on EOs for other reinforcers such as tokens and tangibles to establish the correct response form. However, once the response form is established, it may actually be under the control of these other EOs and not an EO related to information as a reinforcer. That is, a speaker may emit a topographically correct "Wh" question, but the response is a function of the availability of reinforcement, rather than an increase in the value of specific verbal reinforcement (Michael, 1982, 1988; Skinner, 1957; Sundberg, Loeb, Hale, & Eigenheer, 2002). In common sense terms, the child may not really want to know the answer to the question, but is emitting the behavior to obtain some other form of reinforcement (e.g., attention, tokens). Below are several examples of contriving or capturing the relevant EOs for teaching mands for information.

*What?: Mands controlled by an EO involving the names of things.* For example, if a student sees a novel stimulus that cannot be tacted, the response "What's that?" should be prompted and differentially reinforced.

*Where?: Mands controlled by an EO involving the location of people or things.* For example, if a student cannot find his toy frog the trainer should prompt and differentially reinforce the response "Where's my frog?"

*Who?: Mands controlled by an EO involving information regarding a specific person.* For example, if a teacher gives a student's favorite toy to another teacher and tells the student "I gave your toy to a teacher" the trainer should then prompt and differentially reinforce the response "Who has it?"

*When?: Mands controlled by an EO involving an EO for information concerning time.* For example, if a student wants to see a movie and it is not currently available, the trainer should prompt and differentially reinforce the response "When will we watch the movie?"

*How?: Mands controlled by an EO involving instructional information or the function of things.* For example, if a student cannot make a certain toy work the trainer should prompt and differentially reinforce the response "How does it work?"

*Why?: Mands controlled by an EO involving the causes of actions or events, and other explanations of behavior.* For example, if a trainer emits a sudden behavior such as stopping while on a walk, and the student looks quizzically at her, trainer should prompt and differentially reinforce the response "Why are you stopping?"

## Additional Types of Mands

There are a wide variety of other mands that occur in day-to-day discourse that often must be directly taught to a language delayed person. Below are a sample of these mands and an identification of the relevant EO.

*General mands controlled by an EO involving human contact or assistance.* For example, if a student is reinforced by a high five, the trainer should prompt and differentially reinforce the response "High five," when an EO is present.

*Mands controlled by an EO involving eye contact or the physical proximity of others.* For example, if a student demonstrates an EO for attention is strong, the trainer should prompt and differentially reinforce a response such as tapping a teacher's arm.

## Mands for the Removal of Aversives

There are several different mands that can be evoked by learned aversive stimuli. Many individuals need to be specifically taught each of them (e.g., "Go away," "Don't," "Stop," "Give that back," "Leave me alone"). It is important that these responses be under EO control rather than evoked by a discriminative stimulus. Therefore, the aversive stimulus must be present during training, and terminating the aversive stimulus must be the main form of reinforcement for the correct response, otherwise the mand will not occur in the natural environment under the appropriate conditions. The language trainer must capture or contrive an EO involving the value of the termination of the aversive stimulus (e.g., pain, something stuck, something broken, darkness, a loud noise, someone too close, a peer who takes reinforcers). For example, if a student often emits head banging when a toy is stuck, the trainer should present the stuck toy (e.g., enclosed in his hands) and echoically prompt "Let go" before the head banging can occur. Correct echoic responses should be initially reinforced, then fade the echoic prompt.

## EOs Can Help to Establish Other Verbal Behaviors

It also appears that mand training, and the use of the EO as an independent variable, can facilitate the later development of echoic, tact, and intraverbal training in at least two ways. First, a successful mand program with a previously nonverbal child often changes the child's willingness to participate in training sessions. The child may experience success, where only failure had occurred in the past. Second, the EO can be used as an additional independent variable in teaching echoics, tacts, and intraverbals (multiple control). Once a specific response form is acquired under multiple sources of control, then procedures to break free from EO control and bring the response solely under the relevant discriminative stimulus control can be implemented (Carroll & Hesse, 1987; Drash, High, & Tutor, 1999; Sundberg & Partington, 1998).

## Summary

EOs play an important role in behavior analysis and have many applications to human behavior, especially in the area of language training for persons with delayed or defective language. However, in order to effectively use EOs as independent variables specialized repertoires are required. Once behavior analysts and practitioners acquire those repertoires, EOs can be identified, captured, and contrived to help establish a wide variety of important verbal behaviors, such as an initial mand repertoire, mands for missing items, mands for information, and mands involving the different parts of speech. Without these important verbal skills a verbal repertoire cannot be complete, and important verbal and social behaviors such as maintaining a conversation are impossible.

## A Call for a New Term

Michael and colleagues (Laraway, Snycerski, Michael, & Poling, 2003; Michael, 2002) recently proposed changing the term "establishing operation" to "motivative operation." While acknowledging that the term EO is gaining acceptance, the authors identify several advantages of the term motivative operation (MO). In addition to the immediate understanding by listeners as to the topic of analysis, the term MO (which would result in the UEO being identified as the UMO, and the CEO identified as the CMO) more easily accommodates the analysis of reduced motivation, and is overall more conceptually complete. According to Michael (personal communication), "the main advantages are that the terms are more logically consistent, are mutually exclusive and collectively exhaustive, and should for this reason be more easily learned and more effectively used for communicating with others and for communicating with oneself in the sense of thinking about the topic."

In the area of teaching language to children diagnosed with autism and other developmental disabilities it seems easier for parents and teachers to understand and implement procedures when the term motivative operation is used rather than establishing operation. The result can be an improved implementation of the recommended intervention procedures. For example, telling a parent to conduct a mand trial when the child's motivation for an object is strong, is more likely to succeed than telling the parent to wait for an establishing operation. Like all terminological changes, time will determine if the term MO will be an improvement over the previous term EO .

## Conclusion

Motivation is perhaps one of the most widely discussed topics in the field of psychology. The relevance of motivation to human behavior is ubiquitous, and most introductory psychology textbooks contain at least one chapter on the topic. However, motivation has not been considered a major topic in the field of behavior analysis, despite the fact that Skinner wrote extensively about motivation as an important antecedent variable. Much of what was once considered by Skinner as the topic of motivation in the early development of behavior analysis has been inappropriately subsumed under the topic of reinforcement. This situation has changed during the past 20 years, mainly due to the work by Michael (e.g., 1993) on the EO. The successful applications of the EO to mand training and the reduction of problem behaviors for persons with developmental disabilities have brought the topic of motivation into a larger focus in behavior analysis. There has been a sharp increase in research, and there are now hundreds of publications relevant to the EO and motivation. However, when compared to the extensive research on the other basic principles of behavior, the quantification of motivative variables encouraged by Skinner (1938) has just begun.

## References

Bijou, S. W., & Baer, D. M. (1965). *Child development II: Universal stage of infancy.* Englewood Cliffs, NJ: Prentice-Hall.

Braam, S. J., & Sundberg, M. L., (1991). The effects of specific versus nonspecific reinforcement on verbal behavior. *The Analysis of Verbal Behavior, 9,* 19-28.

Broadhurst, P. L. (1957). Emotionality and the Yerkes-Dobson law. *Journal of Experimental Psychology, 54,* 345-352.

Carroll, R. J., & Hesse, B. E. (1987). The effects of alternating mand and tact training on the acquisition of tacts. *The Analysis of Verbal Behavior, 5,* 55-65.

Catania, A. C. (1993). Coming to terms with establishing operations. *The Behavior Analyst, 16,* 219-224.

Catania, A. C. (1994). *Learning.* Englewood Cliffs, NJ: Prentice-Hall.

Clark, F. C. (1958). The effects of deprivation and frequency of reinforcement on variable interval responding. *Journal of the Experimental Analysis of Behavior, 1,* 221-228.

Cooper, J., Heron, W., & Heward, W. (1987). *Applied Behavior Analysis.* Englewood Cliffs, NJ: Prentice-Hall.

DeLeon, I. G., & Iwata, B. A. (1996). Evaluation of a multiple-stimulus presentation format for assessing reinforcer preferences. *Journal of Applied Behavior Analysis, 29,* 519-533.

Dougher, M. J., & Hackbert, L. (2000). Establishing operations, cognition, and emotion. *The Behavior Analyst, 23,* 11-24.

Drash, P. W., High, R. L., & Tutor, R. M. (1999). Using mand training to establish an echoic repertoire in young children with autism. *The Analysis of Verbal Behavior, 16,* 29-44.

Fantino, E., & Logan, C. A. (1979). *The Experimental Analysis of Behavior.* San Francisco: W. H. Freeman & Company.

Fisher, W. W., Thompson, R. H., DeLeon, I. G., Piazza, C. C., Kuhn, D. E., Rodriguez-Catter, V., & Adelinis, J. D. (1999). Noncontingent reinforcement: Effects of satiation verses choice responding. *Research in Developmental Disabilities, 20,* 411-427.

Goldiamond, I., & Dyrud, J. E. (1967). Some applications and implications of behavioral analysis for psychotherapy. In J. Schlien (Ed.), *Research in Psychotherapy, Vol. III* (pp. 54-89). Washington, D. C.: American Psychological Association.

Gottschalk, J. M., Libby, M. E., & Graff, R. B. (2000). The effects of establishing operations on preference assessment outcomes. *Journal of Applied Behavior Analysis, 33,* 85-88.

Hall, G. A., & Sundberg, M. L. (1987). Teaching mands by manipulating conditioned establishing operations. *The Analysis of Verbal Behavior, 5,* 41-53.

Hart, B., & Risley T. R. (1975). Incidental teaching of language in the preschool. *Journal of Applied Behavior Analysis, 8,* 411-420.

Hesse, B. (1993). The establishing operation revisited. *The Behavior Analyst, 16,* 215-217.

Holland, J. G., & Skinner, B. F. (1961). *The analysis of behavior.* New York: McGraw-Hill.

Iwata, B. A., Smith, R. G., & Michael, J. (2000). Current research on the influence of establishing operations on behavior in applied settings. *Journal of Applied Behavior Analysis, 33,* 411-418.

Kantor, J. R. (1959). *Interbehavioral psychology.* Granville, OH: Principia Press.

Keller, F. S. (1941). Light-aversion in the white rat. *Psychological Record, 4,* 235-250.

Keller, F. S., & Schoenfeld, W. N. (1950). *Principles of psychology.* New York: Appleton-Century-Crofts.

Lamarre, J., & Holland, J. G. (1985). The functional independence of mands and tacts. *Journal of the Experimental Analysis of Behavior, 43,* 5-19.

Laraway, S., Snycerski, S., Michael, J., & Poling, A. (2002). The abative effect: A new term to describe the action of antecedents that reduce operant responding. *The Analysis of Verbal Behavior, 18,* 101-106.

Laraway, S., Snycerski, S., Michael, J., & Poling, A. (2003). Motivating operations and terms to describe them: Some further refinements. *Journal of Applied Behavior Analysis, 36,* 407-414.

Leigland, S. (1984). On "setting events" and related concepts. *The Behavior Analyst, 7,* 41-45.

Malott, R. W., Whaley, W. L., & Malott, M. E. (1997). *Elementary principles of behavior (3rd ed.).* Englewood Cliffs, NJ: Prentice-Hall.

Martin, G., & Pear, J. J. (1978). *Behavior modification: What it is and how to do it.* Upper Saddle River, NJ: Prentice-Hall.

Martin, G., & Pear, J. J. (1988). *Behavior modification: What it is and how to do it (3rd ed).* Upper Saddle River, NJ: Prentice-Hall.

McComas, J., Hoch, H., Paone, D., & El-Roy, D. (2000). Escape behavior during academic tasks: A preliminary analysis of idiosyncratic establishing operations. *Journal of Applied Behavior Analysis, 33,* 479-493.

McDevitt, M. A., & Fantino, E. (1993). Establishing operations and the discriminative stimulus. *The Behavior Analyst, 16,* 191-206.

McGill, P. (1999). Establishing operations: Implications for assessment, treatment, and prevention of problem behavior. *Journal of Applied Behavior Analysis, 32,* 393-418.

McPherson, A., & Osborne, J. G. (1988). Control of behavior by an establishing stimulus. *Journal of the Experimental Analysis of Behavior, 36,* 375-386.

Michael, J. (1982). Distinguishing between discriminative and motivational functions of stimuli. *Journal of the Experimental Analysis of Behavior, 37,* 149-155.

Michael, J. (1985). Two kinds of verbal behavior plus a possible third. *The Analysis of Verbal Behavior, 3,* 1-4.

Michael, J. (1988). Establishing operations and the mand. *The Analysis of Verbal Behavior, 6,* 3-9.

Michael, J. (1993). Establishing operations. *The Behavior Analyst, 16,* 191-206.

Michael, J. (2000). Implications and refinements of the establishing operation concept. *Journal of Applied Behavior Analysis, 33,* 401-410.

Michael, J. (2002). *Motivation and early language training (video).* Kalamazoo, MI: Association for Behavior Analysis.

Millenson, J. R. (1967). *Principles of behavioral analysis.* New York: The MacMillian Company.

Millenson, J. R., & Leslie, J. C. (1979). *Principles of behavioral analysis* (2nd ed.). New York: The MacMillian Company.

Partington, J. W., & Sundberg, M. L. (1998). *The assessment of basic language and learning skills (The ABLLS).* Pleasant Hill, CA: Behavior Analysts, Inc.

Pavlov, I. P. (1927). *Conditioned reflexes.* London: Oxford University Press.

Pierce, W. D., Epling, W. F., & Boer, D. P. (1986). Deprivation and satiation: The interrelations between food and wheel turning. *Journal of the Experimental Analysis of Behavior, 46,* 199-210.

Powers, R. B., & Osborne, J. G. (1976). *Fundamentals of behavior.* St. Paul MN: West.

Premack, D. (1971). Catching up with common sense, or two sides of a generalization: Reinforcement and punishment. In R. Glaser (Ed.), *The nature of reinforcement* (pp. 121-150). New York: Academic Press.

Sanders, R. R., & Sailor, W. (1979). A comparison of three strategies of reinforcement on two-choice learning problems with severely retarded children. *AAESPH Review, 4,* 323-333.

Schlinger, H. D., Jr. (1993). Establishing operations: Another step toward a functional taxonomy of environmental events. *The Behavior Analyst, 16,* 207-210.

Shafer, E. (1994). A review of interventions to teach a mand repertoire. *The Analysis of Verbal Behavior, 12,* 53-66.

Sigafoos, J., Doss, S., & Reichele, J. (1989). Developing mand and tact repertoires with persons with severe developmental disabilities with graphic symbols. *Research in Developmental Disabilities, 11,* 165-176.

Skinner, B. F. (1938). *Behavior of organisms.* New York: Appleton-Century-Crofts.

Skinner, B. F. (1953). *Science and human behavior.* New York: MacMillan.

Skinner, B. F. (1957). *Verbal behavior.* New York: Appleton-Century-Crofts.

Smith, R. G., & Iwata, B. A. (1997). Antecedent influences on behavior disorders. *Journal of Applied Behavior Analysis, 30,* 343-375.

Stafford, M. W., Sundberg, M. L., & Braam, S. (1988). A preliminary investigation of the consequences that define the mand and the tact. *The Analysis of Verbal Behavior, 6,* 61-71.

Sundberg, M. L. (1983). Language. In J. L. Matson & S. E. Breuning (Eds.), *Assessing the mentally retarded* (pp. 285-310). New York: Grune & Stratton.

Sundberg, M. L. (1993). The application of establishing operations. *The Behavior Analyst, 16,* 211-214.

Sundberg, M. L., Loeb, M., Hale, L., & Eigenheer, P. (2002). Contriving establishing operations to teach mands for information. *The Analysis of Verbal Behavior, 18,* 14-28.

Sundberg, M. L., & Michael, J. (2001). The benefits of Skinner's analysis of verbal behavior for children with autism. *Behavior Modification, 25,* 698-724.

Sundberg, M. L., & Partington, J. W. (1998). *Teaching language to children with autism or other developmental disabilities.* Pleasant Hill, CA: Behavior Analysts, Inc.

Sundberg, M. L., San Juan, B., Dawdy, M., & Arguelles, M. (1990). The acquisition of tacts, mands, and intraverbals by individuals with traumatic brain injury. *The Analysis of Verbal Behavior, 8,* 83-99.

Vollmer, T. A., & Iwata, B. A. (1991). Establishing operations and reinforcement effects. *Journal of Applied Behavior Analysis, 24,* 279-291.

Whaley, D. L., & Malott, R. W. (1971). *Elementary principles of behavior.* Englewood Cliffs, NJ: Prentice-Hall.

Wilder, D. A., & Carr, J. E. (1998). Recent advances in the modification of establishing operations to reduce aberrant behavior. *Behavioral Interventions, 13,* 43-59.

## Footnotes

The author wishes to acknowledge Jack Michael and Cindy A. Sundberg for their comments on earlier versions of this paper.

Address correspondence concerning this chapter to the author, Behavior Analysts, Inc., 1941 Oak Park Blvd., Suite 30, Pleasant Hill, CA 94523.

# Chapter 10

# Emotional Recognition
# and Mental Retardation

Kyle E. Ferguson and W. Larry Williams
*University of Nevada, Reno*

Following the Wyatt v. Stickney (1972) ruling mandating the reduction of institutionalized individuals with mental retardation[1], there has been a movement away from institutionalization to community placement (McAlpine, Kendall, & Singh, 1991). Even though this trend generally reflects an improvement in living conditions, many individuals lack the social skills to integrate successfully with society (Mathias, 1990). This is a serious problem given that an adequate repertoire of social skills is essential in achieving a good quality of life and gaining acceptance from the community (McAlpine, Singh, Kendall, & Ellis, 1992, p. 543). As a case in point, poor social functioning is related to reinstitutionalization (Schalock & Harper, 1978), employment loss (Greenspan & Shoultz, 1981), and depression (Benson, Reiss, Smith, & Laman, 1985).

In response to this pressing concern, a considerable amount of research efforts have focused on social skills training. Largely the emphasis of such endeavors has been on behavioral response elements necessary for competent interpersonal functioning. Assuming deficits in specific motor-response channels (Singh & Winton, 1983), previous studies tended to underscore such response modalities as gesturing and non-aggressive touch (Gable, Hendrickson, & Strain, 1978), eye contact (Williams, Martin, McDonald, Hardy, & Lambert, 1975), and verbal behavior (Dy, Strain, Fullerton, & Stowitscheck, 1981), to name only a few. Recent findings, however, suggest that the response skill model is inadequate in explaining the intricacies of interpersonal behavior (Morrison & Bellack, 1981). The ability to discriminate relevant social stimuli also appears to be necessary in effective social behavior[2] (Mathias, 1990; Shantz, 1975; Simeonsson, 1978; Simeonsson, Monson, & Blacher, 1984). For instance, supporting this claim, Warren (cited in Rojahn, Rabold, & Schneider, 1995) found that subjects' scores on the Social Performance Survey Schedule (Matson, Helsel, Bellack, & Senatore, 1983) are significantly correlated with performance on an emotional recognition task[3].

Although there are several media through which social stimuli are conveyed (e.g., proxemics, kinesics, prosody, body posture, paralinguistics, and touch; McAlpine et al. 1992), arguably, facial expression communicates with the greatest precision (Ekman & Friesen, 1971, 1975, 1983). Indeed, a tremulous voice, a slouched body posture, and an unkempt appearance might indicate that the conveyor is probably upset in a very general sense; yet, given these stimuli the observer is unable to discriminate (or accurately tact; Skinner, 1957[4]) whether or not he or she is angry, afraid, melancholy, or sickened by our company.

The expressions appearing on the face convey very precise signals of the specific emotions, and as such, allow for tighter stimulus control (McCrosky & Wheeless, 1976). Granted that our individual in the above example has drawn and lowered his or her brows, causing vertical lines to appear between the brows, with eyes bulging and nostrils flared, we may safely assume that he or she is angry (Ekman & Friesen, 1975, pp. 96-97). Considering these discriminative stimuli, we would make behavioral adjustments accordingly, such as trying to assuage his or her anger, or leave the situation entirely. On the other hand, if our subject presents with the inner corners of the eyebrows drawn up, triangulating the skin below the eyebrow, with the corners of the lips pulled down, perhaps trembling, we might conclude that he or she is sad (Ekman & Friesen, 1975, p. 126). Given this set of stimuli, nurturing behavior would likely be appropriate in this situation.

In addition to emitting emotional messages in and of themselves, facial expressions also augment other channels of communication. Facial expressions are especially important in extending the stimulus dimensions of vocal behavior (Skinner, 1957, pp. 14-19). For example, facial expressions compliment or qualify utterances of the speaker and may also substitute speech, such as winking or raising an eyebrow to show approval or disapproval, respectively (Knapp, 1978, p. 265). As complementing stimuli, facial expressions are especially important in accurately tacting the intentions of others. When an observer fails to do so, often results in responding inappropriately.

In addition to determining other peoples' emotional state, facial expressions also provide information as to the fidelity of that spoken. Indeed, incongruencies between that said and an individual's facial expressions, often leads one to conclude that the speaker is being deceitful (see Ekman & Friesen, 1975, Chapter 11). A failure to appreciate this distinction often places an individual at risk of being exploited.

Other types of communicative channels are also modified through facial expressions. Technically speaking, facial expressions serve as overarching contextual stimuli (Wahler & Fox, 1981). Consider how facial expressions act as setting events in the following situations. A firm touch, such as squeezing someone's arm, is usually construed as aggressive when the person doing the squeezing is snarling. Conversely, place a grin from ear to ear on that same individual, and he or she is behaving lovingly. In either context, the person's facial expression has the final say in how his or her intentions are interpreted by the onlooker, be they hostile or friendly.

Another example takes us to a work environment. When a supervisor frowns at a worker, this generally indicates that the employee is doing something wrong. The supervisor's facial expression, thus, sets the occasion for the worker to modify his or her behavior, otherwise he or she is likely to get fired.

The forgoing discussion has dealt with emotional expressions in very general terms. Facial stimuli are, however, intrinsically multifaceted. In which case, the invocation of a finer-grained analysis is in order to parcel out topographical indices. To this end, Ekman and Friesen (1975) have made efforts to isolate topographical features essential to each emotional expression.

## A Taxonomy of Facial Expressions[5]

Ekman and Friesen (1975) set out to isolate specific features that inhere in facial expressions. In effect, they developed a "facial atlas" that depicts the topographical features of the emotions surprise, fear, disgust, anger, happiness, and sadness. These topographical features were extrapolated from three areas capable of independent movement: "The brow/forehead, the eyes/lids and the root of the nose; and the lower face, including the cheeks, mouth, and most of the nose and chin" (Ekman & Friesen, 1975, p. 103). As one might expect, each of the six emotions results from a variety of combinations and permutations of several facial regions.

*Surprise.* Surprise is the most transient emotion (p. 34). It rises and dissipates abruptly and does not linger as other expressions do. The topographical features of surprise are demarcated as follows: The eyebrows appear arched and high; the skin above the upper eyelid becomes more exposed as the brow is stretched; horizontal wrinkles arise across the forehead; the eyes are open wide with the lower eyelids relaxed; the above eyelids are raised; and the jaw drops causing the lips and teeth to part (pp. 37-40). Of course, surprise as with other expressions to follow, falls along continua by which certain features are accentuated, given individual differences (e.g., age, race, history of exposure to the sun, among others) as well as disparate contingencies (e.g., cultural and situational determinants) affecting expressive nuances (Kantor, 1982).

*Fear.* The expression fear co-occurs with a threat of harm to the organism. The nature of harm may vary from something rather innocuous such as a pop quiz to life-endangering circumstances like escaping the clutches of a grizzly bear. Though unlike surprise, fear can last much longer. Fear lingers. The topographical characteristics of fear are as follows: Raised and straightened eyebrows; with converging brows; horizontal wrinkles appear across the forehead, though, not traversing the entire forehead as they do in surprise; the eyes are open and tense; the upper eyelids are raised and the lower eyelids appear rigid; and the mouth opens, perhaps drawing back tightly (pp. 50-55).

*Disgust.* Disgust coincides with aversive contingencies, though in situations not as injurious or potentially lethal as those engendering fear. Tasting tainted meat, touching a slimy surface, or catching wind of someone's decaying garbage usually elicits the expression identified as disgust. Complex social situations also occasion subtle or not so subtle shades of disgust, say, the response of a prudish onlooker just as a soapbox orator makes an off-colored remark. Regardless of the circumstances in which it occurs, the most important topographical features of disgust manifest in the mouth and nose, and to a lesser extent in the lower eyelids and eyebrows (p. 68). Specifically, these and other features appear as follows: The upper lip is raised, modulating the appearance of the tip of the nose; the nose becomes increasingly wrinkled in more extreme presentations of disgust; and the cheeks are raised producing a change in the appearance of the lower eyelid (pp. 68-69).

*Anger.* Arising under similar contingencies as disgust is anger. Anger is the emotional pattern that accompanies revolt and has a well marked effect upon operant behavior, including a heightened disposition to act aggressively while reciprocally weakening nonaggressive behavior (Skinner, 1953, p. 362). As with other emotions, the countenance of anger varies along a continuum, ranging from obvious to very slight manifestations. What's more, as seen in other expressions, there are distinguishing characteristics inhering in the expression of anger. These topographical features culminate as follows: The eyebrows are drawn and converge together; the forehead is devoid of horizontal wrinkles; the eyelids are tense and stare out in a penetrating fashion; and the mouth is forced open, appearing square at the bottom; moreover, the lips might also be pressed tightly together (pp. 82-88).

*Happiness.* There is a wide gulf between the emotional expressions of anger and happiness. Unlike anger, a happy facial expression suggests an increased probability or a predisposition that the conveyor will act in a reinforcing manner (Skinner, 1953, p. 162). There are distinct features entailed in this facial expression. Here are several topographical characteristics that are associated with this emotional expression: The corners of the lips are drawn back and slightly raised; the lips may remain together, disjoin, or manifest with the teeth and jaw together in a grin; the cheeks become raised; the skin under the lower eyelid is pushed up, and lines emerge from below the eye (a.k.a. "crow's-feet"). As with the forgoing expressions, happiness varies in intensity, ranging from mildly happy to full elation.

*Sadness.* Sadness is generally associated with depriving an organism of reinforcement or results from a loss of an opportunity in engaging in a reinforcing activity. Sadness varies along dimensional gradations as does every other emotional expression. Its topographical features are as follows: The inner corners of the eyebrows are raised, forming a triangular appearance in the skin directly below; the corner of the upper eyelid is raised; the corner of the lips are down; additionally, the lips may also be trembling.

Sadness, like other emotional expressions, plays an integral role in the constellation of social stimuli. The inability in recognizing expressions as such, precludes an individual from successfully integrating in all social milieus. An inability in perceiving emotional stimuli prevents one from effectively relating with other members of society. As will be elucidated later, individuals with mental retardation are often deficient in discriminating between emotional stimuli (Mathias, 1990).

The precise mechanisms involved in emotional recognition are presently unknown. The process by which an individual accurately identifies these social stimuli are undoubtedly multiply determined. Recognizing emotional expressions entail a long series of stimulus-response exchanges.

Some might argue that emotional recognition is simply conditional discrimination. However, recognizing facial expressions, and the development and refinement of this behavioral repertoire, appears to be more involved than that. For example, effectively identifying emotional expressions in all instances cannot possibly be solely explained by conditional discrimination, because individuals are able to identify emotions for the first time in the absence of direct training. As is the case in identifying such complex emotions as embarrassment or jealousy, there is usually no one-to-one correspondence between the appropriate verbal response and reinforcement during behavioral acquisition. A more comprehensive system of analysis ought to import theories that deal with more complex behavioral repertoires.

## The Mechanisms of Emotional Recognition

*Observing Response.* The first stage in identifying emotional stimuli is that of making an observing response. An observing response orients the individual to the behaving organism more generally, and to emotional stimuli in particular (Holland, 1958). By bringing the individual into contact with such stimuli, this will enable the stimulus functions of objects (i.e., facial features) to exert influence upon the observer (Kantor & Smith, 1975). As is the case with other operants, the functional relationship between the emotional stimulus and the observing response is under the control of the prevailing contingencies. Moreover, when certain emotional stimuli are present, and when these properties acquire specific influence, we call this process discrimination (Skinner, 1974, p. 82), or for our present purposes emotional discrimination.

*Tacting Emotional Stimuli.* After individuals are attending to the pertinent emotional stimuli, the next stage in emotional recognition is tacting those emotional features. Paraphrasing Skinner's (1957) definition, this term may be defined as a verbal operant of a particular form, which is evoked by certain stimulus or event characteristics (pp. 81-82). Moreover, the strength of this functional relationship depends upon the extent to which the verbal operant has been reinforced by the verbal community. With respect to tacting facial expressions, this would entail emitting the appropriate verbal stimulus (e.g., anger, surprise, sorrow, and so forth) in the presence of critical nonverbal stimuli (e.g., a grin, trembling lips, furrowed brows, and the like).

*Rule-Governance.* Once an individual appropriately tacts an emotional expression he or she must then evaluate whether such stimuli is positive or negative. That is to say, the observer must determine based on the individual's emotional display, the likelihood that certain classes of behavior will be reinforced, extinguished, or punished. In either case should the observer emit responses incongruent with the contingencies that prevail, the observer's behavior will likely follow with an aversive outcome (e.g., telling jokes when the person is angry). Conversely, should the individual act in agreement with the contingencies at hand, the observer's behavior will likely result in reinforcement be it positive or negative.

Let us turn to an example to help illustrate this point. An individual has just violently struck her thumb while attempting to hammer in a nail. Moreover, she has a ruddy complexion, is clenching her teeth, and is screaming out every expletive in a sailor's verbal repertoire. Even upon correctly tacting this cluster of stimuli as anger, we still need to respond to this event in accordance with idiosyncratic rules pertaining to one's history with her, and with respect to rules of a more global nature.

Should we tact "anger" only to begin complimenting her on her hairstyle, we will undoubtedly run into trouble. A more appropriate response might entail nurturing or leaving the situation entirely in the event that she becomes volatile.

The behavior to which we have been referring is called rule-governed behavior. Although there is much debate as to what are particular instances of rule-governed behavior, a widely accepted definition is that originally proffered by Skinner (1966), which had been elaborated upon by others (See Parrott, 1987, for an alternative position on this subject). Rules are special classes of discriminative verbal stimuli (Baum, 1994; Catania, Shimoff, & Matthews, 1989, p. 120). Rules are said to specify contingencies of reinforcement (Pierce & Epling, 1995).

Zettle and Hayes (1982) propose three principle functional units of rule-governed behavior which are pliance, tracking, and augments. Of the three, tracking and augmenting rules are most germane for our discussion here. First, we will describe what tracking is, which will be followed with an example. Second, augments will also be taken up in this section.

The second principle unit of rule-governed behavior is termed tracking (Zettle & Hayes, 1982, p. 81; the rule per se is called a track). Tracking is rule-governed behavior under the influence of the degree to which a rule corresponds to the way the world is arranged (Zettle & Hayes, 1982, p. 81). That is, tracks specify the circumstances by which a reinforcer or punisher will likely follow the emission or absence of a given operant. Moreover, the more deferred the anticipated consequences, the less likely we are to follow rules of this sort.

Examples of tracks illustrating the above points are as follows. The advice "Do not drink caffeinated beverages just prior to retiring for the evening," will likely be observed given the immediacy of the consequences of failing to comply. Anyone who has imbibed a cup or two of coffee at this time will undoubtedly realize that this rule corresponds well with the way the world is arranged. Conversely, the rule "You should not smoke for it causes cancer," is less likely to influence behavior to the same degree. The consequences to which this rule refers are far too remote. Indeed, the chances of a pre-teenager getting cancer in the near future are slim. Additionally, the rule "Smoking is in," will supersede this rule as a result of the immediate social consequences for following it (i.e., support from one's peer group, who smoke).

Zettle and Hayes (1982, pp. 81-82) also describe a third unit of rule-governed behavior they term augmenting (the rule itself is called an augmental). Augmenting is rule-governed behavior under the "apparent changes in the capacity of events to function as reinforcers or punishers" (Zettle & Hayes, 1982, p. 81). As Hayes, Zettle, and Rosenfarb (1989, p. 206) note, an augmental is a verbal stimulus that also serves as an establishing stimulus as described by Michael (1993, Chapter 7). That is to say, an establishing stimulus has two momentary effects (Michael, 1993, p. 58), one it establishes other stimuli as reinforcers, and two, it has an evocative effect.

Much of the arts employ the use of literary devices that serve as augmentals. Indeed, it is through such verbal stimuli, which engender the elicitation of conditioned emotional responses on the part of the reader or observer (Skinner, 1957). Consider this famous passage from Edgar Allan Poe's, *The Fall of the House of Usher* (1951) as a case in point:

During the whole of a dull, dark, and soundless day in the autumn of the year, when the clouds hung oppressively low in the heavens, I had been passing alone, on horseback, through a dreary tract of country...with an utter depression of the soul which can compare to no earthly sensation...There was an iciness, a sinking, a sickening of the heart...(p. 115).

In this passage, Poe provides a graphic description that in a literary sense portends impending doom. Moreover, through this passage a panoply of aversive conditioned emotional responses will likely be elicited as one reads through every line. Using Michael's (1993) analysis, autoclitics such as "dull," "dreary," and "iciness" are evocative in that they engender "depressing" imagery, "feelings," and so forth. They are also reinforcer-establishing in a sense that they increase the aversive properties of events around us, after reading this passage.

At any rate augmentals are critical in our understanding of the processes involved in emotional recognition. For instance, following the augmental, "Her facial expression looks as if she is ready to explode," should evoke effective behavior with respect to assuaging her anger, and it increases the reinforcing properties of leaving the situation if in doing so has led to auspicious outcomes in the past.

*Stimulus Equivalence.* Stimulus equivalence has much to contribute to our understanding of how individuals come to recognize subtler shades of emotional expressions. At the heart of this theory is the whole notion of transfer of functions. That is to say, this theory addresses the transfer of evocative and consequential functions from one stimulus to the next (Hayes, Devany, Kohlenberg, Brownstein, & Shelby, 1987). In this regard we, in part, account for supposed mechanisms by which individuals learn about emotional stimuli without being explicitly taught.

Stimulus equivalence has received much attention within recent years. The principal reason for this rapid outgrowth is because the concept of stimulus equivalence lends support for a behavioral account of cognition and language (Sidman, 1992). Another reason is due to the fact that equivalence is not readily accounted for by the concept of conditional discrimination: The three-term contingency does not predict the emergence of untrained performances (Barnes, 1994). In particular, in a typical stimulus equivalence preparation, subjects are directly trained to choose Stimulus B and Stimulus C given Stimulus A, and then during testing, most subjects select Stimulus B in the presence of Stimulus C without further reinforcement. Readers should note that neither Stimulus B nor Stimulus C has been differentially reinforced in relation to one another. It follows, therefore, that neither stimulus should reliably exert stimulus control given this arrangement. The concept of conditional discrimination has no ready explanation for why this is so.

Sidman (1971, 1980, 1987) advanced the matching-to-sample procedural definition of equivalence. This definition is cast in terms of mathematical equivalence (Sidman, 1992). Mathematical equivalence entails three properties, the first of which is reflexivity. Reflexivity refers to a conditional relation in which stimuli that are conditionally related to one another must show the same relation to themselves. The specific term for this test is generalized identity matching, or simply, untrained identity matching. In short, when provided with an array of stimuli, reflexivity is shown when an individual matches stimuli that are identical across all dimensions.

The second requirement for equivalence is the property of symmetry. Symmetrical relations consist of untrained matching of stimuli with sample-comparison positions reversed with respect to training (Cowley, Green, & Braunling-McMorrow, 1992). Each sample and its positive comparison thus comprise a functionally equivalent stimulus class (Skinner, 1953) – they are not identical with respect to formal characteristics (Mackay & Sidman, 1984). The specific term for this test is arbitrary matching, although it is sometimes called "symbolic" matching. The point to notice here is that samples and comparisons need not resemble each other.

Let us now consider the third and final property of mathematical equivalence, that being transitivity. The learner must be taught at least two discriminations which are linked via a common stimulus. The training would proceed as follows. First, the conditional relation of set A along with set B would be trained. Second, an additional conditional relationship involving set B is taught with respect to a novel set of stimuli, let us call this group C. If the learner then matches those stimuli in set C in the presence of A, the relation among the stimuli has the property of transitivity.

This relationship is said to be derived or emergent, in light of the fact that the stimuli contained in groups A and C were never presented together in training – they were linked by common stimuli, namely, set B (Rehfeldt & Hayes, 1998). Technically speaking, when a particular function is trained to a given stimulus, that function will transfer to other stimuli symmetrically or equivalently related to that stimulus (Barnes & Keenan, 1993; Hayes, Kohlenberg, & Hayes, 1991).

This whole notion of transfer of function is especially pertinent to understanding possible processes involved in emotional recognition. Moreover, it is through these purported mechanisms by which individuals might come to respond appropriately in accordance with emotional stimuli without being explicitly taught how to do so.

Once individuals have been trained in relational learning of this sort, and have demonstrated mastery within this set of procedures, then these skills tend to transfer to other settings. Research indicates that equivalence class formation is highly generalizable across settings and procedures (Rehfeldt & Hayes, 1998). After a history of reinforcement for responding relationally to arbitrarily applicable stimuli in a particular context, responding will generalize to novel stimuli given similar contextual parameters (Hayes, 1991). Equivalencing is therefore a generalized operant class that is contextually controlled.

It follows, therefore, that equivalence technology has much potential both in terms of understanding the development of perceptual phenomena, as in the case of emotional recognition, as well as providing techniques by which perceptual behavior might be taught.

## Studies Investigating Emotional Recognition
## with Mental Retardation

Research has demonstrated repeatedly that individuals with mental retardation do not fare as well on emotion recognition tasks. In what follows, we review several seminal studies on emotional recognition and mental retardation. For a comprehensive and up-to-date review the reader should consult an excellent article by Moore (2001).

Some researchers suggest that there is a distinct deficit related to mental retardation called the emotion-specificity hypothesis. As such, "mental retardation is associated with deficits in decoding facially expressed emotions (that are not) fully accounted for by Mental Age (MA)" (Rojahn et al. (1995, p. 477, parenthesis added). Emotion-specificity refers to an impairment in dealing strictly with affective information as opposed to cognitive processes in general.

Rojahn and his colleagues (1995) set out to test the emotion-specificity hypothesis. They tested this hypothesis on three groups of 16 participants: adults with mild to moderate mental retardation (called the "mentally retarded" group; 7 men, 9 women), adults of about the same age not diagnosed with mental retardation (the "adult control group," 11 men, 5 women), and children matched with respect to MA (the "child control group," 7 boys, 9 girls).

To evaluate participants' emotional recognition skills Rojahn et al. (1995) employed the use of The Facial Discrimination Task (Erwin et al., 1992). This instrument is comprised of two subtasks. One of which tests the ability to discriminate facial emotional stimuli while the other targets participants' ability in distinguishing disparity among different sets of facial-age cues. Each subtest is composed of 40 black-and-white 13 cm x 18.5 cm photographs of faces. For their study, test administration was slightly modified between groups. For instance, with the child control group and the group comprising the mentally-retarded adults, the test was presented in this manner. Using a 5-point scale participants were asked to respond vocally or were required to point to a 3 cm x 12 cm horizontal bar consisting of three cells set on a letter-sized sheet of paper. The left cell had the word "happy" printed on it, the middle cell was blank, and printed on the remaining cell positioned to the right was the word "sad." For the age-task the words "old" and "young" appeared in the left and right cells, respectively. Positioned below the cells were two vertical columns, a short line (5 cm) representing "a little" and situated adjacently, was a longer line (12 cm) that denoted the response "a lot." Such provisions were not employed with the adult control group. The adult control group used the 7-point scale without such response aids, as originally intended by Erwin et al. (1992).

On the emotion task, participants were asked to indicate whether the photograph depicted a happy face, a sad face, or a face that was neither happy nor sad. Following a response suggesting the presence of either emotion, participants were then asked to indicate whether the model was a "little happy or sad" or a "lot happy or sad."

Adults with mental retardation were tested in two sessions. During the first session The Facial Discrimination Task was employed. To minimize order effects, the task sequence was counterbalanced across subjects (emotion task first vis-à-vis the age task first). As an additional experimental control, three different experimenters were also employed in administering this set of exercises.

Answers were transformed into three different response measures comprising an overall correct score, a sensitivity score, and a specificity score. Correct responses were those that matched Erwin et al.'s (1992) recommendations derived from a consensus rating procedure. So conceived, the overall correct score was the number of items correctly identified divided by the total number of items. Sensitivity scores were defined as the number of correctly recognized items of a particular emotional or age category, divided by the total number of items of that emotion or age category. The third measure, specificity, was defined as the total number of correctly identified neutral items divided by the number of neutral items. In analyzing the data, Rojahn et al. (1995) used overall correct score as the main dependent variable, while employing sensitivity and specificity measures in post hoc error analyses.

Descriptive statistical analyses indicated that the group with mental retardation achieved an average of .60 (SD = 0.15) overall correct score on the emotion recognition task; the child control group obtained a mean of .78 (SD = 0.13); and the adult control group's mean performance was .79 (SD = 1.00). Reflecting a similar trend across groups, on the age task, the overall correct scores were .53 (SD = 0.19), .57 (SD = 0.15), and .82 (SD = 0.44), respectively.

The primary statistical analysis was a 3 (groups) x 2 (tasks) mixed design analysis of variance with a between-subjects factor (group) and a within-subject factor (task). As aforementioned, the dependent variable was the overall correct score. In sum, analyses revealed a significant Tasks x Groups interaction effect (p < .001), and both main effects were significant (group, p < .001; task, p < .01). Two posteriori one-way analyses of variance were also employed to parse out differences between groups with respect to the two tasks. As predicted, the three groups differed significantly from one another on both tasks (p < .001). Subsequent analysis (Tukey tests) indicated that the group with mental retardation scored significantly lower (p < .01) on the emotion recognition task than both the adult and child control groups. The analysis also revealed that the two control groups were not statistically significant from one another. On the age task, both groups, the retarded and child control group scored significantly lower (p < .001) than the adult control group.

The error data for the emotion and age tasks were examined apart from the above analyses. These data may be summed up as follows. The three groups differed significantly on sensitivity happy and sad (p < .001 and p < .01, respectively), and specificity (p < .01). Specifically, pairwise comparisons revealed that the adult control group performed significantly better than both the child control group and the mentally retarded group, whereas the latter groups did not significantly differ with one another. Sensitivity for sadness indicated that both control groups outperformed the retarded group, but did not significantly differ from each other. Lastly, upon examining specificity scores, the adult groups differed significantly from the child group. With respect to sensitivity and specificity scores on age tasks, sensitivity for young faces, sensitivity for old faces, and specificity for neither young nor old faces eventuated in a significant main effect among groups (p<.001). Results also showed that groups differed significantly on both sensitivity scores (young, < .01; old, <.05); the adult control group performed significantly better than the child control group and the mentally retarded group; and the child control group and the mentally retarded group were not statistically significant with respect to one another. Lastly, on sensitivity for old faces, both adult groups performed significantly higher than the child control group, though did not differ with respect to one another.

Based on these results, Rojahn et al. (1995) conclude that adults with mental retardation have significant difficulties in discriminating between emotional stimuli depicted facially. They further add that deficient performance could not be attributed to impaired intellectual functioning in light of evidence that MA-matched children showed superior performance. As a corollary, they argue that the results of their study confirm the emotion-specificity hypothesis.

These conclusions, however, are premature in regards to emotional recognition in general. One must examine emotional recognition utilizing other emotional stimuli as well, such as tone of voice, posture, touch, and the like – not to mention employing more facial expressions than just happy and sad. Indeed, just narrowing our analysis to facial stimuli reveals that individuals with mental retardation respond differentially (i.e., they are better able to identify some emotions (e.g., happy) compared to others (e.g., surprise; McAlpine et al., 1992).

An additional criticism concerns their choice of including a neutral category. In consideration of Ekman and Friesen's (1975) taxonomy, no facial expression is devoid of emotional content. Let us recall that facial expressions are compound stimuli comprised of at least three areas capable of independent movement. Perhaps neutrality might be construed as a milder form of sadness or nascent disgust, given that the model is not ostensibly smiling or pressing his or her lips tightly together as in the case of anger.

The emotion-specificity hypothesis aside, in light of Rojahn et al.'s data and others to follow, individuals with mental retardation clearly show diminished ability in emotional recognition. Touching this point, McAlpine et al. (1991) also investigated facial emotional responding in persons with mental retardation. McAlpine et al. cast their study in terms of emotional discrimination with respect to overall intellect, though these researchers parceled out a finer-grained analysis of the nature of impairment, as well as provided a more thorough inquiry into other emotional genera as well.

McAlpine et al. (1991) investigated 501 children, adolescents, and adults with mental retardation ability in recognizing the six basic facial expressions[6] as described by Ekman and Friesen (1975). The demographic characteristics of the participants were broken down as follows: 179 children and adolescents, ranging in age from 5 to 19 years, with a mean age of 13 years; 194 adults, ranging in age from 19 to 67, with a mean age of 33 years. Participants were recruited from the community and a public residential facility. In accordance with the American Association on Mental

Retardation (AAMR; Grossman, 1983), regarding the cohort of children and adolescents: 19 were labeled as having borderline intelligence; 62 were classified as mildly retarded; 78 as moderately retarded; and 20 were labeled as having severe mental retardation. Using the same diagnostic criteria suggested by the AAMR, the adult population was comprised of 6 as having borderline intelligence; 35 were classified as being mildly retarded; 104 as moderately retarded; 40 were labeled severely retarded; and 9 participants were classified as profoundly retarded. In addition to the experimental groups, a control group comprised of 128 children without mental retardation was employed. The participants in the control group were recruited from an elementary and junior high school. The age of the control subjects ranged from 5 to 13 years, with a mean age of 9.5 years. Prior to the study, all subjects were asked the meaning of the various emotions.

McAlpine et al.'s study employed an emotional recognition task as opposed to an emotional labeling task[7]. As such, subjects were required to select one photograph from a set representing the target emotion. Each participant was presented with four sets of six photographs depicting one of each emotion (i.e., happiness, sadness, anger, fear, surprise, and disgust). The stimulus material were enlargements (24 cm X 16 cm) of Ekman and Friesen's (1975) standardized blank-and-white photographs. Moreover, correct and incorrect performance, scored on a trial-by-trial basis, were the dependent variables.

The results of the McAlpine et al.'s study indicate that, when considering group performance, children with mental retardation accurately identified 10 out of a possible 24 facial expressions; adults with mental retardation correctly recognized only seven; and school children without mental retardation identified 21. A more detailed analysis revealed that, in the control group, accuracy increased progressively with age ($p < .001$); happiness was correctly identified far more than any other emotional expression by all groups (children without mental retardation, 100%; children with mental retardation, 85%; and adults with mental retardation, 83%); children with moderate mental retardation were particularly deficient in recognizing anger (34%) and surprise (37%); children with mild mental retardation performed worse with respect to fear (48%) and surprise (43%); relative to the other emotions, children with borderline intelligence were particularly poor identifying disgust (62%) and surprise (61%); across intellectual categories, adults with mental retardation recognized least the emotions surprise and fear (39%); lastly, as a group, individuals without mental retardation recognized all emotions with a high degree of accuracy: happiness (100%), sadness (90%), anger (90%), disgust (88%), surprise (83%), and fear (79%).

In light of their findings, McAlpine et al. concluded that in their sample, children, adolescents, and adults with mental retardation were less adept at identifying emotional expressions when compared to children without mental retardation. Particularly the emotions surprise and fear posed the greatest challenge for these individuals. This too was seen in the control group as well. Further still, as subjects moved from greater severity to less impairment along the intellectual continuum, the ability in accurately recognizing emotions increased commensurately. In the same vein, as previously stated, a similar effect was also seen as we moved along the age scale in the group of children without mental retardation.

In a follow-up study, McAlpine, Singh, Ellis, Kendall, and Hampton (1992) examined the ability of seven adults with mental retardation in recognizing facial expressions depicting various emotions. Additionally, participants were provided with discrimination training in an effort to teach them how to accurately recognize the facial expressions of posed photographs.

What makes this study so significant is the fact that it was the first to demonstrate that individuals with mental retardation can be taught skills that enable them to better recognize facial expressions depicting emotional content (McAlpine, et al. 1992, p. 559). To this end, these researchers evaluated three techniques as a means of training facial emotional recognition. The first of which entailed teaching subjects basic rules of facial movements associated with each of the six universal emotions. These rules were based on work conducted by Ekman and Friesen (1975). The second approach utilized a method as described by Lenz, Singh, and Hewett (1991) called directed rehearsal. Lastly, the third procedure employed in their study involved using the "flashing photograph" technique, developed by Ekman and Friesen (1975), as a means of increasing the fluency with which participants discriminate among facial expressions.

McAlpine et al. (1992) used the following inclusion criteria in their study: participants could at least explain the meaning of the six basic emotions; had obtained a score of 50% or less on a prebaseline discrimination test employing the use of Ekman and Friesen's (1975) stimulus cards; and had obtained a score of 50% or less on a labeling test of the six basic emotions using the same photographs as those used in the discrimination test.

McAlpine et al. (1992) used Ekman and Friesen's (1975) stimulus material. Specifically, they enlarged eight sets of photographs that portrayed the emotions happiness, sadness, anger, fear, surprise, and disgust. Six of the eight sets served as test material while the other two were utilized as demonstration photographs. In addition to cards, the authors used videotaped role-plays as a means of assessing whether or not subjects' skills generalized from the posed photographs to video. This involved 24 role plays depicting life situations in which actors emitted the six basic facial expressions.

McAlpine et al. (1992) employed a multiple-baseline across subjects design (Baer, Wolf, & Risley, 1968), in which a generalization probe across baseline and training conditions was presented. During baseline subjects were asked to indicate how actors were feeling upon being presented with 18 test photographs (three sets, each depicting the six basic emotional expressions). Following the baseline phase, training went as follows. The training proper was delivered in four phases, with advancement made contingent on achieving criterion performance on earlier stages (see below). As with baseline subsequent to every successful training phase, subjects were tested using the 18 photographs from the Ekman and Friesen (1975) set.

In Phase One of training, participants were presented with one set from the 12 demonstration photographs. Subjects were asked to point to the critical facial features involved in independent movement as mentioned earlier in this chapter (i.e., the forehead wrinkles, nose, lips, eyes, and eyebrows). Participants advanced to Phase Two when they had achieved 100 % accuracy in identifying all of these five features. For those individuals who were unsuccessful they employed the directed rehearsal procedure (Lenz et al., 1991) as a way of remediation, which entailed having the experimenter name the facial region and point to it on the photograph. After which, subjects were instructed to repeat the correct response five times.

Phase Two went as follows. For each of the six basic emotions, two photographs showing the same facial expression (using different models) were placed in front of the participant. At which time the experimenter tacted the emotional expression and then described and pointed to the facial features associated with that particular emotion (e.g. nose, cheeks, eyebrows, and lips). Once the experimenter was finished, the subject was required to point or trace those specified features. As in Phase One, incorrect responses were remedied using the direct rehearsal procedure. Successful subjects advanced through the remaining five emotions until they had achieved perfect performance. Subsequent to achieving criterion performance, participants proceeded to Phase Three.

In Phase Three, one of the two sets of demonstration photographs was set out in front of the subject. The experimenter then asked the subject to tact the emotional expression depicted on the card. Once again, incorrect responding resulted in directed rehearsal training, whereas correct performance advanced the subject through the remaining five emotions. After accurately naming all six emotions, participants progressed to Phase Four.

Phase Four consisted of a type of fluency training. Subjects were shown a set of demonstration photographs that were presented over a decreasing time period. The limited hold was originally set at 5 seconds for the first set of six photographs, this interval was later reduced to 1 second. Phase Four terminated when subjects could correctly tact each of the demonstration cards within the 1 second hold, for five consecutive trials with 100% accuracy.

After training, as a generalization probe, subjects were presented with twenty-four videotaped scenarios. The generalization probe was delivered as follows. Subsequent to viewing each of the scenarios, subjects were asked how the actor was feeling. Despite the accuracy of performance, this procedure was repeated through-out each discrete trial until all of the remaining 23 scenarios had been viewed. Incidentally, this generalization probe was exactly the same as that employed in the baseline phase. After the generalization probe, subjects were tested three successive times during the ensuing 8 to 9 months without any additional training. Testing was identical to those conditions used in the baseline phase and during the generalization probe condition.

As a result of their intervention McAlpine et al.'s (1992) subjects demonstrated marked improvement over baseline performance. Upon inspecting within-series data (i.e., A-B), there was a steep upward trend and substantial increase in level relative to baseline measures seen in all seven subjects (Barlow & Hersen, 1984; Johnston & Pennypacker, 1993). By the same token, examining between-series patterns corroborated these findings as training was introduced across legs (i.e., into subjects' baseline phase).

For the most part this effect maintained at follow-up, which translates into almost a year's time. Of course, the further removed we are from training the less confident we can be in attributing the endurance of this change to the treatment package.

All subjects increased their mean performance by 29% to 67% during training, relative to baseline levels. Moreover, aside from two individuals, the remaining five participants were able to emit between 88% and 91% during the last five days of training (McAlpine et al. 1992, p. 569). Generalization effects were also seen in their cohort, albeit there was some variability across subjects, with respect to both baseline and the training conditions. For instance, while mean correct responses ranged from 14% to 35%, one subject emitted 63% correct responses. Once again, as previously stated, there was little change in performance at follow-up.

As McAlpine et al. (1992, p. 544) maintained, those individuals with social skills deficits might not have acquired the requisite behaviors needed for appropriate social interaction. With this in mind, those individuals with developmental disabilities especially those who have been reared in an institutional setting, are at a unique disadvantage. Contrary to those individuals who function typically and acquire social skills effortlessly through natural contact with others (via observational learning) individuals with mental retardation require explicit training in this area (Griffiths, Feldman, & Tough, 1997, p. 254).

## Concluding Remarks

Following the Wyatt v. Stickney (1972) ruling, individuals with mental retardation are being relocated into the community. At first blush this seems to be an improvement over previous conditions; however, there are those who are ill equipped to reap the benefits of living in the community and in effect are just as "institutionalized" as their counterparts in institutional settings. That is to say, institutional life (e.g., requiring much support) has followed them upon discharge. Although there is considerable debate as to why such individuals struggle in the community, one of the most reasonable explanations is that of focusing on participants' social skills. For the most part this approach has targeted various motor response channels for intervention. As Morrison and Bellack (1981) have indicated, however, such a system falls short of providing an adequate treatment of the intricacies of interpersonal behavior. It seems that the ability in discriminating the emotional displays of others is a critical aspect of effective social functioning (Mathias, 1975; Simeonsson, 1978; Simeonsson, Monson, & Blacher, 1984).

## References

American Psychiatric Association. (1994). *Diagnostic and statistical manual of mental disorders* (4th ed.). Washington, DC: Author.

American Psychiatric Association. (1987). *Diagnostic and statistical manual of mental disorders* (3rd ed.). Washington, DC: Author.

Baer, D. M., Wolf, M. M., & Risley, T. R. (1968). Some current dimensions of applied behavior analysis. *Journal of Applied Behavior Analysis, 1*, 91-97.

Barlow, D. H., & Hersen, M. (1984). *Single case experimental deigns: Strategies for studying behavior change* (2nd ed.). New York: Pergamon Press.

Barnes, D. (1994). Stimulus equivalence and relational frame theory. *The Psychological Record, 44*, 91-124.

Barnes, D., & Keenan, M. (1993). A transfer of functions through derived arbitrary and nonarbitrary stimulus relations. *Journal of the Experimental Analysis of Behavior, 59*, 61-81.

Baum, W. M. (1994). *Understanding behaviorism*. New York: Harper Collins College Publishers.

Benson, B. A., Reiss, S., Smith, D. C., & Laman, D. S. (1985). Psychosocial correlates of depression in mentally retarded adults II: Poor social skills. *American Journal of Mental Deficiency, 6*, 657-659.

Bloom, M., Fischer, J., & Orme, J. G. (1995). *Evaluating practice: Guidelines for the accountable professional*. Boston: Allyn and Bacon.

Catania, A. C., Shimoff, E., & Matthews, B. A. (1989). An experimental analysis of rule-governed behavior. In S. C. Hayes (Ed.), *Rule-governed behavior: Cognitions, contingencies, and instructional control* (pp. 119-150). Plenum Press: New York.

Cowley, B. J., Green, G., & Braunling-McMorrow, D. (1992). Using stimulus equivalence procedures to teach name-face matching to adults with brain injuries. *Journal of Applied Behavior Analysis, 25*, 461-475.

Dunn, L. M, & Dunn, L. M. (1981). *Peabody Picture Vocabulary Test-Revised*. Circle Pines, MN: American Guidance Service.

Dy, E. B., Strain, P. S., Fullerton, A., & Stowitscheck, J. (1981). Training institutionalized, elderly mentally retarded persons as intervention agents for socially isolate peers. *Analysis and Intervention in Developmental Disabilities, 1*, 199-215.

Ekman, P. (1993). Facial expression and emotion. *American Psychologist, 48*(4), 384-392.

Ekman, P., & Friesen, W. V. (1971). Constants across cultures in the face of emotion. *Journal of Personality and Social Psychology, 17*, 124-129.

Ekman, P., & Friesen, W. V. (1975). *Unmasking the face: A guide to recognizing emotions from facial clues*. Englewood Cliffs, NJ: Prentice-Hall.

Ekman, P., & Friesen, W. V. (1983). Research on expressions of emotion. In A. M. Katz & V. T. Katz (Eds.), *Foundations of nonverbal communication* (pp. 97-107). Carbondale, IL: Southern Illinois University Press.

Erwin, R. J., Gur, R. C., Gur, R. E., Skolnick, B., Mawhinney-Hee, M., & Smailis, J. (1992). Facial emotion discrimination: I. Task construction and behavioral findings in normal subjects. *Psychiatry Research, 42*, 231-240.

Gable, R. A., Hendrickson, J. M., & Strain, P. S. (1978). Assessment, modification, and generalization of social interaction among severely retarded, multihandicapped children. *Education and Training of the Mentally Retarded, 13*, 279-286.

Greenspan, S., & Schoultz, B. (1981). Why mentally retarded adults lose their jobs: Social competence as a factor in work adjustment. *Applied Research in Mental Retardation, 2*, 23-38.

Griffiths, D., Feldman, M. A., & Tough, S. (1997). Programming generalization of social skills in adults with developmental disabilities: Effects on generalization and social validity. *Behavior Therapy, 28*, 253-269.

Grossman, H. J. (Ed.). (1983). *Classification in mental retardation*. Washington, DC: American Association on Mental Deficiency.

Hall, G. A., & Chase, P. N. (1991). The relationship between stimulus equivalence and verbal behavior. *The Analysis of Verbal Behavior, 9*, 107-119.

Hayes, S. C. (1991). A relational control theory of stimulus equivalence. In L. J. Hayes & P. N. Chase (Eds.), *Dialogues on verbal behavior* (pp. 19-40). Reno, NV: Context Press.

Hayes, S. C., Devany, J. M., Kohlenberg, B. S., Brownstein, A. J., & Shelby, J. (1987). Stimulus equivalence and the symbolic control of behavior. *Revista Mexicana de Análisis de la Conducta, 13*(3), 361-374.

Hayes, S. C., Kohlenberg, B. S., Hayes, L. J. (1991). Transfer of specific and general consequential functions through simple and conditional equivalence relations. *Journal of the Experimental Analysis of Behavior, 56*, 119-137.

Hayes, S. C., Zettle, R. D., & Rosenfarb, I. (1989). Rule-Following. In S.C. Hayes (Ed.), *Rule Governed Behavior: Cognition, Contingencies, and Instructional Control* (pp. 191-220). New York, New York: Plenum Press.

Holland, J. G. (1958). Human vigilance. *Science, 128* (3315), 61-67.

Johnston, J. M., & Pennypacker, H. S. (1993). *Strategies and tactics of human behavioral research* (2nd ed.). Hillsdale, NJ: Erlbaum.

Kantor, J. R. (1958). *Interbehavioral psychology*. Chicago: Principia Press.

Kantor, J. R. (1982). *Cultural psychology*. Chicago: Principia Press.

Kantor, J. R., & Smith, N. W. (1975). *The science of psychology: An interbehavioral survey*. Chicago: Principia Press.

Knapp, M. L. (1978). *Nonverbal communication in human interaction* (2nd ed.). New York: Holt, Rinehart, & Winston.

Kull, R. (1990). Emotional self regulation and facial muscle measurement training. In J. R. Cram & Associates (Eds.), *Clinical EMG for surface recordings: Volume 2* (pp. 371-388). Nevada City, CA: Clinical Resources.

Leader, G., Barnes, D., & Smeets, P. M. (1996). Establishing stimulus equivalence relations using a respondent-type training procedure. *The Psychological Record, 46*, 685-706.

Lenz, M., Singh, N. N., & Hewett, A. E. (1991). Overcorrection as an academic remediation procedure: A reappraisal. *Behavior Modification, 15*, 64-73.

Mackay, H. A., & Sidman, M. (1984). Teaching new behaviors via equivalence relations. In P. H. Brooks, R. Sperber, & C. McCauley (Eds.), *Learning and Cognition in the Mentally Retarded* (pp. 493-513). Hillsdale, NJ: Lawrence Erlbaum Associates, Publishers.

Mathias, J. L. (1990). Social intelligence, social competence, and interpersonal competence. In N. W. Bray (Ed.), *International review of research in mental retardation* (pp. 125-160). New York: Academic Press.

Matson, J. L., Helsel, W. J., Bellack, A. S., & Senatore, V. (1983). Development of a rating scale to assess social skill deficits in mentally retarded adults. *Applied Research in Mental Retardation, 4,* 399-407.

McAlpine, C., Kendall, K. A., & Singh, N. N. (1991). Recognition of facial expressions of emotion by persons with mental retardation. *American Journal of Mental Retardation, 96,* 29-36.

McAlpine, C., Singh, N. N., Kendall, K. A., & Ellis, C. R. (1992). Recognition of expressions of emotion by persons with mental retardation. *Behavior Modification, 16,* 543-558.

McCroskey, J., & Wheeless, L. (1976). *Introduction to human communication.* New York: Allyn and Bacon.

Michael, J. L. (1993). *Concepts and principles of behavior analysis.* Kalamazoo, MI: Association for Behavior Analysis.

Moore, D. G. (2001). Reassessing emotion recognition performance in people with mental retardation. *American Journal on Mental Retardation, 106,* 481-502.

Morrison, R. L., & Bellack, A. S. (1981). The role of social perception in social skill. *Behavior Therapy, 12,* 69-79.

Parrott, L. J. (1987). Rule-governed behavior: An implicit analysis of reference. In S. Mogil & C. Mogil (Eds.), *B. F. Skinner: Consensus and controversy.* London: Falmer.

Piaget, J. (1972). *The psychology of intelligence.* Totowa, NJ: Littlefield Adams.

Pierce, W. D., & Epling, W. F. (1995). *Behavior analysis and learning.* Englewood Cliffs, NJ: Prentice Hall.

Poe, E. A. (1951). The fall of the house of usher. In T. O. Mabbott (Ed.), *The selected poetry and prose of Edgar Allan Poe* (pp. 115-130). New York: The Modern Library (original work published 1839).

Raven, J. C. (1960). *The standard progressive matrices: A, B, C, D, E.* London: Lewis.

Rehfeldt, R. A., & Hayes, L. J. (1998). The operant-respondent distinction revisited: Toward an understanding of stimulus equivalence. *The Psychological Record, 48,* 187-210.

Rojahn, J., Rabold, D. E., & Schneider, F. (1995). Emotion specificity in mental retardation. *American Journal on Mental Retardation, 99,* 477-486.

Schalock, R. I., & Harper, R. S. (1978). Placement from community-based mental retardation programs: How well do clients do? *American Journal of Mental Deficiency, 17,* 189-293.

Shantz, C. U. (1975). The development of social cognition. In E. M. Hetherington (Ed.), *Review of child development research* (Vol. 5, pp. 257-323). Chicago: University of Chicago Press.

Sidman, M. (1971). Reading and auditory-visual equivalences. *Journal of Speech and Hearing Research, 14,* 5-13.

Sidman, M. (1980). A note on the measurement of conditional discrimination. *Journal of the Experimental Analysis of Behavior, 33*, 285-289.

Sidman, M. (1987). Two choices are not enough. *Behavior Analysis, 22*, 11-18.

Sidman, M. (1992). Equivalence relations: Some basic considerations. In S. C. Hayes & L. J. Hayes (Eds.), *Understanding verbal relations: The second and third international institute on verbal relations* (pp. 15-27). Reno, NV: Context Press.

Sidman, M., & Tailby, W. (1982). Conditional discrimination vs. matching-to-sample: An expansion of the testing paradigm. *Journal of the Experimental Analysis of Behavior, 37*, 5-22.

Simeonsson, R. J. (1978). Social competence. In J. Wortis (Ed.), *Mental retardation and disabilities: An annual review* (Vol. 10, pp. 130-171). New York: Bruner/Mazel.

Simeonsson, R. J., Monson, L. B., Blacher, J. (1984). Social understanding and mental retardation. In P. H. Brooks, R. Sperber, & C. McCauley (Eds.), *Learning and cognition in the mentally retarded* (pp. 389-417). Hillsdale, NJ: Erlbaum.

Singh, N. N., & Winton, A. S. W. (1983). Social skills training with institutionalized severely and profoundly mentally retarded persons. *Applied Research in Mental Retardation, 4*, 383-398.

Skinner, B. F. (1953). *Science and human behavior*. New York: Macmillan Publishing Co., Inc.

Skinner, B. F. (1957). *Verbal behavior*. New York: Appleton-Century-Crofts.

Skinner, B. F. (1966). 'An operant analysis of problem solving.' In B. Kleinmuntz (Ed.), *Problem solving: Research, method, and theory*. New York: Wiley.

Skinner, B. F. (1974). *About behaviorism*. New York: Vintage Books.

Skinner, B. F. (1987). *Upon further reflection*. Englewood Cliffs, NJ: Prentice-Hall, Inc.

Sundberg, M. L., & Partington, J. W. (1998). *Teaching language to children with autism and other developmental disabilities*. Pleasant Hill, CA: Behavior Analysts, Inc.

Taylor, A. R. (1982). Social competence and interpersonal relations between retarded and nonretarded children. In N. R. Ellis (Ed.), *International review of research in mental retardation* (Vol. 11, pp. 247-283). Orlando, FL: Academic Press.

Wahler, R. G., & Fox, J. J. (1981). Setting events in applied behavior analysis: Toward a conceptual and methodological expansion. *Journal of Applied Behavior Analysis, 14*, 327-338.

Williams, L., Martin, G., McDonald, S., Hardy, L., & Lambert, L. (1975). Effects of a backscratch contingency of reinforcement for table serving on social interaction with severely retarded girls. *Behavior Therapy, 6*, 220-229.

*Wyatt v. Stickney*. 344 F. Supp. 373 (M.D. Ala. 1972).

Zettle, R. D., & Hayes, S. C. (1982). Rule-governed behavior: A potential theoretical framework for cognitive-behavior therapy. In P. C. Kendell (Ed.), *Advances in cognitive-behavioral research and therapy* (Vol. 1, pp. 73-118). New York: Academic Press.

## Endnotes

1. According to DSM IV criteria the essential features of Mental Retardation are "subaverage intelligence (Criterion A) that is accompanied by significant limitations in at least two of the following skill areas: communication, self-care, functional academic skills, work, leisure, health and safety (Criterion B)." (p. 39). With respect to Criterion A, subaverage intelligence is defined as an Intelligence Quotient (IQ) using standardized, individually-administered intelligence tests (Wechsler Intelligence Scales for Children, and Stanford-Binet), of about 70 or below. Using the same metric, Mental Retardation is broken down further into four categories. The first, Mild Mental Retardation, consists of an IQ level ranging from around 50-55 to approximately 70. This group constitutes 85 % of those with Mental Retardation. With respect to functional outcome, individuals who fall within the mild category can be expected to live independently or in supervised settings. The next level of severity is Moderate Mental Retardation, falling on the continuum between an IQ level of 35-40 to 50-55. Comprising about 10 % of those individuals with Mental Retardation, these individuals can be expected to work under supervision in sheltered workshops or in the general workforce, and are expected to adapt well to living in the community usually in supervised settings. The next level of intellectual impairment is Severe Mental Retardation. Severe Mental Retardation is delineated by an IQ falling between 20-25 to 35-40, comprising 3 % - 4 % of people with Mental Retardation. Unlike the former groups, such individuals are expected to perform simple tasks in supervised settings only. The third category is profound Mental Retardation. Profound Mental Retardation is defined as an individual having an IQ below 20 or 25. Comprising 1 % - 2 % of individuals with Mental Retardation such individuals may be able to perform simple tasks in closely supervised and sheltered setting. The last category is Mental Retardation, severity unspecified. Individuals given this label are those who cannot be successfully tested by standardized tests, yet there is a strong presumption that Mental Retardation is present.

2. As an aside, at a more fundamental level, such discriminative processes are also essential for virtually all forms of learning functionally tied to socially-mediated consequences (Rojahn, Rabold, & Schneider, 1995).

3. It is so common that individuals with mental retardation exhibit difficulties in adapting socially, that the American Association on Mental Retardation (AAMR) has repeatedly cast mental retardation in terms of diminished social competency along with the ubiquitously held intellectual deficiencies (Mathias, 1990; Grossman, 1983).

4. Skinner (1957) defined a tact as "a verbal operant in which a response of a given form is evoked (or at least strengthened) by a particular object or event or property of an object or event" (pp. 81-82).

5. Some individuals have actually measured through Electromyography and specifically located the individual muscles involved in emotional expression. For

example, see Kull (1990, pp. 383-384) for a recent discussion of the muscles involved in emotional expression.

6. As an aside, there are those who maintain that there are only six basic facial expressions which are constant across cultures – the debate, however, continues (see Ekman, 1993, for a decision of this debate).

7. McAlpine and his associates (1991) chose an emotional recognition task over an emotional labeling task because recognition tasks are less ambiguous and allow participants with only a limited understanding of language, with more severe retardation, to be tested (p. 31).

# Chapter 11

# Developmental Disabilities and Psychopathology: Rehabilitation and Recovery Focused Services

Nirbhay N. Singh, Mohamed Sabaawi, and Judy Singh
*ONE Research Institute, Midlothian, VA*

Individuals with developmental disabilities often have co-occurring mental illness. This co-occurrence, often referred to as dual diagnosis, has estimated prevalence rates higher than the rates of mental illness among individuals in the general population (Došen & Day, 2001). The prevalence of mental illness in individuals with developmental disabilities varies from 10% to 80%, depending on a number of factors including the diagnostic criteria used, disorders screened and the size and characteristics of the sample surveyed (Singh, Ellis & Wechsler, 1997).

It is particularly challenging to treat mental illness in this population because behavior problems and language and neurocognitive deficits interfere with the assessment of signs and symptoms of psychiatric disorders and preclude the use of some forms of treatment. Other factors contributing to these challenges may include medical conditions that result in or mimic signs and symptoms of psychiatric disorders; the lack of operational criteria for diagnosing mental illness; physical illness; and various behavioral, environmental, and service provider issues (Pyles, Muniz, Cade, & Silva, 1997; Singh, Sood, Sonenklar, & Ellis, 1991). In addition, although multiple treatments are often needed to treat a range of presenting problems, clinical strategies for integrating multiple treatment modalities have yet to be fully developed (Singh et al., 2002).

Most of our knowledge of assessment and treatment effects, particularly relating to psychopharmacological, psychosocial, and behavioral treatments, is derived from studies undertaken in institutions. For example, until very recently, virtually all randomized controlled drug trials included only institutionalized participants (Aman & Singh, 1988). Further, the majority of behavioral studies has been conducted in institutions or specialized treatment centers. For example, a recent review of the behavioral treatment literature on self-injury showed that only about 10% of the studies reported between 1964 and 2000 included participants from community-based settings (Kahng, Iwata, & Lewin, 2002).

The vast majority of individuals with developmental disabilities and mental illness (DD/MI), however, reside in community settings (Lakin, Prouty, Polister, & Coucouvanis, 2003). The lack of rigorous clinical research in these settings has resulted in a paucity of community-based treatment models for this population. With a few exceptions, individuals with DD/MI and their families do not have access to comprehensive community-based services that fully meet their needs (Menolascino, 1994). We describe a strength-based, holistic service delivery model that can be adapted by community agencies to meet the particular needs of individuals with DD/MI in their care. Our model extends the biopsychosocial approach by incorporating current concepts of psychosocial rehabilitation and recovery.

## Strength-Based Holistic Approaches

Meeting current professional standards of care in the field of developmental disabilities requires a paradigm shift from treating individuals for their disease, disorder, deficits, and disabilities to providing them with skills and supports that enhance their quality of life in specific contexts. It means moving from a treatment model that focuses on neutralizing their negative conditions to actually putting them on a pathway to wellness by providing them with skills and supports that will enable them to make appropriate choices at the level of their functioning.

Interventions that focus just on individuals' target behaviors have not been successful in producing sustained changes in their quality of life. Challenging behaviors exhibited by individuals with DD/MI are multidetermined, and involve the individuals, service providers (e.g., family members, care staff), living environments, and system factors. Findings from primary and secondary prevention programs suggest that effective interventions must address multiple systems in which the individuals are embedded and target the known correlates of their serious and persistent challenging behaviors. In addition, our own research and clinical work suggests that we must intensively focus on building and enhancing these individuals' strengths and wellness, so that they have alternative methods of coping in the real world.

A medical model of treatment focuses almost exclusively on the individual and his challenging behaviors and mental illness. Typically, the process involves history-taking, assessments of specific presenting problems, case formulation, and development of behavior- or disorder-specific interventions. The emphasis is on understanding the cause of an individual's "problem" as viewed by clinicians, which then leads to a treatment program for controlling, managing, or eliminating the problem. Transactional models are broader and include assessment of multiple factors that may bear on the individual's presenting problems (Sameroff, 1995). That is, staff and peer factors may be considered in the case formulation. Further, the transactional model can be extended to include the effects that systems may have on the individual. For example, if the individual is in a group home, then the effects of being in this system of care, and the effects of the individual on the system, must be factored in the case formulation. In addition to the presenting problems, the strengths of the individual, his[1] care providers (e.g., parents, foster parents, facility care staff, teachers), and the system have to be assessed and considered in the case formulation.

A strength-based holistic model assumes that an individual navigates daily life in layers of contexts that are dominated by people who care for and provide services to the individual and by systems that provide the framework for such care. The internal and external environments (i.e., biological and ecological) of the individual provide the basis for a transactional analysis of his behavior. Transactions occur not only within the individual (e.g., as in what the body does to a drug and what the drug does to the body) but also between the individual and his social and physical environments. Service providers (e.g., parents, family members, school personnel, professional staff in hospitals and group homes) are embedded in the individual's social environment and, therefore, the individual's transactions with the service providers form a cornerstone of his quality of life. Layers of systems provide the context for the service providers' transactions with the individual and, thus, systems form another cornerstone that governs an individual's quality of life. Together, the individual, care providers, and systems form the critical components of a strength-based holistic service delivery system. Assessment of the goodness-of-fit amongst the three components indicates where the fit is weak or fragile, and the intervention is formulated so as to strengthen the fit (Singh, 2001). Thus, case formulation takes into account the strengths and weaknesses of the three components, and identifies the solutions by considering changes that can be made in one or more of the components.

The first step of a strength-based holistic approach requires a broad-based assessment of the individual in all areas of functioning. For example, this can be achieved within the framework of a Plan of Life, a second-generation person-centered plan (J. Singh, 2002). The Plan of Life provides the context for all assessments, development of supports and services that are based on assessed needs, and a monitoring system for service/supports provision as well as "real life" outcomes. Real life outcomes are those that are meaningful in everyday life and are not focused solely on reduction of challenging behaviors. The needs assessment is undertaken in conjunction with a strengths conversation (as opposed to a strengths "interview") because it is designed to build a collaborative relationship with the individual and the care providers. The strengths conversation highlights for the providers areas that the individual (and his family and significant others) perceives as being important to him. The second step requires an assessment of the providers' functioning through strengths conversations that explore their own strengths as well as their perceptions of the way they provide supports and services for the individual within the current system. The third step requires an assessment of the policies, operating procedures, processes, practices, and strengths of the layers of systems in which the individual and providers are embedded.

This approach assumes that the strengths of the individual form the basis for all interventions and that all interventions are designed to facilitate an enhanced quality of life rather than just to control or manage problems. It also assumes that the strengths of the people who provide the skills training, supports or services (e.g., facility staff, parents, administrators) have been assessed, enhanced, and woven into the interventions for the individual. Finally, it assumes that the strengths of the system (e.g., responsivity, flexibility, adaptability) or layers of systems (e.g., facility, community, district, state, and federal policies and procedures) have been assessed and used to enhance the individual's well being. A strength-based holistic approach is designed to take the individuals, providers and systems from where they are to where they want to be through a series of structured steps that will enable them to maintain their gains without continual external assistance from experts. The supports, services, and interventions are based on assessed needs and are provided in an atmosphere of nonjudgmental acceptance and compassion, obviating the need for faultfinding, blaming, and punishing consequences. In addition, this approach enhances the strengths and effectiveness of the service providers as well as of the service system itself.

## Psychosocial Rehabilitation and Recovery

In our approach, we provide services to individuals with DD/MI, particularly those with mild or moderate levels of mental retardation, in the context of the rehabilitation and recovery philosophy. We believe that our role as service providers is to empower/help individuals to develop skills and supports that strengthen their current levels of overall functioning, foster desired role functioning (e.g., being a student, employee, or tenant), and enhance their quality of life and sense of purpose in specific contexts. In this view, rehabilitation capitalizes on the individual's strengths to facilitate increased effectiveness, success, and satisfaction in the contexts of the individual's choice, with the minimum degree of professional involvement. Thus, rehabilitation complements and extends treatment and other interventions that are primarily aimed at symptom relief, safety, and the accessing of available services; at a minimum, it adds self-determination and empowerment, as well as a process for achieving them.

Rehabilitation is based on a set of values that provides the foundation for its practice. Minimally, as described by Anthony, Cohen, Farkas, and Gagne (2002), these include the following:

(a) *Person orientation.* The focus is on the individual as a person rather than as a patient, a diagnostic label, or an illness. Thus, person-first language is normative. The relationship between the service provider and the individual is one of mutual respect and reciprocity; it is a dynamic relationship with each one learning from the other. One specific process outcome of person orientation is that treatment planning is person-centered rather than focused on a disease or disorder.

(b) *Functioning.* Rehabilitation aims to improve an individual's functional status and quality of life in specific contexts rather than to reduce, control or neutralize the effects of a disorder, disease, deficit, and disability. As with the Positive Behavior Supports approach to behavioral intervention (Carr et al., 2002), the focus is on developing skills and strengthening positive behaviors rather than on controlling or managing challenging behaviors.

(c) *Supports*. Supports are provided for as long as they are needed so that the individual can maintain and fulfill desired role functioning. For example, an individual may need supports to learn vocational skills while being employed (i.e., supported employment); other examples include supported education and supported living environments.

(d) *Environmental specificity*. Social demands and performance are contextual. Therefore, rehabilitation is focused on real-world contexts in which the individual will be required to live, learn, work, and socialize. Thus, assessments are undertaken in or for the context in which the individual fulfills or will fulfill a desired role function. Skills building and supports provided match the needs of the individual in specific rather than generic contexts.

(e) *Involvement*. Individuals are included in every decision that affects their life and functioning. Instead of decisions being made *for* the individual, decisions are made *with* the individual. Their level of involvement mirrors their functional status; the higher their functional status, the more responsibility they take for their own rehabilitation and recovery.

(f) *Self-Determination and choice*. Self-determination and choice-making are basic rights afforded to everyone, including those with disabilities (Wehmeyer, 1998; 2001). Thus, individuals with disabilities must be supported to exercise their rights to the greatest degree possible in choosing where they live, learn, work, and socialize. In a therapeutic context, they should be supported to choose how they wish to be involved with and take responsibility for their own rehabilitation and recovery.

(g) *Outcome orientation*. Rehabilitation focuses on measurable outcomes for the individual in specific rather than in generic contexts. Is the individual able to engage in specific skills that will lead to a desired role function in a given context and be satisfied with the experience? As noted by Anthony et al. (2002, p. 83), success is are "measured in terms of the person's ability to respond to the demands of the chosen environment, while satisfaction is measured in terms of the person's own reported experience there."

(h) *Growth potential*. People with or without disabilities have the potential to grow and flourish in their chosen environments. The process of rehabilitation and recovery can be seen as an exploration of the boundless possibilities inherent in all human beings. Thus, change is driven by a positive vision of what can be achieved rather than hindered by the limitations of one's disabilities.

These values are incorporated in the services and technologies that service providers offer individuals as they engage in recovery from their mental illness—that is, as they regain their functional skills, socially valued roles in society, and their sense of self.

Recovery is an experiential dimension of wellness, hope, optimism, and self-affirmation. The concept of recovery arose from the writings of individuals who were recovering or had recovered from serious mental illness about their experiences including effects of treatments they had received for their illness, discrimination due to their illness, and poor mental health service delivery systems (Anthony et al., 2002; Deegan, 1988; Fisher, n.d.; Ralph, 2000). While recovery is an emerging concept without a firm definition, Deegan (1988, p. 15) suggested that it "is a process, a way of life, an attitude, and a way of approaching the day's challenges. It is not a linear process. At times our course is erratic and we falter, slide back, regroup and start again. The need is to meet the challenge of the disability and to reestablish a new and valued sense of integrity and purpose within and beyond the limits of the disability; the aspiration is to live, work, and love in a community in which one makes a significant contribution."

Recovery is a mode of being; a journey in living rather than a destination. There are no presumed outcomes that apply to all individuals because each individual's course of life is different. The individual learns to live with the illness or disorder and to minimize its effects on his daily functioning, withstands its subjective experience in terms of hopelessness and internalized stigma, and overcomes its social consequences, such as discrimination, loss of employment, and social isolation. Recovery is being hopeful and optimistic about the future by maintaining and enhancing one's skills and accessing social, emotional, physical, and community supports.

Autobiographies (e.g., Jamison, 1995; Manning, 1994; Schiller & Bennett, 1994) and interviews with individuals who have recovered from their mental illnesses provide us with some sense as to what helped or hindered their recovery (Onken, Dumont, Ridgway, Dornan, & Ralph, 2002). These guidelines have much relevance for people with DD/MI, especially those with mild or moderate levels of developmental disabilities, because they too can recover from their mental illnesses. Rehabilitation is what service providers engage in to facilitate individuals with DD/MI to recover from their challenging behaviors and the effects of mental illness. The strengths-based holistic approach provides the basis for the assessment and treatment of challenging behaviors; rehabilitation provides the foundation for developing skills and increasing supports that will enable the individual to recover from the debilitating effects of mental illness.

## Rehabilitation- and Recovery-Focused Services

Use of the medical model requires the physician or psychiatrist to assess the nature of the disease, disorder, deficit, or disability, to diagnose the condition, and to prescribe a treatment. While the physician may need to gather and synthesize information from multiple sources, there is little need to go beyond this level of professional involvement to understand the condition and provide treatment. The biopsychosocial model requires the physician to develop a clinical formulation that draws on formal assessments and informal observations of multiple clinicians, but it is not essential to have multiple clinicians present to assist with the clinical formulation (Ross, 2000). However, because holistic models require much more extensive assessments that cover virtually every aspect of an individual's life, an interdisciplinary treatment team that includes the individual is a necessary condition for assessment, diagnosis, clinical formulation, development and implementation of interventions, and outcome monitoring.

The use of interdisciplinary treatment teams is a *sine qua non* in the field of developmental disabilities and provides an ideal setting for making clinical decisions about integrating multiple treatment modalities (Drotar & Sturm, 1996; Natvig, 1991). Treatment teams are critical to the process of developing effective treatment plans, including activities such as conducting multidisciplinary assessments, determining and implementing treatments, and monitoring treatment outcomes. The development of a coordinated treatment plan is essential for integrating psychopharmacological, nursing, psychosocial, psychoeducational, and cognitive behavioral treatments. Thus, we see the treatment team that is consistent and enduring in its membership as the smallest unit that is responsible for an individual's treatment. Further, we see the individual as an integral member of his treatment team.

## Assessments

The treatment team undertakes a comprehensive set of assessments focused on adaptive behavior, social skills, strengths, disorders, deficits, disabilities, and diseases (Matson, Mayville, & Laud, 2003; Singh et al., 1991; Silka & Hauser, 1997). In addition to these assessments, a rehabilitation and recovery focus requires an assessment of the individual's functional status across multiple domains and of skills and supports needed to fulfill specific role functioning. Although skill deficits, interests, and strengths are sometimes assessed, these assessments are based on the individual's history and current mental status, and not on an observation of the person attempting to perform these skills in the appropriate context. Further, generic skills are assessed regardless of whether the individual will need those skills or not. Our approach is to conduct formal functional assessments only of those skills that the individual will need to have to perform specific tasks in the individual's chosen role(s). Further, we assess key categories of supports and resources that the individual will need such as specific people, places, things, and activities relative to his chosen roles and environments.

Our assessments are directly linked to the development of interventions because assessments identify the individual's disabilities, problems, needs, and barriers to fulfilling chosen roles and an enhanced quality of life. Identified disabilities, problems, needs, and barriers lead to the development of goals and objectives, and interventions are developed that match these goals and objectives. Given the basic premise that rehabilitation is done with and not to an individual, we involve them in the assessment process to the full extent of their current functional status and desire to be involved. This process gives us an indication of the individual's interests, hopes, motivation, optimism, and confidence in recovery from his disabilities and behavioral challenges. Furthermore, this process often provides insights relative to some individuals' overt lack of motivation for change; for example, it could be due to low environmental awareness, incomplete knowledge of real choices, lack of knowledge about alternative ways of achieving the same ends, and fear of change. Such insights provide the basis for planning and developing services.

## Diagnosis

Much has been written regarding diagnostic uncertainty in individuals with DD/MI, especially relating to co-occurring psychiatric disorders (Jacobson & Mulick, 1996; Holden & Gitlesen, 2003). As we have noted previously, the goal is to understand the individual's presenting psychiatric problems at the highest level of diagnostic sophistication that can be achieved based on a comprehensive interdisciplinary assessment (Singh & Sabaawi, in press). There are four levels of diagnostic sophistication: (a) symptomatic, which includes isolated symptoms (e.g., auditory hallucinations) that provide an indication of a possible diagnosis (e.g., psychotic disorder not otherwise specified); (b) syndromic, which includes the constellation of signs and symptoms that have been present for a given time, to which standardized inclusionary and exclusionary criteria can be applied to derive a diagnosis (e.g., depression); (c) pathophysiologic, which includes structural or biochemical changes that indicate the diagnosis (e.g., an individual presenting with anxiety, depression or manic excitement, weakness, excessive sweating, tremors and, in some cases, disturbances of thought and cognition may have elevated thyroid function tests that suggest a diagnosis of hyperthyroidism); and (d) etiologic, in which the diagnosis is based on known causative factors.

The diagnostic formulation follows the standard biopsychosocial model, which means that biomedical, psychological, and social factors are integrated into a comprehensive framework for understanding the individual's symptomatic and syndromic presentation. With individuals with mild or moderate levels of developmental disabilities, most psychiatric diagnoses are at the symptomatic and syndromic levels of sophistication because we currently do not have a thorough understanding of the pathophysiologic or etiologic bases of many psychiatric disorders. Thus, it is not uncommon to find wide variability in treatment outcomes in individuals diagnosed with the same syndrome because they have similar presentations but substantially different underlying mechanisms. This means that, at times, we are treating these individuals' behavioral symptoms or psychiatric disorders without fully appreciating the biological and genetic underpinnings or how these factors transact with the individual's emotional, physical, psychosocial, and cultural environments.

## Clinical Formulation

All relevant information about the individual is synthesized into a clinical formulation that provides the basis for making clinical predictions in a fairly scientific manner. Clinical formulation typically leads to clinical hypotheses regarding the individual's current status, clinical course, and future treatments. Typically, all members of the treatment team contribute to the clinical formulation, which is summarized by the team leader. The clinical formulation can be structured in several ways depending on the theoretical orientation of the professional. One effective way of formulating the case is by systematically discussing the following sequence of data: (a) pertinent history—a brief sketch of who the individual is; (b) predisposing factors—biological (e.g., prenatal and genetic factors, complications during pregnancy or delivery, mother's use of substances during pregnancy, head trauma, etc.) and psychosocial (e.g., emotional, physical, or sexual abuse, parental divorce and separation, etc.); (c) precipitating factors—prescribed medications, medical conditions, major psychosocial stressors, and substance and alcohol abuse; (d) perpetuating factors—personality disorders, chronic medical conditions, substance and alcohol abuse, and non-compliance with prescribed medication; (e) present status—current signs and symptoms of psychiatric disorders, reason for admission or hospitalization, and challenging behaviors; and (f) previous treatments—treatments utilized during the course of the individual's psychiatric illness, response to previous treatments, adverse effects of psychotropic and other medications, and culture-based treatments. When stated in this sequence, the clinical formulation leads directly to the goals and objectives of the current admission or hospitalization.

## Cultural Context of Clinical Formulation

We believe that mental health services must be culturally informed and that all professionals should engage in culturally sensitive practices from assessment to intervention. Our experience of mental illness is informed by our cultural backgrounds. However, some professionals may think that because the population of individuals we are dealing with has compromised cognitive capacity, we need not pay much attention to their cultural belief systems. This is undoubtedly a false assumption because all of us, regardless of our cognitive status, have belief systems that impact the quality of care and treatment we receive. Thus, as clinicians we need to be broadly culturally informed, and be able to integrate our cultural knowledge and skills in our clinical interactions with culturally diverse individuals (James & Prilleltensky, 2002). Indeed, as Gaw (2001, pp. 15-18) has noted, incorporating a cultural perspective in the delivery of mental health services (a) enhances diagnosis and treatment, (b) fosters clinicians' sensitivity towards the individuals being treated, (c) enriches clinical knowledge, (d) provides guidelines for judgment of "normality" versus "abnormality" of behavior, and (e) provides an understanding of human beings, whether their behavior is normative or deviant.

Several frameworks recently advanced in the research literature for incorporating cultural aspects of mental health care can be adapted for use with individuals who have DD/MI (e.g., Arredondo et al., 1996; Sue et al., 1998). At the very least, we believe that clinicians should (a) inform themselves of the individual's explanatory model of mental illness, and (b) engage in some self-analysis of their own cultural reactions to an individual's mental illness. While it is not expected that clinicians be

fully informed about the mental health aspects of all cultures, they can systematically inquire about the individual's explanatory model of mental illness.

In our own work, we have adapted a series of questions that were first developed
by Arthur Kleinman, a psychiatrist and medical anthropologist at Harvard Medical
School, and subsequently reworded by Fadiman (1997, pp. 260-261):

1.  What do you call the problem?
2.  What do you think has caused the problem?
3.  Why do you think it started when it did?
4.  What do you think the sickness does? How does it work?
5.  How severe is the sickness? Will it have a short or long course?
6.  What kind of treatment do you think you should receive? What are the
    most important results you hope to receive from this treatment?
7.  What are the chief problems the sickness has caused?
8.  What do you fear most about the sickness?

These questions can be adapted for use with significant others (e.g., family
members, care providers) of those individuals who cannot respond fully to the
questions themselves. When using these questions as a basis for conversation about
the individual's mental illness, we find that we begin to appreciate from the
individual's perspective what the illness means to him and how we can together
overcome it and respond to its consequences. In addition, we use this information
to guide the entire treatment planning process.

The other aspect of our cross-cultural work includes self-analysis of our own
cultural biases towards mental illness itself, as well as towards people with mental
illness. In this, we have been guided by the work of Hughes (1992) who has provided
an excellent outline for such an inquiry. As summarized by Gaw (2001, pp. 16-17),
the outline includes the following considerations:

1.  What about this patient's appearance or behavior makes me think what
    I am seeing and hearing is pathology?
2.  What are the sources of the putative "pathologic" characterization?
3.  What label(s) am I subconsciously applying to this patient, and where
    did they come from?
4.  What social class or group am I assuming the patient belongs to, and
    what do I know about that? What are my own prejudices about that
    group, and where do such characterizations come from—childhood
    directives and role-modeling, family-inculcated out-group attitudes,
    scanning of current events that may reinforce preexisting stereotypes?
5.  Other than "pathology," what other hypotheses come to mind to
    explain this unusual behavior?
6.  What other label could I use to describe this behavior instead of
    pathology?

7.  What are the circumstances of the referral (if a referral), and what is the descriptive spoken language used by other health care providers in conveying information about the patient?

8.  What labels and summary inferences are used in the patient's chart or in the referral? How many of the empirical observations such labels purport to reflect can I recreate from the written record (knowing that a medical record needs to be highly selective in the amount of data reported)? What do I know about the person or persons making such comments in the record?

Information from the individual and the clinician's self-analysis provide the initial context for developing a cultural formulation, outlines and examples of which can be found in the Diagnosis and Statistical Manual of Mental Illness (DSM IV-TR; APA, 2000, pp. 897-898), Tseng and Streltzer (2001), and Committee on Cultural Psychiatry (2002).

## Treatment Planning and Reviews

An important principle of psychosocial rehabilitation is that the individual is increasingly involved in his rehabilitation as his functional status improves. Thus, the individual is an integral member of the treatment planning process and works with the treatment team to determine the foci and nature of the interventions. There are various ways to increase the individual's meaningful involvement in the treatment planning process. However, it is important that all treatment team members, as well as the individual being served, understand what meaningful involvement means in the context of developing, implementing, and reviewing outcomes of intervention plans. This requires preparing the individual for assessments that may occur prior to or between treatment team meetings and for the treatment planning process itself. The individual needs to understand and feel comfortable with the treatment planning or review process. Thus, the team members should prepare the individual for his input and be ready to mindfully listen and thoughtfully discuss with the individual his input in a mutually respectful manner.

For inpatient services, the traditional treatment plan can be replaced by a plan that focuses on the individual's discharge to a lesser level of care or prepares the individual for a chosen role in a specific environmental context. Further, the traditional treatment plan can be replaced by a wellness plan that focuses on building the individual's strengths, enabling the individual to respond early to vulnerabilities that may otherwise lead to or exacerbate an episode of mental illness, and to maintain good mental, physical and emotional health. Given that good health is not just the absence of disease, it behooves us as service providers to assist individuals with DD/MR to maintain and enhance their wellness rather than focus narrowly on treating diseases, disorders, disabilities, and deficits.

In treatment planning, it is critical to remember that the goals of intervention are the individual's goals as opposed to those of the treatment team and that the foci of interventions are consistent with core psychosocial rehabilitation principles and values, especially self-determination and choice, individualization, outcomes valued by the individual, and growth potential. Further, the individual's record, which includes the treatment plan, should be jargon-free and written at his or her reading and comprehension level. At the very least, the individual must be able to review and understand his own intervention plan.

## Interventions

In mental health, as well as in developmental disabilities, our treatments have generally focused on controlling the individual's mental illness and challenging behaviors. The assumption has been that these individuals will be able to function better if the effects of their mental illnesses were neutralized and their challenging behaviors controlled or managed. This kind of thinking has led to mechanical, compartmentalized treatment approaches without much thought given to the individual as an active participant in shaping his own life.

The main mode of treating mental illness has been the use of psychotropic medications. While such medications do provide relief from the effects of mental illness, they do not teach the individual how to respond to their vulnerabilities to episodes of mental illness when such conditions arise in the future. The main mode of treating challenging behavior has been through the use of behavior management principles. Typically, behavior management plans are externally driven and focused on controlling or managing the individual's behavior in specific contexts for time-limited periods. In the main, they are not designed to treat the individual; that is, they are typically not designed to teach the individual to make different, socially valid choices that would help them achieve the same ends (Gardner & Cole, 1987). Although there are exceptions, especially those that are based on a Positive Behavior Supports approach (Carr et al., 2002), most behavioral interventions are simply not behavioral treatments as defined by Gardner and Cole.

In addition to these treatments, we have traditionally included skills training as a component of most treatment plans (or habilitation plans as they are sometimes called). Typically, generic activities of daily living and other skills are assessed for deficits, and then the deficits are remediated through skills training programs. However, what is not appreciated in this approach is that it is not enough to assess deficits within a static framework in order to enhance an individual's rehabilitation outcomes. The individual may or may not need the generic skills being taught in their chosen or desired roles in specific environments. Given that an individual lives in specific environments and performs specific role functions, it follows that they will require specific skills and specific skill performance levels. That is, not all individuals need the same skills, performed at the same level, to be successful and satisfied in their chosen roles. Individuals need to be taught those skills that they require for their rehabilitation with regard to specific role functions in specific contexts. This would require service providers to list, describe, and evaluate the skills that an individual would need for a specific role in a specific environment. Such dynamic thinking in skill development is typically absent in most skill training programs.

Similar thinking is lacking in terms of assessing individuals for supports that they will require in their chosen roles. Once an individual has been assisted to choose one or more social roles and the environment or place where he will perform these roles, then we must perform an individualized assessment of needed supports and resources. The needs are assessed with the individual rather than for the individual, and supports and resources are established in the individual's chosen environments.

Traditional treatment plans include activities and active treatments. In many such plans, an individual is assigned various activities throughout the day. These activities certainly fill an individual's time, reduce boredom, and may even provide essential stimulation, but they are not driven by the individual's assessed needs in terms of rehabilitation. These activities cannot be defined as active treatment, which is essentially linked to the assessed needs of the individual and expressed as goals and objectives in the treatment/discharge or wellness plan. Further, the individual and the service provider must regularly monitor the outcomes of active treatment in terms of the individual's performance, rehabilitation and satisfaction.

One way of conceptualizing activities is to think about them in terms of what they enable the individual to do as a consequence of engaging in them. We can broadly define these activities as leading to enrichment, treatment, or rehabilitation. For example, enrichment activities would include those that facilitate the individual to increase knowledge, interests, and abilities. Treatment activities would include those that assist the individual to manage symptoms and decrease the distress associated with the symptoms or impairments. Rehabilitation activities include those that enable the individual to counter the effects of disabilities and to function in a valued community role. Currently, most interventions function as either enrichment or treatment activities; far fewer function as rehabilitation-related activities. However, to make a real difference in an individual's life, there must be full integration of the three types of activities.

## Summary

We see a rehabilitation and recovery focused approach to providing services as the next step in our progression towards enabling individuals with DD/MR to participate fully in our communities. Full implementation of this approach will require the field of developmental disabilities to (a) embrace a rehabilitation and recovery approach, (b) provide training and support for service providers in this approach, (c) develop policies, procedures, and mechanisms necessary to implement this approach, (d) develop methodologies for rehabilitation-focused assessments of skills and supports for valued community roles, (e) integrate enrichment, treatment, and rehabilitation activities for individuals with DD/MI, (f) meet their recovery needs by providing individualized, experiential rehabilitation interventions, and (g) provide the necessary supports and resources that will enable them to live successfully in the community.

# References

Aman, M. G., & Singh, N. N. (1988). *Psychopharmacology of developmental disabilities.* New York: Springer-Verlag.

American Psychiatric Association. (2000). *Diagnostic and statistical manual of mental disorders* ( 4th ed. text revision). Washington, DC: Author.

Anthony, W., Cohen, M., Farkas, M., & Gagne, C. (2002). *Psychiatric rehabilitation* (2nd ed.). Boston, MA: Center for Psychiatric Rehabilitation.

Arrendondo, P., Toporek, R., Brown, S. P., Jones, J., Lock, D.C., Sanchez, J., & Stadler, H. (1996). Multicultural counseling competencies. *Journal of Multicultural Counseling and Development, 24,* 42-78.

Carr, E. G., Dunlap, G., Horner, R. H., Koegel, R. L., Turnbull, A. P., Sailor, W., Anderson, J. L., Albin, R. W., Koegel, L. K., & Fox, L. (2002). Positive behavior support: Evolution of an applied science. *Journal of Positive Behavior Interventions, 4,* 4-16.

Committee on Cultural Psychiatry. (2002). *Cultural assessment in clinical psychiatry.* Washington, DC: American Psychiatric Press, Inc.

Deegan, P. E. (1988). Recovery: The lived experience of rehabilitation. *Psychosocial Rehabilitation Journal, 11*(4), 11-19.

Došen, A., & Day, K. (2001). Epidemiology, etiology, and presentation of mental illness and behavior disorders in persons with mental retardation. In A. Došen & K. Day (Eds.), *Treating mental illness and behavior disorders in children and adults with mental retardation* (pp. 3-24). Washington, DC: American Psychiatric Press.

Drotar, D. D., & Sturm, L. A. (1996). Interdisciplinary collaboration in the practice of mental retardation. In J. J. Jacobson & J. A. Mulick (Eds.), *Manual of diagnosis and professional practice in mental retardation* (pp. 393-401). Washington, DC: American Psychological Association.

Fadiman, A. (1997). *The spirit catches you and you fall down: A Hmong child, her American doctors, and the collision of two cultures.* New York: Farrar, Straus and Giroux.

Fisher, D. B. (n.d.). *New vision of recovery: You too can recover from "mental illness."* Lawrence, MA: The National Empowerment Center, Inc.

Gardner, W. I., & Cole, C. L. (1987). Behavior treatment, behavior management, and behavior control: Needed distinctions. *Behavior Residential Treatment, 2,* 37-53.

Gaw, A. C. (2001). *Cross-cultural psychiatry.* Washington, DC: American Psychiatric Publishing, Inc.

Holden, B., & Gitlesen, J. P. (2003). Prevalence of psychiatric symptoms in adults with mental retardation and challenging behavior. *Research in Developmental Disabilities, 24,* 323-332.

Hughes, C. C. (1992). Culture in clinical psychiatry. In A. C. Gaw (Ed.), *Culture, ethnicity, and mental illness* (pp. 1-41). Washington, DC: American Psychiatric Press.

Jacobson, J. W., & Mulick, J. A. (1996). *Manual of diagnosis and professional practice in mental retardation.* Washington, DC: American Psychological Association.

James, S., & Prilleltensky, I. (2002). Cultural diversity and mental health: Towards integrative practice. *Clinical Psychology Review, 22,* 1133-1154.

Jamison, K. R. (1995). *An unquiet mind.* New York: Vintage Books.

Kahng, S., Iwata, B. A., & Lewin, A. B. (2002). Behavioral treatment of self-injury, 1964-2000. *American Journal on Mental Retardation, 107,* 212-221.

Lakin, K. C., Prouty, R., Polister, B., & Coucouvanis, K. (2003). Selected changes in residential service systems over a quarter century, 1977-2002. *Mental Retardation, 41,* 303-306.

Manning, M. (1994). *Undercurrents: A therapist's reckoning with her own depression.* San Francisco: HarperCollins.

Matson, J. L., Mayville, S. B., & Laud, R. B. (2003). A system of assessment for adaptive behavior, social skills, behavioral function, medication side-effects, and psychiatric disorders. *Research in Developmental Disabilities, 24,* 75-81.

Menolascino, F. J. (1994). Services for people with dual diagnosis in the USA. In N. Bouras (Ed.), *Mental health in mental retardation* (pp. 343-352). Cambridge, UK: Cambridge University Press.

Natvig, D. (1991). The role of the interdisciplinary team in using psychotropic drugs. *Journal of Psychosocial Nursing in Mental Health Services, 29,* 3-8.

Onken, S. J., Dumont, J. M., Ridgway, P., Dornan, D. H., & Ralph, R. O. (2002). *Mental health recovery: What helps and what hinders?* Alexandria, VA: National Technical Assistance Center for State Mental Health Planning (NTAC).

Pyles, D. A. M., Muniz, K., Cade, A., & Silva, R. (1997). A behavioral diagnostic paradigm for integrating behavior-analytic and psychopharmacological interventions for people with a dual diagnosis. *Research in Developmental Disabilities, 18,* 185-214.

Ralph, R. O. (2000). *Review of recovery literature: A synthesis of a sample of recovery literature 2000.* Alexandria, VA: National Technical Assistance Center for State Mental Health Planning (NTAC).

Ross, D. E. (2000). A method for formulating a biopsychosocial formulation. *Journal of Child and Family Studies, 9,* 1-6.

Sameroff, A. J. (1995). General systems theories and developmental psychopathology. In D. Cicchetti & D. J. Cohen (Eds.), *Developmental psychopathology* (Vol. 1, pp. 659-695). New York: Wiley.

Schiller, L., & Bennett, A. (1994). *The quiet room: A journey out of the torment of madness.* New York: Warner Books.

Silka, V. R., & Hauser, M. J. (1997). Psychiatric assessment of persons with mental retardation. *Psychiatric Annals, 27,* 162-169.

Singh, J. (2002). *My plan of life: A guide to strength-based practice.* Midlothian, VA: ONE Publications.

Singh. N. N. (2001). Holistic approaches to working with strengths: A goodness-of-fit wellness model. In A. Bridge, L. J. Gordon, P. Jivanjee, & J. M. King (Eds.), *Building on family strengths: Research and services in support of children and their families* (pp. 7-16). Portland, OR: Portland State University, Research and Training Center on Family Support and Children's Mental Health.

Singh, N. N., Ellis, C. R., & Wechsler, H. A. (1997). Psychopharmacoepidemiology in mental retardation. *Journal of Child and Adolescent Psychopharmacology, 7,* 255-266.

Singh, N. N., & Sabaawi, M. (in press). Pharmacotherapy. In M. Hersen (Ed.), *Encyclopedia of behavior modification and cognitive behavior therapy, Vol. 2: Child clinical applications.* Thousand Oaks, CA: Sage.

Singh, N. N., Sood, A., Sonenklar, N., & Ellis, C. R. (1991). Assessment and diagnosis of mental illness in persons with mental retardation. *Behavior Modification, 15,* 419-443.

Singh, N. N., Wahler, R. G., Sabaawi, M., Goza, A. B., Singh, S. D., Molina, E. J., & the Mindfulness Research Group. (2002). Mentoring treatment teams to integrate behavioral and psychopharmacological treatments in developmental disabilities. *Research in Developmental Disabilities, 23,* 379-389.

Sue, D. W., Carter, R. T., Casas, J. M., Fouad, N. A., Ivey, A. E., Jensen, M., LaFrambiose, T., Manese, J. E., Ponterotto, J. G., & Vazquez-Nutail, E. (1998). Multicultural counseling competencies: Individual and organizational development. In *Multicultural aspects of counseling (Vol. 2).* Thousand Oaks, CA: Sage.

Tseng, W. S., & Streltzer, J. (2001). *Culture and psychotherapy: A guide to clinical practice.* Washington, DC: American Psychiatric Press, Inc.

Wehmeyer, M. L. (1998). Self-determination and individuals with significant disabilities: Examining meanings and misinterpretations. *Journal of the Association for Persons with Severe Handicaps, 23,* 5-16.

Wehmeyer, M. L. (2001). Self-determination and mental retardation. In L. M. Glidden (Ed.), *International review of research in mental retardation* (Vol. 24, pp. 1-48). San Diego, CA: Academic Press.

## Footnote

1. The terms "his" and "him" are used throughout to refer to "his or her" and "him or her," respectively, unless otherwise specified.

# Chapter 12

# Depression in Persons
# with Mental Retardation

Kyle E. Ferguson
*University of Nevada, Reno*
John M. Guercio
*Center for Comprehensive Services, Carbondale, Illinois*
Akihiko Masuda and W. Larry Williams
*University of Nevada, Reno*

The topic of human emotions has been examined and debated for millennia in philosophical arenas (e.g., Aristotle, 1998; Hume, 1977; Sartre, 1948) and recently, for just over a century, in psychology (e.g., Cabanac, 2002; Cannon, 1927; Damasio, 1994; Ekman, 1992; James, 1890; Lazarus, 1991; Schachter & Singer, 1962). Despite widespread interest across disciplines, this subject has remained largely unexamined by behavior analysts.

Despite the fact that emotional disturbances are implicated in virtually all psychiatric conditions (Berenbaum, Raghavan, Huynh-Nhu, Vernon, & Gomez, 2003), the received view in applied behavior analysis is that inquiry into human emotions is of no value. There are two major reasons why this is so (Anderson, Hawkins, & Scotti, 1997; Forsyth & Eifert, 1996; Friman, Hayes, & Wilson, 1998). First, some argue that the study of human emotions is complete and therefore further investigation is unwarranted. Accordingly, emotional behavior of the "reflexive" variety (e.g., shock-induced aggression) are typically conceptualized and explained in terms of classical conditioning[1], while emotional behavior that concerns cognition and overt actions (e.g., jealousy) are explicated using operant conditioning principles. Either, or a combination of these, thus provide an exhaustive account of human emotional behavior. Second, some argue that human emotion is not a legitimate subject matter in its own right (e.g., Lamal, 1998). Skinner (1971), for example, saw emotions as mere "by-products" of contingencies of reinforcement (p. 16); exploring these have only "stood in the way of the inspection of more important things" (Skinner, 1974, p. 170).

Although there are traditional accounts of private events (e.g., Skinner, 1953), many behavior analysts have recently argued for a more extensive empirical analysis of these, including emotion, in order to gain a better understanding of complex human phenomena (e.g., Forsyth & Eifert, 1996; Hayes, 1994; Hayes, Barnes-

Holmes, & Roche, 2001; Hayes & Wilson, 1993; Rehfeldt, & Hayes, 1998). This movement has been facilitated by recent progress in behavior analytic accounts of human language and cognition. Instead of viewing emotion as an independent entity (e.g., epiphenomenon), as is the case traditionally, the role of emotion is treated as a function of the social-verbal context.

The present chapter discusses human emotional behavior in general, followed by a discussion on the emotional behavior of persons with mental retardation. First, traditional behavioral views of emotions and their limitations are discussed. Second, we then provide a brief overview of traditional operant accounts of verbal behavior, as these serve as the foundations for a contemporary view of language and cognition, called relational-frame theory (RFT) (Hayes & Wilson, 1993). RFT is taken up in the third section of the chapter. RFT provides a viable program of research capable of exploring the full spectrum of human emotions. Fourth, our current discussion would be incomplete without mentioning the cognitive or, using current parlance, cognitive-behavioral perspective on emotional regulation, as these approaches have received the most attention and empirical support in treating emotional problems. The fifth section briefly addresses the implications of psychiatric disorders observed in persons with developmental disabilities. Sixth, depression is highlighted next. The chapter closes by showcasing a behavioral approach to treating depression, called behavioral activation (BA) (Jacobson, Martell, & Dimidjian, 2001; Martell, Addis, & Jacobson, 2001). One of the benefits of this treatment modality is that it is much easier to learn than its therapeutic counterparts in cognitive psychology (Hollon, 2001). Accordingly, while it has yet to be tested, it appears well suited for this population.

Before proceeding, an important point deserves mention, as it may bear on how readers approach this chapter. Readers should note that the authors do not necessarily endorse the notion that psychiatric diagnostic categories *exist* in an ontological sense (e.g., the Diagnostics and Statistical Manual implies that psychiatric disorders are *real entities*, just as a malignant tumor is a real entity; American Psychiatric Association, 1994). Rather, our aim is pragmatic. In addition to typical behavior that is commonly dealt with in applied settings (e.g., self-injurious behavior), subtler emotional behavior (e.g., "depressed" behavior) is often overlooked by behavior analysts; which should come as no surprise, given their training (i.e., they are not trained to look for so-called "symptoms" of anxiety and depression). Hopefully, this chapter will better orient readers to these subtle behaviors that also affect the ability of persons with mental retardation to live more independent and productive lives.

## Traditional Behavioral Views of Emotion

### Respondent Conditioning

Emotional behavior was originally studied and conceptualized by behaviorists in terms of respondent conditioning (Pavlov, 1927; Watson & Rayner, 1920). According to this view, a neutral stimulus (NS) (e.g., bell) is directly paired with an event (UCS) (e.g., loud noise) that reflexively elicits emotional responding (UCR) (e.g., the organism startles, the Sympathetic branch of the Autonomic Nervous System is engaged, etc.). By repeating the NS-UCS contiguous association, the neutral stimulus assumes some or many of the functions of the UCS; it becomes a conditioned stimulus (CS). Namely, the CS comes to elicit a response (CR) that is comparable to the original UCR (i.e., the organism startles, etc.).

An elaborated form of respondent conditioning is called second-order (or higher-order) respondent conditioning (see Pierce & Epling, 1999). According to this principle, upon frequent pairings with the $CS_1$, another neutral stimulus can elicit a similar emotional reaction ($CS_2$). Additionally, other stimuli, in the absence of training, may also acquire an emotion-eliciting function based simply on overlapping physical similarities with the established $CS_1$ (e.g., similar frequency of tone). This principle is called stimulus generalization (Catania, 1992).

*Limitation of respondent paradigm.* One major limitation of this view is that respondent conditioning cannot explain events that obtain emotion-eliciting functions not directly associated with the UCS (i.e., overlapping formal properties or non-arbitrary similarities). Respondent conditioning attempts to explain indirect emotional learning by stimulus generalization and higher-order conditioning. That is, transfer of stimulus function only occurs under these circumscribed conditions.

Although respondent conditioning accounts for some of the variability observed in emotional behavior, recent studies have demonstrated the transfer of stimulus functions among stimuli that do not share formal properties with an existing emotion-eliciting stimulus (e.g., Dougher, Augustson, Markham, Greenway, & Wulfert, 1994; Roche & Barnes, 1997; Roche, Barnes-Holmes, Smeets, Barnes-Holmes, McGeady, 2001). Moreover, research has also shown the failure to produce third-order respondent conditioning (Cicero & Tryon, 1989; Tryon & Cicero, 1989). If higher-order conditioning were indeed a robust phenomenon, naturally one would expect that third-, fourth-, or fifth-order conditioning would be achievable with relative ease. This, of course, has not been the case.

Another major limitation includes its inability to account for bidirectional stimulus relations, which is observed among verbally-able humans (Jenkins, 1963). From a strict respondent perspective, stimulus-stimulus relationships can only occur unidirectionally (UCS → CS) – not the other way around (Sidman, 1994).

As an ad hoc maneuver, one of the attempts to resolve these limitations is to include in the respondent account, cognitive and symbolic behaviors as underlying mediational factors (e.g., Staats & Eifert, 1990). This approach is driven by observations that human cognitive activities (e.g., thinking) entail human emotional experience. That is, language and cognition serve important functions by providing humans with emotional experiences without direct exposure to the actual physical stimuli or events that typically elicit emotional reactions. One of the theories derived from this perspective is paradigmatic behavior theory (PBT).

## Paradigmatic Behavior Theory

PBT (Forsyth & Eifert, 1996; Staats & Eifert, 1990) conceptualizes human emotions in a social-verbal context by integrating respondent and operant conditioning as one unit. PBT states that the acquisition and maintenance of the emotion-eliciting function of an event does not require direct experience. Rather, the association between *verbal events* with certain stimulus events (e.g., situations, objects, images, or words) is sufficient for those objects or situations to acquire certain emotion-eliciting functions. While respondent learning entails the peripheral nervous system (e.g., reflex), PBT treats human emotions as central nervous system learning, the likes of which involves cognitive and symbolic behaviors.

While seemingly a more flexible account than the traditional respondent paradigm, PBT has limitations in resolving the issue of indirect emotional learning (Forsyth & Eifert, 1996). These are due to its account of human language, regarding cognition as mediational variables, and the subsequent abandonment of further analysis of these events.

While incorporating respondent and operant conditioning into one unit, PBT's account of emotional behavior is still conceptually anchored in the classical conditioning paradigm. PBT only states that human verbalizations can function as stimuli that elicit emotional responses by frequent pairings with the UCS. The integration of the two principles is described such that, these verbal stimuli (e.g., words), which acquire emotion-eliciting functions, function as discriminative and consequential stimuli in operant conditioning. Insofar as it applies a unidirectional approach (i.e., the respondent paradigm) to the nature of verbal phenomena, PBT fails to account for the core nature of verbal events, that being bidirectional stimulus relations.

## Two-Factor Theory

Another behavioral theory that also combines respondent and operant processes is two-factor theory (Mowrer, 1947, 1951, 1956). Two-factor theory provides a model of avoidance behavior. According to Mowrer (1947), avoidance entails both classical conditioning and operant conditioning. First, through classical conditioning, the warning signal (i.e., CS) comes to elicit fear. Second, every time the organism is successful at removing the feared stimulus (i.e., escape behavior), the operant (avoidance) response is thus negatively reinforced. Hence, avoidance behavior is maintained by way of operant conditioning. As it applies to clinical phenomena, the conditioned emotional response is a CR (i.e., fear and anxiety) and the eliciting stimulus, a CS (e.g., crowds where panic attacks frequently occur).

The CS is crucial in two-factor learning theory. While it serves as an eliciting stimulus, it also serves as an antecedent stimulus that occasions the avoidance response. Although studies have demonstrated the utility of two-factor theory, both in terms of basic research (e.g., Miller, 1948) and clinically (e.g., Hogan & Kirchner, 1967), one major problem remains: as with PBT, it cannot account for bidirectional stimulus relations (i.e., S $\leftrightarrow$ S; See McAllister & McAllister, 1995, p. 158ff., for further criticisms of two-factor theory).

## Skinner's Perspective on Human Language and Cognition

Skinner views human cognition as a functional set of responses, called operants (Skinner, 1957; 1969; 1974). Skinner (1957, 1990) maintains that verbal behavior is selected by way of social contingencies. According to Skinner, the only difference between verbal behavior and other operants is that the contingencies of reinforcement operating on verbal behavior are mediated solely by other people (Skinner, 1957). Accordingly, provided that another organism mediates the delivery of the reinforcer or punisher, nonhumans are also capable of verbal behavior (e.g., the experimenter mediates the reinforcement of lever pressing, hence, the behavior of the rat is verbal).

Skinner (1957) describes various types of functional relationships between controlling variables and verbal responding. In what follows, we take up two in particular called tacts (the verb is tacting) and mands (the verb is manding).

*Tacting.* Tacting is a verbal response of a particular form that is evoked by certain stimulus or event characteristics (Skinner, 1957, pp. 81-82)[2]. Tacting can occur publicly or privately (i.e., within the "organism's" own skin) in response to public or private stimulation. The strength of this functional relationship depends on the extent to which the verbal community reinforces correspondence between verbal responding and its referents.

In regards to emotional behavior, while the verbal community does not have direct access to an individual's private events, there are a number of collaterally occurring, publicly observable behaviors. Take the clinical manifestations of depression, for example. Publicly observable behaviors implicated in depression are as follows: crying spells, social withdrawal, and psychomotor retardation (markedly slower movements), among others.

*Mands.* Another functional class of verbal behavior is what Skinner (1957, p. 35) calls mands. A mand is defined as a verbal operant in which the response is reinforced by certain consequences and as such, is under the momentary control of relative states of deprivation (e.g., hunger) or aversive stimulation (e.g., pain) (Michael, 1993). Mands usually directly or indirectly identify the reinforcer (e.g., "I'm thirsty") or aversive stimulus of which these are a function.

The notion of manding is of particular import in training individuals with mental retardation how to appropriately make requests, emotionally (e.g., accessing personal contact in times of need) or otherwise. Those individuals with severely compromised verbal abilities, for example, develop maladaptive ways of manding (see Sundberg & Partington, 1998; Sundberg, present volume; for a thorough discussion on how to train manding, as well as tacting, to special populations).

*Rule-governed behavior.* Skinner (1969; 1974) classifies operant behavior as either contingency-shaped or rule-governed. Contingency-shaped behavior is behavior shaped by the natural world. For example, a hangover results from drinking too much alcohol the night before. A person's drinking behavior can be shaped by this aversive consequence without being told that drinking too much causes hangovers. Contingency-shaped behavior is comparable to what the philosophers

Ryle (1949) and Russell (1961) call "knowing that" and "knowledge by acquaintance," respectively.

Rule-governed behavior entails a verbal antecedent or rule, which is said to specify the contingencies of reinforcement. Thus, rule-governed behavior is analogous to what Ryle (1949) and Russell (1961) call "knowing how" and "knowledge by description" (i.e., "book learning"), respectively. Rule-governed behavior provides a conceptual model for thinking and cognition (Skinner, 1989, p. 16). According to Skinner, cognitions in the form of rules can function both as antecedent stimuli (e.g., prompting overt behavior or further private stimulation) and as responses (i.e., private event, as an epiphenomenon) (Anderson, Hawkins, & Scotti, 1997; Skinner, 1989).

*Criticisms of Skinner.* Although Skinner's account of verbal behavior encourages a naturalistic approach to human language and cognition, some verbal processes fall outside this model. Over and above the fact that Skinner's approach to verbal behavior is too broad, being incapable of demarcating verbal behavior from other social behavior or a rule from other antecedent stimuli, the major criticism is its limitation in explaining bidirectional, arbitrarily-applicable stimulus relations and indirect learning beyond stimulus generalization (Hayes, Blackledge, Barnes-Holmes, 2001). Here, again, Skinner's (1957) analysis of verbal behavior only accounts for unidirectional stimulus-response relationships.

## A Contemporary View of Emotion: Relational Frame Theory

Relational frame theory (RFT) is a behavior analytic theory of complex human behavior, such as language and cognition (Hayes, 1994; Hayes, Barnes-Holmes, & Roche, 2001; Hayes & Wilson, 1993). One of the most encouraging features of RFT is that it can explain so-called "indirect learning;" it thus extends beyond stimulus generalization.

According to this perspective, indirect learning is attributable to human language and cognition (i.e., derived stimulus relations as verbal processes and outcomes). This idea is, of course, similar to other behavioral theories such as paradigmatic behavioral theory and cognitive theories. However, what sets RFT apart from other theories is its inductive, descriptive, and functional approach to human language and cognition; all the while it avoids the use of language and cognition as mediational variables. RFT addresses human language and cognition as generalized functional operants of arbitrarily applicable relational responding, that are brought under contextual control. Said differently, verbal responding (e.g., relationally framing events) is conceptualized as a dependent variable that is influenced by contextual or independent variables (technically, *Cfunc* and *Crel*; Hayes et al., 2001).

A number of researchers have shown that humans learn derived, bidirectional stimulus relations easily (Hayes, 1994; Hayes, Fox, Gifford, Wilson, Barnes-Holmes, & Healy, 2001; Hayes & Wilson, 1993). When a verbally-able human, while in the presence of one stimulus (i.e., stimulus A) learns to select an arbitrarily related stimulus (B), then this trained unidirectional relation will lead to a derived bidirectional relation without further training. This principle is termed *mutual entailment.* Similarly, when A-B and A-C relations are directly trained, B-C, and C-B relations are derived indirectly (*combinatorial entailment*). Furthermore, the function of stimuli framed in the relational network tends to change or transform in accordance with the arbitrarily derived stimulus relation (*transformation of stimulus function*). The transformation of stimulus function has been reported in the domains of conditioned reinforcement (e.g., Auguston, & Dougher, 1997; Hayes, Kohlenberg, & Hayes, 1991), discriminative function (e.g., Dymond & Barnes, 1995), and elicited conditioned emotional responding (e.g., Dougher, Augustson, Markham, Greenway, & Wulfert, 1994; Roche & Barnes, 1997).

It is important to note that RFT does not dispute the existing accounts of direct learning and other derived processes, such as stimulus generalization among nonarbitrary stimuli, held by respondent and operant conditioning paradigms. For example, RFT stresses the importance of nonarbitrary stimuli, their stimulus relations, and their relations with arbitrary stimuli in relational learning (Barnes-Holmes, Barnes-Holmes, & Cullinan, 2000; Fields, Reeve, Adames, & Verhave, 1991; Stewart, Barnes-Holmes, Roche, & Smeet, 2002). RFT thereby synthesizes the concept of arbitrarily applicable derived learning with traditional behavioral accounts in order to explain behavioral processes unaccounted for by these paradigms (Barnes-Holmes, Barnes-Holmes, & Cullinan, 2000; Chase & Danforth, 1991). Therefore, from this contextual perspective, RFT does not conceptualize human emotion as a discrete behavior process or entity. Rather, RFT views emotion within the context of dynamic interactions of respondent, operant, and derived operant processes – any, or all of which are potentially operating at any given time (Barnes-Holmes, Barnes-Holmes, Roche, Hearly, Lyddy, & Cullinan, 2001).

*RFT's account of human emotional learning.* While other theories are hindered by arbitrary, bidirectional aspects of human emotional learning, RFT can account for these phenomena without too much difficulty. RFT simply explains indirect, bidirectional, and arbitrary aspects of emotional learning in terms of the transformation of stimulus function taking place within relational networks (i.e., mutual entailment and combinatorial entailment). As mentioned, any novel stimulus can obtain a certain stimulus function when framed with other stimuli, which have certain emotion-eliciting functions. The acquired stimulus function is thus dependent on the relation with other stimuli that enter into the relational frame.

The transformation of stimulus function in the area of human emotions is reported in the relational frame of coordination (sameness; Dougher et al., 1994; Barnes-Holmes, Keane, Barnes-Holmes, 2000; Roche & Barnes, 1997) and other varieties of relational networks (e.g., oppositeness; Roche & Barnes, 1997; Roche, Barnes-Holmes, Smeets, Barnes-Holmes, & McGeady, 2000). As a case in point, let us consider a study conducted by Dougher and his associates (1994). Participants in the study were first trained to establish two different relational networks of coordination (i.e., equivalence classes). Next, one stimulus from one of the relational networks was paired with electric shock using a respondent conditioning procedure; the consequence of which elicited a robust physiological (emotional) reaction. As a result of this experimental preparation, participants' physiological arousal was also observed in the presence of other stimulus members, sharing the same relational network (i.e., associated with electric shock). By contrast, no appreciable physiological arousal occurred in the presence of stimuli that participated in other relational networks (i.e., not associated with electric shock).

*RFT's account of experiential avoidance.* The previous section addressed the indirect acquisition of emotion-eliciting function of a novel stimulus through its participation in a relational network. The following describes clinical extensions of RFT. Namely, how emotion-eliciting relational networks contribute to experiential avoidance (Hayes, Wilson, Gifford, Follette, & Strosahl, 1996).

From an RFT perspective, like other non-human organisms, humans in early stages of development learn various forms of avoidance behavior from direct contact with contingencies. As humans develop and their verbal repertoires become more elaborate, avoidance behavior becomes increasingly verbal. For example, individuals begin formulating rules about their direct contact with aversive stimuli (Hayes, 1989; Hayes, & Gifford, 1997). Through bidirectional transformations of stimulus function, the responses themselves take on aversive properties (i.e., the verbal stimuli become punishers). Thus, the individual not only avoids the events in question but also begins avoiding their responses to these (colloquially, he or she avoids everything that "reminds" him- or herself about the aversive experience). Furthermore, the ever-evolving framing process facilitates the development of more complex and abstracted relational networks, which are often seen among individuals with anxiety disorders (historically, these were called "neuroses;" Auguston & Dougher, 1997; Friman, Hayes, & Wilson, 1998; Hayes et al., 1996).

## Cognitive View of Emotion

Clinically speaking, the four major cognitive or cognitive-behavioral views of emotion are Beck's (1976) Cognitive Therapy (CT), Ellis's Rational-Emotive Therapy (RET; 1962; more recently, Rational-Emotive Behavior Therapy; REBT), Meichenbaum's (1977) Self-Instructional Training, and Burns's popular self-help protocol, "Feeling Good" Therapy (1989). Among many others (hundreds of empirical demonstrations), alcoholism (Steigerwald & Stone, 1999), severe social phobia (Mattick & Peters, 1988), the trauma of rape (Foa & Rothbaum, 1998), and depression (Jacobson et al., 1996) are some of the clinical problems that have been successfully treated using these. Let us next consider Ellis's treatment called Rational-Emotive Therapy (RET) as an illustration of a cognitively-oriented perspective on emotional regulation.

*Rational-Emotive Therapy.* Ellis's (1962, 1994) RET is implicitly based on the notion of augmental rules. Augmenting (the verb form of augmental) is rule-governed behavior under the "apparent changes in the capacity of events to function as reinforcers or punishers" (Zettle & Hayes, 1982, p. 81). Observe, therefore, that an augmental is a verbal stimulus that also serves as an establishing stimulus (Hayes, Zettle, & Rosenfarb, 1989, p. 206). That is, it has an evocative effect on related behavior and momentarily increases the reinforcing effectiveness or punishing properties of other events (Michael, 1993; cf. Skinner's, 1957, concept of mand).

RET "concentrates on people's current beliefs, attitudes and self-statements as contributing to or 'causing' and maintaining their emotional and behavioral disturbances" (Ellis et al., 1988, pp. 1-2). What logically follows, therefore, is the notion that *appropriate emotions* are preceded by *rational beliefs* and *inappropriate emotions* like hostility are preceded by *irrational beliefs* (Ellis, 1971). While the list of potential irrational beliefs would seem endless, Ellis and colleagues (1988) have narrowed it down to just four: demandingness, awfulizing, human worth ratings, and low frustration tolerance (Ellis, 1994; Ellis et al., 1988):

1. *Demandingness* – the tendency to substitute demands for wishes, as mirrored in word choices such as "should," "ought," "must," and "have to" (e.g., "I must go to college in order to live a meaningful life").
2. *Awfulizing* – extreme and exaggerated negative evaluations of events – colloquially, blowing the situation out of proportion (e.g., "My life is over if I don't get into college").
3. *Human worth ratings* – evaluations or denigrations of people including the self (e.g., "Not going to college makes me worthless to everyone in my life").
4. *Low frustration tolerance* – the perceived inability to withstand the discomfort of an activating event – activating events evoke emotional and behavioral responding (e.g., "I can't live another day").

From an Ellisian perspective irrational core beliefs ought to be disputed rationally. Cognitive disputations are attempts at changing the client's erroneous beliefs through persuasion, didactic presentations, Socratic dialogue, vicarious experiences, and other forms of verbally-mediated approaches (Ellis, 1962, 1971, 1994). In what follows are three major techniques upon which irrational beliefs are disputed in therapeutic milieus (Walen, DiGiuseppe, & Dryden, 1992):

• *Logical Disputation Questions* – (getting clients to evaluate the logical consistency or semantic clarity in their thinking) (p. 159). *Example*: Just because a person knows right from wrong does not *logically* follow that he or she must behave in accordance with these.
• *Reality-Testing Disputation Questions* – (asking whether their beliefs are consistent with empirical reality). *Example*: Awfulizing beliefs can be challenged by asking such questions as (p. 161):

1. *What is the proof*…"that you always screw up?"
2. *Where's the evidence*…"that you blow every social situation?"
3. *What would happen if*…"you panicked in front of your friends?"
4. *Let's be scientists*. What do the data show?

5.  What is the *probability* of a bad consequence – is it 2 to 1, 200 to 1, 2000 to 1, etc.?

•  *Pragmatic Disputation Questions* – (getting clients to assess the "hedonic" value – i.e., desire for pleasure and avoidance of pain – of their belief system) (pp. 161-162). *Example*: The belief is used to regulate emotional upset.

Tversky and Kahneman (1974) demonstrate how humans tend to make predictable errors in judgment and decisions when in ambiguous situations. In particular, under these circumstances humans routinely fail to take the representativeness of phenomena into account (i.e., do not use information about base rates), and place too great an emphasis on their initial impressions (i.e., "intuitions" or "gut reaction"). Clients diagnosed with Panic Disorder are obvious examples of this phenomenon (Sullivan, Kent, & Coplan, 2000). Sympathetic arousal triggers "the fight or flight response" or what Selye calls the "Alarm Reaction" (1974, p. 38ff.). Activating the sympathetic branch "speeds up the organism"; heart rate increases along with metabolism, and end organs not required in protecting the organism are suppressed (e.g., digestive system; hence, stomach upset) (Asteria, 1985).

While most individuals "normalize" these internal events by taking base rates into account (e.g., "What are the odds of having a heart attack at 20 years of age?"), those individuals with Panic Disorder catastrophize attacks as something potentially lethal. Such individuals frequently misinterpret the "meaning" of panic attacks and fear that they are dying, experiencing a stroke, having a heart attack, or going insane. Over time, many clients develop a recurrent pattern of irrational fears, aptly called the "fear of fear" cycle (Barlow, 1988).

*Problems with cognitive-behavioral orientations to therapy.* Cognitive-behavioral approaches "literalize" language (i.e., they are "content oriented") – hence, they can potentially become part of the client's problem (producing more experiential avoidance, via their participation in relational frames), not a solution (Hayes, Strosahl & Wilson 1999). All psychological avoidance is born out of "excess literality." For example, individuals with Obsessive-Compulsive Disorder will engage in ritualistic behavior (e.g., hand washing) as a means of ridding themselves of obsessional thoughts (e.g., contamination), which are as real as the things they represent (e.g., contamination obsessions = disease).

From an empirical standpoint, there is some question as to the utility of including cognitive techniques in treatment packages. In some instances, these techniques appear to be superfluous, providing little or no incremental validity over and above behavioral preparations. Take cognitive-behavior therapy for depression, for example. Jacobson et al. (1996) conducted a dismantling study and found that the cognitive component could not account for any more variance already accounted for by behavioral activation. Simply getting the person "moving," engaged in preferred activities, seemed to suffice in alleviating most of the symptoms of depression as well as prevent subsequent relapse (Gortner, Gollan, Dobson, & Jacobson, 1998). Moreover, adaptive thinking patterns more often than not followed behavioral activation, as opposed to the other way around. Martell, Addis, and Jacobson (2001) conclude,

> The take-home message seemed fairly clear: Treating depression by helping to activate people is just as effective as helping them to change their thinking. Perhaps, on average, cognitive interventions are unnecessary (p. xxiii).

## Psychiatric Disorders in Persons with Mental Retardation

The consensus in healthcare is that individuals with mental retardation are at increased risk of developing psychiatric disorders, especially in institutional settings. For example, one report estimated that over 50% of institutionalized persons had at least one diagnosable psychiatric disorder; comparatively speaking, the rate of those residing in the community fell between 20% and 35% (Singh, Sood, Sonenklar, & Ellis, 1991). On the whole, epidemiologic studies have shown that, almost invariably, the rate of psychiatric disturbances in this population is markedly higher than those of the general population (Borthwick-Duffy, 1994). Some estimates of this discrepancy are four- to six-fold higher (Matson & Barrett, 1982).

Before proceeding, a cautionary note is warranted: Due to diminished cognitive functioning, developmentally disabled individuals are less likely to identify symptoms as well as report these should they arise clinically (Kostinas, Scandlen, & Luiselli, 2001). To be sure, as is the case in all psychiatric disorders that affect persons with mental retardation, there is an underreporting of cases.

While describing the prevalence rates of all of the disorders is beyond the scope of the present chapter, before turning to depression, let us consider one anxiety-related disorder: Obsessive-compulsive disorder.

### Obsessive-compulsive Disorder (OCD)

The incidence of OCD in special populations ranges from 0.63% to 3.5%; again, several fold higher than the general population (Crews, Bonaventura, & Rowe, 1994). There are a number of behaviors observed in individuals without disabilities that include ritualistic hand washing, ordering, and checking, among others. These behaviors may take on a different complexion in persons with developmental disabilities. Behaviors such as hoarding, perseveration on certain topics, and rigid structural patterns in their daily routines are more prevalent in this group.

Interventions are characterized in three ways. The first of these involves interventions that try to eliminate antecedent stimuli that trigger the obsessive-compulsive cycle. Examples of this would be identifying patterns of ritualistic hand washing or other behaviors and eliminate some of the stimuli that consistently precede these behaviors. The second approach involves teaching appropriate functional replacement behaviors that the individual can use in place of the maladaptive behavioral rituals. The third approach uses contingent consequences based on the observation of the targeted OCD behaviors (e.g., overcorrection). Of all of these methods, the latter is the least recommended due to increased potential in concomitant aggressive responding.

In one of the few controlled studies investigating these procedures in special populations, Matson (1982) employed a package consisting of positive reinforcement, integrated into a DRO schedule, along with contingent overcorrection and modeling of appropriate responding. He found that this package was effective in reducing the checking rituals of the participants in the study.

In a related study, Kostinas and associates (Kostinas et al., 2001) also examined OCD behaviors and the use of behavioral interventions. They identified perseverative verbalizations related to inappropriate topics as the target behavior. A design was implemented that included Differential Reinforcement of other behaviors (DRO), as well as a response cost procedure to decrease these behaviors. They found that the response cost procedure was more effective than the DRO procedure in reducing the perseverative verbalizations.

## Depression in Persons with Mental Retardation

*Diagnosis.* To receive a diagnosis of Major Depressive Disorder (MDD), the following criteria must be met (American Psychiatric Association, 2000, p. 173ff.).

A. The occurrence of a single *Major Depressive Episode (MDE)*. A MDE entails *5 or more* of the following symptoms that have been present within a *two-week period*. At least one of the symptoms are either (1) *depressed mood* or (2) *loss of interest* or *pleasure* (anhedonia), and are *not due to a general medical condition* or *mood-incongruent delusions* or *hallucinations*. The symptoms cause *marked distress*.

   1) *depressed mood* most of the day within the observation interval.
   2) *diminished interest* or *pleasure* in usual, preferred activities.
   3) significant *weight loss* (i.e., over 5%), not due to dieting or increased exercise, or marked increase or decrease in appetite.
   4) *insomnia* or *hypersomnia* almost every day.
   5) *psychomotor agitation* (restlessness) or *retardation* (slowed movements) nearly every day.
   6) *fatigue* or *loss of energy* almost daily.
   7) *feeling worthless* or *excessive guilt.*
   8) *impaired concentration* or marked *indecisiveness.*
   9) recurrent thoughts of *death, suicidal ideation,* or *suicide attempts.*
B. The MDE is *not better accounted for by other disorders* (e.g., Schizoaffective Disorder or Delusional Disorder).
C. There has *never been a Manic Episode, Mixed Episode,* or *Hypomanic Episode.*

The DSM-IV makes a further distinction between *MDD, Single Episode* and *MDD Recurrent.* Simply, MDD, Single Episode entails only one Major Depressive

Episode and the latter, two or more – the interval of which must be at least two consecutive months.

Depression occurs in the general population at a rate of "4.5% to 9.3% for females and 2.3% to 3.2% for females" (American Psychiatric Association, 1994, p. 229). Relatively speaking, the rate of depression in persons with mental retardation is several-fold higher (Singh, Sood, Sonenklar, & Ellis, 1991).

*Assessment issues.* One of the prerequisites for mood assessment is the ability to provide self-report to others about covert behaviors. As alluded to earlier, this becomes a significant barrier to assessment, when working with individuals whose language abilities are severely compromised due to severe mental retardation (Charlot, Doucette, & Mezzacappa, 1993). As a result, most of the research that has been pursued in this area has been related to those with mild to moderate disabilities (Campo, Sharpton, Thompson, & Sexton, 1997).

For those with more severe disability, direct observation methods have proven to be effective indices of mood (Green & Reid, 1996). Examples of such indices have included operationally defining behaviors that have been correlated with inferred pleasant private events. Based on the data garnered from these measures, Green and Reid were able to demonstrate a functional relationship; namely, a systematic increase of indices of "happiness" and reduction in indices of "unhappiness."

The inability to effectively identify or seek assistance related to possible depressed behaviors leaves the onus on the service provider to assist in this process. There are a number of behaviors that are associated with each disorder that can be readily observed by direct care staff, family members, and others. Among these behaviors is excess somnolence, changes in eating patterns, less interest in preferred activities, fluctuations in weight, among others (see DSM-IV criteria above).

Current research has negated the view that people with developmental disabilities are too "psychologically primitive" to develop psychiatric issues (Sovner & DesNoyers Hurley, 1983). The tendency to overlook such disorders has been termed "diagnostic overshadowing" – leaving the clinician no other choice but to attribute most of the behavioral and cognitive difficulties in special populations to their diagnosis, without entertaining the possibility that the two could co-exist, co-morbidly (Luiselli, 1998; Walters, Barrett, Knapp, & Borden, 1995).

*Risk factors.* Some researchers indicate that there may be a greater tendency for individuals with mental retardation to experience symptoms of depression or other mood disorders, given their lowered probability at accessing positive reinforcement and in light of recent genetic findings (Matson et al., 1991). First, let us consider environmental issues. In many instances, individuals with developmental disabilities spend a great deal of their lives away from family members and other important social contacts. They may reside in facilities that are located a great distance from their homes. These factors are linked to depressed states (i.e., lowered reinforcement densities). Second, there is mounting physiological evidence that these individuals have certain genetic predispositions that contribute to higher rates of depression. For example, persons with Down's syndrome are more vulnerable to hypothyroidism;

a condition positively correlated with the onset of depression (Davis, Judd, & Hermann, 1997).

*Future directions.* The transition to a more behavior analytic approach has commenced through the identification of "atypical symptoms" of depression (Ross & Oliver, 2003). Among these are irritability, self-injurious behavior, and aggression. These behaviors have now been added to the diagnostic framework of more common behaviors such as excess sleep, changes in eating patterns, and loss of interest in preferred activities. These "atypical symptoms" have been reported in approximately 83% of individuals with severe disabilities, and 55% in those with mild mental retardation (Meins, 1995). Meins also suggests that an irritable mood could be a core diagnostic criterion for depression in special populations.

The association between unwanted behavior and mood disorders has been implicated in the literature. This applies to both depression and Bipolar disorder. For example, self-injury has been noted to occur only during depressed episodes in some individuals, and aggression has been related to manic features of Bipolar disorder (Lowry & Sovner, 1992). The observable nature of such behaviors allows clinicians to better track and document the origins and progression of mood disorders in these populations (Sturmey, 1998).

## Behavioral Activation

Behavioral Activation (BA) was born out of a tradition of behavior analytic views of depression. These views are based on the notion that depressed individuals contact fewer positive reinforcers and consequently, experience fewer pleasurable emotions or private stimulation (e.g., joy). Ferster (1973), for example, suggests that depressed persons emit fewer behaviors that eventuate in positive reinforcement – because they are preoccupied with avoiding contact with aversive stimuli. Observe that this perspective is wholly consistent with Hayes and colleagues notion of experiential avoidance mentioned earlier (Hayes, Strosahl, & Wilson, 1999). Lewinsohn (1974) elaborates further. Namely, depressed individuals tend to be 1) insensitive to positive stimuli and thus, find few activities reinforcing; 2) there is a paucity of reinforcers available (e.g., consider the lives of depressed shut-ins); 3) he or she might have an impaired social repertoire, deficient in evoking socially-mediated positive reinforcement on the part of others. Readers should note that any or all of these might enter into the contingency at any given time. While Ferster, unfortunately, has been largely overlooked, Lewinsohn's model has received a fair amount of empirical support in the literature. For example, studies show that depressed persons engage in far fewer pleasant activities relative to nondepressed individuals and in social settings, emit far fewer, interpersonally-relevant, positive behaviors (Garland, Fox, & Williams, 2002; Lewinsohn & Amenson, 1978; Lewinsohn & Graf, 1973; Lewinsohn & Libet, 1972; Libet & Lewinsohn, 1973).

BA is a stand-alone treatment for depression that conceptualizes much of the behavior of depressed individuals as avoidance behavior (Jacobson et al., 2001). It places an emphasis on increasing the client's activity levels which ultimately increases contact with positive reinforcement in his or her life. Accordingly, this overall increase in reinforcement density serves to decrease symptoms of depression.

BA focuses on identifying external events that trigger episodes of depression and the ineffective coping strategies that follow (e.g., passive coping; Martell, Addis, & Jacobson, 2001). Hollon (2001) summarizes this relationship nicely:

> It (BA) relies heavily on an examination on the consequences of different behaviors, particularly those that serve to avoid imminent distress at the cost of blocking access to subsequent reinforcement. The therapist works with the client to conduct a functional analysis of his or her current life situations (triggers), emotional and behavioral responses, and the consequences that ensue. A real premium is placed on developing stages or plans that deal more effectively with the life problems, particularly with respect to substituting active efforts to cope for the avoidance behaviors clients tend to prefer. Therapists frequently refer to a visual diagram that differentiates between TRAP versus TRAC models, with the former referring to trigger-response-avoidance pattern and the latter referring to trigger-response-alternative coping. Thoughts and beliefs are largely ignored. Attention is paid to the function that they serve (ruminating distracts the patient from efforts to cope) (p. 272, parenthesis, authors).

The course of treatment proceeds as follows: 1) establish a therapeutic relationship (i.e., therapeutic alliance); 2) present the behavioral model to the client (i.e., the vicious cycle of depressed mood → decreased activation → depressed mood, etc.); 3) establish treatment goals – with the expressed aim of reengaging the client, such that he or she is more likely to contact positive reinforcement; 4) conduct a functional analysis of the client's present circumstances (i.e., What contextual features disrupted his or her normal routine, triggering the depressive cycle?); and 5) relapse prevention (clients and therapist devise a plan in the event of relapse) (Jacobson et al., 2001; Martell et al., 2001).

Readers should note that BA therapists are typically very specific and concrete with clients (Martell et al., 2001). Accordingly, this treatment modality is far easier to learn, relative to extant cognitive-behavioral therapies (Hollon, 2001). Of course, to be sure, protocols will have to be simplified for persons with developmental disabilities. While BA awaits more empirical support, preliminary findings are promising (Gortner et al., 1998; Jacobson et al., 1996; Hollon, 2000).

## Concluding Remarks

Given their limited coping and problem-solving repertoires, persons with developmental disabilities are highly susceptible to abuse and neglect. Although, residential and institutional settings employ safeguards to prevent this, the fact of the matter remains: Abuse and neglect statistics are staggering. Considering just one form of abuse, sexual abuse, while it occurs in the general population at a rate of 20% for females and 5-10% for males, more than 90% of persons with developmental disabilities will experience sexual abuse at some point in their lives (Sobsey, & Doe, 1991). In actual numbers, it has been estimated between 15,000 and 19,000 individuals with developmental disabilities are sexually assaulted each year in the United States (Sobsey, 1994). To make matters worse, roughly half of those individuals will experience 10 or more incidents of abuse over the course of their lives (Valenti-Hein & Schwartz, 1995).

Researchers have attempted to explicate the potential link between sexual abuse and psychopathology. While highly controversial and, as it stands, inconclusive, there is increasing evidence that supports a positive correlation. In particular, if sexual abuse is not effectively treated, long-term symptoms may persist (Jumper, 1995; Neumann, Houskamp, Pollock, & Briere, 1996). These include: substance abuse (Gearon, Kaltman, Brown, & Bellack, 2003); self-mutilation (King, Coxell, & Mezey, 2002); suicidal attempts (Leverich et al., 2003); anxiety (McCreary & Thompson, 1999); eating disorders (Steiger & Zankor, 1990; Welch & Fairburn, 1994); and depression (Cheasty, Clare, & Collins, 1998; Weiss, Longhurst, & Mazure, 1999), to name only a few. While this association has yet to be established in persons with mental retardation, let alone in the population on the whole, a reasonable conclusion is that a significant number of individuals who have been abused suffer from emotional problems related to trauma. In the worst cases, such individuals develop diagnosable psychiatric disorders.

In closing, for readers interested in learning more about emotional disorders and their treatments, we recommend consulting Chambless and colleagues (Chambless et al., 1998) list of empirically-supported treatments, as a point of departure. While far from perfect, this list is comprised of the industry's "gold standard" therapies.

## References

American Psychiatric Association. (2000). *Quick reference to the diagnostic criteria from DSM-IV-TR*. Washington, DC: Author.

American Psychiatric Association. (1994). *Diagnostic and statistical manual of mental disorders* (4th ed.). Washington, DC: Author.

Anderson, C. M., Hawkins, R. P., & Scotti, J. P. (1997). Private events in behavior analysis: Conceptual basis and clinical relevance. *Behavior Therapy, 28*, 157-159.

Aristotle. (1998). *Nicomachean ethics* (D. P. Chase, Trans.). New York: Dover Publications, Inc.

Asteria, M. F. (1985). *The physiology of stress*. New York: Human Sciences Press.

Auguston, E. M., & Dougher, M. J. (1997). The transfer of avoidance evoking functions through stimulus equivalence classes. *Journal of Behavior Therapy and Experimental Psychiatry, 28*, 181-191.

Barlow, D. H. (1988). *Anxiety and its disorders*. New York: Guilford Press.

Barnes-Holmes, D., Barnes-Holmes, Y., & Cullinan, V. (2000). Relational frame theory and Skinner's verbal behavior: A possible synthesis. *The Behavior Analyst, 23*, 69-84.

Barnes-Holmes, D., Barnes-Holmes, Y., Roche, B., Hearly, O., Lyddy, F., & Cullinan, V. (2001). Psychological development. In S. C. Hayes, D. Barnes-

Holmes, & B. Roche, (Eds.), *Relational frame theory: A post-Skinnerian account of human language and cognition* (pp. 157-180). New York: Kluwer Academic/Plenum Publishers.

Barnes-Holmes, D., Keane, J., & Barnes-Holmes, Y. (2000). A derived transfer of emotive functions as a means of establishing differential preferences for soft drinks. *The Psychological Record, 50*, 493-511.

Beck, A. T. (1976). *Cognitive therapy and the emotional disorders.* New York: International Universities Press.

Berenbaum, H., Raghavan, C., Huynh-NHu, L., Vermon, L. L., & Gomez, J. J. (2003). A taxonomy of emotional disturbances. *Clinical Psychology: Science and Practice, 10*, 206-226.

Borthwick-Duffy, S. (1994). Epidemiology and prevalence of psychopathology in people with mental retardation. *Journal of Consulting and Clinical Psychology, 62*, 17-27.

Burns, D. D. (1989). *The feeling good handbook.* New York: A Plume Book.

Cabanac, M. (2002). What is emotion? *Behavioural Processes, 60*, 69-83.

Campo, S. F., Sharpton, W. R., Thompson, B., & Sexton, D. (1997). Correlates of the quality of life of adults with severe or profound mental retardation. *Mental Retardation, 35*, 329-337.

Cannon, W. B. (1927). The James-Lange theory of emotions: A critical examination and an alternation. *American Journal of Psychology, 39*, 106-124.

Catania, A. C. (1992). *Learning* (3rd ed.). Englewood Cliffs, NJ: Prentice Hall.

Chambless, D. L., Baker, M. J., Baucom, D. H., Beutler, L. E., Calhoun, K. S., Crits-Christoph, P., Daiuto, A., DeRubeis, R., Detwiler, J., Haaga, D. A. F., Johnson, S. B., McCurry, S., Mueser, K. T., Pope, K. S., Sanderson, W. C., Shoham, V., Stickle, T., Williams, D. A., & Woody, S. R. (1998). Update on empirically-validated therapies, II. *The Clinical Psychologist, 51*, 3-16.

Charlot, L. R., Doucette, A. C., & Mezzacappa, E. (1993). Affective symptoms of institutionalized adults with mental retardation. *American Journal on Mental Retardation, 98*, 408-416.

Chase, P. N., & Danforth, J. S. (1991). The role of rules in concept learning. In L. J. Hayes and P. N. Chase (Eds.), *Dialogues on verbal behavior* (pp. 205-222). Reno NV: Context Press.

Cheasty, M., Clare, A. W., & Collins, C. (1998). Relation between sexual abuse in childhood and adult depression: Case-control study. *British Medical Journal, 17*, 198-201.

Cicero, S. D., & Tryon, W. W., (1989). Classical conditioning of meaning II: A replication and triplet association. *Journal of Behavior Therapy and Experimental Psychiatry, 20*, 197-202.

Crews, W. D., Bonaventura, S., & Rowe, F. (1994). Dual diagnosis: prevalence of psychiatric disorders in a large state residential facility for individuals with mental retardation. *American Journal of Mental Retardation, 98*, 688-695.

Damasio, A. R. (1994). *Descarte's error: Emotion, reason, and the human brain*. New York: Avon Books.

Davis, J. P., Judd, F. K., & Herrman, H. (1997). Depression in adults with developmental disability: Part 1. A review. *Australian and New Zealand Journal of Psychiatry, 31*, 232-242.

Dougher, M. J., Augustson, E., Markham, M. R., Greenway, D. E., & Wulfert, E. (1994). The transfer of respondent eliciting and extinction functions through stimulus equivalence classes. *Journal of Experimental Analysis of Behavior, 62,* 331-351.

Dymond, S., & Barnes, D. (1995). A transformation of self-discrimination response functions in accordance with the arbitrarily applicable relations of sameness, more than, and less than. *Journal of the Experimental Analysis of Behavior, 64,* 163-184.

Ekman, P. (1992). An argument for basic emotions. *Cognition and Emotion, 6,* 169-200.

Ellis, A. (1962). *Reason and emotion in psychotherapy*. New York: Lyle Stuart.

Ellis, A. (1971). *Growth through reason*. North Hollywood, CA: Wilshire.

Ellis, A. (1994). *Anger: How to live with and without it*. New York: Carol Publishing Group.

Ellis, A., McInerney, J. F., DiGiuseppe, R., & Yeager, R. J. (1988). *Rational-emotive therapy with alcoholics and substance abusers*. Boston: Allyn and Bacon.

Ferster, C. B. (1973). A functional analysis of depression. *American Psychologist, 28,* 857-870.

Fields, L., Reeve, K. E., Adames, B. J., & Verhave, T. (1991). Stimulus generalization and equivalence classes: A model of natural categories. *Journal of the Experimental Analysis of Behavior, 55,* 305-312.

Foa, E., B., & Rothbaum, B. O. (1998). *Treating the trauma of rape: Cognitive-behavioral therapy for PTSD*. New York: Guilford Press.

Forsyth, J. P., & Eifert, G. H. (1996). The language of feeling and the feeling of anxiety: Combinations of the behaviorisms toward understanding the function-altering effects of language. *The Psychological Record, 46,* 607-649.

Friman, P. C., Hayes, S. C., & Wilson, K. G. (1998). Why behavior analysts should study emotion: The example of anxiety. *Journal of Applied Behavior Analysis, 31,* 137-156.

Garland, A., Fox, R., & Williams, C. (2002). Overcoming reduced activity and avoidance: A five areas approach. *Advances in Psychiatric Treatment, 8,* 453-462.

Gearon, J. S., Kaltman, S. I., Brown, C., & Bellack, A. S. (2003). Traumatic life events and PTSD among women with substance use disorders and schizophrenia. *Psychiatric Services, 54,* 523-528.

Gortner, E. T., Gollan, J. K., Dobson, K. S., & Jacobson, N. S. (1998). Cognitive-behavioral treatment for depression: Relapse prevention. *Journal of Consulting and Clinical Psychology, 66,* 377-384.

Green, C. W., & Reid, D. H. (1996). Defining, validating, and increasing indices of happiness among people with profound multiple disabilities. *Journal of Applied Behavior Analysis, 29,* 67-78.

Hayes, S. C. (Ed.). (1989). *Rule-governed behavior: Cognition, contingencies, and instructional control.* New York: Plenum Press.

Hayes, S. C. (1994). Relational frame theory: A functional approach to verbal event. In S. C. Hayes, L. J. Hayes, M. Sato, & K. Ono, (Eds.), *Behavior analysis of language and cognition* (pp. 9-30). Reno, NV: Context Press.

Hayes, S. C., Barnes-Holmes, D., & Roche, B. (2001). Relational frame theory: A precis. In S. C. Hayes, D. Barnes-Holmes, & B. Roche, (Eds.), *Relational frame theory: A post-Skinnerian account of human language and cognition* (pp. 141-154). New York: Kluwer Academic/Plenum Publishers.

Hayes, S. C., Blackledge, J. T., & Barnes-Holmes, D. (2001). Language and cognition: Constructing an alternative approach within the behavioral tradition. In S. C. Hayes, D. Barnes-Holmes, & B. Roche, (Eds.), *Relational frame theory: A post-Skinnerian account of human language and cognition* (pp. 3-20). New York: Kluwer Academic/Plenum Publishers.

Hayes, S. C., Fox, E., Gifford, E. V., Wilson, K. G., Barnes-Holmes, D., & Healy, O. (2001). Derived relational responding as learned behavior. In S. C. Hayes, D. Barnes-Holmes, & B. Roche, (Eds.), *Relational frame theory: A post-Skinnerian account of human language and cognition* (pp. 21-49). New York: Kluwer Academic/Plenum Publishers.

Hayes, S. C., & Gifford, E. V. (1997). The trouble with language: Experiential avoidance, rules, and the nature of verbal events. *Psychological Science, 8,* 170-173.

Hayes, S. C., Kohlenberg, B. K., & Hayes, L. J. (1991). Transfer of consequential functions through simple and conditional equivalence classes. *Journal of Experimental Analysis of Behavior, 56,* 119-137.

Hayes, S. C., & Wilson, K. G. (1993). Some applied implications of a contemporary behavior-analytic account of verbal events. *The Behavior Analyst, 16,* 283-301.

Hayes, S. C., Strosahl, K. D., & Wilson, K. G. (1999). *Acceptance and commitment therapy.* New York: Guilford Press.

Hayes, S. C., Wilson, K. G., Gifford, E. V., Follette, V. M., & Strosahl, K. (1996). Experiential avoidance and behavior disorders: A functional dimensional approach to diagnosis and treatment. *Journal of Consulting and Clinical Psychology, 64,* 1152-1168.

Hayes, S. C., Zettle, R. D., & Rosenfarb, I. (1989). Rule-Following. In S.C. Hayes (Ed.), *Rule governed behavior: Cognition, contingencies, and instructional control* (pp. 191-220). New York: Plenum Press.

Hogan, R. A., & Kirchner, J. H. (1967). Preliminary report of the extinction of learned fears via a short term implosion therapy. *Journal of Abnormal Psychology, 72,* 106-109.

Hollon, S. D. (2000). Do cognitive change strategies matter in cognitive therapy? *Prevention and Treatment, 3, Article 25.* Available on the World Wide Web: http://journals.apa.org/prevention/volume3/pre0030025c.html.

Hollon, S. D. (2001). Behavioral activation treatment for depression: A commentary. *Clinical Psychology: Science and Practice, 8,* 271-274.

Horne, P. J., & Lowe, C. F. (1996). On the origins of naming and other symbolic behavior. *Journal of the Experimental Analysis of Behavior, 65,* 185-241.

Hume, D. (1977). *An enquiry concerning human understanding.* Indianapolis: Hackett Publishing Company.

Jacobson, N. S., Dobson, K. S., Truax, P. A., Addis, M. E., Koerner, K., Gollan, J. K., Gortner, E., & Prince, S. E. (1996). A component analysis of cognitive-behavioral treatment for depression. *Journal of Consulting and Clinical Psychology, 64,* 295-304.

Jacobson, N. S., Martell, C. R., & Dimidjian, S. (2001). Behavioral activation treatment for depression: Returning to contextual roots. *Clinical Psychology: Science and Practice, 8,* 255-270.

James, W. (1890). *The principles of psychology* (Vols. 1 and 2). New York: Holt.

Jenkins, J. J. (1963). Mediated associations: Paradigm and situations. In C. N. Cofer & B. S. Musgrave (Eds.), *Verbal behavior and learning: Problems and processes* (pp. 210-245). New York: McGraw Hill.

Jumper, S. (1995). A meta-analysis of the relationship of child sexual abuse to adult psychological adjustment. *Child Abuse and Neglect, 19,* 715-728.

King, M., Coxell, A., & Mezey, G. (2002). Sexual molestation of males: associations with psychological disturbance. *British Journal of Psychiatry, 181,* 153-157.

Kostinas, G., Scandlen, A., & Luiselli, J. K. (2001). Effects of DRL and DRL combined with response cost on perseverative verbal behavior of an adult with mental retardation and obsessive compulsive disorder. *Behavioral Interventions, 16,* 27-37.

Lamal, P. A. (1998). Advancing backwards. *Journal of Applied Behavior Analysis, 31,* 705-706.

Lazarus, R. S. (1991). *Emotion and adaptation.* Oxford: Oxford University Press.

Leverich, G. S., Altshuler, L. L., Frye, M. A., Suppes, T., Keck, P. E., Jr., McElroy, S. L., Denicoff, K. D., Obrocea, G., Nolen, W. A., Kupka, R., Walden, J., Grunze, H., Perez, S., Luckenbaugh, D. A., & Post, R. M. (2003). Factors associated with suicide attempts in 648 patients with bipolar disorder in the Stanley Foundation Bipolar Network. *Journal of Clinical Psychiatry, 64,* 506-515.

Lewinsohn, P. M. (1974). The behavioral study and treatment of depression. In K. S. Calhoun, H. E. Adams, & K. M. Mitchell (Eds.), *Innovative treatment methods in psychopathology.* New York: Wiley.

Lewinsohn, P. M., & Amenson, C. S. (1978). Some relations between pleasant and unpleasant mood-related events. *Journal of Abnormal Psychology, 87,* 644-654.

Lewinsohn, P. M., & Graf, M. (1973). Pleasant activities and depression. *Journal of Consulting and Clinical Psychology, 41,* 261-268.

Lewinsohn, P. M., & Libet, J. (1972). Pleasant activities, activity schedules, and depression. *Journal of Abnormal Psychology, 79*, 291-295.

Lowry, M. A., & Sovner, R. (1992). Severe behavior problems associated with rapid cycling bipolar disorders in two adults with profound mental retardation. *Journal of Intellectual Disability Research, 36*, 269-281.

Luiselli, J. K. (1998). Introduction to the special issue. *Journal of Developmental and Physical Disabilities, 10*, 315-316.

Martell, C. R., Addis, M. E., & Jacobson, N. S. (2001). *Depression in context: Strategies for guided action.* New York: W. W. Norton.

Matson, J. L., & Barrett, R. P. (1982). *Psychopathology in the mentally retarded.* New York: Grune & Stratton.

McCreary, B. D., & Thompson, J. (1999). Psychiatric aspects of sexual abuse involving persons with developmental disabilities. *Canadian Journal of Psychiatry, 44*, 350-355.

Meichenbaum, D. (1977). *Cognitive-behavior modification: An integrative approach.* New York: Plenum Press.

Meins, W. (1995). Symptoms of major depression in mentally retarded adults. *Journal of Intellectual Disability Research, 39*, 41-45.

Matson, J. L. (1982). Treating obsessive-compulsive behavior in mentally retarded adults. *Behavior Modification, 6*, 551-567.

Matson, J. L., Gardner, W. I., Coe, D. A., & Sovner, R. (1991). A scale for evaluating emotional disorders in severely and profoundly mentally retarded persons : development of the Diagnostic Assessment for the Severely Handicapped (DASH) Scale. *British Journal of Psychiatry, 159*, 404-409.

Mattick, R. P., & Peters, L. (1988). Treatment of severe social phobia: Effects of guided exposure with and without cognitive restructuring. *Journal of Consulting and Clinical Psychology, 56*, 251-260.

McAllister, W. R., & McAllister, D. E. (1995). Two-factor theory: Implications for understanding anxiety-based clinical phenomena. In W. O'Donohue & L. Krasner (Eds.), *Theories of behavior therapy: Exploring behavior change* (pp. 145-171). Washington, DC: American Psychological Association.

Michael, J. L. (1993). *Concepts and principles of behavior analysis.* Kalamazoo, MI: Western Michigan University, Society for the Advancement of Behavior Analysis.

Miller, N. E. (1948). Studies of fear as an acquirable drive: I. Fear as motivation and fear reduction as reinforcement in the learning of responses. *Journal of Experimental Psychology, 38*, 89-101.

Mowrer, O. H. (1947). On the dual nature of learning: A re-interpretation of "conditioning" and "problem-solving". *Harvard Educational Review, 17*, 102-148.

Mowrer, O. H. (1951). Two-factor learning theory: Summary and comment. *Psychological Review, 58*, 350-354.

Mowrer, O. H. (1956). Two-factor learning theory reconsidered, with special reference to secondary reinforcement and the concept of habit. *Psychological Review, 63*, 114-128.

Neumann, D. A., Houskamp, B. M., Pollock, V. E., & Briere, J. (1996). The long-term sequelae of childhood sexual abuse in women: A meta-analytic review. *Child Maltreatment, 1*, 6-16.

Pavlov, I. P. (1927). *Conditioned reflexes: An investigation of the physiological activity of the cerebral cortex* (G. V. Anrep, Trans.). London: Oxford University Press.

Pierce, W. D., & Epling, W. F. (1999). *Behavior analysis and learning* (2nd ed.). Upper Saddle River, NJ: Prentice Hall.

Rehfeldt, R. A., & Hayes, L. J. (1998). The operant-respondent distinction revisited: Toward an understanding of stimulus equivalence. *The Psychological Record, 48*, 187-210.

Roche, B., & Barnes, D. (1997). A transformation of respondently conditioned stimulus function in accordance with arbitrarily applicable relations. *Journal of the Experimental Analysis of Behavior, 67*, 257-301.

Roche, B., Barnes-Holmes, D., Smeets, P. M., Barnes-Holmes, Y., & McGeady, S. (2000). Contextual control over the derived transformation of discriminative and sexual arousal functions. *The Psychological Record, 50*, 267-291.

Ross, E., & Oliver, C. (2003). The assessment of mood in adults who have severe or profound mental retardation. *Clinical Psychology Review, 23*, 225-245.

Russell, B. (1961). Knowledge by acquaintance and knowledge by description. In R. E. Egner & L. E. Denonn (Eds.), *The basic writings of Bertrand Russell* (pp. 217-224). New York: Simon and Schuster (originally published in 1912).

Ryle, G. (1949). *The concept of mind.* New York: Barnes and Noble Books.

Sartre, J. P. (1948). *The emotions: Outline of a theory.* New York: Philosophic Library.

Schachter, S., & Singer, J. E. (1962). Cognitive, social, and physiological determinants of emotional state. *Psychological Review, 69*, 379-399.

Selye, H. (1974). *Stress without distress.* New York: J. B. Lippincott Company.

Shepherd, M., Cooper, B., Brown, A. C., & Kalton, C. W. (1966). *Psychiatric illness in general practice.* London: Oxford University Press.

Sidman, M. (1994). *Equivalence relations and behavior: A research story.* Boston, MA: Authors Cooperative.

Singh, N. N., Sood, A., & Ellis, C. R. (1991). Assessment and diagnosis of mental illness in persons with mental retardation: Methods and measures. *Behavior Modification, 15*, 419-443.

Skinner, B. F. (1953). *Science and human behavior.* New York: Macmillan.

Skinner, B. F. (1957). *Verbal behavior.* New York: Appelton-Century-Crofts.

Skinner, B. F. (1969). *Contingency of reinforcement: A theoretical analysis.* New York: Appelton-Century-Crofts.

Skinner, B. F. (1971). *Beyond freedom and dignity.* New York: Alfred A. Knopf.

Skinner, B. F. (1974). *About behaviorism.* New York: Knopf.

Skinner, B. F. (1989). The origin of cognitive thought. *American Psychologist, 44*, 13-18.

Skinner, B. F. (1990). Can psychology be a science of mind? *American Psychologist, 45*, 1206-1210.

Sobsey, D. (1994). *Violence and abuse in the lives of people with disabilities: The end of silent acceptance?* Baltimore: Paul H. Brookes Publishing Company.

Sobsey, D., & Doe, T. (1991). Patterns of sexual abuse and assault. *Sexuality and Disability, 9* (3), 243-259.

Sovner, R., & DesNoyers Hurley, A. (1983). Do the mentally retarded suffer from affective illness? *Archives of General Psychiatry, 40*, 61-67.

Staats, A. W., & Eifert, G. H. (1990). The paradigmatic behavior theory of emotions: Basis for unification. *Clinical Psychology Review, 10*, 539-566.

Steiger, H., & Zankor, M. (1990). Sexual traumata among eating-disordered, psychiatric, and normal female groups: Comparison of prevalences and defense styles. *Journal of Interpersonal Violence, 5*, 74-86.

Steigerwald, F., & Stone, D. (1999). Cognitive restructuring and the 12-step program of Alcoholics Anonymous. *Journal of Substance Abuse Treatment, 16*, 321-327.

Stewart, I., Barnes-Holmes, D., Roche, B., & Smeets, P. M. (2002). Stimulus equivalence and nonarbitrary relations. *The Psychological Record, 52*, 77-88.

Sturmey, P. (1998). Classification and diagnosis of psychiatric disorders in persons with developmental disabilities. *Journal of Developmental and Physical Disabilities, 10*, 317-330.

Sullivan, G. M., Kent, J. M., & Coplan, J. D. (2000). The neurobiology of stress and anxiety. In D. I. Mostofsky & D. H. Barlow (Eds.), *The management of stress and anxiety in medical disorders* (pp. 15-35). Boston: Allyn and Bacon.

Sundberg, M. (2004). A behavior analysis of motivation and its relation to mand training. In W. L. Williams (Ed.), *Developmental disabilities: Etiology, assessment, intervention, and integration.* Reno, NV: Context Press.

Sundberg, M. L., & Partington, J. W. (1998). *Teaching language to children with autism or other developmental disabilities.* Pleasant Hill, CA: Behavior Analysts, Inc.

Tversky, A., & Kahneman, D. (1974). Judgment under uncertainty: Heuristics and biases. *Science, 185*, 1124-1131.

Tryon, W. W., & Cicero, S. D. (1989). Classical conditioning of meaning I: A replication and higher-order extension. *Journal of Behavior Therapy and Experimental Psychiatry, 20*, 137-142.

Valenti-Hein, D., & Schwartz, L. 1995. *The sexual abuse interview for those with developmental disabilities.* Santa Barbara, CA: James Stanfield Company.

Walen, S. R., DiGiuseppe, R., & Dryden, W. (1992). *A practitioner's guide to Rational-Emotive Therapy* (2nd ed.). Oxford: Oxford University Press.

Walters, A. S., Barrett, R. P., Knapp, L. G., & Borden, M. C. (1995). Suicidal behavior in children and adolescents with mental retardation. *Research in Developmental Disabilities, 2*, 85-96.

Watson, J. B., & Rayner, R. (1920). Conditioned emotional reactions. *Journal of Experimental Child Psychology, 3,* 1-14.

Weiss, E. L., Longhurst, J. G., & Mazure, C. M. (1999). Childhood sexual abuse as a risk factor for depression in women: Psychosocial and neurobiological correlates. *American Journal of Psychiatry, 156,* 816-828.

Welch, S. L., & Fairburn, C. G. (1994). Sexual abuse and bulimia nervosa: Three integrated case control comparisons. *American Journal of Psychiatry, 151,* 402-407.

Zettle, R. D., & Hayes, S. C. (1982). Rule-governed behavior: A potential theoretical framework for cognitive-behavior therapy. In P. C. Kendell (Ed.), *Advances in cognitive-behavioral research and therapy* (Vol. 1, pp. 73-118). New York: Academic Press.

## Footnotes

1 Readers should note that the terms classical conditioning and respondent conditioning are used interchangeably throughout the chapter. Relatedly, the terms mental retardation and developmental disability are also alternated throughout the text, and used synonymously.

2 As a side note, tacting is not the same as naming because the evoking stimulus must be present at the time of the verbal response (Zettle & Hayes, 1982, p. 79). With naming, the verbal response can occur outside of the physical presence of the stimulating object (Horne & Lowe, 1996).

# Chapter 13

# Supporting Behavioral Repertoires in Elderly Persons with Developmental Disabilities

Craig A. Yury, Kyle E. Ferguson,
Michael A. Cucciare, and Jane Fisher
*University of Nevada, Reno*

The population of the world is aging at an unprecedented rate. It is estimated that between 1975 and 2025 the earth's population will double, with the number of persons over the age of sixty increasing by 224% (United Nations, International Plan of Action, 1998). In 1900 only 4% of Americans were over the age of 65. From 1900 to 2000 the number of Americans 65 years old and older rose from 3.1 million to 34.6 million or 13% of the population. This "greying of America" will increase significantly as the first wave of the baby-boom generation, the largest birth cohort in U.S. history, reaches 65 in the year 2011. By the year 2020, the population aged 65 to 74 is projected to grow 74 percent. By the year 2030 the proportion of elderly persons in the population will have increased to over 20% (U.S. Census, 2003).

The population of persons with developmental disabilities (DD) is following the same trend, due to both the aging of baby boomers with DD and increases in the average life expectancy of persons with DD associated with improvements in healthcare. Increased longevity of persons with DD has been shown in Austria, Germany, and Switzerland (Wieland, 1987; Dupont, Vaeth, & Videbech, 1987); Netherlands (Maaskant, 1993); Ireland (Mulchany & Reynolds, 1984); the United Kingdom (Hogg, Moss, & Cooke, 1988), the United States (Janicki, Dalton, Henderson, & Davidson, 1999) and Australia (Ashman, Suttie, & Bramley, 1995). With this increase in the number of persons with DD living to old age the importance of understanding the effects of aging on persons with DD is at an unprecedented point in history.

## Overview of the Aging Process: Primary vs. Secondary Aging Effects

The aging process can be conceptualized as involving normal biological changes that are inevitable and universal to a species. These changes have been termed *primary aging*. In contrast, *secondary aging* involves noninevitable age-related deterioration that is due to disease, disuse, or abuse (Rowe & Kahn, 1987). In this chapter we will examine the effects of primary aging on the functioning of persons with DD and factors associated with secondary aging effects with a focus on interventions that decrease the likelihood of *excess* disability. We will first examine how cohort related factors such as historical shifts in the care of persons with DD have impacted the current cohort of older persons with DD.

## A Historical Perspective on Aging and Developmental Disabilities

To understand the current cohort of elderly persons with DD one must take into account the environment that shaped their lives. Major changes in society's treatment of persons with DD have occurred over the past 40 years. Although social changes and research have significantly enhanced the care and education of persons with DD it can be argued that the current population of elderly persons with DD have not benefited from the relatively recent improvements to the extent that future generations will.

*Education.* The educational opportunities that were available to the current cohort of elderly persons with DD illustrate how a history graded factor on the trajectory of their lives. Most have lived their lives with little or no formal education. There were no publicly funded special education services in place during the childhoods of the current cohort of elderly persons with DD. *U.S. Public Law 94-142* was enacted by the U.S. Congress in 1975. This law required that a free, appropriate public education would be available for all handicapped children aged 3-21, no later than September 1, 1980. In 1983, the programs under the *Education of the Handicapped Act (EHA)* were amended by Public Law 98-199 to encourage the expansion of services to preschool aged children. This important law was enacted too late to fully benefit the current elderly population with DD.

*Residential Options.* Historical changes in the regulations involving community-based housing versus institutionalization have also changed dramatically during the lives of the current cohort of older adults with DD. With the advent of PL 94-142 and its emphasis on least restrictive environments, families for the first time had access to educational programs that were accessible within their community. It was no longer necessary to place children with DD in institutional settings in order to access treatment and education services.

The community mental health movement that began in the 1960s also impacted the lives of the current cohort of elderly persons with DD. As states attempted to meet the requirement of the decentralization of mental health services, persons with DD were likely to be moved from state institutions into long-term care nursing facilities for the elderly. Nursing homes, designed for the medically ill elderly, were ill-prepared to provide appropriate services for persons with DD. In 1987 the U.S. Congress passed the Omnibus Reconciliation Act of Nursing Home Reform (OBRA) to prohibit this practice. This law requires states to evaluate the mentally retarded in nursing homes and move those who do not need nursing care to a specialized facility. OBRA requires that people seeking admission to Medicaid-certified nursing homes be "screened" to determine if they meet criteria for a mental illness or mentally retardation. The purpose of the law is to prevent persons with mental illness or retardation, who need treatment for these conditions, from being placed in nursing homes unless nursing home care is medically necessary. OBRA also requires that current residents of Medicaid-certified nursing homes be evaluated once a year to determine if they are mentally ill or retarded and if nursing home care is required. Except for certain circumstances, residents of nursing homes with mental illness or mental retardation who do not need nursing home care will be required to move to other housing. If the person has been discharged from a hospital and needs 30 days or less of convalescent care for the condition treated, or the person is in a coma, then the person may be admitted to a nursing home.

Medicaid programs within the U.S. have implemented home and community-based services waivers that target special populations. Section 1915(c) of the Social Security Act, Medicaid law authorizes the Secretary of the U.S. Department of Health and Human Services to waive certain Medicaid statutory requirements. These waivers enable states to cover a broad array of home and community-based services for specific populations as an alternative to institutionalization. Essentially, the waiver system allows an elderly person to exchange the services offered by institutionalization for home-based services. Four basic types of waivers are now available to meet the needs of specific populations. The waivers are based on the level of alternative long-term institutional care needed. Intermediate care facility-mental retardation, and psychiatric hospital level of care for individuals who are severely or chronically mentally ill make up two specific levels of care. The remaining two are chronic or rehabilitative hospital level of care for individuals who are medically fragile, chronically ill, or severely disabled, and nursing facility level of care for individuals who are elderly. This division recognizes both those persons with DD and those who are elderly, but does not specifically address the needs of elderly persons with DD.

For those elderly persons with DD who do not require institutionalization, community living is a viable option when services that support independent living are available. Services such as personal care, respite care, personal emergency response system, extended home health care, environmental modifications, case management, home delivered meals, family or consumer training, dietician or nutritionist services, assistive devices and behavioral consultation services are all necessary to ensure the safety each person. Section 1915(c) of the Social Security Act covers the aforementioned services in lieu of institutionalization.

The current cohort of young adults with DD will be the first in U.S. history to fully benefit from a system of social services that can meet the needs of persons with DD across the lifespan. Given that the cohort of older adults with DD lived out their lives in environments that were not designed to support them they are at high risk for excess disability in old age. The following section will discuss the effects of primary aging in the context of a developmental disability and the risks of secondary aging effects in persons with DD.

## Primary and Secondary Aging Effects in the context of a Developmental Disability

The majority of older adults who do not have a DD are able to compensate for normal age associated losses through the use of prosthetics or learned behavioral strategies that serve to prevent a functional impairment. In contrast, when normal age-associated losses (e.g., in cardiovascular, sensory, motor, and cognitive function) occur in an older adult with DD, the risk of excess disability is quite high as the behavioral effects of the age-associated losses are likely to be unreported, undetected, and hence not treated with appropriate medical care and/or environmental prosthetics. Currently, there are no sound epidemiological data detailing the incidence and prevalence of age-associated functional impairments in elderly persons with DD. Extrapolating from data on the general population can be informative for understanding the significant risk of excess disability experienced by older adults with DD.

## Primary Aging and Functional Impairment in the Aged Population

Chronic disability is experienced by about 20% of the general population of elderly (Manton & Gu, 2001). Sensory impairments are especially prevalent with 33% of elderly U.S. citizens having hearing impairments and 20% having vision impairments (Desai, Pratt, Lentzer, & Robinson, 2001). Approximately one third of all elderly persons have mobility limitations (Freedman & Martin, 1998), and 7% to 8% have cognitive impairments (Freedman, Aykan, & Martin, 2001). Minorities and persons of low socioeconomic status are especially vulnerable to developing physical limitations and not having these limitations properly treated (Ostchega, Harris, Hirsch, Parsons, & Kingston, 2000; McNeil, 2001). Elderly persons with DD are at particularly high risk for excess disability associated with lifestyle (e.g., poor nutrition, limited exercise) and are likely to encounter significant difficulty in accessing adequate assistance for their special needs.

### Age-Related Changes in Sensory Function

Mild deterioration in sensory function is considered a primary aging effect. Still, sensory impairment can affect quality of life for older adults. A study of the effects of vision and hearing impairments on over two thousand elderly individuals living in San Francisco found that sensory impairments caused significant difficulties in social relationships, self-sufficiency, activities of daily living (ADLs), and mood (Wallhagen, Strawbridge, Shema, Kurata, & Kaplan, 2001). The following sections briefly describe common functional difficulties that occur with decline in the sensory systems.

*Changes in Vision.* Several functional visual changes take place as the body ages. Two of the most prominent include changes in visual processing speed and the presence of eye clutter. Visual acuity in older adults is often substantially diminished. Older adults can experience as much as an 80% reduction in visual acuity by the age of 85. Declines in both static and dynamic visual acuity occur (Atchley & Anderson, 1998). Static acuity is the identification of stationary objects; dynamic acuity is the ability to identify objects that are moving. Visual processing speed begins to slowly decline after the age of 30 (Spence, 1995). Even with mild impairment in visual acuity, older adults may experience problems selecting objects out of crowded fields such as when in a busy, public area.

*Changes in Hearing.* Presbycusis, tinnitus, deafness, dizziness, and vertigo, are common changes in hearing experienced by normally aging individuals. Presbycusis refers to normal age-related hearing loss of high frequency hearing. Hearing loss can occur in both ears (usually noticeable by 50) and takes the form of both impaired sensitivity to high and low frequency sounds. Impairment in sensitivity to high and low frequency sounds can result in difficulty comprehending speech. Tinnitus refers to the experience of having persistent background noise in either or both ears, which can take many forms including a constant hissing or whistling. Roughly 10% of those over the age of 65 have this problem and it appears to be more common in women than in men. Lastly, dizziness and vertigo affect as many as 90% of elderly primary care patients. Dizziness refers to a feeling of unsteadiness while experiencing movement in one's head, while vertigo refers to the false impression that the world was circulating around the individual or that the individual is moving in space. Both dizziness and vertigo may lead older adults to appear confused or feel less secure when engaging in movement. For example, older adults who have these experiences may change the way they stand, or hold onto things in an attempt to gain security.

*Changes in Taste and Smell.* Aging is associated with a general decrease in the sensitivity of the taste sensation. There are several theories as to what causes our taste sensation to diminish with age. Possible causes include, (1) the diminishment of taste buds, (2) changes in the way our central nervous system processes olfactory stimuli, (3) and a reduction in the amount of saliva production. Functionally, a diminished sense of taste can lead to a general decline in motivation to eat. For most people, the sense of smell begins to decline in the 30s and continues to progress slowly as they age. Several factors including the loss of olfactory sensory cells have been posited as the cause. A diminished sense of smell can lessen a person's sense of taste, and their ability to identify smoke, gas, and harmful substances.

*Changes in Temperature Regulation and Reflex Responses.* As we age, our body displays a lessened ability to both regulate our temperature and engage in reflexes. First, with aging comes a decreased ability for the autonomic nervous system to respond to changes in the environment. For example, the bodies of older persons have a decreased ability to regulate their temperature. As a result, a person's ability to maintain a normal body temperature in cooler weather (e.g., below 68) is made more difficult. Second, a general decrease in reflex response is common in older adults. The absence of the ankle, knee, bicep and tricep muscles is found in a substantial number of persons over the age of 70. Furthermore, all jerk reactions are essentially gone by the age of 90.

## Secondary Aging Effects: Prevalence of Medical Problems in Older Adults with DD

The primary cause of mental retardation is known in only about 25 percent of the population with DD. A common known etiology of mental retardation in North America is trisomy 21 (Van Allen, Fung, & Jurenka, 1999; Chudley, this volume). Baird and Sodovnick (1989) report that survival in individuals with DS is less than in the general population, however, 50% live into there fifties, and roughly 14% will survive to age 68. There is a growing concern that while a substantial portion of health care services are delivered by primary care physicians, little information is known about the chronology of health care issues in adults with trisomy 21 (Van Allen et al., 1999). In order to examine the risk of medical comorbidities in adults with trisomy 21, Van Allen et al. reviewed the medical charts of 38 adults with trisomy 21 living a residential facility in British Columbia. Of the 38 participants, 20 adults were considered "older" with age ranging from 50 to 68 years (mean age =59). The researches found several co-occurring medical problems in the older adult group. The most prevalent sensory impairment was vision impairments (75%) followed by hearing impairments (35%). Other co-occurring medial problems were respiratory (60%), cardiovascular (55%), gastrointestinal (25%), genitourinary (40%), osteoarthritis (65%), seizures (55%), Alzheimer's disease (75%), and Parkinsonian symptoms (5%).

Patel, Goldberg, & Moss (1993) examined the prevalence of psychiatric disorders in older adults with mental retardation. Their study sample consisted of 105 adults over the age of 50. The sample of participants consisted of 58% men and 42% women. Furthermore, 32% of the sample was between the ages of 50-59, 45% between 60-69, 15% between 70-79, and 8% e•80. The following prevalence rates were found: any psychiatric disorder (excluding dementia; 11.4%), dementia (11.4%), depressive disorders (4.8%), anxiety disorders (5.7%), bipolar disorder (1.9%), and schizophrenia (1.9%).

***Dementia in Older Adults with Trisomy 21.*** Tyrrell et al. (2001) investigated the prevalence of dementia (Alzheimer's type) in 285 persons diagnosed with Trisomy 21. They included adults between the ages of 35-74 years, with a mean age of 47 years (SD= 8.2 years). The researchers found a 13.3% prevalence rate of dementia, with adults diagnosed with dementia significantly older than non-dementia individuals. Prevalence rates for each age group were as follows:

- <40                    (1.4%)
- ≥40 < 50               (5.7%)
- ≥50 < 60               (30.4%)
- ≥60                    (41.7%)
- ≥70                    (50%)

Those living in institutional settings were more likely to have a diagnosis of dementia than those living in community-dwellings due to the fact that individuals living in institutional settings were older. Gender and premorbid cognitive level were not found to account for any differences in rates of dementia diagnoses.

Persons with DD *and* dementia have also been found to have higher prevalence rates of other medical conditions when compared with persons with DD who do not have dementia: epilepsy (66%), myoclonus (muscle jerks) (13%), and head injury (5%).

## Prevention of Excess Disability among the Elderly

Even with the high prevalence of disabilities in the elderly, over the past two decades in the United States there has been an overall decline in disability among the elderly (Manton & Gu, 2001). Based on the National Long-Term Care Survey data accumulated between 1982 and 1999, Manton and Gu demonstrated that the prevalence of chronic disability decreased from 26.2% to 19.7%. Further, disability rates of elderly populations are also declining for minority groups, and that rates are decreasing more rapidly over time.

Appollonio, Carabellese, Fratolla, & Trabucchi, (1996) examined the effect of correction of sensory impairments on individual's functioning. The researchers examined over 2000 elderly persons within San Francisco to determine the impact of correction of sensory impairment on social relationships, self-sufficiency, ADLs, and mood. Correction of sensory impairments was found to mitigate the negative effects of the sensory impairments. Thus, enhancing elderly individuals' current sensory abilities is an effective technique in dealing with a wide variety of issues. Factors such as improved medical treatments, effective public health prevention campaigns directed at promoting healthy living, and the spread of assistive devices (e.g. grab-bars, walkers, specifically designed appliances) have had a clear impact on the general population of older adults.

## Treatment Research on Aging and Developmental Disabilities

Very little published research exists on treatment for elderly persons with DD. Any treatment designed for this population must take into account the history of these persons, the normal aging process, effective techniques used with similar techniques, much of the treatments designed for children and adults with DD can be applied to the elderly population. Special considerations must be kept in mind when applying these treatments to the elderly. First, as mentioned earlier the elderly population did not benefit from laws providing them with free education, thus they do not have the same level of education. Secondly, as also mentioned earlier, the elderly population suffers from increased disabilities. Diseases and disabilities can interact together creating a more difficult set of problem behaviors. Thus treatments designed for populations with fewer disabilities must be altered to deal with age related changes.

## Contextual Learning Factors

Environmental context can play a vital role in the acquisition of motor behavior and reproducing that specific behavior. For instance, Lee and Hirota (1980) and Lee and Magill (1985) demonstrated that accurate reproduction of motor tasks can be improved if the initial training environment is re-established at time of testing. Interpretation of these results suggests that stimuli within the environment play an important role in maintaining behaviors. Through the normal aging process, and the comorbidity of other diseases, difficulties in perceiving the contextual variables emerge for the elderly. Thus, more salient and intentional stimuli are necessary to elicit target behaviors.

Wright and Shea (1991) have defined intentional stimuli as "Explicitly identified information necessary to successfully perform a task", where as incidental stimuli are "not explicitly identified as crucial to task performance but have the potential to become associated with particular responses because of their selective presence in the training environment." Based on these definitions, Kimbrough, Wright and Shea (2001) have demonstrated that reducing the saliency of intentional stimuli creates greater dependence on incidental stimuli. In other words, contextual factors take on a greater role in eliciting specific behaviors in the absence of information on how and when to perform the specific behavior.

Aged related sensory impairments and disorders such as dementia make it very difficult for an elderly individual to accurately perceive incidental stimuli, and understand what should be performed in the presence of these incidental stimuli. A more effective approach involves always utilizing intentional stimuli. Intentional stimuli that are easy to identify and understand aid the elderly individual orienting them to their environment. This approach does not rely on memory or sensory perception as heavily as context-dependence, thus eliminating several difficulties associated with aging.

## Functional Role of Disruptive Behaviors

Functional relationships between the environment and the behavior of elderly individuals with DD play an important role in understanding their behavior. Two popular models are Lindsley's (1964a, b) *geriatric behavioral prosthetic model* and Lawton's (1982) *environmental press model*. There is a certain degree of overlap between the two models; for instance, both are functionally based.

According to Lindsley (1964b): "Human behavior is a functional relationship between a person and a specific social or mechanical environment" (p. 41). This functional relationship has often been expressed by the following ecological equation, made famous by Kurt Lewin (1951): $B = f(P, E)$; where behavior (B) is a function of the person (P) and the environment (E). It is important to note that person variables are seen as relatively independent of those variables outside the individual. For example, competence is seen as a characteristic of the individual (Lawton, 1982).

It follows, therefore, that behavioral deficiencies can be remedied in two ways: by modifying the person (i.e., P side of the equation) or modifying the person's environment (i.e., E side of the equation). The former suggests that it is the individual or his or her behavioral repertoire that is "defective," not the environment. From a deficient-person perspective, to rectify the problem surgery (e.g., in the case of hydrocephalus), medication (e.g., antibiotics for infection-induced delirium), or skills training might be in order (e.g., teaching mnemonic devices to individuals with memory impairments). Another approach is to furnish individuals with prosthetic devices. Common prostheses include though are not limited to, devices that amplify the intensity of stimuli (e.g., hearing aids), augment the person's movements or responses (e.g., electric can openers), and reduce avoidance behavior on the part of others (so-called cosmetic prosthesis; e.g., glass eye) (Lindsley, 1964a).

The second way behavioral deficiencies can be rectified is by modifying a "defective environment," by employing environmental prosthesis. The most important feature of this orientation is matching the functional capacities of the individual with the level of environmental support (Kahana, 1975)[1]. Simply, individuals with highly compromised repertoires (high discrepancy) require considerable support. By contrast, other individuals with more adaptive repertoires (low discrepancy) require less support in order to perform optimally.

Insofar as we provide support for physical challenges, so too can we provide support for behavioral challenges. Namely, are there behavioral excesses or deficits that are associated with functional impairment? In building prosthetic environments, Lindsley (1964a, b) bases these on operant conditioning principles (e.g., reinforcement). In applying these principles, Lindsley maintains that behavioral engineers must provide 1) precise behavioral descriptions; 2) functional definitions of stimulus, response, and reinforcement; and 3) pay particular attention to behavioral processes. Let us describe and elaborate on each of these in turn.

*Behavioral description.* The first step in designing a prosthetic environment is to provide a precise behavioral description. The most important feature of precise behavioral descriptions is that they facilitate communication among professionals. Lindsley suggests using a topographical definition, which enables observers to record responses. Direct observation methods are the most suitable assessment strategies in building prosthetic environments (see Bloom, Fischer, & Orme, 1995, for specific strategies). General points to consider in implementing a measurement system are: who does the recording (e.g., professionals or direct care staff), at what times is behavior observed (e.g., at specific times or per diem), for how long is the observation interval (e.g., in one-minute blocks or hourly), and what specific response dimensions are targeted? (i.e., frequency, duration, or permanent products of behavior; Bloom, Fischer, & Orme, 1995, p. 95) In any event, the measurement system should be sensitive enough so as to capture most of the target behavior.

*Functional definitions and identifying contingent relationships.* The relationship between the environment and behavior is called a *contingency* (Sulzer-Azaroff & Mayer, 1991). A contingency simply means that some aspects of the environment influence behavior in characteristic ways. These contingencies are usually described linearly, as antecedent, behavior, and consequences (Bijou, Peterson, & Ault, 1968). In regards to antecedent stimuli, one asks what are the contextual variables that are associated with the target response? (e.g., physical, social, and temporally-related environmental factors). Is there a systematic relationship between potential antecedents and the response in question? Do certain consequent stimuli reinforce or punish the target response, as evidenced by an increase or decrease in rate of responding, respectively? That is to say, is there a contingent relationship between these stimuli and behavior? There are two assessment strategies that help us identify the controlling environmental features of which behavior is a function; one is a descriptive (ABC) analysis, the other is an experimental analysis or more commonly known as a functional analysis (Lerman, & Iwata, 1993; Wallace et al., this volume).

*Pay attention to behavioral processes.* Lastly, by "paying attention to behavioral processes," behavioral engineers adjust their programs in accordance with prevailing contingencies of reinforcement. What is being urged here is to attend closely to what's "missing" in the contingency (Lindsley, 1964b). Are the antecedent stimuli too weak to evoke effective performance? Is the individual incapable of emitting the response in question? Is the reinforcement schedule too thin to support the target behavior? Have otherwise effective reinforcers lost their potency? From a prosthetic environmental perspective, these issues are addressed by way of stimulus building, response building, contingency building, and consequence building, respectively.

1. *Stimulus building.* The purpose of stimulus building techniques is to give weak or neutral antecedent stimuli the ability to evoke effective behavior. For example, staff might consider changing the intensity or size of discriminative stimuli (e.g., increasing letter size on a sign) or combining antecedents, so as to increase overall valence (e.g., combining a loud tone with a bright light).

2. *Response building.* Response building techniques take movements that are regularly emitted but not currently in use, and making these serviceable for the problem at hand (Lindsley, 1964a). Manual or physical guidance is one such example. An individual who has never used a walker can be taught by gently moving their limbs into position and providing the needed support to ambulate. Guidance is thus removed once the person is able to use the walker independently.

3. *Contingency building.* Contingency building entails maintaining a response by shifting reinforcement density from richer schedules to thinner schedules of reinforcement (Skinner, 1953). Initially, every response is followed by the delivery of the reinforcer. The reinforcer-to-response ratio is thus 1:1. Once a steady state of responding is achieved, gradually thin out reinforcement delivery to an intermittent schedule of reinforcement (e.g., every 3rd response produces the reinforcer; Ferster & Skinner, 1957).

4. *Consequence building.* Neutral events can become reinforcers when they are frequently paired with powerful reinforcers. Generally speaking, the closer the temporal relationship between reinforcer and neutral stimulus increases the likelihood that neutral stimuli will acquire reinforcing functions. In the event that a reinforcer loses its reinforcing effects due to satiation, it can regain its potency by withholding the stimulus for a period of time (technically, producing a state of deprivation).

*Classifying environments.* Environmental determinants serve to activate behavioral competencies; the effects of which exert positive, negative, or neutral presses. An example of a positive press would be a person getting a depressed sedentary relative out of bed by engaging him or her in a pleasant activity. An example of a negative press would entail a broken air conditioner, as this might elicit physical exertion, or possibly death, during summer months. An example of a neutral press might entail a broken radio. It is still considered a press because radios in general (when they are operating) activate the listening and dancing behavior of many elderly individuals. The following are environmental determinants that can potentially activate behavior.

1.  *Personal environment.* The personal environment includes significant others, such as a family member or spouse.
2.  *Group environment.* The group environment includes individuals who are proximally situated in relation to the individual, such as other residents in the person's neighbourhood.
3.  *Social environment.* The social environment consists of socio-cultural factors that impact the individual, such as the culture to which he or she identifies.
4.  *Physical environment.* The physical environment is the natural or manufactured nonpersonal, nonsocial aspect of the person's environment.

Comparable to the geriatric behavior model, the environmental press model suggests that behavior is a function of the competence of the individual and the environmental press of the contingencies that prevail (Lawton, 1982). The specific relationship is thus: As competency decreases, the greater the impact of environmental factors on the individual. Lawton and Simon (1968) call this the environmental-docility hypothesis. In accordance with this model, to improve adaptive functioning, one would either improve competence along implicated behavioral continua, modify the person's environment, or both (see Lawton, 1975, for numerous examples as to how one might initiate such compensatory efforts).

## Minimizing Restraint

A line of research dedicated to the elderly population involves dementia patients. Dementia populations suffer from aged related changes as well as cognitive impairments. Several issues have emerged as critical to overcoming behavioral problems, with a diminishing repertoire of abilities being a major contributing factor to problem behaviors.

Recent research has found that many of the problem behaviors exhibited by dementia patients reliably occur under very specific environmental conditions (rather than randomly or constantly). This research suggests that the problem behaviors serve a purpose for the patient in that they serve as alternative methods of communication for a patient who has lost the ability to communicate through "normal" means (e.g., language, nonverbal gestures) due to the disease (Bourgeois, Burgio, & Schultz, 1995; Buchanan & Fisher, 2002; Burgio, Scilly, Hardin, Janosky, Bonino, Slater, & Enberg, 1994).

Several behavior analytic forms of treatment for disruptive behaviors have demonstrated that they can be effective in reducing problems behaviors. Burgio et al. (1994) have eliminated disruptive vocalizations by offering the patients either auditory stimulation in the form of music or tactile stimulation in the form of stuffed animals. Cohen-Mansfield and Werner (1998) have utilized visual, auditory and olfactory stimuli to simulate a home or natural outdoor environment in order to decrease wandering behavior. Burgio and Stevens (1999) have also demonstrated that reinforcement procedures can reduce physical aggression in dementia patients. Buchanan and Fisher (2002) employed a noncontingent reinforcement procedure to reduce disruptive vocalizations in dementia patients.

Given that persons with DD are at high risk for developing excess disability as they age it is critical that providers give priority to interventions that target the maintenance of behavioral repertoires. Behavior analytic strategies have unique advantages for sustaining the fragile repertoires of elderly persons with DD by targeting the function of behaviors rather than eliminating behaviors that are topographically challenging. Functional analytic strategies that target the reason a behavior occurs do not contribute to further eliminating behaviors but instead allow for the design of environments that make problem behaviors unnecessary while strengthening adaptive behaviors.

## References

Appollonio, I., Carabellese, C., Fratolla, L., & Trabucchi, M. (1996). Effects of sensory aids on the quality of life and mortality of elderly people: A multivariate analysis. *Age and Ageing, 25*, 89-96.

Ashman, A. F., Suttie, J. N., & Bramley, J. (1995). Employment, retirement and elderly persons with an intellectual disability. *Journal of Intellectual Disability Research, 39*, 107–115.

Atchley, P., & Andersen, G. J. (1998). The effect of age, retinal eccentricity and speed on the detection of optic flow components. *Psychology and Aging, 13*, 297-308.

Baird, P. A., & Sodovnick, A. D. (1989). Life tables for down syndrome. *Human Genetics, 82*, 291-292.

Bijou, S. W., Peterson, R. F., & Ault, M. H. (1968). A method to integrate descriptive and experimental field studies at the level of data and empirical concepts. *Journal of Applied Behavior Analysis*, 1, 175-191.

Bloom, M., Fischer, J., & Orme, J. G. (1995). *Evaluating practice: Guidelines for the accountable professional* (2nd ed.). Boston: Allyn and Bacon.

Buchanan, J. A., & Fisher, J. E. (2002). Functional assessment and noncontingent reinforcement in the treatment of disruptive vocalization in elderly dementia patients. *Journal of Applied Behavior Analysis, 35*, 68-72.

Bourgeios, M. S., Burgio, L. D., & Schultz, R. (1995, November). *Modifying the repetitive verbalizations of patients and Alzheimer's disease.* Paper presented at the Annual Meeting of the Gerontological Society of America, Los Angeles.

Burgio, L. D., Scilly, K., Hardin, J. M., Jankosky, J., Bonino, P., Slater, S. C., & Engberg, R. (1994). Studying disruptive vocalization and contextual factors in the nursing home using computer-assisted real-time observation. *Journal of Gerontology: Psychological Sciences, 49*(5), P230-P239.

Burgio, L. D., & Stevens, A. B. (1999). Behavioral interventions and motivational systems in the nursing home. In R. Schultz, G. Maddox, & M. P. Lawton (Eds.), *Annual Review of Gerontology and Geriatrics* (pp. 284-320). New York: Springer.

Cohen-Mansfield, J., & Werner, P. (1998). The effects of an enhanced environment on nursing home residents who pace. *Gerontologist, 38,* 199-208.

Cutler, D. M. (2001). The reduction in disability among the elderly. *Proceedings of the National Academy of Sciences,* 98, 6546-6547.

Desai, M., Pratt, L. A., Lentzer, H., & Robinson, K. N. (2001). *Trends in vision and hearing among older Americans.* Hyatsville, MD: National Center for Health Statistics. Aging Trends (2).

Dupont A., Vaeth, M., & Videbech, P. (1987). Mortality, life expectancy, and causes of death of mildly mentally retarded in Denmark. *Upsala Journal of Medical Sciences, 44,* 76–82.

Ferster, C. B., & Skinner, B. F. (1957). *Schedules of reinforcement.* New York: Appleton-Century-Crofts.

Freedman, V. A., Aykan, H., & Martin, L. G. (2001). Aggregate changes in severe cognitive impairment among older Americans: 1993 and 1998. *Journal of Gerontological Behavioral Psychological Sciences and Social Sciences, 56,* 100-111.

Freedman, V. A., & Martin, L. G. (1998). Understanding trends in functional limitations among older Americans. *American Journal of Public Health, 88,* 1457-1462.

Hogg, J., Moss, S., & Cooke, D. (1988). *Ageing and Mental Handicap.* London: Croom-Helm.

Janicki, M., Dalton, A., Henderson, M., & Davidson, P. (1999). Mortality and morbidity among older adults with intellectual disabilities: Health services considerations. *Disability and Rehabilitation, 21,* 284–294.

Kahana, E. A. (1975). A congruence model of person-environment interaction. In P. G. Windley, T. Byerts, & E. G. Ernst (Eds.), *Theoretical development in environments for aging* (pp. 181-214). Washington, DC: Gerontological Society.

Kimbrough S. K., Wright, D. L., & Shea, C. H. (2001). Reducing the saliency of intentional stimuli results in greater contextual-dependent performance. *Memory,* 9(2), 133–143.

Lawton, M. P. (1975). *Planning and managing housing for the elderly.* New York: Wiley.

Lawton, M. P. (1982). Competence, environmental press, and the adaptation of older people. In M. P. Lawton, P. G. Windley, & T. O. Byerts (Eds.), *Aging and the environment: Theoretical approaches* New York: Springer Publishing Company.

Lawton, M. P. (1986). *Environment and aging* (2nd ed.). Albany, New York: Center for the Study of Aging.

Lawton, M. P., & Simon, B. (1968). The ecology of social relationships for the elderly. *Gerontologist, 8,* 108-115.

Lee, T. D., & Hirota, T. T. (1980). Encoding specificity principle in motor short-term memory for movement extent. *Journal of Motor Behavior, 12,* 63–67.

Lee, T. D., & Magill, R. A. (1985). On the nature of the movement representations in memory. *British Journal of Psychology, 76,* 175–182.

Lerman, D. C., & Iwata, B. A. (1993). Descriptive and experimental analyses of variables maintaining self-injurious behavior. *Journal of Applied Behavior Analysis, 26,* 293-319.

Lewin, K. (1951). *Field theory in social science.* New York: Harper & Row.

Lindsley, O. R. (1964a). Direct measurement and prosthesis of retarded behavior. *Journal of Education, 147,* 62-81.

Lindsley, O. R. (1964b). Geriatric behavioral prosthetics. In R. Kastenbaum (Ed.), *New thoughts on old age* (pp. 41-60). New York: Springer Publishing Company.

Maaskant, M. A. (1993). *Mental handicap and ageing.* Kavanah, Dwingeloo.

Manton, K. G., & Gu, X. (2001). Changes in the prevalence of chronic disability in the United States black and nonblack population above age 65 from 1982 to 1999. *Proceedings of the National Academy of Sciences,* May 8.

McNeil, J. (2001). *Americans with disabilities, 1997: Current population reports.* Washington, DC: US Census Bureau; 70-73.

Mulcahy, M., & Reynolds, A. (1984). *Census of Mental Handicap in the Republic of Ireland.* Medico-Social Research Board, Dublin.

Nursing Home Reform Act. (1987). *Part 2, Section 4211, of the Omnibus Budget reconciliation Act (OBRA), Public Law 100-203.*

Ostchega, Y., Harris, T., Hirsch, R., Parsons, V. L., & Kingston, R. (2000). Prevalence of functional limitations and disability in older person in the US: Data from national health and nutrition examination survey. *Journal of American Geriatric Society, 48,* 1132-1135.

Patel, P., Goldberg, D. P., & Moss, S. C. (1993). Psychiatric morbidity in older people with moderate and severe learning disability (mental retardation). Part II: the prevalence study. *British Journal of Psychiatry, 163,* 481-491.

Rowe, J. W., & Kahn, R. L. (1987). Human aging: Usual and successful. *Science, 237,* 142-149.

SEC. 1915. [42 U.S.C. 1396n] (2003). Provisions respecting inapplicability and waiver of certain requirements of this title. www.socialsecurity.gov.

Skinner, B. F. (1953). Science and human behavior. New York: Macmillan.

Sulzer-Azaroff, B., & Mayer, G. R. (1991). *Behavior Analysis for Lasting Change.* New York: Harcourt Brace College Publishers.

Tyrrell, J., Cosgrave, M., McCarron, M., McPherson, J., Calvert, J., Kelly, A., et al. (2001). Dementia in people with down's syndrome. *International Journal of Geriatric Psychiatry, 16,* 1168-1174.

United Nations. (1998). International Plan of Action on Ageing. United Nations/Division for Social Policy and Development. New York, NY.

U.S. Census Bureau, Special Populations Branch. (2003). http://www.census.gov/population/www/socdemo/age.html#older

U.S. Public Law 94-142 (S. 6) (1975). Education for All Handicapped Children. http://asclepius.com/angel/special.html

U.S. Public Law 98-199 (1983). Education of the Handicapped Act (EHA). http://www.ed.gov/policy/speced/leg/idea/history.html

Van Allen, M. I., Fung, J., & Jurenka, S. B. (1999). Health care concerns and guidelines for adults with down syndrome. *American Journal of Medical Genetics, 89*, 100-110.

Wallhagen, M. I., Strawbridge, W. J., Shema, J. A., Kurata, J., & Kaplan, G. A. (2001). Comparative impact of hearing and vision impairment on subsequent functioning. *Journal of American Geriatrics Society, 49*, 1086-1092.

Wieland, H. (1987) *Geistig behinderte Menschen im Alter: Theoretische und empirische Beitrage zu ihrer Lebenssituation in der Bundesrepublik Deutschland, in Osterreich und in der Schweiz*. Ed Schindele, Heidelberg.

Wright, D. L., & Shea, C. H. (1991). Contextual dependencies in motor skills. Memory & *Cognition, 19*, 361–390.

World Health Organization. (WHO) (2000). *Healthy Ageing – Adult's With Intellectual Disabilities: Summarative Report*. World Health Organization, Geneva.

## Footnote

1. Kahana calls this person-environment congruence.

# Chapter 14

# Improving Educational Opportunities for Students with Developmental Disabilities: Advancement through Changes in Special Education Law

### Thomas S. Higbee
*Utah State University*

For children both with and without disabilities, school is a major part of life. A child's school experience begins at either preschool or kindergarten and extends through high school and sometimes beyond. School is the place where children learn not only academic but also many important social skills. Typically developing children acquire these skills through experiences that take place both inside and outside the classroom. Only in relatively recent years, however, have these same educational opportunities afforded to typically developing children been more closely approximated for children with disabilities.

The history of education for children with disabilities in the United States is similar to that of other groups who were "different" from the norm. In the past, education for children with disabilities was seen as a privilege rather than a right and many individuals with disabilities were excluded from publicly funded education programs (Huefner, 2000). While students with mild disabilities were often provided with services in regular schools, students with more severe disabilities were relegated to special schools, institutions, or received no services at all (Huefner, 2000). Prior to the 1970's, many states had laws on the books that allowed public schools to deny enrollment to students with disabilities (Murdick, Gartin, & Crabtree, 2002). Local school personnel were under no legal obligation to provide students with disabilities the same educational access and opportunities that were given to "normal" students. Educational services for students with disabilities varied greatly from place to place because there were no uniform guidelines or requirements for public school systems. The state of affairs is summarized in Section 601 of the 1997 IDEA amendments:

> Before the date of the enactment of the Education for All Handicapped Children Act of 1975 (Public Law 94-142) –
> (A)  the special educational needs of children with disabilities were not being fully met;

(B) more than one-half of the children with disabilities in the United
    States did not receive appropriate educational services that would
    enable such children to have full equality of opportunity;
(C) 1,000,000 of the children with disabilities in the United States were
    excluded entirely from the public school system and did not go
    through the educational process with their peers;
(D) there were many children with disabilities throughout the United
    States participating in regular school programs whose disabilities
    prevented such children from having a successful educational
    experience because their disabilities were undetected; and
(E) because of the lack of adequate services within the public school
    system, families were often forced to find services outside the public
    school system, often at great distance from their residence and at their
    own expense. (IDEA, 1997)

As the civil rights movement brought equal educational access for children of
minority races, parents of children with disabilities sought to follow a similar process
of advocacy, litigation, and ultimately legislation to secure equal educational
opportunities for their children. A landmark court case in 1972, the Pennsylvania
Association for Retarded Children (PARC) vs. Commonwealth of Pennsylvania
case, established requirements for a free and appropriate public education (FAPE) for
children with mental retardation within the jurisdiction of the federal court. Heward
(2003) points out that the court ruling was particularly influential because the
language of the ruling not only guaranteed a free and appropriate public education
but also stated that placements in regular classrooms and regular public schools were
preferable to segregated settings.

As a result of the debate that followed the PARC and other court cases, congress
passed Public Law 94-142, the Education for All Handicapped Children Act in
1975. This law literally opened the doors of public education for all students with
disabilities. As summarized by Heward (2003, p. 21), its purpose was to:

assure that all children with disabilities have available to them…a free and
appropriate public education which emphasizes special education and
related services designed to meet their unique needs, to assure that the rights
of children with disabilities and their parents or guardians are protected, to
assist states and localities to provide for the education of all children with
disabilities, and to assess and assure the effectiveness of efforts to educate
children with disabilities.

The law has subsequently been reauthorized and amended four times (it is
currently undergoing its fifth reauthorization). The law was renamed the Individuals
with Disabilities Education Act (IDEA) in 1990 and the current version was
authorized in 1997. While additional regulations and requirements have been added
to the law during each reauthorization, the core features of IDEA have remained

fairly constant since its original version. These core features of IDEA can be summarized in six basic principles: 1) Zero reject, 2) Nondiscriminatory assessment, 3) Individualized education programs (IEP), 4) Education in the least restrictive environment (LRE), 5) Procedural due process, and 6) Parental participation. Each of these principles is outlined in detail below.

## Zero Reject

IDEA guarantees that all children with disabilities are eligible for a free and appropriate education (FAPE) (Peterson & Hittie, 2003). FAPE is defined in 34 C.F.R. § 300.13 of the IDEA, as educational services that:

(a)   are provided at public expense, under public supervision and direction, and without charge;
(b)   meet the standards of the SEA [State Educational Agency]…;
(c)   include preschool, elementary school, or secondary school education in the State involved; and
(d)   are provided in conformity with an IEP [Individualized Education Program] that meets the requirements of Secs. 300.340-300.350.

This principle represents the philosophical core of IDEA and is based on the idea that all children with disabilities, regardless of type or level of severity of the disability, are deserving of and entitled to a free and appropriate education (Murdick et al., 2002). The Zero Reject principle is also based on the belief that all children are capable of learning and as such are deserving of educational services.

IDEA not only requires schools to provide educational services to all children with disabilities, it requires them to actively seek out these students (Smith, Polloway, Patton, & Dowdy, 2003). This process has been called a "child find" system. This was an important feature in the original 1975 law because so many children had previously been excluded from public education. Schools meet this requirement of actively seeking out students with disabilities in a number of ways including: "child find" posters, television public service announcements, articles in newspapers, and other public relations campaigns (Smith et al., 2003). The 1999 amendments to IDEA also require schools to identify children who may qualify for special education from highly mobile populations such as migrant and homeless children (Huefner, 2000).

## Nondiscriminatory Assessment

In order to qualify for special education services under IDEA, students must be given a comprehensive evaluation. Schools are required to use nonbiased assessment methods that gather information from multiple sources to determine whether or not a child has a disability and is eligible for special education services. Testing procedures are not allowed to discriminate based on culture, race, or native language and placement decisions cannot be made based on the results of only one testing instrument or a single source of information (Heward, 2003).

This requirement for nondiscriminatory assessment was incorporated into the law because it was observed that there was an overrepresentation of minority students being identified for special education (Murdick et al., 2002). When this finding was subjected to further investigation, evidence was produced indicating that certain norm-referenced standardized tests are inherently discriminatory towards students from disadvantaged socioeconomic and minority racial groups (Smith et al., 2003). Misclassifying a student as having a disability when he/she does not, or classifying them with the wrong disability has obvious negative consequences. Misclassifying a student can lead to a stigmatizing label that can produce isolation from school experiences, rejection by peers and teachers, and lowered expectations which can lead to a "self-fulfilling prophecy" (Murdick et al., 2002).

Given these findings and the potential negative consequences of misclassification, it is important for teachers and administrators to interpret information from norm-referenced standardized tests with caution as they may not represent the true abilities of the student. IDEA regulations and case law produced by subsequent litigation have provided specific guidelines for school districts for conducting nondiscriminatory assessment including, a requirement to administer all tests in the native language of the student in an attempt to prevent language bias in testing (see Chapter 4, Nondiscriminatory Assessment, of Murdick et al., 2002 for a summary of guidelines).

## Individualized Education Program (IEP)

The primary tool provided by IDEA for individualizing educational services and committing educational resources to students with disabilities is the individualized education program (IEP) (Huefner, 2000). The IEP has been described as the "centerpiece of the special education process" (Heward, 2003, p. 59). The IEP is both a document and a process. As a document, it is ideally developed through the cooperation and collaboration of parents and school personnel. It describes the abilities and needs of the child with disabilities and specifies the school placement and educational services that are designed to meet the unique needs of the child (Gorn, 1997). The IEP is also the end product of a process mandated by IDEA where educators and parents work together first to determine if a child's disability negatively impacts his/her education, and second, to design the educational plan for the child if it does.

The IEP team is charged with the development of the IEP while the state educational agency, usually represented by the local school district, is responsible for implementing the IEP. Historically, the IEP team was made up of a special educator, the parent(s), a representative of the school district (LEA), and when appropriate, the student (Huefner, 2000). The 1997 amendments to IDEA [20 U.S.C. § 1414(d)(1)(B)] expanded the team to include the following:

(i)   the parents of the child with a disability;
(ii)  at least one regular education teacher of such child (if the child is, or may be, participating in the regular education environment);

(iii) at least one special education teacher, or where appropriate, at least one special education provider of such child;

(iv) a representative of the local educational agency (LEA) (usually the school district) who—

  (I) is qualified to provide, or supervise the provision of, specially designed instruction to meet the unique needs of children with disabilities;

  (II) is knowledgeable about general education curriculum; and

  (III) is knowledgeable about the availability of resources...

(v) an individual who can interpret the instructional implications of evaluation results, who may be a member of the team...

(vi) at the discretion of the parent or the agency, other individuals who have knowledge or special expertise regarding the child, including related service personnel as appropriate; and

(vii) whenever appropriate, the child with a disability.

This expanded IEP team specifically makes provision for more than one special education teacher or no special education teacher if a related service provider (e.g., speech pathologist) is the primary provider of special education services (Huefner, 2000). The new list also requires a regular education teacher to be present if the student is, or may be, participating in a regular education classroom. This reflects the emphasis of IDEA '97 on the expanded role of the general education teacher in providing special education services and the importance of special education students accessing the general curriculum. The "general curriculum" is defined by the 1999 IDEA regulations as "the same curriculum as for nondisabled children" [34 C.F.R. § 300.12(a)(1)(i)], or in other words, what typically developing children study instead of some special curriculum. The regular education teacher on the team should be the individual who is responsible for the implementation of the portion of the IEP that is to take place in the regular education classroom (Huefner, 2000).

The role of the school district (LEA) administrator is also more explicitly outlined under IDEA '97. The administrator is required to be knowledgeable about not only the availability of district resources, as was required in the past, but also about the general curriculum. The administrator is also required to be competent in the provision or supervision of the provision of special education services. This language is somewhat looser than in previous versions of IDEA and does not require that a key administrator participate in the IEP if the special education provider is knowledgeable about district resources as well as the general curriculum (Huefner, 2000).

Under previous versions of IDEA, the IEP team only had to include an individual qualified to interpret the instructional implications of evaluation results in the initial IEP meeting. IDEA '97 changed this requirement so that this individual must be present at all IEP meetings. This person could be someone already on the team, such as one of the special or regular education teachers, or an additional person, such as a school psychologist or other professional.

The parents or school districts may invite others who have special knowledge or expertise related to the child. Regardless of who invites the additional participant, the IEP team determines if he/she has the necessary experience or expertise to participate on the team. Related service providers and independent evaluators often fill this role.

When a child is of the age where transition planning for the transition to the "post-school world" is taking place (at age 14 and above), representatives of agencies participating in the transition process must be invited to the IEP meeting. These might include vocational rehabilitation providers, supported employment service providers, and others. If the student has not been involved in the IEP process before, every effort should be made to include him/her at this point so that individually appropriate objectives and services that will facilitate transition can be considered.

The law makes clear that parental (or guardian) participation in the IEP process is critical. In fact, the regulations specify that one or both parents must be invited to attend the IEP meeting and that the meeting must be scheduled at a mutually convenient time and place (Huefner, 2000). Parents must be notified in advance of who will be attending the IEP meeting. If neither parent is able to attend the meeting, then school district personnel are required to use other means to include them such as conference telephone calls. Multiple, documented, unsuccessful attempts to include parents are required before a school district is permitted to formulate an IEP without parental input (Huefner, 2000). Appendix A of the 1999 final regulations makes the following important points about the role of parents in the IEP process:

1. The parents of a child with a disability are expected to be equal participants along with school personnel, in developing, reviewing, and revising the IEP for their child. This is an active role in which the parents (1) provide critical information regarding the strengths of their child and express their concerns for enhancing the education of their child; (2) participate in discussions about the child's need for special education and related services and supplementary aids and services; and (3) join with the other participants in deciding how the child will be involved and progress in the general curriculum and participate in State and district-wide assessments, and what services the agency will provide to the child and in what setting [34 C.F.R. Part 300, app. A at question 5].

2. Agency staff may come to an IEP meeting prepared with evaluation findings and proposed recommendations regarding IEP content, but the agency must make it clear to the parents at the outset of the meeting that the services proposed by the agency are only recommendations for review and discussion with the parents. Parents have the right to bring questions, concerns, and recommendations to an IEP meeting as part of a full discussion, of the child's needs and the services to be provided to meet those needs before the IEP is finalized. Public agencies must ensure that, if agency personnel bring drafts of some or all of the IEP

content to the IEP meeting, there is a full discussion with the child's parents, before the child's IEP is finalized, regarding drafted content and the child's needs and the services to be provided to meet those needs [34 C.F.R. Part 300, app. A at question 32].

3. In addition, the concerns of parents and the information that they provide regarding their children must be considered in developing and reviewing their children's IEPs. In addition, the concerns of parents and the information that they provide regarding their children must be considered in developing and reviewing their children's IEPs [34 C.F.R. Part 300, app. A at subsec. II: Involvement of Parents and Students].

According to Murdick et al. (2002), the IEP team must consider five additional factors that are potentially important for the development of an appropriate IEP. First, the team must consider the behavior of the student which may impede "his or her learning or that of others" [IDEA, 1997, 20 U.S.C. § 1414(d)(3)(C)]. If this is found to be the case, then the IEP team must consider "positive behavioral interventions, strategies, and supports that address that behavior" [IDEA, 1997, 20 U.S.C. § 1414(d)(4)(B)]. Typically, a functional behavioral assessment is conducted to determine the function of the challenging behavior and then a positive behavioral intervention plan (PBI or BIP) is written describing specific behavioral interventions to be used that are appropriate to the function of the challenging behavior (see Chapter 4 of this book for a description of these procedures by Wallace, Kenzer, and Penrod). If a change to a more restrictive placement because of behavioral challenges is being considered, then the law requires a functional behavioral assessment (Huefner, 2000). The second special factor that must be considered is the language needs of the child with limited English proficiency. If language is an issue for a specific child, then the IEP team should develop specific strategies to address this. Third, unless it is determined to be unnecessary by the IEP team, children who are blind or visually impaired must have consideration provided for their need for instruction in Braille. Fourth, for students who are deaf or hard-of-hearing, communication needs must be considered since direct instruction to meet the communication needs of the child is required in the IEP development process. Finally, the assistive technology (AT) needs of each child must be considered during the IEP meeting.

The AT consideration requirement was added during the 1990 amendments to IDEA and occurred as a result of the increased availability of AT devices and services for people with disabilities and increased demands by parents that these devices and services be available in school settings. IDEA '97 [20 U.S.C. § 1401(1)] defines an AT device as "[a]ny item, piece of equipment, or product system, whether acquired commercially off the shelf, modified, or customized, that is used to increase, maintain, or improve functional capabilities of a child with a disability." Further, an AT service is defined in IDEA as:

…any service that directly assists a child with a disability in the selection, acquisition, or use of an assistive technology device. Such term includes–

(A)  the evaluation of the needs of such child, including the functional evaluation of the child in the customary environment;

(B)  purchasing, leasing, or otherwise providing for the acquisition of assistive technology devices;

(C)  selecting, designing, fitting, customizing, adapting, applying, maintaining, repairing, or replacing of assistive technology devices;

(D)  coordinating and using other therapies, interventions, or services with assistive technology devices, such as those associated with existing education and rehabilitation plans and programs;

(E)  training or technical assistance for such child, or, where appropriate, the family of such child; and

(F)  training or technical assistance for professionals (including individuals providing education and rehabilitation services), employers, or other individuals who provide services to, employ, or are otherwise substantially involved in the major life functions of such child. [IDEA, 1997, 20 U.S.C. § 1401(2)].

As a result of this expanded focus on AT in IDEA, the identification of AT needs and the acquisition of AT devices and services has become a key issue for IEP teams. Before AT consideration was required in the IEP, school districts often failed to consider the need for AT devices and services for all children (Murdick et al., 2002). In many cases, AT was only considered for individuals with significant physical and/ or communication needs. A wide variety of AT devices are currently available ranging from communication boards for students with severe disabilities to computer programs that help students with learning disabilities organize their creative writing. New AT is being developed every year and the requirement of IDEA that AT be considered for all students will help facilitate access to it by students and their families.

After the preceding five factors have been considered, the IEP team should develop an IEP for each child that is determined to be eligible for special education. Under IDEA '97 [20 U.S.C. § 1414(d)(1)(A)], the IEP document must be written to include eight components:

1.  a statement of the present levels of educational performance of the child;

2.  a statement of measurable annual goals, including benchmarks or short-term instructional objectives;

3.  a statement of the specific educational services, related services (e.g., speech therapy, occupational therapy, etc.), and program modifications or supports for school personnel that will be provided;

4.  an explanation of the extent to which the child will be able to participate with nondisabled children in regular class and activities;

5. the extent to which the child will participate in state- or district-wide assessments, modifications that should be used, or alternative assessments that might be implemented;
6. the projected date for initiation of services and modifications with the anticipated frequency location and duration specified;
7. beginning at age 14, and updated annually, a statement of transition service needs and, at age 16, a statement of the interagency responsibilities or any linkages; and
8. how the progress towards the annual goals will be measured, how the parents will be informed of the child's progress including whether the child's progress is adequate to meet the annual goals established by the IEP team, and with a frequency no less than that of parents of nondisabled children.

The initial component of the IEP is the child's present levels of educational performance (PLEP). The PLEP contains information gathered from a thorough, nondiscriminatory assessment of the child and the child's identified needs for specifically designed instruction. The child's disability classification alone is not sufficient information for developing IEP goals. In fact, IDEA does not require that a child's disability classification be included on the IEP, though many states choose to do so (Huefner, 2000). It is important to remember that a thorough evaluation of the child's strengths and needs must be completed before the IEP in order to facilitate the selection of appropriate goals and objectives. Beginning in 1997, IDEA required that the PLEP include how the child's disability affects his/her ability to access and make progress in the general curriculum [20 U.S.C. § 1414(d)(1)(A)(i)].

Once the child's PLEP are known, the next task for the IEP team is to generate measurable annual goals including either intermediate short-term objectives or benchmarks (milestones indicating progress towards annual goals). Annual goals, objectives, and benchmarks must address the student's academic and nonacademic need areas for the upcoming school year and be related to:

(I) meeting the child's needs that result from the child's disability to enable the child to be involved in and progress in the general curriculum; and

(II) meeting each of the child's other educational needs that result from the child's disability [20 U.S.C. § 1414(d)(1)(A)(ii)].

According to Huefner (2000), prior to IDEA '97, only the objectives but not the annual goals had to be stated in measurable terms. This changed in IDEA '97 as Appendix A of the 1999 final regulations makes clear:

Measurable annual goals, including benchmarks or short-term objectives, are critical to the strategic planning process used to develop and implement the IEP for each child with a disability. Once the IEP team has developed measurable annual goals for a child, the team (1) can develop strategies that will be most effective in realizing those goals and (2) must develop either measurable, intermediate steps (short-term objectives) or major milestones (benchmarks) that will enable parents, students, and educators to monitor progress during the year, and, if appropriate, to revise the IEP consistent with the student's instructional needs [34 C.F.R. Part 300, app. A at question 1].

The regulations also specify the purpose of short-term objectives and benchmarks and the frequency with which this information is to be reported to parents:

As noted above, each annual goal must include either short-term objectives or benchmarks. The purpose of both is to enable a child's teacher(s), parents, and others involved in developing and implementing the child's IEP, to gauge, at intermediate times during the year, how well the child is progressing toward achievement of the annual goal. IEP teams may continue to develop short-term instructional objectives, that generally break the skills described in the annual goal down into discrete components. The revised statute and regulations also provide that, as an alternative, IEP teams may develop benchmarks, which can be thought of as describing the amount of progress the child is expected to make within specified segments of the year. Generally, benchmarks establish expected performance levels that allow for regular checks of progress that coincide with the reporting periods for informing parents of their child's progress toward achieving the annual goals. An IEP team may use either short term objectives or benchmarks or a combination of the two depending on the nature of the annual goals and the needs of the child [34 C.F.R. Part 300, app. A at question 1].

IEP teams are given the flexibility to use either benchmarks, short-term objectives, or a combination of the two, whichever choice is appropriate in each individual situation. Whichever method is used, if the student is not making adequate progress, then the IEP should probably be revised. IEP goals are intended to be completed in one year's time. An IEP that contains the same goals from year to year should raise red flags for the IEP team and should probably be examined to determine the appropriateness of the goals or instructional methods used to achieve them (for more information on writing effective goals, objectives, and benchmarks, see Lignugaris/Kraft, Marchand-Martella, & Martella, 2001)

Other sections of the IEP require statements about the specific special education and related services, and the program modifications or supports for school personnel to be provided to the student. These statements are to include all of the special education and related services needed by the student to achieve the goals on the IEP and receive FAPE (Gorn, 1997). A broad range of services and supports (even those that may appear non-educational in nature) can be included in this section of the IEP including, for example: transportation services, health-related services (e.g., tube feeding, catheterization), the assistance of an instructional aide, counseling, speech therapy, physical therapy, adaptive physical education, and others. Only services that the IEP team determines are necessary for the student to receive FAPE in his or her LRE are included in the IEP. All services and supports that are included in the IEP are to be provided at no cost to the student or his/her family (Murdick et al., 2002).

If the child will not be participating in the regular education class and in nonacademic and extracurricular activities with his/her peers without disabilities, then the IEP must explain the extent of nonparticipation [20 U.S.C. § 1414(d)(1)(A)(iv)]. The requirement was changed to the extent of *nonparticipation* from the extent of *participation* in IDEA '97 and reflects the changed philosophical focus of the law towards more inclusive education. This small change in language is a legally significant one because now in situations where IEPs are challenged, the school district's burden of evidence has changed from one of showing when the child *can* participate to one of showing when the student *cannot* participate in regular education programs (Huefner, 2000).

The 1997 IDEA amendments also added requirements that students with disabilities participate in state- and district-wide assessments or other alternative assessments when appropriate [20 U.S.C. § 1414(d)(1)(A)(v)]. The extent of participation, including modifications or accommodations necessary for participation, is included in the IEP. If the student is not going to participate in state- or district-wide testing, then reasons for nonparticipation and descriptions of alternative assessments must be included. What constitutes an "alternative assessment" is not specified in the law and was to be developed by individual states (although scheduled to be completed by July 2000, this process is still ongoing).

The IEP also includes the projected dates for initiation of services and modifications and specifies the frequency, duration, and location of services. Location of services is specified to provide a means of monitoring whether or not services are being provided within the regular education classroom, suggesting that related services should not significantly reduce the child's opportunity to access the general curriculum and participate in a regular education classroom (Huefner, 2000).

The IEP also must contain information about transition planning for older students who are preparing to transition to the "post-school" world. For students between the ages of 14 and 16, the IEP must include a statement of transition service "needs" [20 U.S.C. § 1414(d)(1)(A)(vii)(I)]. For students ages 16 and up, the IEP must contain a statement about actual transition services that will facilitate the student's transition out of the school setting [20 U.S.C. § 1414(d)(1)(A)(vii)(II)]. "Post-school" options for students with disabilities could include: postsecondary education, vocational training, supported employment, continuing and adult education, adult services, independent living, and community participation (Huefner, 2000). The IEP team, including the student, should evaluate the skills, wants, and needs of the student in transition planning.

In addition to planning for the student's educational success, the IEP team is mandated to monitor the child's progress on IEP goals. As summarized in the above section on annual goals, short-term objectives, and benchmarks, parents are to receive reports on progress towards IEP goal completion at the same frequency with which parents of children without disabilities receive progress reports (generally at least four times per year). Again, if progress is not being made towards IEP goals, then modifications to the goals or to instructional strategies should be made by the IEP team.

### Least Restrictive Environment

Another critical feature of IDEA is the mandate that children with disabilities be educated in the least restrictive environment (LRE). Given special education's exclusionary past, this mandate is of particular importance. The phrase "least restrictive environment" is often used as a synonym for "mainstreaming" or "inclusion." However, as Murdick et al. (2002) summarize, this usage is incorrect because the terms "mainstreaming" and "inclusion" refer to the educational practice of placing students with disabilities in regular educational classrooms while the term "least restrictive environment" refers to the IDEA mandate:

1.  that children with disabilities be educated with children who are not disabled whenever possible;
2.  that educational placement be based on the child's education needs and be as close to the child's home as possible;
3.  that the child be provided access to nonacademic and extracurricular activities; and
4.  that each public agency provide a continuum of alternative placements with increasing levels of educational supports.

As previously stated, the intent of IDEA is that children with disabilities be educated in the regular education classroom as much as possible. IDEA also mandates, however, that a *continuum* of alternative placements (CAP) be available to meet the educational needs of individual students. While it is the ideal, a full-time regular education placement may not be the best educational option for some students with disabilities and CAP ensures that other options will continue to be available to serve these students. In general, CAP consists of the following placements listed from least to most restrictive: regular class, special class, special school, home instruction, and instruction in a hospital and/or institution (Murdick et al., 2002). The regulations state that the more severe the child's needs, the more the educational environment may become segregated or restrictive. The fewer the needs, the less restriction and segregation should be allowed. The IEP team is charged with determining the LRE where a student can achieve his/her IEP goals.

## Procedural Due Process

Due process is a constitutional right granted to all citizens under the 5th and 14th amendments of the U.S. Constitution. Huefner (2000) outlines the two basic elements of due process: 1) notice: informing the person of the contemplated governmental action to restrict one's life, liberty, or property and the reason for the action, and 2) a chance to respond: allowing the person to tell his/her side of the story at some kind of formal or informal hearing. Influenced by early court cases in the 60's and 70's where disability advocates successfully invoked due process rights for people with disabilities, congress included extensive due process safeguards into IDEA. These safeguards are provided to parents in written form at several points during the IEP process. Huefner (2000, pp. 172-173) provides a summary of the due process rights of parents:

> The procedural safeguards notice must include an explanation of parents' rights to:
> 1. Written prior notice before an educational agency proposes (or refuses) to initiate or change the child's identification, evaluation, educational placement or provision of FAPE
> 2. Give or withhold consent at specific times
> 3. Access their child's educational records
> 4. Obtain an independent educational evaluation (IEE) of their child
> 5. Present complaints to initiate an appropriate due process hearing with respect to any of the items mentioned in number 1
> 6. Mediation prior to a hearing
> 7. A due process hearing
> 8. A second-tier (state-level) hearing-review procedure if the impartial due process hearing is conducted by an LEA (district) rather than the SEA (state)
> 9. Appeal the final administrative hearing decision to state or federal court
> 10. Attorney's fees if the parent is the prevailing party
> 11. The requirement that the child remain in his or her current placement while administrative or judicial proceedings are pending, unless the parents and the educational agency agree otherwise (also known as the stay-put provision)
> 12. The procedures allowing an exception to the stay-put provision for students who are subject to a disciplinary placement in an interim alternative educational setting
> 13. The requirement for prior notification from parents if they unilaterally seek a private school placement at public expense for a child with a disability

14. The right to file a complaint with the SEA on any matter mentioned
    in number 1 above. (Others besides parents also have a right to file such
    a complaint—for example, teachers.)

Huefner suggests that the first ten rights are basically an elaboration of the basic
elements of due process: notice and some kind of hearing prior to the intended
governmental action. The last four safeguards extend beyond basic due process
rights. They are intended to protect the welfare of students, they require parents to
give notice to schools, and they inform parents of an alternative method of dispute
resolution to mediation and hearings.

Because due process is a concept that is protected under the U.S. Constitution
and IDEA regulations, it must be respected by school district personnel. It is
designed to protect students from unilateral decisions about educational placements
and programs by school personnel. Due process safeguards ensure that parents and
school districts will be equal partners in the educational process (Smith et al., 2003).

## Parental Participation

Parents are undoubtedly the persons who know their children best and are
critical to the success of the educational process. Parents have been the driving force
behind educational reforms for children with disabilities. Parents have organized
advocacy groups and lobbied congress to make changes in the law to protect the
educational rights of their children. These efforts have succeeded in establishing the
role of parents on the educational team. According to Murdick et al. (2002), the role
of the parent is to serve as a, "counterbalance to the schools and as a protector of the
rights of the students." The application of IDEA provisions are ensured by the
careful vigilance of parents. As discussed above, the parent is a required member of
the IEP team and plays a critical role in making decisions concerning educational
placement and programming for their child with a disability. The law makes this
point clear:

> Each local educational agency or State educational agency shall ensure that
> the parents of each child with a disability are members of any group that
> make decisions on the educational placement of their child [20 U.S.C. §
> 1414(f)].

Because parents are such a critical piece of the educational team, IDEA specifically
defines who can fill this role if a child's natural parents are unable or unwilling to do
so. As defined in federal regulations, "parent" can include not only a natural parent,
but also a guardian, a surrogate parent appointed by the LEA, and anyone acting in
the place of a parent such as a relative or anyone else with whom the child lives [34
C.F.R. § 300.19].

## Special Education Services for Infants, Toddlers, and Preschoolers under IDEA

In the 1986 amendments to IDEA, Congress extended special education services to infants, toddlers, and preschool age children. Prior to enactment of these changes to the law, many preschoolers with disabilities were not receiving special education services and systematic early intervention services for infants and toddlers with disabilities from birth through age two were virtually nonexistent in many states (Heward, 2003). The rationale for providing special education services to young children is made clear in the law:

> FINDINGS- The Congress finds that there is an urgent and substantial need –
> (1) to enhance the development of infants and toddlers with disabilities and to minimize their potential for developmental delay;
> (2) to reduce the educational costs to our society, including our Nation's schools, by minimizing the need for special education and related services after infants and toddlers with disabilities reach school age;
> (3) to minimize the likelihood of institutionalization of individuals with disabilities and maximize the potential for their independently living in society;
> (4) to enhance the capacity of families to meet the special needs of their infants and toddlers with disabilities; and
> (5) to enhance the capacity of State and local agencies and service providers to identify, evaluate, and meet the needs of historically underrepresented populations, particularly minority, low-income, inner-city, and rural populations [20 U.S.C. § 1431(a)].

If, through early educational intervention, a child with a disability's potential can be maximized and the negative effects of his/her disability minimized, this benefits both society and the individual. Society is benefited by having a more productive member and also saves money if the individual does not require special services or if these services are less extensive than they would have been had early intervention services not been provided. The benefit to the individual and his/her family is obvious and cannot be easily quantified. The preventative model of educational service delivery for young children specified in this portion of IDEA is arguably the most forward thinking in all of special education law.

### Conclusion

While the system is far from perfect (ask any parent of a child with disabilities or special education professional), educational services for children with disabilities are undoubtedly more available and are having a greater impact on the lives of children with disabilities because of federal legislation. The process of obtaining special education services and agreeing upon educational programs and placements can sometimes be contentious and cumbersome. Despite its drawbacks, though, this process protects the rights of children with disabilities and their families and helps ensure that they have access to a free and appropriate education in the least restrictive environment. Of equal importance, the law also ensures that they have a deciding voice in determining this education and environment. By mandating that parents and educators work as a team to design educational programs for children with disabilities, the law prevents either group from making unilateral decisions and requires that they work together to produce positive outcomes for children with disabilities.

## References

Gorn, S. (1997). *The answer book on individualized education programs.* Horsham, PA: LRP Publications.

Education for All Handicapped Children Act of 1975, 20 U.S.C. § 1400 *et seq.* (1975).

Heward, W. L. (2003). *Exceptional Children: An introduction to special education* (7th ed.). Upper Saddle River, NJ: Merrill/Prentice Hall.

Huefner, D. S. (2000). *Getting comfortable with special education law: A framework for working with children with disabilities.* Norwood, MA: Christopher-Gordon.

Individuals with Disabilities Education Act Amendments of 1997, 20 U.S.C. § 1400 *et seq.* (1997).

Lignugaris/Kraft, B., Marchand-Martella, N., & Martella, R. C. (2001). Strategies for writing better goals and short-term objectives or benchmarks. *TEACHING Exceptional Children, 34*, 52-58.

Murdick, N., Gartin, B., & Crabtree, T. (2002). *Special Education Law.* Upper Saddle River, NJ: Merrill/Prentice Hall.

PARC v. Commonwealth of Pennsylvania, 343 F. Supp.297 (E.D. Pa. 1972).

Peterson, J. M., & Hittie, M. M. (2003). *Inclusive teaching: Creating effective schools for all learners.* Boston: Allyn and Bacon.

Smith, T. E. C., Polloway, E., Patton, J. R., & Dowdy, C. A. (2003). *Teaching students with special needs in inclusive settings* (4th ed.). Boston: Allyn and Bacon.

# Chapter 15

# Implementing and Researching Person-Centered Planning

Steve Holburn

*New York State Institute for Basic Research in
Developmental Disabilities*

John W. Jacobson

*Sage Colleges Center for Applied Behavior Analysis, Troy, NY*

## Implementing and Researching Person-Centered Planning

### What is Person-Centered Planning?

The principles and approaches of person-centered planning (PCP) are popular topics in the field of developmental disabilities today. Person-centered planning emerged in the mid 1980's as a way to better understand the experiences of people with developmental disabilities, and enhance those experiences with the help of allies (O'Brien, O'Brien, & Mount 1997). Service systems commonly began to adopt practices consistent with PCP in the mid 1990s. The general goals of PCP are to decrease social isolation, establish friendships, increase engagement in preferred activities, develop competencies, and promote respect. Many policy makers and service agencies in the field of developmental disabilities have embraced the underlying tenets of PCP with vigor (Holburn & Vietze, 1999; Schwartz, Jacobson, & Holburn, 2000), but implementation of PCP as described by its founders, is neither brief nor easy, and as a result, person-centered planning has been largely misapplied, or implemented only in part, in many service agencies that have sought to adopt it (O'Brien et al., 1997).

Person-centered planning can be considered to be an extension of the social inclusion movement for people with intellectual disabilities, articulated in the principles of normalization (Nirje, 1969). Wolfensberger (1972) introduced normalization to a wider audience of administrators, managers, educators, and clinicians in the United States, and later reformulated it as social role valorization (Wolfensberger, 1983). Although the principles of normalization and social inclusion remain largely theoretical frameworks upon which changes in service delivery practices have been premised over the years, PCP combines these principles with *procedures* to accomplish goals consistent with the principles (O'Brien & Lovett, 1992). Thus, PCP encompasses methods for planning designed to result in substantive changes in supports, activities, involvements, and services for people with developmental disabilities. This blending of ideology and strategy has been conducive to adoption of person-centered planning as an integral component of the progressive zeitgeist in developmental disabilities.

The principles and practices of person-centered planning have some distinct features and shared features with other practices that are progressive, and commonly appear in various forms in agency policy, procedure manuals, and governmental regulations. In numerous states, the processes of person-centered planning are now embodied in law (Schwartz, et al., 2000; Wagner, 1999). In noting that "Person-centered planning has moved from the fringes of service systems to the center" (p. 379), Smull and Lakin (2002), concluded that many policy makers have already decided to require that the approach be implemented throughout service systems. This observation is consistent with reports of attempts to implement person-centered planning statewide (e.g., Butkus, Rotholz, Lacy, Abery, & Elkin, 2002; Maine Department of Mental Retardation, 1994).

Different forms of PCP exist, varying in emphasis and specific processes. Popular forms include Personal Futures Planning (Mount, 1992; 1994; Mount, & Zwernick 1988); Essential Lifestyle Planning (Smull & Harrison, 1992); The McGill Action Planning System or MAPS (Vandercook, York, & Forest, 1989); Whole Life Planning (Butterworth et al., 1993), and Planning Alternative Tomorrows with Hope or PATH (Pearpoint, O'Brien, & Forest (1993). Each of these processes are multifaceted, and involve long-term problem solving interventions embedded within more comprehensive changes in the organization, including organizational processes of planning, developing, managing, and appraising. Differences in the specific processes within the various approaches suggests that each may have dissimilar strong points or may be suitable for different applications (e.g., may be more readily undertaken in simpler or more complex organizations, or for certain subgroups), but there has been no comparative research regarding relative benefits of the various approaches under differing circumstances (Smull & Lakin, 2002). A recent PCP approach, Planning for Inclusive Communities Together Using Reinforcement and Evaluation (PICTURE; Holburn, Gordon, & Vietze, 2004), incorporates professional interventions and quantitative evaluation into its method.

## A Summary of the Person-Centered Planning Process

There are certain procedural or strategic components that are salient to most variants of the process. Essentially, PCP brings together the most important people in the life of a person, envisions a better life for the person, and discovers ways to achieve the vision. Participation is voluntary and the group is typically diverse, including both human-service workers and other significant people, including family members, and advocates. Team dynamics are designed to emphasize non-hierarchic roles of team members and to focus on abilities and personal interests, rather than a service requirements orientation more typical of a conventional clinical team planning process. Instead, the views of family members, friends, and the focus person (the person being helped) are guiding influences, and the process is moderated by a facilitator who runs meetings and keeps the group focused on core goals and values (as noted above).

Many tangible features of the planning process are purposively structured to be different from those common in clinical teams, for example, the facilitator typically records or maps what people say on large sheets of paper rather than standardized forms. Information developed in the course of meetings is consolidated into pre-arranged themes such as *personal history, preferences, community places, dreams, fears, and capabilities,* which become the basis for developing the vision of a better future. The facilitator identifies ways to accomplish the vision through consensus and secures commitments for follow through. Many person-centered planners (e.g., O'Brien & Lovett, 1992; Smull, 1998) emphasize that the focus person's preferences may be negotiated in light of potentially competing issues of health and safety, available resources, and what others want for the person.

The group remains committed to creating a lifestyle based on the aspirations of the focus person. As circumstances and aspirations change, the group adjusts its strategy. It continues to meet periodically to reflect on successes and setbacks and may establish new strategies and address additional aspects of lifestyle and engagement with the individual. Person-centered planning processes do not prescribe timelines on how long planning should last; instead, the duration of the process is associated with the principal focus of the group, and may be time-limited or continue indefinitely based on these considerations. Examples of variations in the focus of groups are: including a child in a general education classroom, finding a graduating teenager a typical job, or developing supports that enable an adult to live in a neighborhood. In most instances it will be difficult to foresee how much time and effort these endeavors will take. Some advocates may suggest that the person-centered process is never really over, and that achievement of any or all of the three goals mentioned above is just the beginning of a much longer journey, as individual preferences, opportunities, and aspirations change (Kinkaid, 1996).

## Challenges to the Integrity of Person-Centered Planning

Unfortunately, PCP may be frequently misapplied in systems that serve people with disabilities (O'Brien et al., 1997). Implementation problems should not be surprising with any long-term intervention that consists of multiple components and requires a team of individuals to carry it out. The problem of misapplication may be more serious than it seems with respect to the survival of given practice: No matter how powerful an approach is, if it cannot be instituted properly or if its implementation complexities limit its benefit to a relatively small number of people, it will be of insufficient consequence, and therefore, unlikely to endure or thrive.

Nearly all of the published work on PCP refers to challenges in instituting PCP. Failed PCP attempts have been traced to numerous factors, such as fundamental misunderstandings of the process (O'Brien et al., 1997), lack of sufficient components of the process (Mount, 1994), failure to integrate PCP into the existing team culture and process (Sanderson, 2002), unwillingness by professionals to relinquish power to the consumer (Marrone, Hoff, & Helm, 1997), insufficient effort to increase social and service resources (O'Brien & O'Brien, 1998), and administrative reluctance to openly acknowledge difficulties in adopting the approach (Holburn & Vietze, 1999). Some investigators have identified inadequate facilitation as an obstacle to effective person-centered planning (Hagner, Helm, & Butterworth, 1996; Reid & Green, 2002). Organizational and system strategies for overcoming difficulties in implementing PCP have been suggested by Holburn and Vietze (1999).

## Can Person-Centered Planning Help Institutionalized People with Behavior Problems?

People with the most challenging behavior tend to be grouped closely together in environments that are replete in aversive qualities, although with the deinstitutionalization movement, people with such behavior typically live in community-based living arrangements (Frawley, 1994). In the United States, congregate environments have been noisy, routinized, chaotic, boring, and even dangerous. Fortunately, many institutions and other congregate settings in the United States have been closed. In the remaining facilities, some of these negative qualities remain constant, while others seem to occur sporadically. Although the residents of such environments do not control the contingencies responsible for adverse conditions, it can appear to an onlooker that the conditions are brought about by their disruptive behavior. However, it is other people who create the physical aspects of the environments, determine the groupings, organize the daily routines, and administer the programs. These include local administrators and staff of the facilities, but also more distant individuals such as system administrators or federal policymakers who stipulate to those at the facility what rules shall govern, and what resources will be available for which purposes. The occupants of congregate facilities often have little say over where they go, what they do, or with whom they spend their time. Much of their time may be spent waiting for programming to ameliorate behavior problems to establish skills for living in the community, or to develop leisure skills, but research suggests that, with the exception of specially-dedicated settings that are designed for intensive services, very little new learning takes place in large congregate settings (e.g., Hayden, 1998; Hile & Walbran, 1991; Parsons, Cash, & Reid, 1989; Richman, Riordan, Reiss, Pyles, & Bailey, 1988; Stancliffe, Abery, & Smith, 2000; Stefan, 1993).

Professionals who work in the clinical trenches of bureaucratically-governed living environments sometimes refer to them as pathetic (Himadi, 1995). Administrative control governs nearly all aspects of the life of a person living in such a setting, including the activities of eating, sleeping, and bathing. There is little give-and-take in such environments, in part because of logistical constraints imposed by congregation. It is not possible for staff members to come under the influence of (or differentially respond to) the behavior of the individual when they are responsible for the health and safety of a sizable group of people, who collectively, exhibit a myriad of behavior problems and health care requirements. Under such conditions, excessive behavior often results in consequences to everyone in the group, while smaller changes in behavior (desirable or undesirable) are usually of little consequence. When the capacity of the employee to establish reciprocal response patterns is restricted by competing system-centered contingencies, reinforcers are infrequent, and often noncontingent or counter-habilitative (e.g., people who could acquire more independence may not receive the services that would achieve this aim, Meinhold & Mulick, 1990). Such conditions would seem to generate system-centered conformity, and eventually the person's repertoire would likely appear dull and limited. Such conditions may also potentiate automatic sensory reinforcement that can maintain unusual behavior such as stereotypy and self-injury. An observer might say the person has few choices, or nothing to do, is unmotivated, and has turned inward. Blame for the conditions described above should not be attributed to employees who are trying to assist people with developmental disabilities in institutions. Behavior analysts or any other clinicians working in an undesirable bureaucratic system can fall victim to the same contingencies that ultimately negatively influence a person living there (Reppucci & Saunders, 1974). It is institutional structure and the inherent contingencies of operation that are to blame (Goffman, 1961).

It is not the purview of traditional interdisciplinary planning teams to address the adverse conditions described above. Instead, these teams address issues such as health, skill development, and deceleration of problem behavior *within the given environment*. Alternatively, a PCP team deliberately seeks to identify and eliminate non-preferred aspects and routines in the person's immediate environment, and at the same time arrange for a better lifestyle such that the person is doing what he or she enjoys and experiencing more satisfaction.

Improvements in behavior problems should occur if the PCP team can truly reduce social isolation and segregation, establish friendships, increase opportunities to preferred activities, develop competence, and promote respect. However, such broad environmental changes, by themselves, will not resolve all of the person's behavior problems, but they are likely to constitute an environment in which direct contingency management and other technical interventions can be more be effective (Emerson & Hatton, in press; Holburn, 1997), and where services such as psychiatric and psychological intervention may be implemented to further alleviate intrusive impacts of mental or behavioral disorders on opportunities for socialization and community participation. However, there is little evidence that lifestyle change alone, i.e., living a non-institutionalized lifestyle, without specifically increasing choice making and participation in preferred activities, diminishes challenging behavior (Emerson & Hatton, in press).

## What Does Research Say about Person-Centered Planning?

One might assume that the goals of PCP alone make PCP a useful endeavor and that research is not necessary to confirm it as a worthwhile. After all, where are the data confirming the value of the parent movement or legal advocacy for people with developmental disabilities? However, when PCP is applied in systems, it is bound to compete with other approaches and resources, and this fact automatically calls forth questions of effectiveness. Person-centered planning may even replace some system-centered practices viewed as unhelpful or bureaucratic, but can we demonstrate that PCP is superior to such practices? Given both the limited resources in systems and the long-term, complex nature of the PCP, it is reasonable to conclude that PCP should be at least as effective as other approaches in achieving goals such as inclusion, choicemaking, and relationships. Efficiency in service provision, which is typically perceived as a problematic aspect of system-centered approaches (Mount, 1994), cannot be ignored when multiple methods purport to accomplish the same objectives. On the other hand, one cannot ignore the reality that there are few other methods that attempt to effect such broad life changes for people with developmental disabilities.

There are few published studies that have attempted to evaluate outcomes of PCP. Qualitative studies, mostly relying on participant observation and interviews, have reported favorable changes in quality of life, such as improvements in: housing and decision-making (Malette, 2002); respect and opportunities for choice-making (Parley, 2001); community participation and relationships (Sanderson, 2002); and communication, job finding, and inclusive education (Dumas, De La Garza, Seay, & Becker, 2002; Hagner, Helm, & Butterworth, 1996). Qualitative researchers have consistently noted difficulties in implementing PCP within service systems, and have often reported unmet goals (e.g., Hagner et al., 1996). In a review of qualitative studies, Rowe and Rudkin (1999) concluded that because of methodological limitations, it was not yet possible to compare qualitative outcomes among various PCP approaches or across contexts, although measurement of each of the outcomes noted above can be achieved through quantitative methods as well.

There are pronounced limitations to the generalizability of quantitative studies as well. These studies tend to examine selected aspects of PCP process or intended outcomes, but do not claim to evaluate the efficacy of PCP as such (e.g., Factor, Sutton, Heller, & Sterns, 1996; Miner & Bates, 1997). Several investigations have examined the validity or utility of preferences identified through PCP (Davis & Faw, 2002; Green, Middleton, & Reid, 2000; Reid, Everson, & Green, 1999). Another line of PCP research has demonstrated reductions in challenging behavior following PCP using single-case designs (Holburn & Vietze, 2002a; Klatt et al., 2002; Rea, Martin, & Wright 2002). Although these designs are quasi experimental, their findings suggest that PCP, when combined with applied behavior analytic methods, can be a viable approach for people with challenging behavior.

A notable study of PCP was conducted by Magito-McLaughlin, Spinoza, and Marsalis (2002), in which typical PCP outcomes were quantified and data from four adults in a person-centered service model were compared to those of four matched participants receiving traditional services for a one-week period. Results revealed that the PCP group showed more community participation, choicemaking, relationships, and competencies. However, individuals in the traditional group spent more time in jobs, while those in the PCP group tended to sample jobs and job related activities. The study is unique in that it attempted to achieve individualized services for PCP participants through systematic organizational changes such as staff allocation, transportation, and decentralizing clinical, administrative, and support staff.

At least two longitudinal studies reported implementation of a full PCP process and also evaluated a range of outcomes that are typically targeted. In the first study, participants in PCP showed moderate but significant improvements on proxy measures of QOL compared to a matched contrast group participating in traditional service planning (Holburn, Jacobson, Schwartz, Flory, & Vietze, 2004). The other study was a singe-case investigation in which improvements on proxy measures of QOL and reductions in observed levels of challenging behavior occurred following person-centered planning (Holburn & Vietze, 2002a). However, the first study did not use randomization for group assignment and the second lacked true control phases. Both studies used proxy data, and it should be noted that researchers differ in the degree to which they accept assessments via proxy measures as representative of valid participant responses (Cummins, 2002; McVilly, Burton-Smith, & Davidson, 2000). In short, presently there are few rigorous evaluations of the outcomes of PCP.

## Challenges in Measuring the Process and Outcomes of Person-Centered Planning

Given the complexity of PCP interventions, it is remarkable that no studies have systematically reported on degree of adherence to particular forms of PCP. However, measuring the process of PCP is challenging for several reasons. First, it is important that assessing adherence to PCP principles or prescribed procedures does not interfere with the actual process by distracting group members or deterring the course of planning. Formative evaluation should involve feedback given to the group periodically on how well members are conforming to the process (Holburn et al., 2000). Although some might contend that feedback will contaminate the process because it will become part of it, feedback poses no threat to replication so long as it is described as part of the procedure. Moreover, the feedback would likely increase awareness of and conformance to the process, and may thereby reduce the likelihood of misapplication.

For all interventions, greater standardization and precision in procedural detail decreases the likelihood that the intervention will drift from its originally stated course. In this regard, a fundamental incompatibility seems to emerge because person-centered planning resists standardization and uniformity both conceptually and methodologically. As a dynamic process, PCP is designed to adapt to or drift with the circumstances as they develop. As Drake (1999) noted, "It morphs." As new goals and problems emerge, new strategies develop, and new people are likely to enter the picture. Yet, there are certain components of the process that remain stable across individuals and meetings. Like other approaches, PCP prescribes certain techniques that involve characteristic processes. The techniques differ, depending on the type of PCP employed, but they tend to consist of sequenced activities in a curriculum-like format. All PCP methods tend to prescribe guidelines, ground rules, checklists, mapping methods, and problem-solving strategies that can be described and assessed for accuracy of implementation. The multiple-component nature of the process appears to be the most formidable obstacle to assessing intervention integrity, but it must be acknowledged that in all applied research, interventions are never truly precise, identical, or replicable in every respect. Applied interventions, including replications, occur in real-life situations, not in laboratories, and as such, they are subject to the fluctuations of conditions that are themselves influenced by a myriad of factors that also vary. In behavioral science intervention research, the answer to the question, "Did you do what you reported that you did?" might be "yes," but in truth, adherence to the stated procedures only really can be an estimate, irrespective of the simplicity or complexity of the intervention procedures. Unfortunately, the fidelity or integrity of procedures such as organizational change strategies is seldom measured in clinical or management practice with an appreciable degree of precision. In fact, most applied social science research does not even report how faithfully the interventions are applied. In PCP research, such estimates can be developed by (a) confirming that multiple essential components of PCP are present for some people and not others, and then comparing outcomes, or by (b) assessing implementation of PCP with respect to the presence of certain components and then comparing outcomes in relation to natural or observed variation in the presence or implementation of those particular components.

The validity of a PCP process measure appears to be limited by the extent to which the components of the process can be separated into their constituent units for verification. One way to assess the integrity of the PCP process is through questionnaires that permit a team to quantify degree of adherence to such units. For example, Holburn et al. (2000a) reported development of an instrument that a team can use to self-evaluate adherence to six person-centered process elements. These elements are presence of strategic roles, personal relationship with the focus person, desire for change, creation of a personalized vision, commitment to planning and follow-up, and flexible funding and resources. Team members rate their team's performance through questions comprising each element. The questions can be answered anonymously and then averaged to obtain a measure of adherence to each element, or team members can indicate adherence through consensus based on team discussion.

Integrity of the process might be more accurately measured by quantifying adherence through independent observation. An observational measure to assess the fidelity of PCP is The *Assessment of Person-Centered Planning Facilitation Integrity* questionnaire (Holburn, Vietze, & Gordon, 2001). This brief instrument lists 22 aspects of meeting logistics and meeting facilitation. An observer who is present during the meeting specifies the presence or absence of each aspect during meetings, preferably assessing earlier meetings more frequently than later ones. Recording takes place after the meeting to minimize potentially intrusive recording effects. Following the meeting, performance feedback can be provided to members of the planning team. Thus, such assessment permits confirmation that a given method was actually employed, which is fundamental for replication, and it can also guide the team in making adjustments in procedure. Additional detail on instrument development, administration, and inter-rater observer agreement are reported in Holburn (2002a).

Assessing the outcomes of person-centered planning is also a challenging task (Holburn, 2002b). Goals aimed at improving autonomy or gaining respect might be met, yet it can be difficult to determine if the person has truly achieved greater autonomy or respect. More tangible products of planning, such as whether a person got and kept a job or moved to a smaller home in the community are easier to objectify. Difficulties in defining and measuring apparently subjective outcomes is no doubt related to the common practice of displaying the outcomes of person-centered planning in a qualitative, story-like format. Such stories often present an inspiring narrative of a person's new life situation and how pivotal members of the community came together to make that happen. Unfortunately, qualitative research generally does not conform to traditional research standards of believability, and therefore, it tends to be viewed as descriptive, anecdotal, or exploratory rather than analytic or evidence-based. Of course, quantitative research also tells a story, but through more technical language and through the more structured format of research review, methods, results, and discussion.

A critical difference between qualitative and quantitative accounts of PCP is that the latter are based on a more rigorous standard of proof. This difference restricts the subject matter of quantitative research to phenomena that can be assessed and compared through measures of magnitude such as frequency, rate, duration, and scale scores. Qualitative research has no such boundaries, and investigators can delve easily into areas considered too complex or fuzzy for traditional research. The narrative accounts of qualitative research are usually transmitted in colloquial language, and they seem to be more interesting and easier to remember than numerical estimates of what occurred. Importantly, they appear to have strongly influenced the adoption of PCP. Such accounts can also inspire quantitative investigators to evaluate PCP, but it is possible that this influence is potent principally to those who have already adopted a PCP frame of reference, and merely strengthen pre-existing perspectives. In any case, there is a dearth of research on PCP, and all forms of research, including group designs, single-subject analysis, and qualitative investigations, will add to what we know about applying PCP in systems that serve people with developmental disabilities. The convergence of findings of the various forms of research may be a measure of their validity in this area of investigation.

Quantitatively-oriented investigators may be reluctant to evaluate PCP because of the challenges in applying traditional empirical methods to PCP. For example, the flexible nature of the PCP process and the way that goals are developed present one impediment. In traditional intervention research, specific outcomes are targeted in advance to permit measurement methods to be designed before the intervention. However, in PCP, the vision for the person (i.e., goals) develops *during* the intervention. Even if certain outcomes such as community inclusion and improved relationships are anticipated and measurements are designed prospectively, the achievement of planned outcomes themselves can lead to other desirable outcomes that were not initially anticipated, and it is possible that the breadth of effects may be underestimated. In the behavioral sciences, these outcomes are often called *collateral effects*. They can be systematically measured, but generally they are described briefly to better convey possible multiple impacts of the intervention. When examined in their own right, they constitute as an extension of the original research design. This often takes the researcher into interesting territory and requires that the researcher have the flexibility and resources to expand the design, but such searches are consistent with the spirit of scientific inquiry (e.g., as discussed by Rosales-Ruiz & Baer, 1997). Nonetheless, if unmeasured or inadequately measured by the standards of behavioral science, the perspective that particular collateral effects were caused by the intervention should be considered speculative until confirmed in further research.

A common quantitative approach entails comparisons between groups of people who receive different treatments. The groups typically consist of large numbers of participants. Larger numbers of participants increases the generalizability of the findings and it also permits statistical analysis of multiple treatments and outcomes. However, the usually the small numbers of individuals in quantitative research on PCP limits the number of different treatments and outcomes that can be studied.

Perhaps the most formidable challenge in evaluating PCP pertains to the quantification of the seemingly subjective aspirations or goals of PCP. Interestingly, researchers who have not investigated PCP per se have demonstrated methods of quantifying many goals associated with PCP. As examples, the following outcomes have all been operationalized and evaluated, although they were achieved from interventions other than PCP: community inclusion (Kennedy, Horner, Newton, & Kanda, 1990), choice (Cooper & Browder, 1998), relationships (McGee, Almeida, Sulzer-Azaroff, & Feldman, 1992), respect (Asher, Singleton, Tinsley, & Hymel, 1979), and even happiness (Green & Reid, 1996). Because these outcomes *can* be measured, and transcend the features of detailed, individual outcomes, these outcomes, as dependent variables, *can* be included in an evaluation of within-individual, or across-individual benefits of PCP implementation; their nature does not *defy* quantitative measurement. For example, to measure community inclusion, one could readily assess changes in the number and types of community settings in which a person participates; development of affiliative relationships with clubs, organizations, groups, or particular settings; and other forms of engagement or social network expansion. Such an approach was used in the evaluation of PCP by Magito-McLaughlin et al. (2002), described earlier, in which five essential outcomes of PCP were operationalized, quantified, and observed.

Another challenge in evaluating the outcomes of PCP pertains to the practical difficulties in simultaneous assessment of multiple objectives (Holburn, 2001). Technically, an investigator needs only to show that one goal of PCP is functionally related to the process of PCP to demonstrate that PCP is effective. However, PCP teams tend to work toward the achievement of multiple objectives at the same time. Not all of these objectives are significant life-changing aspirations (for one person, they might range from getting a hot lunch each day to developing more satisfying relationships), but many individuals who undergo PCP desire to change their lives in substantial ways on several fronts. Few applied researchers can marshal enough resources to sufficiently and reliably quantify four or five molar outcomes simultaneously. More information about quantification of person-centered outcomes can be found in Holburn (2001) and Holburn and Vietze (2002b), which delineate various practical measurement methods for evaluating PCP. The assessment techniques do not require unusual expertise, and they are described in sufficient detail so that they *can* be reproduced.

There is another factor that may mitigate interest in evaluating PCP, but its nature is more conceptual than pragmatic. It may be that researchers avoid study of activities which seem, from the standpoint of adoption as a standard practice, inevitable, or merely a manifestation or a vehicle of service philosophy. This has been the case with the long history of interdisciplinary teams as a structural component of developmental services. Although there have been a considerable number of studies of the functioning and effects of teams in schools (i.e., Individual Educational Plan teams), there are few investigations of either the interdisciplinary process or the relation between that process and its outcomes in adult developmental services. Like PCP today, interdisciplinary teaming was long considered to be the zeitgeist in service provision, and therefore, evaluations of its effectiveness may have been viewed as iconoclastic challenges to "the right thing to do."

## Summary

Person-centered planning is a popular approach in the United States for people with developmental disabilities. It has been contrasted with the system-centered approach, in which the needs of a system of care dominate over individual interests of the people whom the system is supposed to help. Definitions of PCP differ, but all person-centered approaches promote the goals of community inclusion, better relationships, and more choice-making in the lives of people with developmental disabilities. The PCP process entails group problem solving methods, usually over a long time period, as it attempts to shift more power to the individual receiving services and less to those who are providing the services. Person-centered planning can be employed for people with serious behavior problems because it attempts to alter the environment in favor of the person's preferences, and such alterations may render problem behavior less efficient or effective. At the same time, PCP processes do not in themselves prevent the development of typical behavioral or psychiatric interventions to alleviate the impact of behavior problems or mental disorders on the pacing with which lifestyle opportunities may be expanded and community membership enhanced.

A great deal of research has not yet been conducted on person-centered planning, but the extant literature appears to support its use in general terms. One of the reasons why there is so little research in this area is the challenge of measuring adherence to the process and assessment of the multiple and seemingly subjective outcomes promoted by person-centered planning. Reluctance to evaluate PCP might also derive from a tendency to avoid challenging of prevailing practices that are held as progressive and sanctioned through policy.

Investigators have called attention to a multitude of problems and obstacles in implementing PCP effectively. We believe that the effectiveness will be improved through continued research investigations. Research findings should also lead to discoveries that make the process less complicated and perhaps more efficient. It could lead to methods that identify when PCP is implemented in name but not in substance; methods that could be used by groups to self-correct their PCP group processes. In addition, by conducting more analyses of PCP, innovative measurement approaches that have not been applied within the developmental disabilities field are likely to be included (e.g., Green & Reid, 1996), and perhaps more important, the quantification of subjective goals that have not yet been analyzed as such is likely to occur. Both will permit more thorough examination of more outcomes that are important to people with disabilities. Continued analysis of PCP will bode well for behavioral science in general if new measurement approaches are developed that extend the subject matter of the enterprise.

Note: The first author was supported in part by the New York State Office of Mental Retardation and Developmental Disabilities. The views expressed in this article do not necessarily reflect the views of the supporting organization. Some portions of this chapter have been presented in similar form in Holburn (2002a; 2001; 1997) Inquiries may be sent to holbursc@infionline.net

## References

Asher, S. R., Singleton, L. C., Tinsley, B. R., & Hymel, S. (1979). A reliable sociometric measure for preschool children. *Developmental Psychology, 15,* 443-444.

Butkus, S. Rotholz, D. A., Lacy, K. K., Abery, B., & Elkin, S. (2002). Implementing person-centered planning on a statewide basis: Leadership, training and satisfaction issues. In S. Holburn & P. M. Vietze (Eds.), *Person-centered planning: Research, practice, and future directions* (pp. 335-355). Baltimore: Paul Brookes.

Butterworth, J., Hagner, H., Heikkinen, B., Faris, S., DeMello, S., & McDonough, K. (1993). *Whole life planning: A guide for organizers and facilitators.* Boston: Training and Research Institute for People with Learning Disabilities.

Cooper, K. J., & Browder, D. M. (1998). Enhancing choice and participation for adults with severe disabilities in community-based instruction. *Journal of the Association for Persons with Severe Handicaps, 23,* 252-260.

Cummins, R. A. (2002). Proxy responding for subjective well-being: A review. In L. Glidden (Ed.), *International review of research in mental retardation* (pp. 183-207). San Diego: Academic Press.

Davis P., & Faw, G. (2002). Residential preferences in person-centered planning: Empowerment through self-identification of preferences and their availability. In S. Holburn & P. M. Vietze (Eds.), *Person-centered planning: Research, practice, and future directions* (pp. 203-221). Baltimore: Paul Brookes.

Drake, K. (1999, May). *Providing behavioral consultation within a person-centered framework.* Panel discussion at the annual meeting of the Association for Behavior Analysis, Chicago, IL.

Dumas, S., De La Garza, D., Seay, P., & Becker, H. (2002). "I don't know how they made it happen, but they did": Efficacy perceptions in using a person-centered planning process. In S. Holburn & P. M. Vietze (Eds.), *Person-centered planning: Research, practice, and future directions* (pp. 223-246). Baltimore: Paul Brookes.

Emerson, E., & Hatton, C. (in press). Lifestyle interventions for challenging behavior. In J. W. Jacobson, J. A. Mulick, & R. M. Foxx (Eds.), *Fads and dubious treatments in developmental disabilities*. New York: Erlbaum.

Factor, A., Sutton., E., Heller, T., & Sterns, H. (1996). Impact of person-centred later life planning training program for older adults with mental retardation. *Journal of Rehabilitation, 62*, 77-83.

Frawley, P. (1994, September). *Factors associated with the mental health status of recently de- institutionalized adults with mental retardation*. Doctoral Dissertation, Department of Psychology, University of Vermont.

Goffman, E. (1961). *Asylums: Essays on the social situation of mental patients and other inmates*. New York: Doubleday Anchor.

Green, C. W. Middleton, S. G., & Reid, D. R. (2000). Embedded evaluation of preferences sampled from person-centered plans for people with profound multiple disabilities. *Journal of Applied Behavior Analysis, 33*, 639-642.

Green, C. W., & Reid, D. H. (1996). Defining, validating, and increasing indices of happiness among people with profound multiple disabilities. *Journal of Applied Behavior Analysis, 29*, 67-78.

Hagner, D., Helm, D. T., & Butterworth, J. (1996). This is your meeting: A qualitative study of person-centered planning. *Mental Retardation, 34*, 159-171.

Hayden, M. F. (1998). Civil rights litigation for institutionalized persons with mental retardation: A summary. *Mental Retardation, 36*, 75-83.

Hile, M. G., & Walbran, H. B. (1991). Observing staff-resident interactions: What staff do, what residents receive. *Mental Retardation, 29*, 35-41.

Himadi, B. (1995). Discussion: Reflections from the clinical trenches. *Behavioral Interventions, 10*, 161-172.

Holburn, S. (2002a). The value of measuring person-centered planning. In J. O'Brien & C. L. O'Brien (Eds.), *Implementing person-centered planning: Voices of experience* (pp. 79-98). Toronto: Inclusion Press.

Holburn, S. (2002b). How science can evaluate and enhance person-centered planning. *Research and Practice for Persons with Severe Disabilities, 27*, 250-260.

Holburn, S. (1997). A renaissance in residential behavior analysis? An historical perspective and a better way to help people with challenging behavior. *Behavior Analyst, 20*(2), 61-85.

Holburn, C. S. (2001). Compatibility of person-centered planning and applied behavior analysis. *The Behavior Analyst, 34*, 271-281.

Holburn, C. S., Gordon, A. & Vietze, P. (2004). *Planning inclusive communities together using reinforcement and evaluation (PICTURE): A step-by-step guide*. Staten Island, NY: New York State Institute for Basic Research in Developmental Disabilities.

Holburn, S., Jacobson, J. W., Vietze, P. M., Schwartz, A. A., & Sersen, E. (2000). Quantifying the process and outcomes of person-centered planning. *American Journal on Mental Retardation, 105*, 402-416.

Holburn, C. S., Jacobson, J. W., Schwartz A., Flory, M. J., & Vietze, P. M. (2004). The Willowbrook futures project: A longitudinal analysis of person centered planning. *American Journal on Mental Retardation, 109,* 63-76.

Holburn, S., & Vietze, P. (1999). Acknowledging barriers in adopting person-centered planning. *Mental Retardation, 37,* 117-24.

Holburn, S., & Vietze, P. (2002a). A better life for Hal: Five years of person-centered planning and applied behavior analysis with Sal. In S. Holburn & P. M. Vietze (Eds.), *Person-centered planning: Research, practice, and future directions* (pp. 291-314). Baltimore: Paul Brookes.

Holburn, S., & Vietze, P. (Eds.). (2002b). *Person-centered planning: Research, practice, and future directions.* Baltimore: Paul Brookes.

Holburn, S., Vietze, P. M., & Gordon, A. (2001). *Assessment of person-centered planning facilitation integrity.* Staten Island, NY: New York State Institute for Basic Research in Developmental Disabilities.

Kennedy, C. H., Horner, R. H., Newton, S. J., & Kanda, E. (1990). Measuring activity patterns of adults with severe disabilities using the Resident LifeStyle Inventory. *Journal of the Association for Persons with Severe Handicaps, 15,* 79-85.

Kincaid, D. (1996). Person-centered planning. In L. K. Koegel, R. L. Koegel, & G. Dunlap (Eds.), *Community, school family, and social inclusion through positive behavioral support* (pp. 439-465). Baltimore, MD: Paul H. Brookes.

Klatt, K. P., Bannerman, B., Juracek, D., Norman, K. R., McAdam, D. B., Sherman, J. A., & Sheldon, J. B. (2002). Evaluating preferred activities and challenging behavior through person-centered planning. In S. Holburn & P. M. Vietze (Eds.), *Person-centered planning: Research, practice, and future directions* (pp. 315-332). Baltimore: Paul Brookes.

Magito-McLaughlin, D., Spinoza, T. R., & Marsalis, M. D. (2002). Overcoming the barriers: Moving toward a service model that is conducive to person-centered planning. In S. Holburn & P. M. Vietze (Eds.), *Person-centered planning: Research, practice, and future directions* (pp. 127-150). Baltimore: Paul Brookes.

Maine Department of Mental Retardation. (1994). *A proposed person-centered planning process for Maine.* Augusta: Author.

Malette, P. (2002). Lifestyle quality and person-centered support: Jeff, Janet, Stephanie, and the microboard project. In S. Holburn & P. M. Vietze (Eds.), *Person-centered planning: Research, practice, and future directions* (pp. 291-314). Baltimore: Paul Brooks.

Marrone, J., Hoff, D., & Helm, D. T. (1997). Person-centered planning for the millennium: We're old enough to remember when PCP was just a drug. *Journal of Vocational Rehabilitation, 8,* 285-297.

McGee, G. G., Almeida, M. C., Sulzer-Azaroff, B., & Feldman, R. S. (1992). Promoting reciprocal interactions via peer incidental teaching. *Journal of Applied behavior Analysis, 25,* 117-126.

McVilly, K. R., Burton-Smith, R. M., & Davidson, J. A. (2000). Concurrence between subject and proxy ratings of quality of life for people with and without intellectual disabilities. *Journal of Intellectual Disabilities, 25,* 19-39.

Meinhold, P. M., & Mulick, J. A. (1990). Counter-habilitative contingencies in institutions for people with mental retardation: Ecological and regulatory influences. *Mental Retardation, 28,* 67-75.

Miner, C. A., & Bates, P. E. (1997). The effect of person centered planning activities on the IEP/Transition planning process. *Education and Training in Mental Retardation and Developmental Disabilities, 32,* 105-112.

Mount, B. (1994). Benefits and limitations of personal futures planning. In V. J. Bradley, J. W. Ashbaugh, & B. C. Blaney (Eds.), *Creating individual supports for people with developmental disabilities: A mandate for change at many levels* (pp. 97-108). Baltimore: Paul Brookes.

Mount, B. (1992). *Person-Centered planning: Finding directions for change. A sourcebook of values, ideals, and methods to encourage person-centered development.* New York: Graphic Futures Inc.

Mount, B., & Zwernick, K. (1988). *It's never too early, it's never too late: A booklet about personal futures planning* (Publication No. 421-88-109). St. Paul, MN: Metropolitan Council.

Nirje, B. (1969). The normalization principle and its human management implications. In R. B. Kugal & W. Wolfensberger (Eds.), *Changing patterns in residential services for the mentally retarded* (pp. 179-195). Washington, DC: President's Committee on Mental Retardation.

O'Brien, J., & Lovett, H. (1992). *Finding a way toward everyday lives: The contribution of person centered planning.* Harrisburg, PA: Pennsylvania Office of Mental Retardation. (Available from the Research and Training Center on Community Living, Center on Human Policy, Syracuse University).

O'Brien C. L., & O'Brien, J. (1998). The politics of person-centered planning. In J. O'Brien & C. L. O'Brien (Eds.), *A little book about person-centered planning* (pp. 31-36). Toronto: Inclusion Press.

O'Brien, C. L. O'Brien, J. & Mount, B. (1997). PCP has arrived... or has it? *Mental Retardation, 35,* 480-483.

Parley, F. F. (2001). Person-centered outcomes. *Journal of Learning Disabilities, 5,* 299-308.

Parsons, M. B., Cash, V. B., & Reid, D. H. (1989). Improving residential treatment services: Implementation and norm-referenced evaluation of a comprehensive management system. *Journal of Applied Behavior Analysis, 22,* 143-156.

Pearpoint, J., O'Brien, J., & Forest, M. (1993). *PATH: A workbook for planning positive possible futures and planning alternative tomorrows with hope for schools, organizations, businesses, and families* (2nd ed.). Toronto: Inclusion Press.

Rea, J. A., Martin, M., & Wright, K. (2002). Using person-centered supports to change the culture of large intermediate care facilities. In S. Holburn & P. M. Vietze (Eds.), *Person-centered planning: Research, practice, and future directions* (pp. 73-96). Baltimore: Paul Brookes.

Reid, D. H., & Green, C. W. (2002). Person-centered planning with people who have severe multiple disabilities: Validated practices and misapplications. In S.

Holburn & P. M. Vietze (Eds.), *Person-centered planning: Research, practice, and future directions* (pp. 97-126). Baltimore: Paul Brookes.

Reid, D. H., Everson, J. M., & Green, C. W. (1999). A systematic evaluation of preferences identified through person-centered planning for people with profound multiple disabilities. *Journal of Applied Behavior Analysis, 32*, 467-477.

Reppucci, N. D., & Saunders, J. T. (1974). The social psychology of behavior modification: Problems of implementation in natural settings. *American Psychologist, 29*, 649-660.

Richman, G. S., Riordan, M. R., Reiss, M. L., Pyles, D. A. M., & Bailey, J. S. (1988). The effects of self-monitoring and supervisor feedback on staff performance in a residential setting. *Journal of Applied Behavior Analysis, 21*, 401-409.

Rosales-Ruiz, J., & Baer, D. M. (1997). Behavioral cusps: A developmental and pragmatic concept for behavior analysis. *Journal of Applied Behavior Analysis, 30*, 533-544.

Rowe, D., & Rudkin, A. (1999). A systematic review of the qualitative evidence for the use of lifestyle planning in people with learning disabilities. *Journal of Learning Disabilities for Nursing, Health and Social Care, 3,* 148-158.

Sanderson, H. (2002). A plan is not enough. In S. Holburn & P. M. Vietze (Eds.), *Person-centered planning: Research, practice, and future directions* (pp. 97-126). Baltimore: Paul Brookes.

Schwartz, A. A., Jacobson, J. W., & Holburn, S. (2000). Defining person centeredness: Results of two consensus methods. *Education and Training in Mental Retardation and Developmental Disabilities, 35,* 235-249.

Smull, M. W. (1998). Revisiting choice. In J. O'Brien & C. L O'Brien (Eds.), *A little book about person-centered planning* (pp 37-49). Toronto: Inclusion Press.

Smull, M. W., & Harrison, S. B. (1992). *Supporting people with severe retardation in the community.* Alexandria, VA: National Association of State Mental Retardation Program Directors.

Smull, M. W., & Lakin, K. C. (2002). Public policy and person-centered planning. In S. Holburn & P. M. Vietze (Eds.), *Person-centered planning: Research, practice, and future directions* (pp. 379-397). Baltimore: Paul Brookes.

Stancliffe, R. J., Abery, B., & Smith, J. (2000). Personal control and the ecology of community living settings: Beyond living-unit size and type. *American Journal on Mental Retardation, 105,* 431-454.

Stefan, S. (1993). What constitutes departure from professional judgment? *Mental and Physical Disability Law Reporter, 17,* 207-213.

Vandercook, T., York, J., & Forest, M. (1989). The McGill Action Planning System (MAPS): A strategy for building the vision. *Journal of the Association for Persons with Severe Handicaps, 14,* 205-215.

Wagner, G. A. (1999). Further comments on person-centered approaches. *The Behavior Analyst, 22,* 53-54.

Wolfensberger, W. (1972). The principle of normalization in human services. *Mental Retardation, 33,* 111-119.

Wolfensberger, W. (1983). Social role valorization: A proposed new term for the principle of normalization. *Mental Retardation, 21,* 234-239.

# Chapter 16

# Research to Practice:
# Management, Staff Training, and
# Improvement of Services

**John W. Jacobson**
*Sage Colleges Center for Applied Behavior Analysis, Troy, NY*
**Steve Holburn**
*New York State Institute for Basic Research in*
*Developmental Disabilities*

"The accomplishments of the past 25 years are nothing short of astounding. Almost the entire agenda that the most visionary advocates could have dreamed of in the 1970s has come to pass, from the decline of institutions to the growth of community services, to the passage of new laws..., the adoption of progressive policies, availability of more money, and more flexibility in how to spend that money for needed services and supports" (Sundrum, 1999, p. 62).

The primary means of technology transfer in developmental services today is staff and clinician training. This applies to organizational improvement as well as increasing staff and clinician skills. However, as the population structures of the US, UK, and Canada shift toward older ages, the proportion of the population available to provide direct care services is diminishing, bringing with it increased competition for entry level workers among human service systems, service industries, and other businesses. This problem has long-plagued health-care, mental health, and developmental services programs that rely heavily on front-line personnel to deliver services and maintain organizational capacity. Correspondingly, there have been difficulties with sustained high rates of direct service staff turnover; which are reported to be escalating as competition for these workers increases (Larson, Hewitt, & Anderson, 1999). For providers, this means that staff whom they have trained this year have a relatively low probability of remaining in the workforce for more than one or two years.

As a result, many newly hired workers will be inexperienced, and as they encounter complex consumers, ill-prepared to serve them and to act as clinician extenders without ongoing training, assistance, guidance from managers, and consultation. To address this problem and bolster worker motivation to remain in the field of developmental disabilities and develop needed skills, some have suggested, and some have fielded extensive pre-service or in-service introductory training programs through distance education, community colleges, or alternative educational systems.

The primary implication for technology transfer posed by high staff turnover and low staff longevity, which will be characteristic of front-line personnel for the foreseeable future, is that, when technology is transferred through staff training, renewal of staff training must become a continuous organizational activity as it relates to extending services to enhance participation in community life, and more specifically to address service needs for individuals with complex problems. Nevertheless, today staff and clinician training remains the primary means of technology transfer in developmental services, with respect to either organizational improvement (e.g., changing organizational culture) or increasing broad or narrow sets of staff and clinician skills. In this chapter we address recent developments relating to technology transfer generally, as well as considerations and findings at the levels of policy, administration, and management, and with respect to consultation, staff training, and distance education as they impact transfer of technology with the goal of improving services.

## Technology Transfer

Technology transfer is a process for conceiving of a new application for an existing technology (RERC on Technology Transfer [RERC], undated). As described by the RERC, transfer can be initiated by producers of the application, which is termed "supply push", or by consumers or intermediary implementers of the application, which is termed "demand pull." In supply push, potential disseminators identify a technology and seek applications, while in demand pull there is an existing unmet market need for which an appropriate technology is sought. "...Technology transfer will only occur if a manufacturer ... is able to transform a technology in supply into a product in demand" (RERC, undated).

Key actors in the technology transfer process are the producers of the application, consumers of the application, and resource providers. The latter group is composed of (a) organizations, governmental and non-governmental, who may finance development, of an application to a product, (b) third party payors or insurers, who may finance consumer purchases or use, (c) intermediaries who market the product (who may sometimes also be developers), and (d) professionals or others who may disseminate, apply, or otherwise promote the product (RERC, undated, p. 3).

The potential for technology transfer exists in applied behavioral sciences when an existing technology is underutilized or an innovative technology is developed. Technology transfer can be thought of as an inherent process in transition of products from research to practice. Two cases can be offered to illustrate these circumstances. In the first instance, there has been rising consumer demand for behavior analysis services, particularly in early intervention for children with autism

(Jacobson, 2000a; 2000b). The demand (pull) for services that exceeds supply of behavior analysts has resulted in demand pull for (a) behavior analysis training programs at colleges and universities at the undergraduate and graduate levels, and (b) mechanisms, through certification processes, of verifying the appropriateness and extent of training and supervised experience. Demand pull among prospective practitioners, with respect to obtaining the credential of board certification in behavior analysis, also is derivative of the inception of standards for providers recommended by the Autism Special Interest Group of the Association for Behavior Analysis. Demand pull situations in which capacity to transfer technology lags behind mounting demand may become fraught with misapplications of the technology.

In a second instance, a technology may be developed to address an application need that is determined by producers or resource providers on a pragmatic, political, or ideological basis, rather than by demand pull. Supply push thereby involves tailoring the application to be compatible with inferred or verified consumer purchasing biases. An example of diffusion (supply push) initiated by funding agencies is positive behavior support (PBS), which initially was infused with financing through a combination of government-researcher relations and philosophical perspectives championed within the federal Department of Education. However, it must be recognized that the dichotomous push-pull metaphor is one of several processes among a myriad of metacontingent relations that bear on the emergence and maintenance of a professional practice within a culture.

## Technology Transfer of Clinical, Educational, and Behavior Analytic Practices

Clinical innovation represents a special case of technology transfer where key actors in diffusion of a new technology include licensed or certified professionals (e.g., physicians, educators, see also Johnston, 2000). Mike, Krauss, and Ross (1998) and Fineberg (1985) have identified ten factors affecting adoption, shown below with reference to innovation within the developmental disabilities culture and in the context of clinicians and personnel who are employees of organizations rather than independent practitioners.

1. Prevailing theory: If the innovation is compatible with common theories, philosophies, or beliefs, the innovation may be more readily diffused; as an example, positive behavior support blends applied behavior analytic technology with philosophical positions endemic to some special education and developmental services subcultures.
2. The innovation: If a new procedure is "easy to use, requires little change in practice style, is highly remunerative and satisfying, and has no worthy clinical competitors" (Mike et al., 1998, para. 36) it may be more readily diffused (e.g., facilitated communication, dietary intervention to prevent progression of phenylketonuria).

3.  The clinical situation: If a new procedure appears to address commonly identified and urgent problems in providing services (e.g., failing to produce individualized lifestyles), it may be more readily diffused (e.g., person-centered approaches).
4.  Advocacy: If well-recognized authorities advocate or promote the use of a technology, or the technology is associated with particular high-profile individuals, it may be more readily adopted (see Kauffman, 1996).
5.  The potential adopter: Technical or professional skills and attitudes about innovation affect susceptibility to infusion and adoption of new technologies (e.g., middle managers in developmental services may lack training in management tools to assess potential benefits and costs, which may make them vulnerable to ready adoption of some ineffective practices; or skilled managers may adopt innovations to revitalize staff activity).
6.  The practice setting: The technologies that are adopted and the pace of the adoption are affected by personnel resources, monetary and physical resources, organizational capabilities, and protection of operations from destabilization (in organizations, like not-for-profit human service agencies where there may not be substantial cash reserves, changes are more likely to be adopted incrementally so that potential costs and structural impacts can be more readily controlled).
7.  The decision-making process: "Innovations whose acceptance requires group consensus or prior institutional approval are said to require more time for their diffusion" (Mike et al., 1998, para. 42). Convoluted or otherwise extensive administrative consensus processes may also hinder adoption of technologies. Arbitrary, hierarchical mandates for change can be instituted more rapidly, but the new practices may not be implemented fully or effectively.
8.  Environmental constraints and incentives: On the one hand, regulatory and financing decisions affecting organizational autonomy will affect the capacity of organizations to embrace innovation or adopt a technology, while on the other hand, active promotion of particular innovations (e.g., positive behavior support by the Department of Education, and person- centered approaches by lead state developmental service agencies) may hasten or at least stimulate innovation.
9.  Evaluation and methods of evaluation: In the fields of developmental disabilities and special education it is difficult to discern whether formal evaluation of the impacts of an innovation influences its adoption (see Kauffman, 1996). However, when evaluations are favorable, evaluation may lead to advocacy for selected innovations by practitioners who are trained to attend to evaluation findings. On the other hand, these practitioners may resist innovations that seem insensible or arbitrary in the absence of evaluative support.

10. Channels of communication: Little is known about how administrators or managers obtain information about new technologies that may lead them to support or oppose particular innovations. Likely sources are advocates, colleagues, trade publications, conferences, continuing education, and the media (Mike et al., 1998); but many systems and organizations lack internal mechanisms to assess the credibility and utility of putative innovations, and some programs and services with foundations in research and applied evaluation may go unconsidered by key administrators as a result (e.g., see Weist & Christodulu, 2000 regarding empirically validated intervention and treatment strategies in schools).

## Administrative Factors

### Systemic and Leadership Considerations

Haque (2001) argues that in recent decades, with the advent of privatization and deregulation, the guiding concerns in public administration and public service have changed to "overcome public sector inefficiencies, reduce monopoly, minimize budget deficit, streamline public expenditure, withdraw subsidy, generate revenue, expand competition, improve service quality, and increase customer satisfaction" (para. 4). Hague argues that the primary objectives of public services now emphasize accomplishment of economic goals encompassing efficiency and competition.

Increasingly across the United States, the states have privatized both human services once delivered by government and a growing range of new services not previously delivered, through contracting with the not-for-profit, and for-profit sectors (Johnston & Romzek, 1999). Contracting as a management tool to engender innovation might be most effective and accountable when service outcomes are easy to measure, the outcomes are tangible and have short time frames, and where there is adequate service capacity and sufficient numbers of providers of the service (Johnston & Romzek, 1999). However, in the case of developmental services and other service sectors such as community youth services, or mental health, measures become more difficult to specify, outcomes may take longer and be less tangible, or there may be an inadequate supply of providers (Johnston & Romzek, 1999, also see Jacobson & Otis, 1992; Rago, 1996).

Adapting a cautionary statement on inclusion by Kavale and Forness (2000) to the more general issue of service reform in developmental services, and closely paraphrasing, we can note that:

> "Analysis of ...evidence ...suggests that the effectiveness of practices associated with reforms are mixed at best. Generalizations about reforms thus remain tentative, and it appears unwise to advocate for reforms without ensuring that they are carried out effectively. Too much time has been spent talking about reforms, and not enough time evaluating them..." (Kavale & Forness, 2000, para. 48).

In seeking reform, one of the typically first administrative steps taken is to develop a consensus around a vision of what reform will achieve (Diamond, 1996). One example of this process is the systems of care model that has emerged from national reform collaborations among researchers, academics, practitioners, and administrators in childrens' mental health services. The vision of systems of care

"emphasize(d) .... community-based systems of care based on a set of values and principles and the best available research .... incorporate a range of services, involve several agencies, ... partnerships between parents and professionals, and ... intensive, individualized, and culturally competent services" (Kutash, & Rivera, 1994, para. 1).

It is not difficult to discern similarities of intent in system of care reforms through child-and family-centered services and in developmental services reforms through organizational change. Evaluation findings suggest it is feasible to more closely mirror model systems and programs through provider agency reorganization of processes. But it has proven difficult to verify better, more responsive, coordinated, and financially efficient interventions that achieve improved child and family outcomes (Bickmann, Noser, & Summerfelt, 1999, see also Bickman, Lambert, Andrade, & Penaloza, 2000). One possible lesson from these evaluations is that bureaucratic reform may not necessarily lead to improved service quality and or outcomes.

Such outcomes may be more a function of proximal influences such as practitioner training and skills, accessibility of resources permitting occasional intensive services, and substantial interorganizational and practitioner cooperation. It is probably not sufficient for reforms to change bureaucracy and the structure of services; clinician and managerial practices must change as well. Such changes were observed by Pandiani and Edgar (1994) in a study of changes in attitudes of community mental health case managers about appropriate housing options for clients over a period of 12 years.

Training of personnel throughout organizations becomes critical when implementation of policy involves substantial changes in the structure of, staffing of, and relationships among governmental and private organizations. As a case in point, Minton (1995) reported on implementation of the Alaska Youth Initiative, a shift in state policy that involved returning troubled youth, who required services from numerous agencies to their home communities. Training was a significant problem in implementation and maintenance of this initiative (Minton, 1995). The training plan called for a centralized service that would send training teams to locations where training would otherwise be unavailable. However, "financial difficulties" compromised this plan and training responsibilities were assigned to regional coordinators, who had many other responsibilities, and in some instances, agencies developed training of their own regarding coordination of services. Minton (1995) noted that training money was difficult to obtain and maintain, and that training budgets were often seen by legislators as discretionary.

In characterizing the reform of a state bureaucracy to promote individualization of services, Rago (1996) identified systemic factors that impaired transition to a new model of service. Rago (1996) noted that consumer empowerment requires devolving authority to local organizations, and senior managers are often unwilling to relinquish responsibility for decisions, tasks, or risk management to local decision makers, including local government. Another limiting factor included preoccupation with crisis management and perhaps crisis prevention: " .... in a culture where crisis decision making is all too frequent, policy deployment is viewed as a nonproductive activity" (Rago, 1996, para. 32). However, although reforms may be targeted to de-bureaucratize services, organizational efforts at the national, state, and even the community level to institute service reforms are often extremely complex and extended, and even bureaucratic in character (e.g., Mowbray, Bellamy, Megivern, & Szilvagyi, 2001).

## Local Agency or Organizational Innovation

From a management or administrative standpoint, one of the challenges surrounding technology transfer and infusion of innovation into an agency is which innovations to implement within the limited personnel resources available to cover training time when staff are diverted from direct and clinical service to training. Managers may find innovations focusing on organizational processes and structures inherently appealing, but concerns for efficiency and effectiveness may also indicate need for training to enhance direct service staff performance and clinical services. Selection of training resources involves tough decisions, complicated by the fact that in some cases no clear solution may be apparent for management dilemmas, and the wide array of consultative and training emphases available may be bewildering. Unfortunately, typical clinical practices, which may be recommended by those to whom management turns for advice, include those that are not well-founded. Managers therefore are obligated to consider whether there is evidence that proposed training activities can plausibly and realistically contribute to the improvement of organizational performance and service delivery.

Administrative issues surrounding implementation of new procedures or infusion of new techniques in settings are similar regardless of whether the procedure is administrative or clinical in nature. Koch, Cairns, and Brunk (2000) noted that clinician resistance can contribute to the failure of well-designed outcomes management systems, and suggested a wide variety of management strategies to overcome resistance to change. These strategies included: recognizing and addressing staff concerns, enhancing efficiency of task completion so that the innovation is adopted, addressing staff concerns that the innovation does not add value to services, and complementing implementation of change by staff education through discussion with personnel of implications, benefits, and impacts of innovation. Other strategies included: assuring middle management support for the innovation, piloting the innovation before adopting it on a broad scale, seeking volunteers among clinicians and staff to conduct piloting, reducing burden on staff deriving from other responsibilities, providing timely and useful feedback to staff, and soliciting and using feedback from clinicians to improve implementation and expand benefits from the innovation.

Management fads, that is, promising but unproven strategies, are sometimes employed to increase organizational effectiveness. Bacal and Associates (2002) suggested strategies to maximize organizational benefits when adopting management fads. They recommend assuring that management has sufficient information about the fad and implement it only if measurable results can be pre-specified using "hard, data-based measurements of effectiveness or productivity." Thus, changes wrought by the fad should be more than increased activity, and when implementation difficulties are encountered one should gather data on how implementation actually proceeded instead of abandoning the fad out-of-hand (see also, Lewis undated, and Lewis, Sugai, & Colvin, 1998, on implementation evaluation).

More generally, administrative staff can demonstrate their support for, and the importance of, training for staff and clinicians if they participate in training sessions and in supervision of newly developed skills in follow-up activities (e.g., Baker, 1998a, 1998b; Lewis, Sugai, & Colvin, 1998), as well as by carrying out more generic administrative functions such as providing other relevant supervision, means to monitor implementation of improved services and assure accountability, direct and reorganize personnel and other resources in support of innovations, and promote policies and procedures conducive to innovation (Holburn & Vietze, 1999, 2002; Schepis & Dunlap, 2000).

## Management and Supervision

The research literature continues to indicate that management practices impact on the endurance of benefits in staff performance that result from a wide range of staff training processes. For example, Parsons, Cash, and Reid (1989) implemented systematic instruction to ensure that direct service staff implemented planned services. They scheduled systematic observations of each staff person at least weekly, with delivery of positive or corrective feedback and use of checklists that were reviewed by the managers' supervisor. Highly specific task information was inserted in written schedules, and differentiated staff roles of care coordinator, activity coordinator, and trainer were specified, and roles were demonstrated. Beneficial effects were observed during intervention and maintenance periods, but wide variability in effects among staff was noted. These procedures were adopted as part of the management system for the facility, and Parsons et al (1989) suggested that the focus on consumer behavior as the primary outcome measure, rather than staff behavior per se, may have aided maintenance of benefits.

Richman, Riordan, Reiss, Pyles, and Bailey (1988) instituted self-monitoring procedures with staff in two of four houses constituting an intermediate care facility. The self-monitoring procedure included setting daily goals that were self-monitored, graphing of data, and administering self-praise as part of a multi-faceted program that involved external monitoring of adherence to self-developed schedules. They found that the performance of staff was equivalent or slightly better with self-monitoring and supervisor feedback combined, than with self-monitoring alone (although this may be have been an artifact of sequence effects in the research design), and that drift was evidenced for some staff under the self-monitoring alone condition. Similarly, in a group home study, Harchik, Sherman, Sheldon, and Strouse (1992) found that continued implementation of direct observation of, and individual consultant feedback to, staff on use of behavioral skills, appeared necessary to maintain staff skills and behavior during regular and relatively long periods of observation.

In a study involving four private homes for people with chronic mental disorders, Huberman and O'Brien (1999) instituted staff training in setting measurable treatment goals, providing verbal and graphed feedback to consumers, and praising consumers, together with written and verbal feedback to staff, combined with praise and contingent monetary reinforcement. At baseline, consumer goals were typically not being addressed by staff, and most goals were not meaningful or clear. The authors observed large increases in the number of goals addressed weekly and the specificity of treatment goals, as well as positive changes in consumer behavior and use of time. At the end of the study staff returned to baseline with respect to the quality of goal development and goal-related task performance. The training and oversight was terminated by management due to factors of logistical inconvenience, and management abandoned the systematic delivery of reinforcement to staff.

There has been increasing interest in recent years in the differentiation of rule-governed and contingency-shaped staff behavior and its implications both for training and subsequent staff monitoring, feedback, and supervision. Jahr (1998) identified priorities for future staff training research, including fading of training or training-related discrete supervisory practices, the acquisition of competencies and tendency to implement trained procedures, staff self-generation of rules for applying trained procedures, methods to teach staff to identify functional relations inherent in the procedures, and further investigation of the use of general (i.e., representative) case and single (i.e., individual) case training methods. Jahr suggested that inexperienced staff may not acquire needed skills when supervisors provide prompts for performance, and that supervisory prompting may cause stereotyped responding, or inflexibility in interactions with consumers, and recommends the use of interventions that promote self-generated rules. In the same vein, Embregts (2002) suggested that "Poor performance may be explained by staff members experiencing being attached to rules that compete with adequate responding or inconsistent standards of intervention across colleagues and/or settings" (p. 363).

Summarizing contemporary concerns, Cullen (1999) noted: "There is a real danger of assuming that performance specification, monitoring and emphasising compliance [alone] will lead to good services. They do not" (Cullen, 1999, p. 19). He suggests that a primary emphasis on rule setting for staff results in the following sequence: excessive numbers of rules, an over-concern for compliance, documentation, and frequent monitoring resulting in staff fears of making mistakes, rigid routines, falsifying of data in some cases, and staff dissatisfaction, which in turn increases risk that quality will be assessed as poor, and more rules will be prescribed as the solution (also see Holburn & Jacobson, 1993). Cullen (1999) suggested that humane and benevolent management practices should be implemented to monitor staff performance, identify problems, and determine staff skill needs. Further, the over emphasis on rules should be replaced with effective consequences for quality performance, staff training, and clearer staff responsibilities (see also, Reid, Parsons, & Green, 1989).

## The Issue of What to Teach

"Evidence suggests that while clinical practitioners generally value scientific validity, most clinical practices are not strongly supported by empirical evidence. They are supported by personal experience and strong belief (or faith). Practices that are based on belief and personal experience ... are highly prone to error and misuse" (Beutler, 2000, Abstract).

"... it is apparent that among any group of like-minded practitioners, the standard of evidence for the validity of a clinical practice has often been whether it fits the theory, whether the advocates strongly believe in the truth of their theories, and whether they appear to be sincere in advocating the value of clinical experience in support of their belief." (Beutler, 2000, para. 3)

Smith and Dowdy (1998), in a discussion of factors that affect special education practice, cite many issues that stem from administrative determinations, such as program philosophy, state mandates and mandated student-teacher ratios, the availability of teachers, and teacher certification specialties. However, they also suggest that the philosophical "orientation[s] of individual teachers and administrators" (para. 3) may be far more influential than these background factors.

In speaking of the Surgeon General's (Sacher, 2001) report on children's mental health, Goldman (2001) observed: "... just at the point in time that we can tell you what the evidence-based practices are, and distinguish those that are effective from those that we only know are efficacious, we cannot tell you very well how to implement those practices" (para. 5). Moreover, the notion that techniques or methods that are implemented in service settings or by professionals in their practices should have benefits that have been convincingly demonstrated through applied quantitative research has not been accepted by at least a substantial minority of advocates or professionals in some disciplines (Chambless & Ollendick, 2000; McIntrye, 2001). Administrators, managers, and clinicians alike should be able to articulate a clear and sound rationale for training on interventions that have not been validated by research. It is possible that a treatment or technique may be effective but not yet examined in research or research trials.

Managers should be aware that there has been growing concern in medicine and health-related professions that ethical and economic considerations such as standards for, or conditions of, reimbursement suggest that provider organizations should adopt well-researched clinical and service practices (see also, Sackett, Rosenberg, Gray, Haynes, & Richardson, 1996). Alternative rationales for justifying service practices have largely been articulated in terms of philosophical grounds, but for the practitioner, Isaacs and Fitzgerald (1999) have suggested some alternative rationales to evidence-based medicine and selection of treatments, with seeming applicability to the field of developmental services: (a) Eminence: the complete substitution of evidence from experience for research evidence; (b) Vehemence: the substitution of volume for evidence via browbeating; (c) Eloquence: verbal eloquence as a powerful substitute for evidence; (d) Providence: leaving outcomes to fate; (e) Diffidence: not intervening, referring, or doing anything at all when one does not know how to treat a condition; (f) Nervousness: "over-assessment and over-treatment" stimulated by fear of litigation; and (g) Confidence: confidence unvalidated by research that the treatment solution one has to offer is ultimately the best. Quite possibly, several of these rationales are consistent with the justification of service reforms posited on the basis of philosophical grounds, and unvalidated by traditional (e.g., quantitative) evidence of benefit for consumers.

Clinicians are typically respected, but not necessarily reliable, sources of advice on priorities in selection among training alternatives. Dunst, Trivette, and Cutspec (2002) have suggested that research syntheses or reviews that are conducted by scientists or investigators are often ill-suited for use by practitioners because they do not indicate how the practitioner should act differently (e.g., do not specify the target, content and sequence of skill use) in future encounters with clients, patients, or consumers to achieve desired outcomes. Kazdin (1997) has remarked on several characteristics of general clinical (and possibly educational) practice that differ from clinical research practice, including unclear criteria for selecting treatments, use of often unspecified eclectic treatments or combinations of treatments, neglect of evaluation of quality and fidelity of treatment delivery, non-systematic monitoring of either treatment processes or patient progress, and the infusion of clinical judgment into decision-making. These factors contribute to uncertainty among practitioners regarding the value of controlled studies in indicating valuable innovations, and they also impair the ability of the clinician to detect whether he or she is providing a service that is credible (i.e., a faithful, effective, rational choice; see also Crits-Cristoph, Frank, Chambless, Brody, & Karp 1995; Kazdin, 1997). Such considerations limit the extent to which managers and clinicians will have access to knowledge about the demonstrated value of various training options, or receive recommendations for key, well-founded training content. As a middle ground between practice and research Kazdin (1997) suggested that "Empirical decision making is not necessarily fixed or rigid. One does not have to move from one extreme (clinical judgment based on impressionistic data) to the other (inflexible empirical rules and algorithms that preclude consideration of extenuating circumstances" (p. 127).

Even if one can achieve a fine-grained management analysis of organizational performance, there is the possibility that friction or frank disagreement will emerge between managers and clinicians about training priorities. A number of reasons that clinicians may resist innovation have been suggested by Thompson (1999). Clinicians may not find evidence for adopting novel organizational or clinical procedures to be adequate because of methodological shortcomings of research or insufficient replications of relevant findings. At the same time, they may misconstrue research findings and their implications if they cannot interpret the research or if the setting in which they work discourages full review of relevant sources. This can result from a lack of time or access to journals, failure of management to convey interest in staff being up-to-date in their professional fields, and organizational cultures that discourage questioning of unnecessary, inefficient, ineffective, or possibly outdated practices (see also, Garb, 1989; MacLeod, Jones, Somers, & Havey, 2001). The importance of engaging clinicians in general continuing education regarding organizational or clinical procedures that will increase their organizational consultation skills is highlighted by findings from research on team decision-making, in which it has been found that better performance on teams results from training decision-makers in technical (e.g., professional, clinical) knowledge rather than in ways to improve their uses of that knowledge (e.g., team processes; Ganster, Williams, & Poppler, 1991; see also Baker, 1998a; Eber Sugai, Smith, & Scott, 2002).

Of course, managers, including those without clinical training, will also be susceptible to the same types of biases that affect clinicians. At the same time, research on training suggests that improved clinical practices may often reap secondary benefits in the form of reduced health, health-related, and behavioral service requirements for consumers. Barriers to innovation through implementation of research-based practices include organizational cultures that discourage or do not support a role for research in development of improved services (Thompson, 1999). If staff and clinicians are not allowed to question current practices, and there is little organizational support for applied research, organizations are less likely to be effective in discerning fads from the latest substantive developments.

It is common for clinician-researchers to refer to the methods they disseminate as best practices or promising practices (e.g., Lewis, undated). Best practices are those about which quantitative research has been conducted whereas promising practices may be advocated on theoretical, philosophical, legalistic or ideological grounds, but for which little or no quantitative research substantiates value (see Cullen, 1999). Much finer gradations of substantiality of evidence for benefit are available; for example, guidelines for evidence-based medicine identify "promising" practices as noted above as having little basis for use, whereas three levels of evidence for "best" practices can be demarcated (e.g., Cape & Barkham, 2002; Dunst, Trivette, & Cutspec, 2002).

A variety of practice improvement methods (Cape & Barkham, 2002) that commonly appear in an organization's training materials also lack firm research support. These include clinical guidelines, clinical audit, outcomes monitoring and management, outcomes benchmarking, and continuous quality improvement. Research indicates only modest benefit from these methods; findings tend to support effects on enhancement of knowledge rather than competency. Extended follow-up of changes in consumer outcomes related to clinical use of practice improvement methods is seldom conducted.

A common purpose of developing guidelines is to encourage transfer or adoption of interventions that produce positive changes in people with disabilities, illnesses, and conditions (Barnett, Pepiton, & Bell, 1999) and related outcomes (e.g., improvements in quality of life). Clinical guidelines are a representative example of mixed and modest findings; systematic reviews have concluded that such guidelines can alter practice and lead to better health outcomes (Cape & Barkham, 2002). However, some guidelines may be poor in quality or ignored by clinicians, which has increased administrative interest in developing superior guidelines and research interest in increasing clinician adoption of guideline-based practices (Cape & Barkham, 2002).

A common focus of contemporary training for personnel, purported to have both organizational, as well as clinical and direct service implications, includes either person-centered planning or positive behavior support. For example, Allen, McDonald, Dunn, and Doyle (1997) report on implementation in a residential unit of positive behavior support training with emphasis on multiple aspects of intervention. Allen et al. characterize the improvements found for physical restraint, emergency medication, staff injuries, and client injuries as clinically significant. Allen et al. (1997) candidly note limitations on the conclusions that can be drawn from their study, reflecting experimental design concerns common to many studies that have attempted to verify the impacts of staff training. These included poor quality data recording prior to introduction of new training and management procedures, lack of a control group, lack of data regarding the stability of the staff group (the authors note that 50% staff turnover may have occurred during that period), and relatively few staff and clients participated in the study. Some or all of these limitations are common in research on the impact of training, heightening the need for administrators and managers to carefully weigh the probable benefits of training, especially in making decisions whether to pursue cultural changes in an agency or targeted staff training (e.g., specific behavioral instructional skills, choice making, or establishment of community linkages).

Jahr (1998) has suggested that poor implementation of research-based practices by paraprofessionals may reduce staff to client interaction rates, compromise the extent of outcomes obtained, and encourage client passivity and prompt dependency. Richman et al. (1988) found that staff training delivered solely by didactic methods resulted in modest levels of implementation of interventions and other planned activities (Jahr, 1998). Jahr (1998) stressed four outcome dimensions for staff training success: (a) Changes in staff behavior should achieve changes in client behaviors (i.e., therapeutic or educational impact); (b) Changes in staff behavior should generalize to settings and clients other than those involved in the training (i.e., generalization); (c) Changes in staff behavior should generalize to goals and objectives other than those involved in the training (i.e., generalization); and (d) Changes in staff behavior should persist after the training period has expired (i.e., maintenance). These objectives appear to address the essence of management intent of training regardless of the conceptual or intellectual basis of a training activity.

One broad and common categorization of practice improvement goals discriminates among several dimensions of quality: accessibility, acceptability to patients, appropriateness to need, equity, effectiveness and efficiency. Most practice improvement methods have focused on the dimension of effectiveness (Cape & Barkham, 2002; see also, Barnett, Pepiton, & Bell, 1999). In principle, these dimensions of quality are pertinent to the identification and resolution of needed reforms or innovations at the systemic, organizational, or clinical service levels, and are worthy of consideration as touchstones for managerial appraisal of the range of likely benefits from various training activities.

## Fidelity and Practice

"... I think there is this confusion in the literature that one often sees that model programs don't really generalize. [A service model] may work in ... [one state] but it doesn't work in other parts of the country. You need to modify these things for local factors and local conditions in order for them to work. The literature doesn't support that point of view at all... What the literature shows instead ... is that for any evidence-based practice there is a core group of principles or procedures that have to be implemented faithfully in order to get the good outcomes that one expects. If you deviate very much from that the outcomes drop immediately" (Drake, 2001, para. 11).

How far should programs deviate from practices shown to be effective in the literature? Phillips and Jenkins (1997) report that innovations in practice "that are concrete, practical, and appear usable in the classroom" (para. 5) are most likely to be of interest to teachers. They suggest that continued access to experts and staff development resources tailored to the specific innovation affect practice and continued use. But they also note that once an innovation has been adopted, the fidelity with which it is implemented often varies substantially. In their study, teachers universally introduced changes in the tutoring procedures and often failed to effectively implement the procedures in the manner indicated by research.

Phillips and Jenkins raised the question of whether teachers were aware that modifying validated procedures, in varied ways, might vitiate the benefits that could be reasonably expected from faithful implementation. Neef (1995a) suggested that infidelity in the form of adaptation of procedures taught to supervisors or staff is necessary because of differing ecological opportunities in differing settings. However, adaptation does not require alteration of the essential features of an intervention (Drake, 2001), but rather of strategies for delivery of the intervention.

## Values, Attitudes, and Competency Training

In a discussion of mental health deinstitutionalization policy, Shadish (1984) found that there was a tendency to view adverse events or outcomes (e.g., increase in homelessness) as "merely unfortunate happenstance" unconnected to ideology and policy (cited in Kavale and Forness, 2000). Although administrators, managers, and some practitioners may often view changes in ideological perspectives to be inevitable and a potential stimulus toward service improvement, there are some who sound alarms regarding unintended, perhaps ubiquitous, side-effects of implementing multiple and complex reforms at the same time. In discussing current special and regular education reforms Kauffman (1999) noted "Public schooling in the United States has been defaced by the carnage of many ideological train wrecks, and the current ideological trains of … reform are being ridden into an inevitable high-speed collision …." (para. 7).

Very generally stated, managers often must choose between training options that focus on changing values and those that engender knowledge and skill acquisition for the performance of circumscribed but critical tasks (such as offering and reinforcing choice-making in daily and lifestyle decisions by consumers (e.g., Cooper & Browder, 2001). Cullen (1999) noted that research had not identified a causal relationship between staff performance and organizational culture. In research on values in community service agencies, Balcazar, MacKay-Murphy, and Keys (1998) found that personnel who were most knowledgeable about progressive service practices also tended to characterize the organizations for which they work as more progressive. In another study, Becker, Dumas, and Houser (2000) concluded that organizational values predicted implementation of progressive individualized practices. However, neither the Balcazar et al. nor the Becker et al. study indicate a cause and effect relationship between values or personal appraisal of organizational culture and actual staff performance, and that alternative explanations are available for these findings, such as differences in the services offered by agencies and selection of agencies by prospective employees based in part on their service delivery approaches. At this point there is some suggestive evidence that altering organizational values as a component of culture, together with teaching specific skills associated with person centered planning, for example, has some cumulative effects on changes in staff activity (e.g., see Holburn & Jacobson, this volume). However, effects of cultural change (i.e., as outcomes of values training) appear gradual and incremental.

Given that cultural change is likely to be graduated in its impacts, it is not surprising that training incorporating a values component, like other training, manifests varied impacts under differing circumstances. In a study in which staff were trained in specific physical intervention strategies, de-escalation procedures, and positive approaches through a several-day training session and a three month follow-up, no significant changes in numbers of incidents were found (Baker & Bissmire, 2000). The authors noted, "Nearly all training would claim to emphasize proactive approaches; the extent to which this is carried over to the management of challenging behaviour also requires investigation" (p. 44). In another study, Becker et al. (2000), conducted interviews of staff in several agencies differing in pragmatic and philosophical characteristics of operation following self-determination training for service coordinators (i.e., case managers) and found that results varied, with staff or agencies that already were engaged in closely related activities reporting the most benefit from training in terms of implementing person-centered practices.

Although managers can attempt organizational reform through exposure of staff to selected values or philosophically-driven training, it is also possible to address reform of organizational culture through performance-related training. From a management perspective, "An organization's culture, which consists of deeply imbedded values, beliefs, philosophies, attitudes, and operating norms, essentially boils down to "how things are done around here" (Anthony, 1999, para. 1). From a behavioral science perspective, "A cultural practice includes interlocking behavioral contingencies, or complex interrelations between behavioral repertoires of individuals, interlocking behavioral contingencies, and all of the variations enter into aggregate outcome" (Bohrer & Ellis, 1998, p. 42, see also Glenn, 1988). Thus, the values and practices of an employee are influenced by factors in addition to the organizational culture in which the employee works.

Sulzer-Azaroff, Pollack, Hamad, and Howley (1998) instituted a culture change intervention that included training and performance requirements integral to manager feedback to direct service staff, peers, and supervisors (e.g., reporting outcomes to peers and supervisors). Components of this system emphasized scheduling of managerial feedback, reinforcement of staff, and goal setting, procedures which were developed jointly with administration, managers, and other personnel (e.g., clinicians, direct service staff). The system was maintained, and it was supported both formally and incidentally by the senior administrators, and it became an element of the management and supervisory culture of the facility.

## Consultants and Clinicians

Agency clinicians are often drawn upon as trainers in both competency-based, and values-driven training. However, it is usually not necessary to draw on outside consultants as expert trainers. Consultation is a service delivery strategy, rather than an intervention per se; it is a process for assuring that the people who work directly with consumers acquire information or skills that are necessary to serve individual consumers more effectively, with the goal that the individual consumers *will* be served more effectively (Watson & Sterling, 1997; Williams, 2000; Williams & Cummings, 2000). Although there has been considerable research on a wide range of consultative models, most consultation research that included some form of consumer-related outcome measure (i.e., indirect or direct measurement of improvements) uses one of several behavioral consultation models, and indicate variable benefit (Sheridan, Welch, & Orme, 1996).

Nevertheless, research to ascertain these benefits has seldom involved direct measures of consumer change; rather, it tends to consist of improvement ratings, which are fraught with subjective and possibly self-serving influences because of unintended biases of respondents. Watson and Sterling (1997) severely critiqued what they term "myths" about behavioral consultation, citing lack of empirical support for the premises that, for example, "consultative services are more cost efficient than direct intervention, collaborative consultations are more effective than expert consultation, or that didactic instruction of intermediaries (typical of consultation) results in significant behavior change for the target consumer, or other consumers with similar needs served by the same intermediary" (Watson & Sterling, 1997, p. 467). They also noted that there is a scant evidence for some fairly prevalent assumptions pertinent to both consultation and follow-along activities, in particular, that treatment acceptability is related to treatment integrity (i.e., that a procedure viewed as a more acceptable by a teacher will be more completely or more faithfully implemented) and that consultee satisfaction with consultation or with the target consumer is a valid indicator of whether actual clinical or educational goals were achieved.

Many successful (and less than fully successful) training studies have utilized consultant trainers and follow-along consultation as primary components (e.g., Baker, 1998b). Unfortunately, training in how to carry out an intervention seems seldom to generalize spontaneously to an ability to instruct others effectively in implementing the same intervention (McGimsey, Greene, & Lutzker, 1995), a finding not only relevant to the skills required by consultants from outside an organization, but also to those who would function as consultants within an organization such as residential or day service supervisors engaged in staff training. Although it may often be assumed that competent clinician-employees of an organization are also competent trainers of staff, this is not necessarily the case (McGimsey et al., 1995; Parsons & Reid, 1995).

In considering the utility or necessity of obtaining consultation or using clinician employees to improve organizational functioning or staff training, Lewis (undated) suggested:

> "When analyzing potential procedures, expected staff behavior should be outlined to the point that all staff know exactly how to implement the approach, how to respond to student behavior, and where to get assistance if needed…. If the approach under investigation is vague or does not provide sufficient information to replicate, additional information, or alternative approaches, should be examined" (para. 8).

## Effectiveness of Training Staff and Managers or Supervisors

> "Staff training … has not been shown to be sufficiently powerful as a factor [in improving staff performance], although carefully controlled (and often contrived) staff management strategies seem to work. What is disappointing … is that it is often hard to achieve significant change in real world settings" (Cullen, 1999, p. 17)

> "Some training has been found to be effective in increasing staff knowledge and impacting on practice….Training has not always been found to be cost-effective or to have long-term benefits …." (Weightman, 1999, pp. 2-3).

Demonstrations and evaluations of training programs have measured a wide variety of outcomes, including attitude change, self-ratings, and evidence of changes in practice (Harper, 1994). In a review of about 100 outcomes studies of interventions for problem behavior in developmental services, Ager and May (2001) report these interventions were primarily delivered by teachers or direct care staff, and over one-fourth of the studies were conducted by researchers providing temporary assistance, supervision, or consultation. They also observe that many research-based interventions require delivery at high intensity, or well-developed staff skills in the particulars of the interventions. Moreover, they posit that faithful intervention will often not be feasible when logistics of staffing prohibit high intensity or staff have not been taught, and that when organizations attempt to implement such interventions with appropriate assessments, this may not only compromise effectiveness and efficiency, but sometimes ethics as well.

As noted in reviews by Ager and May (2001) and Jahr (1998), a variety of studies have documented the effectiveness of supervisory feedback on staff behavior as a factor affecting implementation of mundane or innovative therapeutic practices (Parsons & Reid, 1995; Seys & Duker, 1988; Shore, Iwata, Vollmer, Lerman & Zarcone 1995; Fleming & Sulzer-Azaroff, 1989). Similar findings have been reported for continuing professional consultation (Harchik, Sherman, Sheldon, & Strouse, 1992; Northup, Wacker, Berg, Kelly, Sasso, & de Raad 1994). Moreover, Ager and May (2001) noted that:

> "The requirement for such sustained supervision in part reflects the fact that the ideas, understandings and attitudes of care staff often run counter to the principles and philosophy of established behavioural approaches to client management…. Such literature is thus not encouraging of any model that suggests simple inculcation of specified 'best practice' in direct care staff. Indeed, it documents a staff culture frequently hostile to the structure and language of behavioural interventions, which generally constitute the most soundly evidence-based form of intervention" (p. 252).

In a series of articles Jones, Felce and colleagues studied implementation and outcomes of Active Support, an organizational intervention to increase the variety of activities in the typical day of people with mental retardation living in group homes and smaller quarters. They have employed direct training, workshops, and more recently, a train the trainer model. Like many others, this team has done both direct training (e.g., the principals provide training directly to staff in the settings where they work) and has recently reported on use of a train the trainer model.

Jones, Felce, and colleagues (2000) introduced Active Support into five residences serving 19 adults with severe mental retardation. Resources for training included a series of "simply written booklets", including forms staff to organize and monitor performance. Initially, a short workshop was provided for staff and the manager at each site. This workshop encompassed review of consumer preferences, household routines, necessary household tasks, and typical recreational and related activities in which consumers engaged. At this time, preliminary activity plans were generated for each consumer for each day of the week. Following the workshop, staff and the manager received individual instruction including demonstration, observed practice by staff, and feedback, which, altogether required three days for two trainers, for each home. Daily activity and monitoring planning were then established, as was responsibility for assuring completion of the planned tasks were identified, and weekly review meetings were established, all as part of the work routine for staff.

In their recent study (Jones et al., 2001b), Active Support training was replicated in three ways: in houses, led by one of the researchers, with managers assisting; led by managers who had previously assisted one of the researchers, with technical assistance from the researchers; and led independently by managers who had previously both assisted a researcher, and received technical assistance from a researcher. Previous studies had indicated, somewhat unexpectedly, that changes in resident routines and activities could result and be maintained based on brief didactic and coaching interventions provided by the researchers, with follow-up limited to effects associated with collection of observational data (e.g., Jones, et al., 2001a). In the study of manager training outcomes (2001b), similar changes were obtained to those found in previous research occurred when managers assisted researchers or researchers assisted managers. However, when managers implemented active support training without assistance from the researchers, even though they had observed and practiced all components of the training, comparable results were not obtained. Previous research (Jones et al., 2001a) found that staff turnover and an agency's inability to train new staff in Active Support were associated with deterioration in provision of Active Support over time.

Several studies have attempted to validate techniques to train professional supervisors in methods to deliver feedback to staff and improve supervisor and staff performance of teaching skills (Parsons & Reid, 1995), whereas many supervisors do not have the same level of education. Other recent studies involving training of supervisors include Embregts (2002), Fleming, Oliver, and Bolton (1996), Jensen, Parsons, and Reid (1998), and Reid, Parsons, & Green, 1989). Especially important aspects of these studies include clearly stated criteria and composition of teaching skills, explicitly stated details of implementation, including resource (reference, source, record, or guidance) materials provided to supervisors or staff, and measurement of effects on consumers, staff, or supervisors. The provisions assist in replication of training procedures in local organizations and selected service settings.

Several other studies have focused on increasing staff provision of choice training and choice offering to clients. Salmento & Bambara (2000) report on a training package incorporating a consultation meeting, in vivo modeling and practice sessions, and follow-up observations and feedback to staff on their performance. A wide scope of outcomes were assessed and identified, including increases in staff offering of choice opportunities to clients, increases in client choices made, maintenance at follow-up one and three months post training, and generalization across settings (time of day) and clients. Salmento and Bambara (2000) identify the purposes of the consultation meeting and in vivo training as:

"(a) provide a rationale for presenting choice opportunities, (b) teach staff members how to identify routines, (c) teach staff members to recognize choice opportunities within routines, and (d) teach staff members how to identify and respond to approach/rejection behaviors as indicators of choice" (para. 15).

It is readily apparent from this description that one focus of the training was generation of both explicit and implicit (self-generated) rules for implementation and delivery of choice making opportunities (e.g., "provision of choice making is an inherent and necessary aspect of the services we deliver"). Staff were taught a specific seven-step procedural sequence (i.e., explicit rules) for single-stimulus choice presentation. Some of the maintenance effects could have been due to the influence of the collection of observational data.

Unfortunately as recently as 1998, Jensen, et al. noted that few investigations have demonstrated how to train supervisors to provide staff feedback in an effective manner. Training issues are as much at the forefront of special education as they are of residential services. Jensen et al. (1998) focused on training teachers of adults with severe disabilities to supervise their teaching assistants effectively. This supervisory training program was effective in improving the performance of the assistants, but student progress was not measured in this study, leaving open the question of whether this improved as well. Some of Jensen's et al. key findings were (a) satisfactory recording of data and teaching accuracy were maintained by the teachers and assistants for 17 months, (b) improvements in teaching assistant performance resulted from training by their supervisors; and (c) teachers' own instructional skills improved during training.

In a study addressing staff-consumer communication interaction training pertinent to both educational and developmental service settings, Purcell, McConkey, and Morris (2000) conducted a quasi-experimental study that compared staff training outcomes, using either a two whole-day meeting tutored by the researchers, or one-to-one sessions in the workplace with a tutor (a clinician or manager who had been trained in the group format). No differences were found between the two methods. This finding is somewhat surprising, but because the researchers taught the group sessions and clinicians or managers taught the one-on-one sessions, the findings could be confounded.

In Baker's (1998a) study of training with group home staff, a wide range of skills and tasks were addressed using brief manager-led exercises and video vignettes. The skills included basic health and safety provisions such as hand washing and use of gloves, positive interactions with residents, and engagement in valued community activities. Improvements were found in hand-washing, use of gloves, and positive interactions, but not in frequency of valued community activities. Baker (1998a) suggested that the training was more successful with less effortful or simpler tasks, but not more effortful or complex tasks. In this case, Baker suggested that the content of the training itself was more concrete and specific with respect to other outcomes compared to values and this may account for differences in acquisition of simpler and more complex competencies. These findings suggest that, other factors such as the use of multiple training strategies being equal, there may be a relatively direct relationship between the breadth of sub-skills required to conduct complex activities (e.g.., increase valued community activities) and the breadth of required training exposure.

## Management Adjunctive to Training

"Without formal systems to promote transfer of learning, most of what is learned in training will never be used on the job" (Rycus & Hughes, 2000, p. 2).

Indeed, supervisory action and feedback appears necessary as a maintaining influence on initial benefits of staff training in intervention and support provision. This conclusion is supported by research and analysis indicating the multiple, often conflicting contingencies for task completion to which managers, clinicians, and staff are subjected (Critchfield & Kollins, 2001; Jones et al., 2001b; Meinhold & Mulick, 1990a, 1990b; Mulick, 1990; Mulick & Meinhold, 1992).

Some exemplar training efforts are extremely extensive, and supporting these efforts may tax the capabilities of some organizations. For example, Allen, McDonald, Dunn, and Doyle (1997) implemented training to alter staff management of aggressive behavior that incorporated classroom instruction, role play, and extended practice of physical interventions. In this setting, management personnel supported use of alternative methods by instituting changes in procedures for reactive behavior management plans, requiring staff to participate in this training upon entry, and requiring refresher training twice yearly. In another study, in order to address common administrative concerns that training draws staff away from completion of everyday work tasks, Parsons, Reid, and Green (1996) implemented a one-day teaching skills training program for direct service staff, using both quizzes and mastery assessments to verify impacts, and follow-up probes for maintenance (see Saloviita & Lehtinen, 2001, for another format of time-limited training). They found that staff improved performance on quizzes and mastery measures, and that teaching proficiency endured on follow-up.

As mentioned earlier. Sulzer-Azaroff et al. (1998) established a system of observational procedures as well as supervisory procedures and reports in a large residential facility, designed with broad staff participation. The system includes interspersion of skill practice with training sessions, as well as developing protocols for observing behavior, for reports, and for reporting routines. Observational and reporting system elements focused on pertinent resident activity and interaction of staff and residents of the facility, and maintenance of data collection and use of the data at multiple levels of management endured. Although these procedures were instituted across residential units, there were no inherent features of the managerial aspects of the system, focus of data collection, periodicity of data collection, or use of reports that would be incompatible for use in community services organizations.

In training studies, concerns about generalization and maintenance of training effects have been longstanding (Ducharme, Williams, Cummings, Murray, & Spencer, 2001). Training of supervisors in supervisory and intervention skills is intended to address those concerns by providing the capability for continuity of staff activity and delivery of interventions within the service environment. Ducharme et al. found that general case quasi-pyramidal training , including continued presence of consultants and using a general case training approach and selected client program exemplars, may promote generalization of teaching skills among both supervisors and staff (see Demchak, Kontos & Neisworth, 1992; Neef, 1995b; Page, Iwata, & Reid, 1982; Shore, Iwata, Vollmer, Lerman, & Zarcone, 1995, for other variations on pyramidal training). However, they also observed that their previous research found that performance-based training lacking a general case approach failed to obtain desirable generalized responses to untrained exemplars and that "staff may, however, have difficulty generalizing the use of these general teaching skills to client program exemplars that were not included in the staff training session.... Thus .. staff training procedures have produced narrow stimulus control to a limited range of skill exemplars" (Ducharme et al., 2001, para. 3).

In a study of a mutlicomponent training program for four direct service staff, Cooper and Browder (2001) reported on the utility of combined written manuals, verbal presentations, role paying, and use of video exemplars, with performance feedback in situ, and self-monitoring. Important features of this study include the individual instruction, focus on choice-making, on which there are relatively few staff training studies, and the incorporation of formal self-monitoring post-training. However, the staff in this study were also graduate students, and for that reason, probably not representative of direct service staff generally; hence, this study should be replicated for impact on more typical staff members.

Hayden (1994) articulated training practices for service systems and organizations that generally have at least modest pragmatic or research-based support. Hayden (1994) recommended that systems develop and support comprehensive training for supervisors of direct service staff on how to provide effective supervision and feedback, develop high quality competency-based training materials for trainers of direct service staff, and adopt and adapt existing training materials from other systems and sources when they address identified training needs effectively (p. 10). Hayden (1994) further recommended that service organizations implement competency-based training cultures and systems, including training that is specific to certain staff and their work with certain consumers, institute peer mentoring programs, and incorporate teaching methods in training that are both effective and preferred by staff (pp. 10-11). Hayden (1994) also recommended a structure for competency-based training that is complementary to behavioral management practices.

## The Promise of Distance Education

With the advent of readily accessible internet resources, many providers have increasingly expressed interest in distance education for staff, through universities or public agency websites. Distance education encompasses a wide range of video, internet-based, or computer assisted instructional strategies and technologies (Graham 2001). Most published comparisons of effects of traditional and distance education instructional strategies have been conducted with college students rather than employees or other adult learners (Graham, 2001). Evaluators of on-line education or distance education have advocated that learning should be verified by observation of participants applying new skills following completion of training (Benigno & Trentin, 2000). Moreover, evaluators have stressed the importance of verifying return on the investment made in providing or using online training (or for that matter, any training strategies, e.g., Benigno & Trentin, 2000).

Unfortunately, studies of return on investment for either video-mediated or online training, are scarce, and have typically utilized relatively week quasi-experimental designs (Bacon & Jakovich, 2001). A number of studies have found similar or mixed outcomes of comparable material delivered in college courses by either classroom or online strategies (Andrews, Gosse, Gaulton, & Maddigan, 1999); a seemingly reassuring finding, if one ignores longstanding concerns that classroom instruction is not, in and of itself, a particularly efficient method of teaching competencies to college students.

More generally, as Waschull (2001) notes there are potential problems with online or distance education that are not well-ascertained, including relying on student initiative or motivation for participation in instruction, the need for access to computers that meet at least a minimum specification for instruction, possible information overload or social isolation, and increased possibility of academic dishonesty (e.g., transcribing and distributing test items; doing coursework for others in their name). Perhaps most critically, there is a lack of research confirming retention of online training content and related performance improvements.

Some have advocated distance education as a valuable and perhaps necessary strategy for training of developmental and educational services professionals and direct service staff (e.g., Sailor et al., 2000). However, the efficacy and effectiveness of large scale distance education as a modality of post-graduate specialty training, and for competency training of workers who may lack both college education or computer usage skills, is almost completely unexplored. It is not yet clear, despite widespread adoption by colleges and universities of distance education, that such applications, unsupplemented by more traditional training and follow-up, are suitable and sufficiently potent to address critical staff training needs.

## Summary

Research and demonstration studies now effectively illustrate and provide guidance regarding delivery strategies for a wide range of training alternatives, focusing on values, attitudes, culture, and competencies. In most instances, sufficiently detailed information is presented in these studies to allow knowledgeable clinicians and consultants to provide training in most areas of interest to administrators and managers. Although we have not reviewed resources developed by states and under federal programs here, a casual search of the Internet reveals that lead state developmental services agencies and other human services agencies are actively engaged in developing training resources, delivering large scale foundational and special focus training, which is often mandated, and they offer a wide range of training materials that can be used or adapted by local organizations. However, three to four decades ago, the focus of staff training was often on remediating fundamental performance or employee work role deficits, or organizational deficiencies; today, although those priorities continue to exist as the character of the workforce changes, there is a more comprehensive focus on organizational reform and improved responsiveness of personnel to consumer needs.

Nonetheless, there are many pragmatic issues that managers in local organizations need to address regarding training, and that are not well-researched, or for that matter, constitute decision points that are not well-discussed in professional and trade journals. For example, we lack a definitive integrative analysis of the types and range of effects that various instructional procedures have for direct service staff, both in terms of initial acquisition and the integrity with which competencies manifest over time. We also lack a definitive analysis of costs in personnel time and effort of managing innovative practices and providing sound supervision.

In addition, research and demonstration projects have largely been conducted in small scale situations (single organizations, school, or local educational agencies) where there may be a limited number of administrators or managers, and hence little has been done to identify key management or administrative tasks or action steps that must be instituted to assure enduring benefit from training. While some action steps are implied in the studies reviewed in this chapter, they are typically writ large, and do not directly address the range of activities inherent in organizing for effective organizational reform (in substance, as well as words), and can be inferred only in some special circumstances (e.g., Sulzer-Azaroff et al., 1998). More typically, managerial activities within organizational reform may be broadly specified rather than clearly defined (e.g., Eber, Sugai, Smith, & Scott, 2002), increasing the difficulty of implementing reform, and perhaps, as well, discouraging administrators and managers from instituting reforms they might otherwise consider.

Another remaining shortcoming in many demonstrations, and hence the practice base, as noted by Jahr (1998), is the inconsistency with which staff skill acquisition and performance is linked to consumer outcomes. The complexity of research models in pyramidal and quasi-pyramidal models of training, or models that require extended follow-along to ascertain whether training has enduring effects that result in consumer gains, is almost certainly one of the major reasons that such evaluation occurs infrequently (e.g., Purcell, McConkey, & Morris, 2000). Even large scale training efforts also often seem to fail to collect information on consumer outcomes, to verify that changes in practices, if instituted, resulted in intended benefits, rather than merely a change in which organizational functions are carried out (e.g., Dunlap & Hieneman, 2000; Sheras, Cornell, & Bostain, 1996), although there are exceptions (e.g., Luiselli, Putnam, & Sunderland, 2002). In addition, when training is provided on a large scale, or innovative services require extensive staff training, implementation is often not verified (as noted by Domitrovich & Greenberg,

2000), although implementation measures may be reported in some cases (e.g., Sheras, Cornell, & Bostain, 1996).

Research appears to provide a sound foundation for practice with regard to the use of supervisors as trainers (i.e., train-the-trainer models) as long as supervisors learn how to teach specific skills in the course of training, and the practices of their supervisors systematically encourage them to monitor, teach, correct, and consequate effective direct service staff delivery of services (regardless of whether those services entail direct teaching or engaging a consumer in preferred activities). However, in some cases, the use of train-the-trainer models for conveying complex and comprehensive clinical or intervention content may threaten fidelity or integrity of implementation, because consultation is often needed. Lack of extensive follow-up of outcomes, even within model large scale programs, may lead to situations where initial fidelity is evident while trainers provide consultation during training, but diminished integrity occurs as time passes and local applications become more idiosyncratic, indicating the need for effective monitoring as an element of demonstration and practice. Without verification of implementation of components of an innovative practice and of outcomes, the conclusion that an innovative practice is reaping benefit remains largely a matter of faith (Domitrovich & Greenberg, 2000; Watson & Sterling, 1997). More successful training efforts (Dunlap & Heineman, 2000; see also Brethower, 2000; Reid & Parsons, 2000; Williams, 2000; Williams & Cummings, 2000) tend to combine instructional theory, modeling, practice, feedback, and coaching. The training is often supplemented or illustrated by demonstration, analysis of individual or general representative cases, discussions, role playing, simulations. They must be compatible with work roles (e.g., individual or team structure or responsibilities), and involve extensive follow-along activities.

## References

Ager, A., & May, F. O. (2001). Issues in the definition and implementation of "best practice" for staff delivery of interventions for challenging behaviour. *Journal of Intellectual & Developmental Disability, 26,* 243–256.

Allen, D., McDonald, L., Dunn, C., & Doyle, T. (1997). Changing care staff approaches to the prevention and management of aggressive behaviour in a residential treatment unit for persons with mental retardation and challenging behaviour. *Research in Developmental Disabilities, 18,* 101-112.

Andrews, E. A., Gosse, V. F., Gaulton, R. S., & Maddigan, R. I. (1999). Teaching introductory psychology at a distance by two-way interactive video. *Teaching of Psychology, 26,* 115-118.

Anthony, R. (1999, January). Organizational culture and innovation. *Innovative Leader, 8*(1), accessed at http://www.winstonbrill.com/bril001/html/ article_index/articles/351-400/article379_body.html on 1/14/03.

Bacal & Associates. (2002). *Management fads - Things you should know.* Accessed at http://www.work911.com/articles/mgmtfad.htm on 1/10/03.

Bacon, S. F., & Jakovich, J. A. (2001). Instructional television versus traditional teaching of an introductory psychology course. *Teaching of Psychology, 28,* 88-92.

Baker, D. J. (1998a). Effects of video-based staff training with manager-led exercises in residential support. *Mental Retardation, 36*, 198-204.

Baker, D. J. (1998b). Outcomes of behavior support training to an agency providing residential and vocational support to persons with developmental disabilities. *The Journal of the Association for Persons with Severe Handicaps, 23*, 144-148.

Baker, P. A., & Bissmire, D. (2000). A pilot study of the use of physical intervention in the crisis management of people with intellectual disabilities who present challenging behaviour. *Journal of Applied Research in Intellectual Disabilities, 13*, 38-45.

Balcazar, F. E., MacKay-Murphy, M., & Keys, C. B. (1998). Assessing perceived agency adherence to the values of community inclusion: implications for staff satisfaction. *American Journal on Mental Retardation, 102*, 451-463.

Barnett, D. W., Pepiton, A. E., & Bell, S. H. (1999). Evaluating early intervention: Accountability methods for service delivery innovations. *The Journal of Special Education, 33*, 177-188.

Becker, H., Dumas, S., & Houser, A. (2000). How organizational factors contribute to innovations in service delivery. *Mental Retardation, 38*, 385-394.

Benigno, V., & Trentin, G. (2000). The evaluation of online courses. *Journal of Computer Assisted Learning, 16*, 259-270.

Beutler, L. E. (2000). Empirically based decision making in clinical practice. *Prevention & Treatment, 3*, Article 27.

Bickman, L., Lambert, E. W., Andrade, A. R., & Penaloza, R. V. (2000). The Fort Bragg continuum of care for children and adolescents: Mental health outcomes over 5 years. *Journal of Consulting and Clinical Psychology, 68*, 710-716.

Bickman, L., Noser, K., & Summerfelt, W. T. (1999). Long-term effects of a system of care on children and adolescents. *Journal of Behavioral Health Services & Research, 26*, 185-202.

Bohrer, K., & Ellis, J. (1998). Analysis of contingencies and metacontingencies in a private sector workplace. *Behavior and Social Issues, 8*, 41-52.

Brethower, D. M. (2000). Organizational behavior management and instructional systems. In J. Austin & J. E. Carr (Eds.), *Handbook of applied behavior analysis* (pp. 423-448). Reno, NV: Context Press.

Cape, J., & Barkham, M. (2002). Practice improvement methods: Conceptual base, evidence-based research, and practice-based recommendations. *British Journal of Clinical Psychology, 41*, 285-307.

Chambless, D. L., & Ollendick, T. H. (2000). Empirically supported psychological interventions: Controversies and evidence. *Annual Review of Psychology, 52*, 685-716.

Cooper, K. J., & Browder, D. M. (2001). Preparing staff to enhance active participation of adults with severe disabilities by offering choice and prompting performance during a community purchasing activity. *Research in Developmental Disabilities, 22*, 1–20.

Critchfield, T. S., & Kollins, S. H. (2001). Temporal discounting: Basic research and the analysis of socially important behavior. *Journal of Applied Behavior Analysis, 34*, 101–122.

Crits-Cristoph, P., Frank, E., Chambless, D. L., Brody, C., & Karp, J. F. (1995). Training in empirically validated treatments: What are clinical psychology students learning? *Professional Psychology: Research and Practice, 26*, 514-522.

Cullen, C. (1988). A review of staff training: The emperor's old clothes. *Irish Journal of Psychology, 9*, 309-323.

Cullen, C. (1999, October). *A review of some important issues in research and services for people with learning disabilities and challenging behaviour.* Scotland: Social Work Services Inspectorate of the Scottish Office. Accessed at www.scotland.gov.uk/ldsr/cullen.pdf on 1/9/03.

Demchak, M., Kontos, S., & Neisworth, J. T. (1992). Using a pyramid model to teach behavior management procedures to childcare providers. *Topics in Early Childhood Special Education, 12*, 458-477.

Diamond, M. A. (1996). Innovation and diffusion of technology: A human process. *Consulting Psychology Journal: Practice and Research, 48*, 221-229.

Domitrovich, C. E., & Greenberg, M. T. (2000). The study of implementation: Current findings from effective programs that prevent mental disorders in school-aged children. *Journal of Educational and Psychological Consultation, 11*, 193–221.

Drake, R. E. (2001). *Evidence based practices: Challenges and opportunities* (workshop transcription). Accessed at www.omh.state.ny.us on 2/8/03.

Ducharme, J. M., Williams, L., Cummings, A., Murray, P., & Spencer, T. (2001). General case quasi-pyramidal staff training to promote generalization of teaching skills in supervisory and direct-care staff. *Behavior Modification, 25*, 233-256.

Dunlap, G., & Hieneman, M. (2000). Essential elements of inservice training in positive behavior support. *Journal of Positive Behavior Interventions, 2*, 22-32.

Dunst, C. J., Trivette, C. M., & Cutspec, P. A. (2002, September). Evidence-based approaches to early childhood development: Toward an operational definition of evidence-based practices. *Centerscope, 1*(1), 1-10. Accessed at http://www.evidencebasedpractices.org/rtc/whatis.php on 2/3/03.

Eber, L., Sugai, G., Smith, C. R., & Scott, T. M. (2002). Wraparound and positive behavioral interventions and supports in the schools. *Journal of Emotional & Behavioral Disorders, 10*, 171-180.

Embregts, P. J. C. M. (2002). Effect of resident and direct-care staff training on responding during social interactions. *Research in Developmental Disabilities, 23*, 353-366.

Felce, D., Bowley, C., Baxter, H., Jones, E., Lowe, K., & Emerson, E. (2000). The effectiveness of staff support: Evaluating Active Support training using a conditional probability approach. *Research in Developmental Disabilities, 21*, 243–255.

Fineberg, H. (1985). Effects of clinical evaluation on the diffusion of medical technology. In Institute of Medicine (Ed.), *Assessing medical technologies* (pp. 176-210). Washington, DC: National Academy Press.

Fleming, R. K., Oliver, J. R., & Bolton, D. M. (1996). Training supervisors to train staff: A case study in a human service organization. *Journal of Organizational Behavior Management, 16*(1), 3-25.

Fleming, R. K., & Sulzer-Azaroff, B. (1989). Enhancing quality of teaching by direct care staff through performance feedback on the job. *Behavioral Residential Treatment, 4,* 377-395.

Ganster, D. C., Williams, S., & Poppler, P. (1991). Does training in problem solving improve the quality of group decisions? *Journal of Applied Psychology, 76,* 479-483.

Garb, H. N. (1989). Clinical judgment, clinical training, and professional experience. *Psychological Bulletin, 105,* 387-396.

Glenn, S. (1988). Contingencies and metacontingencies: toward a synthesis of behavior analysis and cultural materialism. *The Behavior Analyst, 11,* 161-179.

Goldman, H. H. (2001). *The role of the Surgeon General's report in implementing evidence-based practices* (workshop transcription). Accessed at www.omh.state.ny.us on 2/8/03.

Graham, T. A. (2001). Teaching child development via the internet: Opportunities and pitfalls. *Teaching of Psychology, 28,* 67-71.

Haque, M. S. (2001). The diminishing publicness of public service under the current mode of governance. *Public Administration Review, 61,* 65-83.

Harchik, A. E., Sherman, J. A., Sheldon, J. B., & Strouse, M. C. (1992). Ongoing consultation as a method of improving performance of staff members in a group home. *Journal of Applied Behavior Analysis, 25,* 599-610.

Harper, D. J. (1994). Evaluating a training package for staff working with people with learning disabilities prior to hospital closure. *The British Journal of Learning Disabilities, XL,* 35-53.

Hayden, M. (Ed.). (1994). *Training issues for direct service personnel working in community residential programs for persons with developmental disabilities* (Policy Research Brief Vol. 6, No. 2). Minneapolis-St. Paul, MN: Center on Residential Services and Community Living, College Of Education, University of Minnesota

Holburn, C. S., & Jacobson, J. W. (1993). Impact of federal regulations on desired processes and outcomes in public residential facilities: National perspectives. *Journal of Developmental and Physical Disability, 5,* 109-120.

Holburn, S., & Jacobson, J. W. (2003). Implementing and researching person-centered planning. (this volume)

Holburn, S., & Vietze, P. (1999). Acknowledging barriers in adopting person-centered planning. *Mental Retardation, 37,* 117-24.

Holburn, S., & Vietze, P. (Eds.). (2002). *Person-centered planning: Research, practice, and future directions,* Baltimore: Paul Brookes.

Huberman, W. L., & O'Brien, R. M. (1999). Improving therapist and patient performance in chronic psychiatric group homes through goal-setting, feedback, and positive reinforcement. *Journal of Organizational Behavior Management, 19*, 13-36.

Isaacs, D., & Fitzgerald, D. (1999). Seven alternatives to evidence based medicine. *British Medical Journal, 319*, 1618.

Jacobson, J. W. (2000a). Converting to a behavior analysis format for autism services: Decision-making for educational administrators, principals, and consultants. *The Behavior Analyst Today, 1*(3), 6-16.

Jacobson, J. W. (2000b). Early intensive behavioral intervention in autism: Emergence of a parent driven service model. *The Behavior Analyst, 23*, 149-171.

Jacobson, J. W., & Otis, J. P. (1992). Limitations of regulations as social controls in developmental services. *Mental Retardation, 30*, 163-171.

Jahr, E. (1998). Current issues in staff training. *Research in Developmental Disabilities, 19*, 73-87.

Jensen, J. M., Parsons, M. B., & Reid, D. H. (1998). Supervisory training for teachers: Multiple, long-term effects in an education program for adults with severe disabilities. *Research in Developmental Disabilities, 19*, 449–463.

Johnston, J. M. (2000). Behavior analysis and the R&D paradigm. *The Behavior Analyst, 2*, 141–148.

Johnston, J. M., & Romzek, B.S. (1999). Contracting and accountability in state Medicaid reform: Rhetoric, theories, and reality. *Public Administration Review, 59*, 383-400.

Jones, E., Felce, D., Lowe, K., Bowley, C., Pagler, J., Gallagher, B., & Roper, A. (2001a). Evaluation of the dissemination of Active Support training in staff community residences. *American Journal on Mental Retardation, 106*, 344-358.

Jones, E., Felce, D., Lowe, K., Bowley, C., Pagler, J., Strong, G., Gallagher, B., Roper, A., & Kurowska, K. (2001b). Evaluation of the dissemination of active support training and training trainers. *Journal of Applied Research in Intellectual Disabilities, 14*, 79-99.

Kauffman, J. M. (1996). Research to practice issues. *Behavioral Disorders, 22*, 55-60.

Kauffman, J. M. (1999). Comments on social development research in EBD. *Journal of Emotional and Behavioral Disorders, 7*, 189-191.

Kavale, K. A., & Forness, S. R. (2000). History, rhetoric, and reality: Analysis of the inclusion debate. *Remedial and Special Education, 21*, 279-296.

Kazdin, A. E. (1997). A model for developing effective treatments: Progression and interplay of theory, research, and practice. *Journal of Clinical Child Psychology, 26*, 114-129

Koch, R., Cairns, J. M., & Brunk, M. (2000). How to involve staff in developing an outcomes-oriented organization. *Education and Treatment of Children, 23*, 41-47.

Kutash, K., & Rivera, V. R. (1994). Public sector financing of community-based services or children with serious emotional disabilities and their families: Results of a national survey. *Journal of Mental Health Administration, 21*, 262-291.

Larson, S. A., Hewitt, A., & Anderson, L. (1999). Staff recruitment challenges and interventions in agencies supporting people with developmental disabilities. *Mental Retardation, 37*, 36-46

Lewis, T. J. (undated). *Decision making about effective behavioral support: A guide for educators.* University of Oregon. Accessed at http://idea.uoregon.edu/~ncite/documents/techrep/tech25.html on 12/24/02.

Lewis, T. J., Sugai, G. M., & Colvin, G. (1998). Reducing problem behavior through a school-wide system of effective behavioral support: Investigation of a school-wide social skills training program and contextual interventions. *The School Psychology Review, 27*, 446-459.

Luiselli, J. K., Putnam, R. F., & Sunderland, M. (2002). Longitudinal evaluation of behavior support intervention in a public middle school. *Journal of Positive Behavior Interventions, 4*, 182-188.

MacLeod, I. R., Jones, K. M., Somers C. L., & Havey, J. M. (2001). An evaluation of the effectiveness of school-based behavioral consultation, *Journal of Educational and Psychological Consultation, 12*, 203–216.

Malouf, D. B., & Schiller, E. P. (1995). Practice and research in special education. *Exceptional Children, 61*, 414-424.

Mansell, J. (1995). Staffing and staff performance in services for people with severe or profound learning disability and serious challenging behaviour. *Journal of Intellectual Disability Research, 39*, 3–14.

McCormick, L., Noonan, M. J., & Ogata, V. (2001). Co-teacher relationship and program quality: implications for preparing teachers for inclusive preschool settings. *Education and Training in Mental Retardation and Developmental Disabilities, 36*, 119-132.

McGimsey, J. F., Greene, B. F., & Lutzker, J. R. (1995). Competence in aspects of behavioral treatment and consultation: implications for service delivery and graduate training. *Journal of Applied Behavior Analysis, 28*, 301-315.

McIntrye, J. S. (2001). *Practice guidelines, development and dissemination: Methods, issues, and results* (workshop transcription). Accessed at www.omh.state.ny.us on 2/8/03.

Meinhold, P. M., & Mulick, J. A. (1990a). Counter-habilitative contingencies in institutions for people with mental retardation: Ecological and regulatory influences. *Mental Retardation, 28*, 67-75.

Meinhold, P. M., & Mulick, J. A. (1990b). Risks, choices and behavioral treatment. *Behavioral Residential Treatment, 5*, 29-44.

Mike, V., Krauss, A. N., & Ross, G. S. (1998). Responsibility for clinical innovation. *Evaluation & the Health Professions, 21*, 3-27.

Minton, B. A. (1995). Alaska Youth Initiative: The dream, the reality. *Journal of Mental Health Administration, 22*, 293-300.

Mowbray, C. T., Bellamy, C. D., Megivern, D., & Szilvagyi, S. (2001). Raising our sites: Dissemination of supported education. *Journal of Behavioral Health Services & Research, 28*, 484-493.

Mulick, J. A. (1990). The ideology and science of punishment in mental retardation. *American Journal on Mental Retardation, 95,* 142-156.

Mulick, J. A., & Meinhold, P. M. (1992). Analyzing the impact of regulations on residential ecology. *Mental Retardation, 30,* 151-161.

Neef, N. A. (1995a). Research on training trainers in program implementation: an introduction and future directions. *Journal of Applied Behavior Analysis, 28,* 297-299.

Neef, N. A. (1995b). Pyramidal parent training by peers. *Journal of Applied Behavior Analysis, 28,* 333-337.

Northup, J., Wacker, D. P., Berg, W. K.; Kelly, L., Sasso, G. M., & de Raad, A. O. (1994). The treatment of severe behavior problems in school settings using a technical assistance model. *Journal of Applied Behavior Analysis, 27,* 33-47.

Page, T. J., Iwata, B. A., & Reid, D. H. (1982). Pyramidal training: A large-scale application with institutional staff. *Journal of Applied Behavior Analysis, 15,* 335-351.

Pandiani, J. A., & Edgar, E. R. (1994). A longitudinal study of the impact of changing public policy on community mental health client residential patterns and staff attitudes. *Journal of Mental Health Administration, 21,* 71-80.

Parsons, M. B., Cash, V. B., & Reid, D. H. (1989). Improving residential treatment services: Implementation and norm-referenced evaluation of a comprehensive management system. *Journal of Applied Behavior Analysis, 22,* 143-156.

Parsons, M. B., & Reid, D. H. (1995). Training residential supervisors to provide feedback for maintaining staff teaching skills with people who have severe disabilities. *Journal of Applied Behavior Analysis, 28,* 317-322.

Parsons, M. B., Reid, D. H., & Green, C. W. (1996). Training basic teaching skills to community and institutional support staff for people with severe disabilities: A one-day program. *Research in Developmental Disabilities, 17,* 467-485

Phillips, N. B., & Jenkins, J. R. (1997). The research-to-practice ball game. *Remedial and Special Education, 18,* 143-156.

Purcell, M., McConkey, R., & Morris, I. (2000). Staff communication with people with intellectual disabilities: The impact of a work-based training programme. *International Journal of Language and Communication Disorders, 35,* 147-158.

Rago, W. V. (1996). Struggles in transformation: A study in TQM, leadership, and organizational culture in a government agency. *Administration Review, 56,* 227-234.

Reid, D. H., & Parsons, M. B. (2000). Organizational behavior management in human service settings. In J. Austin & J. E. Carr (Eds.), *Handbook of applied behavior analysis* (pp. 275-294). Reno, NV: Context Press.

Reid, D. H., Parsons, M. B., & Green, C. W. (1989). Treating aberrant behavior through effective staff management: A developing technology. In E. Cipani (Ed.), *The treatment of severe behavior disorders: Behavior analysis approaches* (Monograph no. 12—pp. 175-190). Washington, DC: American Association on Mental Retardation.

RERC on Technology Transfer. (undated). *Overview of the technology transfer process (powerpoint presentation and text)*. Accessed at http://cosmos.ot.buffalo.edu/t2rerc/index.html on12/24/02.

Richman, G. S., Riordan, M. R., Reiss, M. L., Pyles, D. A. M., & Bailey, J. S. (1988). The effects of self-monitoring and supervisor feedback on staff performance in a residential setting. *Journal of Applied Behavior Analysis, 21*, 401-409.

Rycus, J. S., & Hughes, R. C. (2000). *What is competency-based in-service training?* Columbus, OH: Institute for Human Services.

Sacher, D. (2001). *Report of the Surgeon General's conference on children's mental health: A national action agenda* Washington, DC: Office of the Surgeon General, Department of Health and Human Services.

Sackett, D., Rosenberg, W., Gray, J., Haynes, R., & Richardson, W. (1996). Evidence based medicine: What it is and what it isn't (editorial). *British Medical Journal, 312*, 71-72.

Sailor, W., Freeman, R., Britten, J., McCart, A., Smith, C., Scott, T., & Nelson, M. (2000). Using information technology to prepare personnel to implement functional behavioral assessment and positive behavioral support. *Exceptionality, 8*, 217-229.

Salmento, M., & Bambara, L. (2000). Teaching staff members to provide choice opportunities for adults with multiple disabilities. *Journal of Positive Behavior Interventions, 2*, 12-21.

Saloviita, T., & Lehtinen, U. (2001). Paraprofessional staff teaching adults with mental retardation. *Education and Training in Mental Retardation and Developmental Disabilities, 36*, 103-106.

Schepis, M. M., & Dunlap, G. (2000). Factors affecting the outcomes of community-based behavioral support. *Journal of Positive Behavior Interventions, 2*, 161-170.

Seys, D., & Duker, P. (1988). Effects of staff management on the quality of residential care for mentally retarded individuals. *American Journal on Mental Retardation, 93*(3), 290–299.

Shadish, W. R. (1984). Policy research: Lessons from the implementation of deinstitutionalization. *American Psychologist, 39*, 725-738.

Sheras, P. L., Cornell, D. G., & Bostain, D. S. (1996). The Virginia Youth Violence Project: Transmitting psychological knowledge on youth violence to schools and communities. *Professional Psychology: Research and Practice, 27*, 401-406.

Sheridan, S. M., Welch, M., & Orme, S. F. (1996). Is consultation effective? A review of outcome research. *Remedial and Special Education, 17*, 341-354.

Shore, B. A., Iwata, B. A., Vollmer, T. R., Lerman, D. C., & Zarcone, J. R.. (1995). Pyramidal staff training in the extension of treatment for severe behavior disorders. *Journal of Applied Behavior Analysis, 28*, 323-332.

Smith, T. E. C., & Dowdy, C. A. (1998). Educating young children with disabilities using responsible inclusion. *Childhood Education, 74*, 317-320.

Stancliffe, R. J., Hayden, M. F., & Lakin, K. C. (1999). Interventions for challenging behavior in residential settings. *American Journal on Mental Retardation, 104*, 364-375.

Sulzer-Azaroff, B., Pollack M. J., Hamad, C., & Howley, T. (1998). Promoting widespread, durable service quality via interlocking contingencies. *Research in Developmental Disabilities, 19,* 39-61.

Sundram, C. J. (1999). Pitfalls in the pursuit of life, liberty, and happiness. *Mental Retardation, 37,* 62-67.

Thompson, P. E. (1999). Overcoming barriers to research-based practice. *MEDSURG Nursing, 8,* 59-63.

Waschull, S. B. (2001). The online delivery of psychology courses: Attrition, performance, and evaluation. *Teaching of Psychology, 28,* 143-147.

Watson, T. S., & Sterling, H. E. (1997). Demythifying behavioral consultation. *School Psychology Review, 26,* 467-474.

Weightman, A. (1999). *Health Evidence Bulletin 9: Staff training.* Cardiff, Wales: Duthie Library UWCM. Accessed at http://hebw.uwcm.ac.uk/learningdisabilities/chapter9.htm, 12/24/02.

Weist, M. D., & Christodulu, K. V. (2000). Expanded school mental health programs: Advancing reform and closing the gap between research and practice. *Journal of School Health, 70,* 195-200.

Williams, W. L. (2000). Behavioral consultation. In J. Austin & J. E. Carr (Eds.), *Handbook of applied behavior analysis* (pp. 375-398). Reno, NV: Context Press.

Williams, W. L., & Cummings, A. (2000). Service Review: Increasing consumer benefits by linking service outcome data to direct-care staff service delivery and decision making. In L. J. Hayes, J. Austin, R. Fleming, & R. Houmanfar (Eds.), *Organizational change* (pp. 277-292). Reno, NV: Context Press.